Wissenschaftliche Untersuchungen
zum Neuen Testament · 2. Reihe

Herausgeber / Editor
Jörg Frey (München)

Mitherausgeber / Associate Editors
Friedrich Avemarie (Marburg)
Judith Gundry-Volf (New Haven, CT)
Hans-Josef Klauck (Chicago, IL)

246

Stephen E. Witmer

Divine Instruction
in Early Christianity

Mohr Siebeck

Stephen E. Witmer: born 1976; 2003 M.Div. and Th.M. from Gordon-Conwell Theological Seminary; 2007 PhD from the University of Cambridge; since 2008 Pastor of Pepperell Christian Fellowship in Pepperell, Massachussetts, USA.

BS
680
.F3
W58
2008

ISBN 978-3-16-149608-0
ISSN 0340-9570 (Wissenschaftliche Untersuchungen zum Neuen Testament 2. Reihe)

Die Deutsche Nationalbibliothek lists this publication in the Deutsche Nationalbiblio-graphie; detailed bibliographic data is available in the Internet at *http://dnb.d-nb.de.*

The book was printed by Gulde-Druck in Tübingen on non-aging paper and bound by Buchbinderei Held in Rottenburg.

Printed in Germany.

For Emma

Acknowledgements

I am thankful to the many people who have contributed in one way or another to the writing of this monograph, which is the published version of my 2007 Cambridge Ph.D. thesis. Most of the research for the thesis was done in the congenial environment of Tyndale House, and I wish to thank the Warden at that time, Bruce Winter, as well as the excellent staff, especially David Instone-Brewer and Elizabeth Magba. I treasure the life-long friends I made at Tyndale House. They have spurred me on in my desire to understand the Scriptures and to honor God in my scholarship.

I am also thankful to the numerous scholars who have generously given of their time to read and interact with my work: Dr. James Aitken, Prof. Markus Bockmuehl, Prof. Gary Burge, Prof. Graham Davies, Prof. Jan du Rand, Prof. Dan Estes, Dr. Elizabeth Harris, Dr. Peter Head, Dr. Charlotte Hempel, and Prof. Peter Jones. Special thanks are due to my two examiners, Dr. Andrew Chester and Prof. Judith Lieu, and to Prof. Hans-Josef Klauck, each of whom read the work carefully and provided detailed comments and suggestions. Thanks also to my friends Todd Wilson, John Yates, Charles Echols, and Charles Anderson for reading sections of my thesis, and to my teaching assistant Daniel Brendsel, for compiling the indexes and improving the manuscript with his eagle eye.

Parts of this monograph were read in various stages at several seminars: the Cambridge-Oxford New Testament Seminar (May 2005), the 'John' session of the ETS meeting (November 2005), the Cambridge Senior New Testament Seminar (February 2006), the Oak Hill Bible College Graduate Seminar (November 2006), and again at the Cambridge Senior New Testament Seminar (May 2007). I am thankful to participants of these seminars for good questions and helpful interaction.

Many thanks to Jörg Frey for accepting my monograph for publication in the WUNT II series, and to Henning Ziebritzki and the editorial staff at Mohr Siebeck for kindly and competently guiding my work to publication.

I would not have been able to pursue my research without the generous financial assistance of the Overseas Research Students scheme, the Cambridge Overseas Trust, Corpus Christi College, and the University of Cambridge Faculty of Divinity. Very special thanks are due to Doug Birdsall and my wonderful Cambridge Support Team, as well as to the Monson Community Church. For the help and support of all these groups, I am deeply grateful.

My supervisor Graham N. Stanton, with his consistent encouragement and deft touch, guided me exactly as was needed at every stage. I have been privileged to observe firsthand the humility, kindness, and selflessness for which he is known and loved by many.

My parents, Daryl and Mary Witmer, have always supported and encouraged me. I thank them for being the first to teach me the Scriptures, and for modeling lives rooted in the Word of God. No one has had a bigger impact on my life.

Finally, this book is dedicated to Emma Witmer, my wife of two years, who went from the lovely girl at the front of church, to girlfriend, fiancée, and wife in the course of its writing. Emma, you are the greatest treasure of my years in Cambridge.

Soli Deo Gloria

June 2008   Stephen E. Witmer
South Hamilton, Massachusetts

Table of Contents

Part Two:

Divine instruction in the Johannine corpus

Part Three:
Divine instruction in Paul and in Matthew

Abbreviations

Abbreviations and stylistic conventions follow, where possible, *SBL* (1999) and IATG^2 (1992). In addition, the following abbreviations are used, with bibliographical details in the Bibliography:

AOTC	Apollos Old Testament Commentary
BECNT	Baker Exegetical Commentary on the New Testament
BST	The Bible Speaks Today
BIS	Biblical Interpretation Series
BRS	Biblical Resource Series
BBC	Blackwell Bible Commentaries
CB	Calwer Bibelkommentare
CPNIVC	College Press NIV Commentary
CRD	Jacob Neusner (ed.), *The Components of the Rabbinic Documents: From the Whole to the Parts*
CCC	Crossway Classic Commentaries
EDSS	Lawrence H. Schiffman and James VanderKam (eds.), *Encyclopedia of the Dead Sea Scrolls*
FN	*Filologia neotestamentaria*
HBS	Herders Biblische Studien
IVPNTCS	IVP New Testament Commentary Series
JGRChJ	*Journal of Greco-Roman Christianity and Judaism*
LW	Jaroslav Pelikan and Helmut T. Lehmann (eds.), *Luther's Works*
MCNT	Meyer's Commentary on the New Testament
NSBT	New Studies in Biblical Theology
NTFF	New Testament Foundations and Facets
NTT	New Testament Theology
NIVAC	NIV Application Commentary
OBS	Oxford Bible Series
PNTC	Pillar New Testament Commentary
POTTS	Pittsburgh Original Texts and Translation Series
SBL	P. H. Alexander et al. (eds.), *The SBL Handbook of Style: for Ancient Near Eastern, Biblical, and Early Christian Studies*
SBLAS	Society of Biblical Literature Aramaic Studies
SVTQ	*St Vladimir's Theological Quarterly*
SBLit	Studies in Biblical Literature
SDSSRL	Studies in the Dead Sea Scrolls and Related Literature
SNTW	Studies of the New Testament and Its World
SJSJ	Supplements to the Journal for the Study of Judaism
TRENT	Traditions of the Rabbis from the Era of the New Testament
UJT	Understanding Jesus Today
WT	Wesleyan Theological Journal

Chapter 1

Introduction

> *'And may God, who rules over the whole world,*
> *give you wisdom, insight, understanding,*
> *knowledge of his commandments, and patience.*
> *Be instructed by God, seeking out what the Lord seeks from you,*
> *and then do it, in order that you may be found in the day of judgment.'*

Epistle of Barnabas 21.5-6, c. 100[1]

This study is an investigation of one aspect of early Christian self-understanding: the conviction current among some early followers of Jesus that they had been, and were being, taught by God, in fulfillment of OT prophetic promises. I will argue that this aspect of early Christian self-understanding was an important one, and has relevance for an appreciation of the eschatology, Christology, pneumatology, ecclesiology and hermeneutics of the earliest Christian communities. By 'early Christianity,' I refer to the Christianity of the first century. The limits of the present study do not permit any comprehensive examination of the idea of divine instruction in Christian documents later than the NT writings. However, the idea of divine instruction is not infrequent in Christian authors of the second century and later (see the epigraph above), and further study would likely yield interesting results.

The early Christian concept of divine instruction has received insufficient attention in the secondary literature. To my knowledge, no monograph has ever comprehensively investigated the concept. Numerous commentaries and articles treat one or another of the NT passages that refer to divine instruction, sometimes referencing the other 'key' passages in a footnote. However, no study has ever gathered together the important NT passages and sought to locate those passages within the context of a close study of divine instruction in the OT and early Jewish literature. This is surprising in light of the many studies on *Jesus* as a teacher.[2] Perhaps the lack of studies devoted to God as a teacher is reflective of the general neglect of God in New

---

[1] Holmes, *Apostolic Fathers*, 325.

[2] Cf. e.g. Byrskog, *Teacher;* Normann, *Christos Didaskalos;* Riesner, *Lehrer*; Robbins, *Jesus the Teacher*; Yieh, *One Teacher*. Many more works are noted below in chapters 4-5.

Testament theology, a problem identified by Nils A. Dahl thirty years ago, and lamented by other scholars since.[3]

The lack of secondary literature on divine instruction in the NT is similar to the situation in OT and Jewish studies. Only a few monographs investigate the idea of divine instruction in the OT,[4] and no study comprehensively investigates divine instruction in the DSS, Philo, and other early Jewish literature. Therefore, one justification for this study is the almost complete lack of previous studies. This also accounts for the lack of a *Forschungsbericht*. The few works that exist will be noted in the course of the study.

The basis and structure of this thesis

This thesis is built upon two observations. First, the idea that God teaches people is pervasive in the OT, and receives an eschatological thrust in the prophetic literature, particularly in Isaiah, Micah, and Jeremiah. A wide range of early Jewish literature develops the idea of God as a teacher, and some of this literature draws upon the OT prophetic promises of eschatological divine instruction. Secondly, multiple corpora in the NT draw upon and develop the OT prophetic promises of eschatological divine instruction. Two OT passages in particular are cited or alluded to: Isa 54.13 and Jer 31.34. The presence of these OT passages can be shown with a reasonable degree of certainty in the Fourth Gospel and 1 Thessalonians, and to a lesser degree in 1 John, Matthew, and 1 Corinthians. One of the contributions of my project is to demonstrate the presence of these OT allusions. In two published studies, I have argued that John 6.45 cites a written or accurately memorized text of Isa 54.13, and that the neologism θεοδίδακτος in 1 Thess 4.9 is coined on the basis of the LXX or MT of Isa 54.13.[5] The OT allusions in 1 John, Matthew, and 1 Corinthians will be examined in chapters 7-9.

In order to understand how some of the earliest followers of Jesus were interpreting the OT prophetic promises of divine instruction as fulfilled in their experience, it is important first to understand the OT concept of divine instruction. Accordingly, chapter 2 surveys the theme of divine instruction in the OT, focusing particularly upon the prophetic literature. Chapter 3 moves toward the NT writings by examining the theme of divine instruction in the DSS, Philo, Josephus, the Apocrypha, and OT Greek pseudepigrapha, as well

---

[3] Dahl, 'Neglected Factor,' 153-163, esp. 153-55. Cf. Keck, 'Renewal,' 363. On this neglect in Johannine studies, see Thompson, *God*, 6-15; Culpepper, *Anatomy*, 112-15.

[4] Cf. Finsterbusch, *Weisung*; Schawe, *Lehrer*. For articles and essays, see below in chapter 2.

[5] Cf. Witmer, 'Citation,' 134-38; Witmer, 'Neologism,' 239-50. This thesis builds on the results of those studies rather than repeating their arguments.

as the idea of a messianic teacher in these writings. The various developments of the idea in the Jewish writings provide an important backdrop for contrast and comparison with the NT development of divine instruction.

Chapters 4-7 constitute the main section of the thesis. Here, I investigate the idea of divine instruction in the Johannine corpus, focusing upon the Fourth Gospel and 1 John. Chapters 8-9 offer brief explorations of the same theme in the Pauline letters and in Matthew. The wider-than-normal breadth of this thesis arises from the conviction that such an approach can highlight areas of unity and diversity in the NT writings that would go unnoticed in narrower studies. I make no attempt to force the evidence into a pre-conceived pattern or a contrived unity. Rather, what is most interesting is to see both similarities and differences. The Johannine writings, the Pauline letters, and Matthew each draw upon the idea of eschatological divine instruction, but develop it in different ways and for varying purposes. In the end, the flexibility and potency of the concept are among its distinguishing features.

Three questions formulated through study of the NT texts themselves are asked of the Johannine, Pauline, and Matthean writings:

1. How do the authors understand the fulfillment of the promises of eschatological divine instruction? How is the teaching of Jesus related to the teaching of God? What is the role of the Spirit?
2. What is the content and function of divine instruction?
3. Does divine instruction obviate the need for human teaching?

These questions are answered in the course of the thesis, and chapter 10 gathers together the most important results in a conclusion.

There are, of course, references to the gods teaching in Greco-Roman sources (and indeed, in many world religions).[6] In this thesis, I do not examine these references. This omission is due to limits of time and space, rather than to the conclusion that study of these sources would contribute nothing to the thesis. On the contrary, such a study would quite possibly shed further light on some of the NT passages. However, in my judgment the clear dependence of the NT upon the OT prophetic literature for its concept of eschatological divine instruction warrants the precedence given to the OT and Jewish sources in this study.

---

[6] See e.g. Homer, *Il.* 5.51; Aeschylus, *Eum.* 279; Plato, *Menex.* 238b; *Socrat. Ep.* 1.10. Cf. Karrer, 'Lehrende,' 9; Zimmerman, *Urchristlichen*, 77-78; Theobald, 'Gezogen,' 334; Colless, 'Divine Education,' 118-42.

Methodology

While this study is built upon the observation that the Johannine writings, the Pauline letters, and Matthew cite or allude to prophetic promises of divine instruction, it is important to study more than simply the passages that draw upon the OT if the idea of divine instruction in the NT documents is to be examined comprehensively. Therefore, while allusions to Isa 54.13 and Jer 31.34 are of most interest, all references to divine instruction must be examined. The former are a subset of the latter:

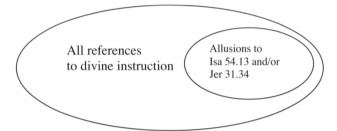

Accordingly, it is necessary to develop a method for identifying the concept of divine instruction in the OT, early Jewish literature, and the NT writings. Because no study similar to mine exists for early Jewish literature and the NT writings, my methodological discussion necessarily interacts with OT treatments of the concept.

In my judgment, the nature of the investigation demands that a study of the concept of divine instruction be based on didactic *terminology*. It is demanded by two factors. First, the concept of 'teaching' is difficult to define. Perhaps the most helpful way of distinguishing teaching from communication in general is to emphasize the continuous, sustained nature of teaching.[7] However, even this distinction is one of degree and is therefore inexact. In some texts, it can be difficult to determine if teaching is occurring, or simply communication in general. These difficulties are reduced in the case of formal instruction. Instruction in a formal setting is fairly easy to identify because we may look for a teacher and pupils and a designated place of instruction.[8] However, instruction can also be informal, and it is far more difficult to identify this type of instruction, since it occurs in the context of everyday life and does not require a teacher or pupils.[9]

Secondly, the problem of identifying the presence of instruction is compounded when we seek to identify the concept of *divine* instruction in the

---

[7] Cf. Louw and Nida, *Lexicon*, 1.413; Rengstorf, 'διδάσκαλος,' *TDNT* 2.148; Rengstorf, 'διδάσκω,' *TDNT* 2.135.

[8] E.g. Acts 11.26; 20.20; Rom 2.17-21; 12.7; 16.17.

[9] E.g. 1 Cor 14.35; Gal 3.2; Phil 4.11.

relevant sources. This is because God does not teach in a classroom or fulfill the recognizable human occupation of 'teacher.' This makes it more difficult to distinguish divine instruction from divine communication (i.e. revelation) in general.

Erich Zenger's recent essay on Yahweh as a teacher in the Psalms is an example of the methodological weakness of approaches that do not rely on didactic terminology.[10] Zenger discusses five Psalms he considers important for the concept of Yahweh as a teacher (Pss 50, 111, 112, 119, 147). Of these, only Ps 119 uses the main didactic terminology, and Zenger does not discuss the verses that use this terminology. Because his methodology is not lexically grounded, it has no control; the Psalms he interprets may refer to the concept of Yahweh as teacher, but they may equally refer only to the general idea of communication from Yahweh. Without lexical grounding, we cannot be certain.

The difficulties of identifying the concept of divine instruction suggest that the best approach is to focus on the terminology of instruction. Accordingly, my method of studying the concept of divine instruction is to examine texts that combine a reference to God with didactic terminology, and then to bring into discussion those texts that (arguably) convey a similar concept even if they do not use this terminology.[11] Ellen Birnbaum's work on Philo is a good example of a careful and methodologically self-aware use of vocabulary in order to study a theme or concept in a complex corpus.[12] Most of the studies of instruction in the OT with which I interact in chapter 2 appropriately anchor their approaches in didactic terminology, and therefore maintain more methodological control than Zenger.[13] Of course, the choice of terminology is important for such an approach, but it is not difficult to isolate a representative list of Hebrew and Greek didactic terminology. In no chapter is my selection of vocabulary comprehensive, but the chosen vocabulary in each case is sufficient to yield an accurate view of the concept of God teaching people.[14]

---

[10] Zenger, 'Lehrer,' 47-67 considers grounding his study in the teaching terminology of the Psalms, but does not employ this method, since it would require too much space for a limited essay.

[11] This method is broad enough to include texts (e.g. Deut 4.10; Jer 31.31-34) that would not be included if the search was only for instances in which God was the grammatical subject of a verb meaning 'to teach.'

[12] Cf. Birnbaum, 'Philo,' 535-52, esp. 536-40.

[13] See the statements of method in Schawe, *Lehrer*, 4-6; Finsterbusch, *Weisung*, 11-12. Cf. Ego, 'Implikationen,' 7-15; Diedrich, 'Lehre,' 59-73.

[14] For a fuller list of Hebrew and Greek verbs for 'teach,' cf. Zuck, 'Hebrew Words,' 228-35; Zuck, 'Greek Words,' 158-68. See also Louw and Nida, *Lexicon*, 1.325-29, 413-16 for the Greek terms under the subdomains 'learn' and 'teach.'

The terminology-based methodology I employ requires two caveats, both concerning the now much-discussed distinction between a word and a concept.[15] First, it is possible for the concept of divine instruction to be present in a given passage without the use of didactic terminology.[16] Nevertheless, several factors suggest that my method has led me to the key passages. Rather than choosing only one word, I have selected a range of didactic terminology. This 'semantic field' leads to a greater number of passages, and so avoids the criticisms of some narrower word studies.[17] Furthermore, while passages that do not use didactic terminology may express the concept of God teaching, I have highlighted above the uncertainty caused by the difficulty of defining the concept of 'instruction.' In my opinion, the safer option is to bring control to the study by staying close to the didactic terminology, even if this means omitting some passages that are on the periphery. Finally, I have noted above that I include passages that do not use didactic terminology, but correspond to passages that do. This is another way of addressing the word/concept distinction.

The second caveat is that not all of my selected didactic terminology will necessarily lead to the same concept of teaching, or (more specifically) divine instruction. This is due to the obvious fact that lexemes can be used in different senses.[18] To take two examples, διδάσκω in 1 Cor 11.14 does not denote instruction of a formal kind, and is so vague in meaning that a more general word could be substituted without a change in meaning (e.g. 'Does not nature *show* you'). Similarly, διδάσκω in Matt 28.15 does not denote a didactic relationship, but has the sense 'tell someone what to do.'[19] Hence, while I have allowed didactic terminology to guide me to the concept of divine instruction, I have not uncritically assumed that all those words will mean the same thing. I note differences in meaning when necessary.

---

[15] See especially the famous work of Barr, *Semantics*, 206-62. Cf. Silva, *Biblical Words*, 17-32.

[16] Cf. Cotterell and Turner, *Linguistics*, 119.

[17] Sawyer, 'Review,' 241 criticizes the discussion of education in *TDNT* 5 because it is restricted to passages where παιδεία, παιδεύω, etc. occur. My methodology has included a broader range of words, including both παιδεύω and διδάσκω, as well as other terminology (including words for 'learn'). Sawyer himself notes that the increasing use of 'semantic fields' in *TDNT* 5 alleviates some of the criticisms of the previous volumes of *TDNT*.

[18] Cf. Cotterell and Turner, *Linguistics*, 120.

[19] Cf. BDAG 241.

Chapter 2

Divine instruction in the Old Testament

'As it says in the prophets, "And they will all be taught by God"'

John 6.45

In this chapter, I provide an overview of the idea of divine instruction in the OT in order to prepare the way for the chapters that follow.[1] The method outlined above in chapter 1 yields a large number of instances in which a reference to God is closely connected with didactic terminology.[2] The various Hebrew and Greek didactic terms have different nuances,[3] but in this chapter I will focus more on the similarities than the differences in meaning. In fact, the terms can sometimes be used synonymously or interchangeably: יסר and למד are placed in synonymous parallelism in Ps 94.10,[4] as are ירה and למד in Ps 25.8–9.[5]

---

[1] In this study, the Apocrypha will be considered in chapter 3, together with other early Jewish sources. This chapter is based on examination of all uses of the following words in the MT: יסר; ירה (Hiphil); למד (Qal); למד (Piel); למד (Pual); למד, לקח, מוסר; מורה. In addition, all uses of the following words in the LXX have been examined: διδακτός; διδασκαλία; διδάσκαλος; διδάσκω; διδαχή; μανθάνω; παιδεία; παιδευτής; παιδεύω; συνετίζω. The LXX consistently translates למד (Qal) with μανθάνω (cf. Kapelrud, 'למד,' *TDOT* 8.10; Rengstorf, 'μανθάνω,' *TDNT* 4.400), and – with the exception of Job and Proverbs – למד (Piel) with διδάσκω (cf. Rengstorf, 'διδάσκω,' *TDNT* 2.136). ירה is translated variously, only once with διδάσκω.

[2] There are over one hundred such passages both in the MT and the LXX.

[3] Cf. the extensive work of Schawe, *Lehrer*, *passim*, and the relevant *TDNT* and *TDOT* articles.

[4] Cf. 94.12. In LXX Ps 17.36, God's παιδεία is said to teach (διδάσκω) the psalmist, and in Jer 32.33, God teaches (למד) instruction (מוסר). In Isa 28.26, יסר and ירה are used in close conjunction.

[5] I find unpersuasive the attempt of Jenni, *Piel*, 119-22 to argue that ירה (Hiphil) denotes teaching within an established student-teacher relationship, while למד (Piel) suggests a more one-off, 'accidental' teaching. There are too many exceptions for Jenni's theory to be convincing. E.g. Deut 11.19 uses למד (Piel) to refer to ongoing instruction within a parent-child relationship. The many uses of למד (Piel) in Deuteronomy for Moses' teaching do not (as Jenni suggests) indicate an 'accidental' teaching, because Moses is seen as the teacher *par excellence*. Cf. למד (Piel) in Isa 48.17: on Jenni's reasoning, one would expect ירה.

As noted in chapter 1, the use of Isa 54.13 and Jer 31.34 in the Johannine corpus, the Pauline letters, and Matthew makes these two texts, and others like them that speak of eschatological divine instruction, of greatest interest for this study. Accordingly, I will focus on these texts in the present chapter. However, it is important to locate the prophetic development of divine instruction within the wider context of divine instruction in the OT. Restrictions of space do not allow here for the kind of comprehensive examination of each of the texts that would be desirable, and I can only sketch the contours of the idea in broad strokes. After examining divine instruction at Sinai and noting some of the most important features of divine instruction in the OT, I will provide a more detailed treatment of the prophetic development of divine instruction, focusing on Isa 54.13 and Jer 31.31–34.

Although not denying the value of some diachronic approaches, I will employ a synchronic approach in my study of the OT writings. The studies of Braulik and Finsterbusch on instruction in Deuteronomy provide good examples of the two approaches. Braulik's aim is to isolate each use of למד in Deuteronomy, and assign it to one of four literary strata, as well as a corresponding sociological context.[6] This approach yields some rather hypothetical results, as Braulik himself admits, due to the lack of scholarly consensus regarding his method and results.[7] Finsterbusch's study, on the other hand, employs a synchronic method, reading the book of Deuteronomy as a compositional unity.[8] For the purposes of this study, a synchronic approach is preferable, since it allows us to deal with the texts as they stand, rather than relying upon hypothetical and disputed theories of authorship and redaction. Moreover, it surely brings us closer to the way in which the authors of the NT writings were reading the OT texts.[9] Therefore, while I am aware of the critical issues surrounding, for instance, the composition of the book of Isaiah,[10] I will not attempt to separate out redactional layers in this study.

---

[6] Braulik, 'Deuteronomium,' 121–22.

[7] Braulik, 'Deuteronomium,' 121.

[8] Finsterbusch, 'Mose,' 27–28. Finsterbusch recognizes the value of diachronic approaches (e.g. the study of Braulik), but asserts that a synchronic approach should come first. Cf. Finsterbusch, *Weisung*, 9–11, and the essays in De Moor, *Synchronic, passim*, particularly Williamson, 'Synchronic,' 211–26.

[9] E.g. John 12.37–41 attributes both Isa 6.10 and Isa 53.1 to what 'Isaiah the prophet' said. Here, the book of Isaiah is seen as a compositional unity. Similarly, there is no hint in 1QIsa[a] of differing authorship for Isa 1–39 and Isa 40–66.

[10] Cf. e.g. Williamson, *Isaiah*, 1–29; Höffken, *Jesaja, passim*.

2.1 Previous research on God as teacher in the OT

Relatively little has been written on divine instruction in the OT. Until recently, the only book-length study was Erwin Schawe's 1979 thesis *Gott als Lehrer im Alten Testament*, an examination of three Hebrew verbs for 'teach' with particular attention to the passages in which God is the grammatical subject.[11] Karin Finsterbusch's thoroughly researched 2005 book *Weisung für Israel* focuses on instruction in Deuteronomy, but also includes substantial chapters on teaching and learning in Isaiah, Jeremiah, and Proverbs.[12] Several essays provide broad overviews of the subject. Brian Colless has written two relevant articles, one outlining the idea of God as a teacher in the OT and NT,[13] and another tracing the idea of divine education in several religions.[14] H.-J. Kraus' article outlines the OT concept of divine instruction, but only in a very partial way, and is more helpful for its theological reflection than for its exegetical contribution.[15]

More recently, several essays have appeared which examine (at least indirectly) the idea of divine instruction in particular OT corpora. As noted above, Georg Braulik has contributed a redaction-history study on the use of למד in Deuteronomy, while Karin Finsterbusch has offered a synchronic study of Moses as teacher in Deuteronomy.[16] Friedrich Diedrich studies the requests for divine instruction in Pss 25, 119, and 143, and concludes that these prayers likely reflect the personal piety of the wisdom tradition and the world of the scribal school.[17] Other work on the Psalms includes that of Erich Zenger, who argues that Yahweh is presented as both a teacher of the nation and the individual in the Psalms.[18] Beate Ego's recent essay takes a broader approach, surveying the concept of instruction in Deuteronomy, the prophetic tradition, the Psalms, Qumran, and the rabbinic literature.[19] In the present

---

[11] Schawe, *Lehrer* studies ירה (Hiphil), למד (Piel), and יסר and its derivatives. Much of Schawe's thesis is only indirectly related to divine instruction, since large portions of it analyze passages in which humans teach.

[12] Finsterbusch, *Weisung, passim.*

[13] Colless, 'Teacher,' 24–38, 112–23, 151–62 draws on Colless' unpublished M.A. thesis, *Yahweh Hammoreh. A Study of the Divine Educator Figure in the Religion of Israel*, 1965. The article leaves much to be desired. It is largely a listing of the OT texts, and includes little interaction with secondary literature.

[14] Colless, 'Divine Education,' 118–42.

[15] Kraus, 'Paedagogia,' 515–27 adopts Calvin's concept of *paedagogia Dei* in his attempt to find a concept that can account for both the unity and differences of the Old and New Testaments.

[16] Braulik, 'Deuteronomium,' 119–46; Finsterbusch, 'Mose,' 27–45.

[17] Diedrich, 'Lehre,' 59–73.

[18] Zenger, 'Lehrer,' 47–67.

[19] Ego, 'Implikationen,' 1–26.

chapter, I will seek to build on the secondary literature noted here, while addressing some issues that have been insufficiently discussed.

2.2 Divine instruction at Sinai

In order to understand the concept of divine instruction in the OT, we begin with the example *par excellence* of divine instruction: the giving of the Law at Sinai.[20] That this is divine instruction is evident in Deut 4.36: 'From heaven he let you hear his voice to instruct [יסר/παιδεύω][21] you; and on earth he let you see his great fire, and you heard his words from the midst of the fire.'[22] In Deut 4.10, the Lord tells Moses that he allowed the people to hear his words so that they would learn (למד [Qal]/μανθάνω) to fear him, and would teach (למד [Piel]/διδάσκω) their children.

An important feature of these Deuteronomic passages is the distinction between direct divine instruction and mediated divine instruction. The 'ten words'[23] are marked off from the rest of the Law as those that were spoken and written (4.13; 5.22; 9.10; 10.4) by God himself, without an intermediary.[24] The texts cited above (4.10, 36) therefore refer to the direct, unmediated divine instruction of the ten words. The Lord speaks the ten words recorded in 5.6–21 'face to face' with the people (5.4),[25] and only then do the people request that Moses act as an intermediary (5.24–27; cf. 18.16). Moses then teaches (למד) Israel the rest of the commandments in the plain of Moab (1.5; 4.1, 5; 5.31; 6.1). God's instruction is demarcated from the teaching of Moses and others in part by the terminology used to describe it. Schawe rightly points out that, in Deuteronomy, God is never the grammatical subject

---

[20] Cf. Braulik, 'Deuteronomium,' 134; Ego, 'Implikationen,' 3 on the archetypal nature of Sinai.

[21] The context of Deut 4.36 suggests that יסר has the sense of 'instruct' rather than 'discipline.' Cf. Schawe, *Lehrer*, 198.

[22] All biblical translations are my own. The 'instruction' of the Lord can also refer to disciplinary action (יסר in 8.5), and his great works on behalf of Israel (מוסר in 11.2). On the didactic nature of these passages, cf. Schawe, *Lehrer*, 199-203.

[23] That is, the 'ten commandments,' referred to as 'words' by the MT (דבר) and the LXX (ῥῆμα).

[24] For recognition of this distinction in the secondary literature, see Nicholson, 'Decalogue,' 422–33; Clines, 'Ten,' 26–45; Baker, 'Decalogue,' 1–24; Finsterbusch, 'Mose,' 35, n. 21.

[25] 5.5 might seem to imply that the communication of the Lord is not direct, since it suggests that Moses stands between the Lord and the people. On this question, cf. Baker, 'Decalogue,' 2, n. 3.

of לִמַּד.[26] Rather, in 4.36, יָסַר is used for God's direct teaching from heaven.[27]

Deuteronomy emphasizes that Moses teaches (לִמַּד) as the Lord commanded him to teach,[28] and this suggests that Moses' teaching mediates the divine instruction – it is not his own.[29] In turn, Moses' instruction is to be taught in public by Levitical priests and judges,[30] and in the family sphere by parents.[31] In sum, the Lord's instruction is mediated by Moses at the request of the people, and in turn mediated by elders, Levitical priests, and parents. However, the ten words were taught *directly* by the Lord to all the people (5.22). Although Israel did not see God's form at Sinai, they did hear his voice and learn from him (4.10, 12).

This distinction between the ten words and the rest of the Mosaic Torah is evident also in the Exodus account, which emphasizes God's direct communication of the ten words (Exod 20.1–17, 22) and his direct action in writing upon two tablets.[32] Like Deuteronomy, Exodus also recounts the people's request for an intermediary after the Lord speaks the ten words (20.19). The divine instruction of 20.22–23.33 (cf. 25.1–31.17) is therefore mediated through Moses, and no longer spoken directly by God. Also like Deuteronomy, Exodus specifies that the words written (and spoken) directly by God are for the instruction of the people: the Lord commands Moses to come up to the mountain so that he can give Moses the stone tablets 'with the Law and the commandment which I have written in order to instruct [יָרָה] them' (24.12).[33]

The distinction noted here between direct and mediated divine communication appears in some early Jewish sources that reflect upon the events at

---

[26] Schawe, *Lehrer*, 92.

[27] Cf. Finsterbusch, *Weisung*, 312–13.

[28] On the importance of לִמַּד in Deuteronomy, cf. Braulik, 'Deuteronomium,' 120. For the references to Moses' teaching at God's command, cf. 4.5, 14; 5.31; 6.1.

[29] לִמַּד in 4.1, 5, 14; 5.31; 6.1; 31.19, 22; לָקַח in 32.2. This is not to say that Moses' teaching consists *only* of repetition of the commands he received from God at Sinai. See Finsterbusch, 'Mose,' 27–45, and the critique of Schawe on this point by Finsterbusch, *Weisung*, 2–3.

[30] יָרָה in 17.10, 11; 24.8; 33.10. Note especially 24.8 for the emphasis that the Levitical priests teach as Moses commanded them. See 31.9–13, and cf. Ego, 'Implikationen,' 2–3.

[31] לִמַּד in 11.19. Note that in this text, parents are to teach 'these words of mine' (i.e. Moses' words). Cf. also 6.6–9, which uses the term שָׁנַן (6.7).

[32] 24.12; 31.18; 32.16. Contrast 24.4, where *Moses* writes commandments.

[33] There are few uses of didactic terminology in Exodus, and almost all these refer to *divine* instruction. Cf. יָרָה in 4.12, 15. יָרָה is also used in 15.25, but not with a didactic connotation. Cf. Schawe, *Lehrer*, 45. Μανθάνω in LXX 2.4 is not used in the sense of formal instruction.

Sinai.[34] Philo devotes much thought to the nature of the divine voice heard by the people at Sinai,[35] and also reflects on the idea that Moses stood between the Lord and the people.[36] In *Spec.* 3.7, he says that God spoke the ten words 'without a spokesman or interpreter...' In *Praem.* 2, he distinguishes the ten words from the rest of the pentateuchal legislation on the basis that the former did not come through a spokesman, while the latter was given 'through the lips of a prophet.' In *Her.* 17–19, he notes that,

> ...wise men [e.g. Moses] take God for their guide and teacher [ὑφηγητῇ καὶ διδασκάλῳ˙], but the less perfect take the wise man; and therefore the Children of Israel say 'Talk thou to us, and let not God talk to us lest we die.'[37]

The OT citation is from Exod 20.19, in which Israel asks for Moses to speak to them in place of God.[38] Philo's reference to God as διδάσκαλος demonstrates that for him, God's speech to Israel before their request for an intermediary was direct divine instruction.

In the *Hellenistic Synagogal Prayers*, likely written between 150 and 300 C.E., the ten words are said to have been spoken by the 'voice' of the LORD and engraved by his hand (5.13).[39] The distinction between the direct speech of God and his communication through an intermediary is clearly evident in *Mek. Bahodesh* 2.115–125,[40] but earlier sources also highlight the same distinction. The synonymous parallelism of Neh 9.13–14 distinguishes the Sabbath command (one of the ten words) from the other laws by virtue of the fact that it was spoken by God 'from heaven,' whereas the other commandments were given 'through Moses.' This is strikingly similar to Philo's *Mos.* 2.213–220, in which Philo retells the story of Num 15.32–36, and notes that the man in the narrative broke the Sabbath command – a command not spoken through God's prophet (i.e. Moses), but by God's voice.[41]

---

[34] I refer to divine 'communication,' because didactic terminology is not always used in these sources.

[35] Cf. *Migr.* 47–52; *Decal.* 32–35, 46–49. Cf. Aristob. frg. 4.3 (written perhaps around the middle of the second century B.C.E.); 1QM 10.10–11 (cited below in chapter 3). For another reference to the divine voice (though not at Sinai), cf. Sir 17.13.

[36] Cf. *Somn.* 2.229. On Moses as an intermediary in Philo's thought, cf. Borgen, 'Philo,' 340. Cf. *L.A.B.* 11.1–14, which probably dates to the early first century C.E.

[37] Unless noted, all Philo translations come from Colson, Whitaker, and Marcus, *Philo,* LCL (PLCL).

[38] On the Exodus passage, cf. Polak, 'Theophany,' 113–47.

[39] Cf. Darnell and Fiensy, 'Hellenistic Synagogal Prayers,' 683.

[40] In the midrash on Exod 19.3–9, Judah ha-Nasi says that Israel told Moses to tell God that, 'It is our wish to hear directly from the mouth of our King. To hear from the attendant is not like hearing from the mouth of the king...' Translation from Lauterbach, *Mekilta,* 2.209. For other rabbinic references, see Agnon, *Present,* 266–82.

[41] The importance of this distinction for Philo is emphasized by his reflection on the nature of that voice in the following context (cf. *Migr.* 47–49).

2.3 Divine instruction in the rest of the OT

As noted above, there are many OT references to God teaching people.[42] In fact, one of the fundamental differences between God and humans is that humans learn and are taught, while God knows all and cannot be taught anything.[43] God is sometimes said to teach those who are not Israelites,[44] but his instruction is almost invariably directed to his people.[45] He teaches extraordinary individuals,[46] but also the average covenant member who fears him (Ps 25.12) and even, in some sense, every human.[47] In this section, I am most interested in examining *when* divine instruction is thought to occur, the *content* of divine instruction, and *how* it is given.

First, when is divine instruction thought to occur? Most of the references to divine instruction in the OT, particularly in the Psalms, are concerned with God's instruction in the past or present.[48] This can be seen by the many requests for God's instruction in the Psalms. These are almost always imperative requests for the Lord to 'teach me.'[49] This indicates that divine instruction in the Psalms is not conceived of eschatologically, but rather as a present, immediate occurrence.[50] This is also the case in much of the rest of the OT and even in numerous passages in the prophetic literature.[51] In Isa 48.17, the Lord is known as the one who teaches Israel to profit, and in Jer 32.33, the Lord is said to have taught Israel and Judah many times in the past.[52] The

---

[42] God is more often said to teach than to be a teacher. The participial forms of לָמַד and διδάσκω ('who teaches') are used with reference to God in the MT and LXX (2 Sam 22.35; Ps 18.35 [ET 18.34]; 94.10; 144.1; Isa 48.17 [MT only]). God is identified as מוֹרֶה in Job 36.22; Isa 30.20.

[43] Cf. Job 21.22; Isa 40.14. Cf. Diedrich, 'Lehre,' 61; Merrill, 'לָמַד,' *NIDOTTE* 2.802.

[44] E.g. possibly Ezek 5.15 and LXX 2 Sam 22.48.

[45] Cf. LXX Isa 46.3 (not found in the MT). Schawe, *Lehrer*, 266 lists only three instances in the OT where God teaches the *Fremdvölker*.

[46] E.g. Moses (Exod 4.12, 15); David's sons (Ps 132.12); Isaiah (Isa 8.11); the Servant (Isa 50.4). Cf. Diedrich, 'Lehre,' 72. Cf. LXX Amos 3.7.

[47] Ps 94.10; Isa 28.26. Cf. Kraus, 'Paedagogia,' 522.

[48] For an example of past divine instruction in the Psalms, cf. Ps 71.17.

[49] Note the imperative of יָרָה (Hiphil) in Ps 27.11; 86.11; 119.33; Job 6.24; 34.32; 2 Chron 6.27; the imperative of לָמַד (Piel) in Ps 25.4; 25.5; 119.12, 26, 64, 66, 68, 108, 124, 135; 143.10. Cf. the imperative of יָדַע (Hiphil) in Ps 90.12; 143.8. Cf. Diedrich, 'Lehre,' 59–73, who focuses on לָמַד (Piel) in Pss 25, 119, 143.

[50] Cf. Ego, 'Implikationen,' 7, who contrasts the eschatological instruction of Israel in Jer 31.31–33 with the Torah piety of the Psalms. God's teaching of David's sons in Ps 132.12 may be partially, although not exclusively eschatological, since it is to continue through each generation.

[51] 1 Kgs 8.36 = 2 Chron 6.27 is probably not eschatological, since it is Solomon's request for God's ongoing response when his people act properly toward him.

[52] Cf. Isa 8.11; LXX Isa 46.3.

concept of *eschatological* divine instruction in Jeremiah and Isaiah stands over against this more common non-eschatological OT understanding of divine instruction.

Secondly, what is the content of divine instruction? The subject matter of divine instruction is quite variable: God teaches agriculture and war, among other things.[53] However, the preeminent objects of instruction, particularly in the Psalms, are the Torah and the way (דרך) of the Lord. The teaching of God's way likely refers to ethical direction,[54] as well as God's saving action.[55]

In Ps 119, we find repeated requests for God to teach his statutes [חק, e.g. 119.12, 26, 64, 124) and ordinances [משפט, e.g. 119.108]. These two terms are among the nine synonyms for Torah used in Ps 119, which begins by pronouncing a blessing upon those who walk in the תורה of the Lord (119.1). It is clear, then, that in Ps 119, God is thought to teach Torah.[56] This raises the much-debated issue of the meaning of Torah in the Psalms and the rest of the OT. The question is important for our discussion of the content of divine instruction. If Torah (and its synonyms) refers to the Mosaic commandments,[57] or to other previously given instruction (e.g. from priests, or wisdom teachers), then the psalmist's request for God to teach the Torah may well refer to the divine revelation of the meaning of a body of previous instruction. This is the view of B. Ego, who suggests that the divine teaching of Torah in Ps 119 refers to the divine revelation and illumination of the meaning of a previously given, *written* (*schriftlich*) revelation. Ego compares this divine instruction with the Levitical instruction in the Law recorded in Neh 8.1–12.[58]

Does Torah in Ps 119 refer to the Mosaic commandments?[59] It is clear that Torah in the Psalms and the OT can have a broader reference than the Mosaic Law. In the wisdom literature, it often has the more general sense of 'instruction,' with no clear reference to the Mosaic Law.[60] This is true also for some of the synonyms for Torah found in the wisdom literature, e.g. דבר, מצוה,

---

[53] For agriculture, cf. Isa 28.26, and the discussion in Finsterbusch, *Weisung*, 29–32, 45. For war, cf. 2 Sam. 22.35 = Ps 18.35 (ET 18.34); Ps 144.1; Hos 7.15; possibly Judg 3.2 (cf. Schawe, *Lehrer*, 131–32). See Ego, 'Implikationen,' 8, n. 31; Colless, 'Teacher,' 154–56. For the subject matter of divine instruction in the OT, cf. Schawe, *Lehrer*, 267.

[54] Schawe, *Lehrer*, 271.

[55] Diedrich, 'Lehre,' 62-63 argues that God's 'way' in Pss 25, 143 does not refer to Torah, but (at least in Ps 25) to his saving action.

[56] Levenson, 'Torah,' 561-63.

[57] It clearly has this sense in Deuteronomy. Cf. Liedke and Petersen, 'תורה,' *TLOT* 3.1420–21.

[58] Ego, 'Implikationen,' 9–12.

[59] Schawe, *Lehrer*, 127, 271 is somewhat unclear on this point.

[60] Liedke and Petersen, 'תורה,' *TLOT* 3.1416 provide examples, e.g. Prov 1.8; 3.1; 7.2; 13.14.

and דרך. Often, these terms refer not to the Mosaic Law, but to the wise commands, instructions, and sayings of parents and wisdom teachers.[61] Dahood refers to Ps 119 as the great 'Psalm of the Law,' but suggests that Torah refers to Law, 'in its widest sense, including all divine revelation as the guide of life and prophetic exhortation as well as priestly direction.'[62]

Jon Levenson also argues that Torah in Ps 119 refers neither to the Pentateuch, nor to the fixed body of Mosaic commandments, and moreover, that it 'lacks a constant identity.' The omission of any reference to Moses in Ps 119, and the lack of any book consciousness, suggests that the psalmist's Torah is not written. Therefore, the psalmist's prayer for divine instruction is not limited to a request for the gift of pneumatic exegesis.[63] For Levenson, the divine instruction of Ps 119.26–29 is unmediated divine teaching that comes through a pneumatic experience and results in *new* Torah. This is very different from Ego's view that Ps 119 speaks of the divine illumination of a previously given, written revelation. Levenson's conclusion is that the author of Ps 119, like Joshua ben Sira, knows at least parts of the Pentateuch, but does not limit Torah to it.[64]

Levenson may be correct in his claim that the Torah of Ps 119 is not identified with the Pentateuch or the Mosaic Law, and that it is more closely related to the instruction of the wisdom tradition. On the other hand, the close lexical links between Deuteronomy and Ps 119 noted by Levenson himself may suggest that the Torah of Ps 119 (together with the 'statutes' and 'commandments') does refer to the Mosaic Law. This may also be supported by the numerous references to the Torah and commandments as God's Torah.[65] God is said to teach the Mosaic Law elsewhere in the OT, and such may be the case in Ps 119.[66]

Even if Levenson is correct that Torah in Ps 119 does not refer solely to the Mosaic commandments, it does not follow that Torah refers to fresh, pneumatic revelations rather than illumination of a previously written body of instruction. Levenson's argument that Ps 119 evidences no book awareness is an *argumentum e silentio*, and even he admits the presence of teachers and

---

[61] Cf. Liedke and Petersen, 'תורה,' *TLOT* 3.1416.

[62] Dahood, *Psalms*, 3.172–73.

[63] Levenson, 'Torah,' 564–65.

[64] Levenson, 'Torah,' 567–68.

[65] E.g. Pss 94.12; 119.12, 26, 64; 132.12 ('my covenant,' 'my testimony').

[66] See Exod 24.12; Deut 4.36, noted above. In Ps 132.12, God teaches (למד) David's descendants either the Sinaitic covenant or the Davidic covenant, though it is hard to say which. Cf. Anderson, *Psalms*, 884. The frequent LXX translation of ירה with νομοθετέω (e.g. Exod 24.12; Deut 17.10; Pss 25.8 [LXX 24.8], 12 [LXX 24.12]; 27.11 [LXX 26.11]) may suggest an association between 'teaching' and the Law on the part of the Septuagint translator, although νόμος in the LXX need not refer to the Mosaic Law. On the translation of ירה with νομοθετέω, cf. Austermann, *Tora*, 177-79.

elders in 119.99–100. Diedrich argues that Ps 119 (and Pss 25, 143) arose out of scribal wisdom circles, which would seem to suggest a broader meaning of Torah than simply the Mosaic commandments, yet Diedrich still maintains that the Torah of Ps 119 is *written*.[67] This discussion of Torah in Ps 119 suggests that the psalmist's frequent requests for divine instruction refer in some cases to the revelation of the meaning of a written Torah (cf. 119.18), whether this is understood as the Mosaic commands, or as wisdom teaching.

Finally, how is divine instruction given? As noted above, God sometimes uses human intermediaries (e.g. Moses, priests, elders) to communicate instruction. However, in the Psalms, the divine instruction is often apparently more direct, and therefore perhaps internal. There is no indication in the psalmist's requests for divine instruction that he anticipates a public, Sinai-like experience of God. The psalmist's request, 'Teach me [לַמְּדֵנִי] thy paths. Lead me in thy truth and teach me [לַמְּדֵנִי]' (Ps 25.4–5) makes no mention of instruction through other humans, and implies an immediacy with God.[68] It is notable that requests for instruction in the Psalms are often placed alongside affirmations of the psalmist's close relationship with God.[69]

One means of divine instruction that emerges in Ps 143.10 is the Spirit:

Teach me [לַמְּדֵנִי] to do your will, for you are my God;
Let your good Spirit [רוּחֲךָ טוֹבָה] lead me on a level path.

The Spirit as a means of divine instruction is found also in LXX Job 32.8; 33.4, as well as Neh 9.20. As we will see in the following chapters, this idea of the Spirit as the agent of divine instruction is present in early Jewish literature and the NT.

2.4 The prophetic development of eschatological divine instruction

The prophetic idea of an *eschatological* divine instruction may be related to the emphasis in some prophets on a widespread eschatological knowledge of God and an outpouring of the Spirit of God.[70] This prophetic development

---

[67] Diedrich, 'Lehre,' 69.

[68] Note the comment of Levenson, 'Torah,' 564 that divine instruction in Ps 119 seems usually to occur without an intermediary (although he recognizes the reference to teachers and elders in 119.99–100). Levenson notes that this unmediated divine instruction contrasts with the Deuteronomic vision of instruction through other humans (particularly through Moses).

[69] E.g. Ps 25.5. Cf. Ego, 'Implikationen,' 13; Diedrich, 'Lehre,' 59–73.

[70] E.g. Ezek 36.26–27; 37.14; Joel 2.27–3.2 [ET 2.27–29]; Hab 2.14.

raises the question of how exactly divine instruction is communicated.[71] Does God continue to use intermediaries in the eschatological future, or is human instruction rendered unnecessary by direct divine instruction? We have already noted in the Exodus and Deuteronomy narratives a distinction between direct and mediated divine instruction. Will God's eschatological instruction be direct, as it was at Sinai before Moses began to act as an intermediary? If so, will it be the internal immediacy evident in the Psalms, or a public, visible theophanic experience as at Sinai? These questions are rarely asked in the secondary literature.

I will argue in this section that, while the prophetic texts (except for Jer 31.34) do not demand the idea of a direct, unmediated eschatological divine instruction, each of them can be plausibly read that way. Isaiah, which has a clear vision of eschatological divine instruction, never mentions human teachers in its descriptions of the eschatological future,[72] even though it refers to human teachers in the present.[73] The same is true for Jeremiah, which mentions human teaching in the past and present,[74] but never in the eschatological future, and in fact explicitly states that there will not be human teaching in the future (Jer 31.34).[75] Both these prophetic visions contrast with Ezekiel, who does not develop the idea of a future divine instruction *and* mentions the teaching (ירד/διδάσκω) of priests in the eschatological Temple (Ezek 44.23).[76] The prophetic expectation of divine instruction goes hand in hand, as Ego has perceptively noted, with a profound skepticism concerning the ability of humans to know God's will apart from divine aid.[77]

Isaiah 2.2–4/Micah 4.1–3

We can see the prophetic notion of a divine eschatological instruction in the material common to Isa 2.2–4 and Mic 4.1–3.[78] The phrase בְּאַחֲרִית הַיָּמִים in Isa 2.2 and Mic 4.1 is a technical expression marking the time of fulfillment

---

[71] A couple texts are uncertain: Hos 10.12 may refer to God teaching righteousness to Israel, and Joel 2.23 may mention a 'teacher for righteousness.' Cf. Riesner, *Lehrer*, 304–6.

[72] Isa 29.24; LXX Isa 32.4; 55.12 speak of future instruction, but leave unclear who teaches.

[73] I.e. the prophets in Isa 9.14 [ET 9.15].

[74] Jer 9.13 [ET 9.14]; 9.19 [ET 9.20]; 10.2.

[75] Jer 12.16 says that if, in the future, the surrounding nations learn (למד/μανθάνω) the ways of Israel, they will be blessed. However, it is unclear who teaches these ways.

[76] Cf. Riesner, *Lehrer*, 304.

[77] Ego, 'Implikationen,' 1–26, esp. 3–5.

[78] It is not necessary for our purposes to decide whether Micah or Isaiah is original, or whether both draw upon previously independent material. Cf. the thorough discussions in Andersen and Freedman, *Micah*, 413–27; Wildberger, *Isaiah*, 1.85–87.

for God's purposes in the world, and is in this sense eschatological.[79] Micah's vision of the future is striking: the peoples will climb to the Temple mount and receive instruction from the Lord. Mic 4.3 demonstrates that the instruction is largely of a juridical nature, but this should not be separated from ethical-religious instruction.[80] Both Isa 2.3 and Mic 4.2 connect divine instruction with the going forth of the תורה from Zion, and the 'word of the Lord' from Jerusalem. The nations (even distant nations, Mic 4.3) submit to the Lord's judgment as he arbitrates between them.

Oddly, many commentators do not ask how this eschatological divine instruction will occur. Some assume that human intermediaries like priests and prophets will be involved.[81] In fact, the text itself makes no mention of any human agency in the Temple.[82] The priests, condemned in Mic 3.11 because they instruct (ירה) for money, do not appear in the Temple. Of course, this does not prove that the prophetic vision is one without human intermediaries, but it opens up at least the possibility that the instruction of the Lord is direct. Andersen and Freedman suggest this idea of direct instruction from Yahweh, pointing to the direct instruction of Moses at Sinai as an analogy.[83] But it seems more likely that if the direct instruction at Sinai is in view, it is the Lord's direct teaching of all Israel (in the ten words) prior to their request for Moses to function as an intermediary. Isa 2 and Mic 4 demonstrate, then, the expectation of an eschatological divine instruction (largely of a juridical nature) that extends to all the nations. These texts open up the possibility, although they do not claim it explicitly, that the eschatological divine instruction is direct, not mediated.

Isaiah 30.20–21

The identity of the teacher[84] in Isa 30.20–21 is somewhat unclear, and it is possible that the language is deliberately obscure.[85] However, as Blenkinsopp

---

[79] Cf. Andersen and Freedman, *Micah*, 401. Wildberger, *Isaiah*, 1.88 notes that the versions (LXX, Targum, Syriac, Vulgate) interpret the phrase eschatologically.

[80] Cf. Schawe, *Lehrer*, 64-65.

[81] E.g. Wildberger, *Isaiah*, 1.96 suggests that the divine word of Isa 2.3 will presumably be 'imparted through the mediation of a priest or a prophet,' but the text itself makes no such claim. Wildberger does not suggest why we should 'presume' the presence of human intermediaries.

[82] Contrast Ezek 44.23 (see above).

[83] Cf. Andersen and Freedman, *Micah*, 404.

[84] With Riesner, *Lehrer*, 304, I read the singular 'teacher' of the MT here, rather than the plural 'teachers' of 1QIsa[a] or the plural 'those that cause you to err' of the LXX. This is supported by the concessive relationship of the two clauses; because the Lord is mentioned in the first clause, it is more likely that the second clause refers to him rather than to other teachers.

[85] Cf. Blenkinsopp, *Isaiah*, 1.420; Ego, 'Implikationen,' 6, n. 24.

notes, Job 36.22 refers to God as a teacher, and Isa 2.3; 48.17 mention him teaching (cf. also 28.26), so it is unsurprising that the Targum interprets the teacher to be God.[86] Blenkinsopp argues that, because the Lord is mentioned in the immediately preceding context, and because the word is said to be behind the listeners, the teacher is probably not the Lord, but a human teacher, perhaps the Servant (cf. 50.4).[87] However, neither of these arguments is convincing. Rather, Wildberger, Watts and Childs, among others, are correct to see the teacher as referring to the instructing presence of Yahweh himself, given the other Isaianic references to God as one who teaches.[88] The references to hearing and seeing the teacher imply an intimacy and direct immediacy with the Lord.[89] In this respect, it is similar to Jer 31.33-34 (see below).[90] Like Isa 2.2–4/Mic 4.1–3, this passage does not necessitate a lack of human intermediaries, but it does allow for that possibility.[91] The claim that the teacher will 'no longer hide himself' is perhaps reminiscent of God's withdrawal at Sinai after the request of the people for an intermediary.[92]

Isaiah 54.13

Several matters require attention in order to clarify the meaning of Isa 54.13. The MT of Isa 54.13 reads: וְכָל־בָּנַיִךְ לִמּוּדֵי יְהוָה וְרַב שְׁלוֹם בָּנָיִךְ. 1QIsaᵃ is identical to the MT, except that it has the *plene* spelling וכול, and reads ב'ניכי for the second בָּנָיִךְ. With the superscript *waw,* the Qumran Isaiah scroll refers to the great peace of 'your builders' rather than the MT's 'your sons.' In the Babylonian Talmud, R. Eleazar assumes the reading 'your sons' twice, but exegetes Isa 54.13 by repointing the text in both cases to read 'your builders': the 'builders' have great peace and are 'taught.'[93] Since Duhm,[94] many scholars have accordingly read בֹנַיִךְ for the first בָּנָיִךְ.[95] However, John

---

[86] Blenkinsopp, *Isaiah*, 1.420–21. The Targum reads: 'your eyes will see the Shekinah in the sanctuary.'

[87] On Blenkinsopp's reading, the word 'from behind' refers to a reminder from the past. But it more likely draws on the imagery of a shepherd who watches his flock from behind. Cf. Finsterbusch, *Weisung*, 36, n. 101; Watts, *Isaiah*, 401.

[88] Cf. Isa 2.3; 8.11; 28.26; 48.17; 50.4; 54.13. Cf. Childs, *Isaiah*, 227; Watts, *Isaiah*, 400–401; Riesner, *Lehrer*, 304.

[89] Cf. Watts, *Isaiah*, 1.401.

[90] Cf. Wildberger, *Jesaja*, 3.1197.

[91] Cf. Fischer, *Tora*, 77. *Contra* Finsterbusch, *Weisung*, 36.

[92] Cf. Watts, *Isaiah*, 1.400–401, who mentions Exod 19.21; 20.21–23.

[93] Cf. *b. Ker.* 28b. See also *b. Ber.* 64a and *b. Tamid* 32b, which end in similar fashion.

[94] Cf. Duhm, *Jesaia*, 411.

[95] This is noted by Watts, *Isaiah*, 2.236. Cf. Elliger, *Deuterojesaja*, 530 for a list of scholars holding this view. It is suggested, without argument, by Westermann, *Isaiah*, 276, 278.

Watts rightly notes that the MT's 'your sons' is well supported by the versions and should be retained.[96]

The lack of any verb in 54.13 raises two possibilities: one can supply וְשַׂמְתִּי (54.12) for the elliptical bicola in 54.13 (so, the LXX). Alternatively, 54.13 may consist of two nominal sentences in which the verb 'to be' is implied. The latter option seems more likely,[97] and in fact some manuscripts of the Isaiah Targum make explicit the verb by adding יהון.[98]

Another matter concerns the time reference of 54.13: are the implied verbs past, present or future? Watts translates 54.13, 'All your children are being taught by Yahweh...' and understands it to refer to the educational efforts of ancient Judaism.[99] Baltzer translates, 'and all your descendants have been taught by Yahweh,' and therefore appears to think the instruction has already occurred.[100] Blenkinsopp,[101] Westermann,[102] and Grimm and Dittert,[103] on the other hand, think 54.13 refers to a future period. This is almost certainly correct. The nearest verb וְשַׂמְתִּי in 54.12 is a conversive perfect, in keeping with the many other future references in Isa 54.[104] 54.7 particularly emphasizes the distinction between Yahweh's past abandonment of his people and his future gathering of them.[105] Moreover, the idealistic description of the future Zion's walls being made of precious stones (54.11–12) suggests that the ideal *eschatological* future is being described.

Finally, it is important to determine the meaning of לִמּוּדֵי יְהוָה in 54.13a. לִמּוּדֵי is a nominal form in construct with יְהוָה, and can be understood as an

---

[96] Watts, *Isaiah*, 2.236. LXX = πάντας τοὺς υἱούς σου διδακτοὺς θεοῦ. Isaiah Targum = 'your sons' (בְנָך).

[97] If 54.13 is dependent upon the verb in 54.12, וְכָל־בָּנַיִךְ would be parallel with שְׁמְשׁתַיִךְ, וּשְׁעָרַיִךְ, and וְכָל־גְּבוּלֵךְ in 54.12. The verb שִׂים can take a double accusative and refer to the act of making something into something else (cf. 1 Sam 8.1 and the examples in *HALOT* 3.1324). But the phrase וְכָל־בָּנַיִךְ לִמּוּדֵי יְהוָה is not precisely parallel with the preceding phrases, and this suggests that it does not depend upon שִׂים, as do the preceding nouns.

[98] Chilton, *Isaiah Targum*, 106 notes that יהון is present in 54.13a in the British Library manuscripts 2211 and 1474, but is omitted in the other witnesses. In 54.13b, it is present in all the Isaiah Targum manuscripts.

[99] Watts, *Isaiah*, 2.235, 239.

[100] Baltzer, *Deutero-Isaiah*, 448, 453. It is unclear why Baltzer thinks 54.13a should be, 'And all your descendants *have been* taught by Yahweh' while 54.13b should be, 'and great *will be* the peace/salvation of your descendants' (emphasis mine). The translation 'descendants' implies a future instruction, not one that has already occurred.

[101] Blenkinsopp, *Isaiah*, 2.365.

[102] Westermann, *Isaiah*, 278.

[103] Grimm and Dittert, *Deuterojesaja*, 447.

[104] E.g. 54.3, 4, 10, 14, 15.

[105] The Isaiah Targum understands 54.13 to be referring to the future, since its יהון is a future verb.

adjective ('taught')[106] or a noun ('student, disciple').[107] If the latter, the meaning is 'disciples of Yahweh.' If the former, the ambiguity of the construct state (literally: 'taught of Yahweh') allows for two possible meanings: 'taught *by* Yahweh,'[108] or 'taught of [i.e. *about*] Yahweh.'[109] The distinction is not inconsequential; in the former, Yahweh is the source and agent of instruction, while in the latter he is the topic of instruction. It is most likely that לִמּוּדֵי in 54.13 is a noun,[110] since the three other uses of לִמּוּד in Isaiah (8.16; 50.4 [2x])[111] are probably to be understood as nouns. If, however, one reads the adjective 'taught' (as does the LXX = διδακτούς), it seems more likely that the genitive construct carries the sense of agency rather than content.[112] In this case, it is basically synonymous with the meaning 'disciples of Yahweh.' In both instances, Yahweh is the source of the instruction rather than its content. The peace promised to Zion's sons in the second bicola is therefore the result of a personal relationship of instruction with Yahweh.

An acceptable translation of Isa 54.13 on the basis of the foregoing exegesis is: 'And all your sons (will be) disciples of Yahweh, and great (will be) the peace of your sons.' Isa 54.13, then, envisions a situation of eschatological divine instruction in Jerusalem. The promise that Zion's children will be 'disciples of Yahweh' implies an ongoing, personal relationship that reverses the people's refusal to accept God's instruction (Isa 30.9), and results in the peace and righteousness denied them previously (Isa 48.18, 22).[113]

Once again employing the categories developed above in our discussion of the divine instruction at Sinai, we may ask whether Isa 54.13 contains the idea of a direct, unmediated divine teaching, and if so, whether that divine instruction is understood to obviate the need for human teachers.[114] Both Schawe, and Grimm and Dittert think so.[115] Certainly, the text allows for

---

[106] Cf. Jer 2.24; 13.23.

[107] Cf. Isa 8.16; 50.4 (2x).

[108] This is what Waltke and O'Connor, *Syntax* 9.5.1b call a 'genitive of agency.'

[109] This is what Waltke and O'Connor, *Syntax* 9.5.3e call a 'topical genitive.'

[110] So *HALOT* 2.531; *DCH* 4.551.

[111] Cf. Williamson, *Isaiah*, 107–9. LXX 50.4–5 speaks of the παιδεία of the Lord, rather than of 'disciples.'

[112] The preceding context of 54.11–12 emphasizes the Lord's action on behalf of Jerusalem, so it is most natural to see the Lord also as the agent of instruction in 54.13. לִמּוּד is used six times in the OT, and only twice adjectivally (Jer 2.24; 13.23). Neither of these two instances is grammatically identical to 54.13, so external evidence for its adjectival use in the construct here is not decisive.

[113] Cf. especially Goldingay, *Isaiah*, 538; Finsterbusch, *Weisung*, 40–41.

[114] Westermann, *Isaiah*, 277–78 does not address these questions.

[115] Schawe, *Lehrer*, 136 suggests that the reference to 'disciples of Yahweh' means that Yahweh himself will instruct his people without need of a human teacher like a priest or prophet. He compares this to Jer 31.34. Grimm and Dittert, *Deuterojesaja*, 447–48 suggest

such a reading, as can be seen by the way in which Isa 54.13 is appropriated in some of the later rabbinic literature.[116] There is no mention of human teachers in Isaiah's eschatological vision, and Jerusalem's inhabitants are said to be disciples of the Lord.

However, Isa 54.13 is ambiguous enough to allow for other readings that do not envision a direct, unmediated divine teaching. The Targum understands Isa 54.13 to refer to the study/teaching of Torah, while *Exod. Rab.* 38.3, citing Isa 54.13, suggests that the priest who labors in Torah becomes a 'disciple of the Holy One.'[117] Accordingly, some modern commentators see no direct divine instruction mentioned in Isa 54.13.[118]

In fact, the striking feature of Isa 54.13 is just how ambiguous it leaves the promise of being 'disciples of Yahweh.' The text does not say whether God will teach his people directly, and it does not say whether the need for human teachers/intermediaries will be obviated. Perhaps it is this lack of specificity in the text itself that has led to varying interpretations and made it useful for differing purposes in various contexts. The emphasis in Isa 54.13 is upon the fact *that* all the children will be 'disciples of Yahweh,' and the consequent שלום they will enjoy, rather than on specifically how the divine instruction will occur or what its content will be.[119]

Jeremiah 31.31–34

Although Jer 31.31–34 does not explicitly claim that God teaches, there is a close combination of God's action in 31.33 and the didactic terminology in 31.34, and this makes the passage relevant to our study.[120] As with Isa 54.13, it is important to establish the time reference of this passage. Within the immediate context of 31.31–34, we may note the repeated phrases 'days are coming' (31.27, 31, 38), 'in those days' (31.29), and 'after those days'

---

that perhaps a 'direct, unmediated Torah-teaching of Jerusalemites is announced,' and also compare Jer 31.34.

[116] Cf. *Gen. Rab.* 95.3; *Exod. Rab.* 21.3.

[117] Cf. *Num. Rab.* 11.7; *b. Ber.* 64a.

[118] Blenkinsopp, *Isaiah*, 2.365 thinks 54.13 refers to study of the Law (citing the Targum). Cf. Watts, *Isaiah*, 2.239; Baltzer, *Deutero-Isaiah*, 453.

[119] Grimm and Dittert, *Deuterojesaja*, 448 note Isaiah's lack of concern with how the promise of being 'disciples of Yahweh' will occur, and contrast this with the Deuteronomist, who names the teaching authorities who function as intermediaries of the teaching of Torah.

[120] See the section on methodology in chapter 1 above. Because it contains the only explicit reference in the OT to a 'new covenant' (בְּרִית חֲדָשָׁה), and is important to the Christian tradition, Jer 31.31–34 has received an enormous amount of attention in the secondary literature. Cf. the bibliographies in Levin, *Verheißung*, 280–94; Holladay, *Jeremiah*, 2.149–50; Keown, Scalise, and Smothers, *Jeremiah*, 82–83. My interests for the purpose of this study allow me to bypass much of this literature.

(31.33).[121] These phrases clearly point to the future,[122] but is it the near future or the eschatological future? Scholars are divided, with some suggesting that the prophecy points to some time in the future (but not the eschatological future),[123] some suggesting that it is an eschatological prophecy,[124] and some not declaring themselves either way.[125] It is helpful to note in this regard that 31.31–34 falls within the larger section of 30.1–33.26, Jeremiah's so-called 'Book of Consolation,' a section framed by the repeated promise of the Lord: 'I will restore their fortunes' (30.3; 33.26).[126] The section is characterized by expressions of hope for the future, found already in 30.3, with its promise of restoration to the land for Israel and Judah.[127] When 31.31–34 is read within this larger context, with its promises of a future Davidic king (30.9; 33.15–17) and restoration to the land (e.g. 30.3, 10, 18; 31.24, 38; 33.11), it seems likely that the promise of the new covenant is indeed eschatological.

31.31–34 is composed of two oracles, each with the double formula 'declares the Lord': 31.31–32 specifies what the covenant will not be, and 31.33–34 suggests what it will be.[128] In 31.33, the Lord promises that he will put his Law within the people and write it on their heart (sing.). The result of this divine action is then described in 31.34: all the people will know the Lord, from the least to the greatest, and therefore will not teach (לִמֵּד) one another, saying, 'Know the Lord.' The question of particular interest for our study is what this means. Does direct divine communication render human teaching otiose in the eschatological future? Interpretations of Jer 31.34 have varied, and we can identify at least three positions:

Table 1. *Interpretations of Jeremiah 31.34*

No human teaching in the future	Some human teaching in the future	Human teaching, but people will learn easily
Thompson; Potter; Holladay; Keown, Scalise, and Smothers; Schawe	Lundbom	Duhm; McKane (?); Swetnam

---

[121] The immediate context of 31.31–34 is the unit of short sections 31.23–26, 27–30, 31–34, 35–37, 38–40. The suggestion by Keown, Scalise, and Smothers, *Jeremiah*, 126–27 of a chiastic arrangement is unlikely, because there is no clear contrast between 31.27–30 and 31.35–37.

[122] McKane, *Jeremiah*, 2.817–18 rightly suggests that Rudolph's attempt to distinguish between 'in those days' and 'after those days' (31.34) is overly precise.

[123] McKane, *Jeremiah*, 2.821 mentions Herrmann and Perlitt as holding this view.

[124] Cf. Keown, Scalise, and Smothers, *Jeremiah*, 127.

[125] Cf. Thompson, *Jeremiah*, 579–81; Lundbom, *Jeremiah*, 2.464–72.

[126] Lundbom, *Jeremiah*, 2.368–69 thinks chapters 30–31 formed an original compositional unit, later expanded to include chapters 32–33.

[127] Cf. Thompson, *Jeremiah*, 551.

[128] Cf. Lundbom, *Jeremiah*, 2.464. The suggestion of a chiastic arrangement by Holladay, *Jeremiah*, 2.164–65 is unconvincing. His arrangement links 31.33a with what precedes, but the זֹאת is clearly proleptic.

In his 1901 commentary, B. Duhm argued that 31.31–34 is written not by
Jeremiah, but by a later scribe, whose greatest affliction is that most Israelites
receive instruction only with difficulty. The hope of 31.34 is not that people
will adhere to a new Law, but that the Torah given at Sinai will be learned
effortlessly by the people. According to Duhm, there is nothing in 31.33–34
to suggest that the writer envisions a direct communication between God and
his people. The truth is much more mundane: the scribal writer envisions his
own ideal, that all God's people would be instructed in the Torah, and thus
become scribes themselves.[129] McKane finds Duhm's interpretation attrac-
tive,[130] but few other scholars have agreed. The problem with Duhm's proposal is that it is almost exactly the opposite of what the text actually says. In
Duhm's view, all will be teachers. The text claims, rather, that none will be
teachers.[131]

But is all human teaching rendered obsolete? Lundbom suggests that formal teaching is not in view at all. He claims that, 'Know Yahweh!' is the instruction of a prophet, and therefore Jeremiah is envisioning a day when there
will be no more prophets like himself.[132] However, Lundbom does not argue
for his claim that formal teaching is not at issue, and neither does he provide
evidence for his claim that 'Know Yahweh!' is the instruction of a prophet.
Contra Lundbom, it does seem that formal teaching is in view. If Jer 31.34 is
read in light of the earlier condemnations of those responsible for providing
formal instruction to Israel (e.g. 2.8; 8.8–11), it seems likely that in 31.34 the
scribal class is declared obsolete in the eschatological future.[133] Moreover,
the closest OT formulation to 'Know Yahweh!' is Prov 3.6, which records the
words of a wisdom teacher, not a prophet.[134] Importantly, there is no explicit
restriction in Jer 31.34 itself to a particular kind of teacher. This suggests that
Lundbom is probably wrong to restrict its reference only to prophets. But it
would be equally wrong to restrict it to the scribal class. It seems rather that
Jeremiah's eschatological vision is of a situation without any human instruc-

---

[129] Duhm, *Jeremia*, 255–57. The view of Swetnam, 'New,' 111–15 is different than
Duhm, but also allows for continued human teaching in the future. Swetnam thinks the
'newness' of the new covenant is that copies of the Mosaic Law will be made available to all
Israelites in the newly formed synagogues. Swetnam suggests that 31.31–34 is connected
with the rise of the synagogue in the exilic period.

[130] McKane, *Jeremiah*, 2.826, although he admits it may be 'unacceptably reductionist.'

[131] This point is brought out clearly by Potter, 'Covenant,' 348. It is therefore inappropri-
ate for Lundbom, *Jeremiah*, 2.470 to describe Potter's view as 'largely a holdover' of
Duhm's argument. Rather, the two views are the opposite of each other.

[132] Lundbom, *Jeremiah*, 2.470.

[133] Cf. Swetnam, 'New,' 112–13; Potter, 'Covenant,' 352–55.

[134] Cf. Keown, Scalise, and Smothers, *Jeremiah*, 135; Holladay, *Jeremiah*, 2.198.

tion, whether it be the instruction of prophets, priests, parents, elders or teachers.[135]

This is brought out even more clearly by the contrast between Jer 31.31–34 and the Deuteronomic vision of instruction. As noted above, Deuteronomy stresses the importance of instruction in both the home and the public sphere. In Deut 6.6–9, the words of the Law are to be 'upon your heart' (cf. Jer 31.33) and each Israelite is to teach the words of the Law to his children (cf. Deut 11.19). In Deuteronomy, the words 'be upon your heart' refer to memorization, and clearly do not preclude human instruction. However, in the eschatological vision of Jeremiah, *God* writes his Law upon the heart of his people (this is not simply memorization) and his action renders human instruction obsolete.[136] In Deut 31.9–13, Moses writes the Law and gives it to the Levitical priests and elders, instructing them to read it publicly every seven years so that all the people will 'hear and learn' to fear the Lord. In Jer 31.33, the Law is written 'on the heart,' and such public instruction is therefore rendered unnecessary.[137]

In light of these differences with Deuteronomy,[138] it seems that the Jeremianic future is contrasted not only with the failure of the scribal, priestly class, but also with the situation in which parents must teach children, and priests and elders must publicly teach the people. In the future, God's Law will be within the human heart, and therefore external instruction of all kinds will be unnecessary.[139] It appears that the past divine instruction that Israel has rejected (למד in 32.33) was communicated, at least in part, through prophets.[140] Jeremiah's claim that all will know the Lord, from the least to the greatest, probably means both 'from young to old' (cf. Jer 6.11–13) and

---

[135] Cf. Thompson, *Jeremiah*, 581; Keown, Scalise, and Smothers, *Jeremiah*, 135; Schawe, *Lehrer*, 103–4. Finsterbusch, *Weisung*, 74–76 argues that parental teaching of children is not in view in Jer 31.34, but I agree with Weinfeld, 'Jeremiah,' 28–29 that it probably is in view.

[136] Potter, 'Covenant,' 350–51 clearly brings out this difference between Jeremiah and Deuteronomy, although I am not persuaded by his thesis that Jeremiah's words are an attack upon the Deuteronomic reform of Josiah. It seems rather that the need for present human instruction is contrasted with the eschatological future, in which human instruction will be unnecessary. Cf. Weinfeld, 'Jeremiah,' 26–29 and Finsterbusch, *Weisung*, 74, who rightly suggests that the divine action in Jer 31.34 guarantees that the individual will always have Torah present to him and will not forget it, the very purpose aimed at in the Deuteronomic teaching.

[137] Cf. Keown, Scalise, and Smothers, *Jeremiah*, 133–34.

[138] Cf. Groß, 'Bund,' 62.

[139] Cf. Holladay, *Jeremiah*, 2.198.

[140] Cf. Schawe, *Lehrer*, 132–34; Finsterbusch, *Weisung*, 77. Cf. the prophets sent by God and rejected by the people (7.25–26). Jeremiah is told to identify Israel as the nation that did not obey the voice of the Lord or accept instruction (מוסר in 7.28; cf. 17.23; 32.33; 35.13, 15).

'from the lowest class to the upper class' (cf. 5.4–5).[141] Older (parents) will not need to teach younger (children), and the educated elite will no longer need to teach the uneducated masses.

I conclude that the eschatological vision of Jer 31.31–34 is one in which human instruction is no longer necessary (31.34) because of the work of God in placing his Law within his people and writing it upon their heart (31.33).[142] 31.31–34 does not explicitly claim that the Lord will teach eschatologically,[143] but it does claim that humans will not teach, because of the Lord's action. Again, this passage may presuppose the categories seen in our discussion of the divine instruction at Sinai: God's direct communication with his people, and his use of human intermediaries for instruction. Later rabbinic discussion interprets the situation envisioned in Jer 31.33–34 in just this way, as a return to God's direct communication at Sinai before the request of the people for an intermediary.[144]

2.5 Conclusion

This overview of divine instruction in the OT has shown that the idea is a significant one in numerous OT writings, and that it is worked out in various ways. Of interest for the NT development of divine instruction are the several OT references to the Spirit teaching (Neh 9.20; Ps 143.10; LXX Job 32.8; 33.4). Also noteworthy is the correlation between divine instruction and revelation of the meaning of a body of previous instruction (e.g. Ps 119). Finally, the questions of how and when divine instruction is communicated are important. In Deuteronomy, the presence of human intermediaries is prominent, while in the Psalms, divine instruction appears to be most often direct and internal. In both Deuteronomy and the Psalms, divine instruction is normally a past or present event. The prophetic development of an eschatological divine instruction goes hand in hand with the prophetic pessimism concerning human inability to understand God's will and act in obedience. God's end-time instruction is the solution to this problem.[145]

Each of the prophetic passages examined (Isa 2.2–4/Mic 4.1–3; Isa 30.20–21; 54.13; Jer 31.33–34) suggests at least the possibility that this fu-

---

[141] Cf. Holladay, *Jeremiah*, 2.198–99.

[142] Cf. Kapelrud, 'למד,' *TDOT* 8.8.

[143] Some rabbinic interpretations of Jer 31.31–34 conclude that the Lord *does* promise to teach his people. In TanB *Yitro* Exod 5.13, the 'Holy One' says that in 'the world to come' he will teach (למד) all Israel the Torah and none will forget it. In support of this claim, Jer 31.33 is cited. Cf. *Pesiq. Rab Kah.* 12.21.1.

[144] Cf. *Cant. Rab.* 1.4, cited below in chapter 5.

[145] Cf. Finsterbusch, *Weisung*, 44.

ture instruction is unique in its directness. There are no human intermediaries described, and in Jer 31.34, their presence is explicitly denied. Isaiah, which develops the idea of divine eschatological instruction, does not mention human instruction in the eschatological future, while Ezekiel, which does not develop the idea of divine eschatological instruction, does mention such instruction (Ezek 44.23). The direct instruction of the prophetic vision does not appear to be the private, internal directness of the Psalms, but rather, a more public one. It may be that the prophets draw upon the categories of direct/mediated divine instruction we saw in the Exodus and Deuteronomic narratives. If this is the case, then the possibility is raised that in the last days, God will be personally, theophanically present to instruct humans. However, Finsterbusch is correct in her assertion that the emphasis of the Isaiah passages is not upon how the Lord will instruct his people, but on the fact that he will make his instruction accessible.[146] While this is true, the idea of an unmediated eschatological divine instruction is nonetheless raised as a legitimate possibility.

---

[146] Finsterbusch, *Weisung*, 45.

Chapter 3

Divine instruction in early Jewish literature

'When his deeds are evident, he shall be expelled from the congregation,
like one whose lot did not fall among the disciples of God.'

Damascus Document 20.4[1]

In this chapter, I examine the idea of divine instruction in early Jewish literature in order to discern whether the idea continued to be an important one after the Old Testament period, in writings more closely contemporary with the New Testament. The concept is developed most fully and interestingly in the Dead Sea Scrolls and the writings of Philo of Alexandria. Accordingly, these sources receive the most extensive treatment. The idea of divine instruction is also present (albeit to a lesser extent) in the writings of Josephus, the Apocrypha,[2] and Old Testament Greek pseudepigrapha,[3] and the relevant passages from these writings are also examined. Finally, I treat the Jewish expectation of a teaching and/or God-taught messianic figure. In the investigation of each of these sources, the methodology outlined in chapter 1 has been employed.

---

[1] Unless otherwise noted, translations of the DSS are taken from García Martínez and Tigchelaar, *Scrolls.*

[2] I follow Charlesworth, 'Apocrypha,' 292-94, who describes the Apocrypha as a 'closed and focused collection' of 13 works: Epistle of Jeremiah, Tobit, Judith, 3 Ezra (aka 1 Esdras), Additions to Esther, Prayer of Azariah and the Song of the Three Young Men, Susanna, Bel and the Dragon, 1 Baruch, Ben Sira, Wisdom of Solomon, 1 Maccabees, 2 Maccabees. Charlesworth does not include 4 Ezra or the Prayer of Manasseh.

[3] I limit myself to *Greek* pseudepigraphal texts because of the importance of controlling the study by means of vocabulary (see chapter 1). I base my work on the Greek texts concorded in A.-M. Denis' volume: *Life of Adam and Eve* (*Apocalypse of Moses*), *1 Enoch* (Greek), *Testament of Abraham*, *Testaments of the Twelve Patriarchs*, *Joseph and Aseneth*, *Psalms of Solomon*, *Paraleipomena Jeremiou* (*4 Baruch*), *3 Baruch*, *Lives of the Prophets*, *Greek Apocalypse of Ezra*, *Apocalypse of Sedrach*, *Testament of Job*, *Letter of Aristeas*, *Sibylline Oracles*, and fragments of 37 other works. Collins, 'Review,' 132-33 notes that Denis omits some works found in Charlesworth's volumes: some of the books of the *Sibylline Oracles*, *Testament of Solomon*, and *3-4 Maccabees*. A search of *3-4 Maccabees* shows that they connect didactic terminology with the Law, but not directly with God.

3.1 Divine instruction in the Dead Sea Scrolls

An examination of the Hebrew, Aramaic, and Greek texts from Qumran reveals that there is no didactic terminology in the few extant Greek texts, and that although the Aramaic texts use some didactic terminology, only 11Q10 (11QTargum of Job) 27.3-4 connects that terminology with God.[4] This text, which probably uses מוסר as a Hebrew loan-word, is a literal translation of Job 36.10: 'And He will open their ears for instruction…'[5] The entire fragment is a translation of Job 36.7-16. The focus of our investigation, therefore, will be the Hebrew texts from Qumran. These texts frequently use didactic terminology, and in approximately 50 instances this terminology is closely connected with a reference to God.[6]

Study and education at Qumran

The matter of what one knows and how one knows it is discussed frequently in the Qumran materials.[7] The viewpoint of many of the non-biblical writings at Qumran is that true knowledge must come from God,[8] for humans are unable to attain it apart from divine aid.[9] Numerous texts speak of God as the 'God of knowledge' (1QS 3.15)[10] and the 'source of knowing' (1QS 10.12). This epistemology may have affected some of the social structures of the community. Alexander Rofé has drawn attention to CD 10.7-10, which stipulates that those over 60 years old are not allowed to judge the congregation.[11] Rofé suggests that the practice of giving leadership to younger men may derive in part from Qumran's concept of revealed wisdom. Their view may reflect a strand of biblical thinking in which, 'Age and

---

[4] I have examined all uses of the following Aramaic words: יסר, אלף, אלפן, אלפון, אלך, מוסר.

[5] García Martínez, Tigchelaar, and Van der Woude, *Qumran Cave 11*, 140-42.

[6] This section is based on an examination of all uses of the following 11 didactic terms: מורה, מוסר, יסר, ירה (to teach, show), לימוד, למוד (Pual), למד (Qal), למד (Piel), שכל, לקח (Hiphil).

[7] Cf. Ringgren, *Qumran*, 114-20. Despite their strong emphasis on knowledge, the DSS should not be identified with Gnosticism due to the differences between the two. For example, knowledge in the Gnostic literature is the means of salvation. At Qumran, salvation comes through repentance and covenant-keeping. Cf. Pearson, 'Gnosticism,' 313-17; Reicke, 'Gnosticism,' 137-141; Davies, 'Knowledge,' 134-41.

[8] E.g. 1QS 11.3-7.

[9] See Goff, *Heavenly Wisdom*, 51, commenting on the epistemology of 4QInstruction. Several texts from the *Hodayot* indicate a similar epistemology: 1QH[a] 5.19-20; 9.21-23; 18.2-7.

[10] Cf. e.g. 1QH[a] 9.26; 20.10; 4Q299 frg. 35.1.

[11] See below for caveats about using CD to reconstruct the practices of the Qumran community.

experience do not grant wisdom; it is the spirit emanating from God that instructs men.'[12]

Together with this view of divine revelation, religious study and education were highly valued at Qumran.[13] Study and teaching were centered on the Scriptures. The community is referred to in CD 20.10, 13 as the 'house of Torah,' and the *pesharim* manifest the community's active engagement with the OT prophetic texts. Several passages from the Rule of the Community (1QS) illustrate the emphasis on study.[14] 1QS 6.6-8 indicates that the community conducted a group study session for about three hours a night in addition to the perpetual study of the Law throughout the day and night.[15] The community in fact defined itself through its interpretation of the Scriptures. It sought to isolate itself not only from those who neglected the Scriptures, but also from those who interpreted them differently.[16] This is suggested by 1QS 5.10-12. The 'men of injustice' who walk in the path of wickedness do not belong to the covenant because they,

…have neither sought [בקשׁו] nor examined [דרשׁהו] his decrees [בחוקוהי] in order to know the hidden matters [הנסתרות] in which they err by their own fault and because they treated revealed matters [והנגלות] with disrespect…

The 'hidden matters' included proper observance of the Sabbath and festivals, which God revealed to the community through the proper interpretation of the Scriptures (cf. CD 3.12-16).[17] During the two-year probationary period required in order to become a full member of the community (1QS 6.21), novices were taught by the Instructor (משׂכיל; cf. 4Q298 frg. 1.1) and then examined with regard to their knowledge and purity by the Examiner (מבקר; cf. CD 15.11).[18]

The titles of several of the community leaders also indicate the great importance of education. The revered founder of the community was called the 'Teacher of Righteousness' (מורה צדק), and the officer who taught the novices during their probationary period was called the 'Instructor' (משׂכיל).[19] The title 'Interpreter of Torah' (דורשׁ בתורה) refers to a future messianic figure (CD 7.18-19; 4Q174 frg. 1i.11), and Charlesworth

---

[12] Rofé, 'Revealed Wisdom,' 1-11.

[13] See now Steudel, 'Weg,' 99-116.

[14] 1QS is only one version of the community's rule, and is likely a later version than that reflected in 4QS^{b,d} and 4QS^e. Cf. Metso, *Development*, 151-55, esp. 152-53; Charlesworth, 'Community,' 133.

[15] Cf. Viviano, 'Study and Education,' 896-98.

[16] Cf. Patte, *Hermeneutic*, 214-15; Betz, *Offenbarung*, 59.

[17] Cf. Patte, *Hermeneutic*, 218-25.

[18] See Charlesworth, 'Community,' 133. The two figures should not be identified with one another. Cf. Hempel, 'Community Structures,' 80-82.

[19] Derived from the Hiphil of שׂכל. See *DCH* 5.504.

speculates that it may sometimes have designated a particular individual during ceremonial events (perhaps recalling the Teacher of Righteousness).[20]

Didactic terminology combined with a reference to God

Didactic terminology is used abundantly in the DSS, and the same verbs are used with both humans and God as their grammatical subject. This is true for all four of the didactic verbs I have examined: שׂכל, למד, ירה and יסר. First, שׂכל is used frequently to refer to the didactic activity of human teachers within the community. The most important official of the community, the Examiner (מבקר),[21] who presides when the community is assembled, is to instruct (שׂכל) the many in the deeds of God (CD 13.7). The Instructor is to teach (שׂכל) the community the 'mysteries of wonder and of truth' (1QS 9.18)[22] and all the legal findings (1QS 9.20).[23] In the future, ideal community, children are to be taught (שׂכל) the statutes of the covenant, and receive instruction (מוסר) in its regulations (1Q28a [1QRule of the Congregation] 1.7-8).[24] In approximately 15 instances, the same verb is used to indicate that *God* teaches.[25]

Secondly, 1QS 3.13 states that it is the responsibility of the Instructor to teach (למד) all the sons of light about the generations of man. In CD 15.14, the Examiner is to teach (למד) new initiates for a full year.[26] למד in the Piel is used with God as its subject seven times.[27] Thirdly, ירה is used for the teaching of the Teacher of Righteousness (CD 20.14) and the Spreader of Lies (1QpHab 10.11), and also in 10 instances for the teaching of God.[28] Finally, the community is to teach (יסר) its members (1QS 3.6) and the Examiner is to teach (יסר) children.[29] יסר is used for the teaching of God in perhaps four instances in the DSS (some texts are too fragmentary for certainty).[30]

---

[20] See Charlesworth, 'Community,' 134. Cf. Knibb, 'Interpreter,' 383-84.

[21] Cf. 1QS 6.11-12, 20; CD 14.13; 15.8, 11, 14.

[22] On the similar didactic duties in CD 13.7 and 1QS 9.18, cf. Hempel, *Laws*, 119-20.

[23] Cf. 1QS 11.1.

[24] Cf. Viviano, 'Study and Education,' 897.

[25] Some of the texts are too fragmentary to be certain, but the following are likely: 1QS 4.22; 1QH^a 15.26; 18.4, 6, 7; 19.4, 10; 20.33; 1QH^a frg. 5.11; 4Q379 frg. 18.6; 4Q381 frg. 24a+b.11; 4Q381 frg. 44.4; 4Q381 frg. 69.4, 5a; 4Q418a frg. 2.1.

[26] Cf. also fragments of CD found in Cave 4: 4Q266 frg. 8i.5; 4Q270 frg. 6ii.7.

[27] 1QM 14.6; 4Q372 frg. 2.4; 4Q491 frg. 8-10i.4; 1QH^a 10.17; 15.10; 4Q438 frg. 4ai.1; 11Q5 24.8.

[28] CD 3.8; 1QS 10.13; 11.17; 1QSb 3.23; 1QH^a 14.9; 4Q216 1.7; 4Q258 frg. 5.2; 4Q264 frg. 1.5; 4Q364 frg. 14.4; 4Q434 frg. 1ii.4.

[29] Cf. 4Q266 (4QDamascus Document^a) 9iii.6; 4Q286 (4QBerakhot^a) frg. 14.2.

[30] 1QH^a frg. 10.7 = 4Q427 frg. 8i.9; 4Q504 frgs. 1-2iii.6; 4Q504 frg. 6.15. The latter two references, both of which allude to Prov 3.12, occur in the Words of the Luminaries, a text

In addition to these four verbs, God is brought into close conjunction with the following didactic terminology: למד Pual (1QM 10.10); למוד (CD 20.4; 1QHᵃ 10.39; 15.10, 14; 4Q428 frg. 3.9; 4Q428 frg. 10.7; 4Q434 frg. 1i.4); מוסר (4Q438 frg. 3.3; 4Q504 frgs. 1-2v.17). In the Isaiah Scroll, God is twice referred to as מורה in Isa 30.20.[31]

Divine instruction at Sinai

I demonstrated above in chapter 2 that in the OT, God's giving of the 'ten words' at Sinai was understood as direct divine instruction. Several texts and fragments suggest that at Qumran, and in the larger world of Second Temple Judaism, Sinai was thought of as a place of divine instruction. The language of Exod 24.12 is echoed in two fragmentary para-biblical texts, 4Q216 (4QJubilees^a) and 4Q364 (4QReworked Pentateuch^b). The former was likely written before the sectarian withdrawal to Qumran, and it is unclear whether the latter was actually composed at Qumran, so these texts may well be representative of wider Judaism.[32] In 4Q216 1.7, God tells Moses that he will give him the stone tablets – the Law and the commandment which he has given to teach (ירה) them. 4Q364 frg. 14.4 cites Exod 24.12: 'the torah and the mitzvah which I have written to teach [ירה] them.'

Further, 4Q381 (4QNon-Canonical Psalms B) frg. 69.5 likely refers to Sinai, using the language of instruction, and is reminiscent of Deut 4.36 and Neh 9.13-14:

...he came down from heaven and spoke to you to teach you [להשכיל] and to turn (you) away from the deeds of the inhabitants of/ [...he gave l]aws, instructions and commandments through the covenant which he established through the hand of [Moses]...

There is no clear evidence that 4Q380 or 4Q381 (likely both part of an originally-unified collection) were composed by the Qumran community, since they do not contain themes or terminology unique to Qumran.[33] Therefore, this reference to divine instruction at Sinai may, like the two passages above, represent a more broadly Jewish view.

Finally, a passage in 1QM may also refer to the events of Sinai as divine instruction. The question of the composition and provenance of 1QM remains an open question among scholars, with some arguing that the document was

---

probably of non-Qumranic origin, but one that was preserved by the community and could well have been used in its prayer ritual. Cf. Chazon, 'Luminaries,' 989.

[31] Unfortunately, the pesher on Isa 30.20 (4Q163 frg. 23ii.17) is fragmentary and neither use of מורה is preserved in the lemma, nor is the interpretation of this verse preserved.

[32] Cf. VanderKam, 'Jubilees,' 434; Crawford, 'Pentateuch,' 776.

[33] Cf. Flint, 'Psalms,' 709; Schuller, '4QNon-Canonical Psalms B,' 90.

composed at Qumran, and others claiming that the whole document, or some of its sources, should be dated earlier.[34] In 1QM 10.10, Israel is described as,

...a nation of holy ones of the covenant, learned in the law[35] [ומלומדי חוק], wise in knowledge, [...] hearers of the glorious voice, seers of the holy angels, with opened ears, hearing glorious things...

The reference to the 'hearers of the glorious voice' (ושומעי קול נכבד), together with the mentions of 'opened ears' and 'hearing glorious things,' may echo the language of Deut 4.12; 5.22 and point to the giving of the Law at Sinai in Exod 20 and Deut 4.[36] As we saw above, in Exod 20, God speaks directly to the people from Sinai until they ask for Moses to function as an intermediary for them. Deut 4.36 says that God let Israel hear his voice (קול) in order to instruct (יסר) them. If Deut 4.36 stands behind 1QM 10.10, the reference to being 'instructed in the Law' may refer to *divine* instruction, and למד may refer to the direct, unmediated divine instruction at Sinai by which Israel received the Law. An extremely fragmentary parallel to this passage is found in 4Q495 frg. 1.2, which preserves the partial words: ברית ומ] [.[37]

Who is taught by God?

In this discussion of the numerous Qumran passages concerning divine instruction, I will pose the three questions asked above in chapter 2: when is divine instruction thought to occur? What is the content of divine instruction? How is divine instruction given? Before answering these questions, however, I will first ask, in the DSS, who are the recipients of divine instruction?

Several texts suggest that the entire community was taught by God. Most importantly, in CD 20.4 we find a reference to the community as the 'disciples of God.'[38] Because none of the CD fragments found in Caves 4-6 at

---

[34] Cf. Duhaime, 'War Scroll,' 84; Davies, 'War,' 966-67.

[35] Vermes, *Dead Sea Scrolls*, 173 translates 'instructed in the laws.'

[36] Yadin, *War*, 306 notes this as a possibility.

[37] Cf. Duhaime, 'War Scroll,' 116-17.

[38] Column 20 comes from manuscript B, found with manuscript A in the Cairo Genizah in 1910, and dates to the twelfth century. The discovery of eight manuscripts of CD in Cave 4 at Qumran, as well as fragments in Caves 5 and 6, has demonstrated that CD is a Qumran document (for description of the fragments, cf. Baumgarten and Davis, 'Fragments,' 59-63). However, the contents of CD may represent a community somewhat different than (although related to) the community at Qumran. On the relationship of the Community Rule to CD, see Hempel, 'Community Structures,' 67-92, esp. 67-70; Knibb, 'Organization,' 136. While 1QS seems to assume a celibate community, CD 7.4-9 depicts a community in which both celibacy and procreative marriage are legitimate lifestyles (cf. CD 14.15-16; 15.5-6; 16.10-12; 19.2-5; Josephus, *B.J.* 2.160-61). Cf. Baumgarten and Schwartz, 'Damascus Document,' 7, 25. Magness, *Archaeology*, 163-87 concludes that the archaeological evidence from the Qumran grave indicates a 'minimal female presence' at Qumran, and an absence of families.

Qumran contains the material found in column 20, we are left to investigate CD-B itself in order to understand this part of the community's self-identity. The reference to the למודי אל comes within a passage that describes the proper measures to take in the case of community members who backslide:

> And thus is the judgment of everyone who enters the congregation of the men of perfect holiness and is slack in the fulfillment of the instructions of the upright. This is the man who is melted in the crucible. When his deeds are evident, he shall be expelled from the congregation, like one whose lot did not fall among the disciples of God [למודי אל].[39] In accordance with his unfaithfulness, all the men of knowledge shall reproach him, until the day when he returns to take his place in the session of the men of perfect holiness…But when his deeds are evident, according to the explanation of the law [מדרש התורה] in which the men of perfect holiness walked, no-one should associate with him in wealth or work, for all the holy ones of the Most High have cursed him. (CD 20.1-8)

In this passage, the punishment of being expelled from the congregation falls upon the one who is disobedient, regardless of whether he is new to the community or not (20.8-9). The offender is sharply contrasted with the community members, who are described in very positive terms (20.2, 4, 5, 7). Line 6 specifies that his works will become apparent according to the 'interpretation of the Torah in which walk the men of perfect holiness.' Timothy Lim has persuasively argued that מדרש here in 20.6, 'has the sense of communal regulation based upon the content of the Torah…A miscreant's deeds, then, are revealed by the authoritative interpretation of the law that regulates the life of the community.'[40]

This raises the question of *why* the community's interpretation is the correct one. I suggest that the phrase למודי אל may function to legitimate the claim that the community possesses the correct interpretation of the Torah. In the *pesharim*, interpretation of the Scriptures is derived from the revealed exegesis of the community, received from the Teacher of Righteousness, and continued in the study of the community. The claim to be taught by God in CD 20.4 may, analogously, refer to the divine revelation of the proper halakhic interpretation of Torah.

Two additional factors must be noted. Recent work on CD has suggested that there are indications of development and redaction within the document itself. Cf. Hempel, *Laws*, *passim*. Also, Davies, *Damascus*, 181-82 has concluded that CD 20.1b-8 is an interpolation. Even if this is so, it is probably related to the Qumran community; Murphy-O'Connor has pointed out the similarity of the passage with 1QS.

[39] למוד may be understood either as an adjective or Qal passive participle of למד, meaning 'taught,' or as a noun meaning 'disciple.' This is the only occurrence of למוד in CD, so it is difficult to favor one meaning over the other. As in Isa 54.13, the two meanings are similar.

[40] Lim, 'Midrash Pesher,' 287.

It is likely that למודי אל alludes to the similar phraseology of Isa 54.13, where the future sons of Zion are referred to as למודי יהוה.[41] Isa 54.13 was available to the community: it is preserved in the Great Isaiah Scroll (1QIsa[a]), which however agrees with the MT in preserving the divine name.[42] A tiny portion of Isa 54.13 is also preserved in the very fragmentary 4QIsa[q]: למו]די.[43] If CD 20.4 does allude to the Isaiah text, it seems likely that the community's identity is shaped through its self-understanding as those who are presently receiving the fulfillment of the Isaianic promise of eschatological divine instruction.

The reference to the entire community as those taught by God in CD 20.4 finds two possible parallels in other Qumran texts. First, the fragmentary 1QH[a] 10.39 contains the single word בלמודיכה, and within the context of the prayer, the second person pronominal suffix clearly refers to God. The question here is whether למוד means 'disciples' or 'teachings.' In its eight uses in the DSS, both meanings are represented.[44] The text of 10.39 is too fragmentary to be sure which is intended, but the pre-fixed preposition ב favors a reference to 'disciples,' in analogy with the בתוך למודי אל of CD 20.4.

Secondly, 4Q381 (4QNon-Canonical Psalms B) frg. 42.1, a tiny fragment, reads:

ת]למד בניך[

E. Schuller has reconstructed the text to read, '[you will] teach your sons...'[45] Although too fragmentary to be sure, the second person singular likely refers to God, since the fragment is part of a psalms collection in which God is addressed in the second person. If so, this is a reference to God teaching 'sons,' possibly recalling the language of Isa 54.13a. However, the text is too fragmentary for certainty.

The above texts suggest that in some sense the entire community understood itself to be taught by God. As noted already, however, evidence from CD must be used cautiously in making claims about the community, and there is no clear evidence that 4QNon-Canonical Psalms B was written by the Qumran community. The fragmentary reference in 1QH[a] 10.39 strengthens the possibility that this was part of the community's self-identity.

Several passages in the *Hodayot* and one passage in 1QS suggest that certain special individuals within the community were seen as recipients of

---

[41] Cf. Riesner, *Lehrer*, 171; Rabin, *Zadokite*, 38, 79.

[42] Cf. Parry and Qimron, *Isaiah Scroll*, 90-91.

[43] Cf. Skehan and Ulrich, 'Isaiah,' 141.

[44] 'Disciple' in CD 20.4; 1QH[a] 15.10; 4Q428 frg. 3.9; 'teaching' in 1QH[a] 15.14; 16.36; 4Q428 frg. 10.7; 4Q434 frg. 1i.4.

[45] Schuller, '4QNon-Canonical Psalms B,' 130.

divine instruction. The idea of God teaching a unique individual comes to expression above all in the *Hodayot*, where the psalmist repeatedly thanks God for teaching him. In this study, I assume it likely, although not certain, that the psalmist is to be identified as the Teacher of Righteousness.[46] In numerous *Hodayot* passages, שכל is used to refer to God's teaching of the psalmist. In 1QH[a] 15 (Sukenik *col.* VII).26-27, the psalmist gives thanks to God for teaching him. In 1QH[a] 18 (Sukenik *col.* X).4, God is said to teach 'man' wonders, but the immediately following context of lines 5-7 suggests that the psalmist has himself in view as the one God teaches.[47]

In addition, two *Hodayot* passages likely use למד to refer to God's teaching of the psalmist. First, in 1QH[a] 15 (Sukenik *col.* VII).10, the psalmist prays,

[ו]אתה אלי נתת‹נ›י לעפים לעצת קודש ות[למדני]בבריתכה ולשוני כלמודיך

Wise, Abegg, and Cook reconstruct the fragmentary ות[as, 'you have taught me.'[48] While other reconstructions are possible,[49] this one is commended by the similar phraseology in 1QSa 1.7 ('taught *in* the Book of Meditation,' 'taught *in* the statutes of the covenant') and the reference to 'disciples' at the end of the line. The clear allusion to Isa 50.4 in 15.10 suggests that למוד means 'disciples': '[And] You, my God, have appointed me as a holy counsel to the weary. You [have taught me] in Your covenant and my tongue is as one of Your disciples [כלמודיך].'

Table 1. *Isa 50.4 and 1QH[a] 15.10*

Isa 50.4 (MT)	אֲדֹנָי יְהוִה נָתַן לִי
1QH[a] 15.10	[ו]אתה אלי נתת‹נ›י
Isa 50.4 (MT) (cont.)	לְשׁוֹן לִמּוּדִים לָדַעַת לָעוּת אֶת־יָעֵף דָּבָר
1QH[a] 15.10 (cont.)	לעפים לעצת קודש ות[...]בבריתכה ולשוני כלמודיך

Mansoor translates למוד in 15.10 as 'teachings,' but this is because he misses the allusion to Isa 50.4.[50] The presence of the allusion is confirmed by another allusion to Isa 50.4, only one column later, which emphasizes the purpose of the psalmist's instruction from God:

---

[46] Present research suggests that the hymns in 1QH[a] were likely written during the lifetime of the Teacher. Cf. Puech, 'Hodayot,' 366-67. Moreover, the exalted claims of the psalmist (at least in the 'Teacher Hymns') point toward an identification as the Teacher of Righteousness. See Knibb, 'Teacher,' 920.

[47] Cf. 1QH[a] 19 (Sukenik *col.* XI).4; 20 (Sukenik *col.* XII).33; 1QH[a] frg. 5.11; although see 1QH[a] 19.9-10. In 20.20, the text is too fragmentary to determine whom God has taught.

[48] Wise, Abegg, Cook, and Gordon, 'Hodayot,' 39.

[49] E.g. Holm-Nielsen, *Hodayot*, 129; Mansoor, *Hymns*, 149.

[50] Mansoor, *Hymns*, 149. Holm-Nielsen, *Hodayot*, 132 rightly notes that the allusion to Isa 50.4 argues for the translation 'disciples.'

Table 2. *Isa 50.4 and 1QH^a 16.36*

Isa 50.4 (MT)	...to support the fatigued with a word	[לָעוּת אֶת־יָעֵף דָּבָר]
1QH^a 16.36	...and to support the fatigued with a word	[ולעות לעאף דבר]

The evidence from 1QH^a 15.10, then, suggests that the psalmist is taught by God (although the reconstruction is not certain) and likens himself to a disciple of God by means of an allusion to Isa 50.4.[51]

A few columns earlier in the *Hodayot*, we encounter a second text that is less clear. In 1QH^a 10 (Sukenik *col.* II).17-18, God is said to teach (למד):

ויהפוכו לשוחה חיי גבר אשר הכינותה בפי ותלמדנו בינה
שמתה בלבבו לפתוח מקור דעת לכול מבינים

It is debated whether in these lines God teaches the psalmist, or an individual ('a man' = גבר) who represents all those who have received the message of the psalmist and become members of the covenant. The main issue in deciding this question is whether the reading בפי should be preserved, or whether an original ו was omitted through haplography, so that the original reading was בפיו.[52] If the former, the line reads, '...a man's life, whom You established *by my word* and whom You taught understanding.'[53] On this reading, God teaches an unspecified man, one who was established by the word of the psalmist. This is supported by Holm-Nielsen, who argues against emending the text to בפיו.[54]

On the other hand, if the original reading is בפיו, the line reads: 'a man *in whose mouth* you established and taught understanding,' presumably referring to the psalmist himself. The emendation to 'his mouth' has in its favor the emphasis upon the psalmist himself in the immediate context,[55] and has been accepted by a number of scholars.[56] In my opinion, it is most likely that an original ו was omitted through haplography. If line 17 reads 'by *my* word,' then line 18 must refer to an individual other than the psalmist when it claims that God 'placed it in *his* heart to open up the source of knowledge to all who understand' (my emphasis). But it seems unlikely that the lofty claim of line 18 refers to someone other than the psalmist. I therefore read lines 17-18 as a reference to the psalmist, who is himself established and taught by God. If this is correct, we have two references, one in 1QH^a 10.17-18 and the

---

[51] Cf. another likely allusion to Isa 50.4 in 4Q428 frg. 3.9.

[52] So Mansoor, *Hymns*, 107.

[53] This is the translation of Wise, Abegg, Cook, and Gordon, 'Hodayot,' 21, my italics.

[54] Holm-Nielsen, *Hodayot*, 36-37.

[55] 10.13 refers to the writer as a 'knowledgeable mediator of secret wonders,' and 10.16 speaks of the persecution of the writer.

[56] So García Martínez and Tigchelaar, *Scrolls*, 1.163; Mansoor, *Hymns*, 107; see those referred to in Holm-Nielsen, *Hodayot*, 36-37, n. 40.

other in 15.10, to God teaching (למד) the psalmist, whom we may (tentatively) identify as the Teacher of Righteousness himself.

Finally, the belief that certain special individuals are the recipients of divine instruction is perhaps supported by the use of ירה in 1QS 10.13, which comes within the prayer of 10.6-11.22. In 10.12-13, the one praying says, 'I shall choose what he teaches [ירה] me, I shall be pleased in how he might judge me.'[57] The prayer of 10.6-11.22 is probably the prayer of the Instructor (משכיל) of the community, rather than the prayer of 'everyman,' because the Instructor is mentioned in 1QS 9.12. In the description of his responsibilities (9.12-10.5), it is said that he is to bless his Creator (9.26), and the prayer of 10.6-11.22 begins, 'With the offering of lips I shall bless him...' Therefore, this passage probably refers to God teaching a leader of the community.

When does divine instruction occur?

In the DSS, divine instruction occurs in the past (e.g. at Sinai), and also in the present and the future. It is clear that divine instruction is seen as a present reality within the life of the community, occurring on an ongoing basis. This accounts for the community's self-perception as those who are taught by God (see above), and for the claims of the psalmist in the *Hodayot* that he is taught by God. In light of the community's view that they were living in the last days, their understanding of this present divine instruction should be viewed as an eschatological one.[58] If, as I suggested above, CD 20.4 alludes to Isa 54.13, the community's status as those taught by God was likely understood as the eschatological fulfillment of the prophetic promise, just as the *pesharim* consistently read the prophetic writings as being fulfilled in their own day.

There also appears to be in the DSS the expectation of a yet-future divine instruction. 1QS 4.21-22 envisions a future scenario:

He will sprinkle over him the spirit of truth like lustral water (in order to cleanse him) from all the abhorrences of deceit and (from) the defilement of the unclean spirit, in order to

---

[57] 4Q258 (4QSerekh ha-Yahad[d]) frg. 5.2, within a variant recension of 1QS 10.12-18, preserves a tiny fragment of 1QS 10.13: 'באשר יורד]'

[58] Cf. Steudel, 'End of Days,' 225-46 for the community's view that they were living in the final period of history. Collins, 'Eschatology,' 256-61 notes that the various models of eschatology in the DSS do not compose a 'fully coherent system.' However, some aspects seem common, i.e. the time of the Messiahs is still future for the community. Collins allows that it is possible that the community saw the End of Days as entailing two phases, and that the first (the time of testing) had already begun. 4QMMT asserts that the End of Days has already begun, and texts like 1QpHab 7.6-13 make it clear that the End of Days was expected as an imminent event.

instruct [הבין] the upright ones with knowledge of the Most High, and to make understand [להשכיל] the wisdom of the sons of heaven to those of perfect behavior.

In this passage, the instruction comes through God's sprinkling of the 'spirit of truth,' which cleanses from defilement and therefore allows for instruction.[59] Moreover, the passage anticipates God's instruction for 'the upright ones' and 'those of perfect behavior.' Both phrases refer to the Qumran community (cf. 1QS 3.1; 8.10, 18-19), and so demonstrate that it expected a future divine instruction for itself.

Another important text in this regard is 1QH[a] 14 (Sukenik *col.* VI).12-13:

...For you have brought [your truth and] your [glo]ry to all the men of your council [עצתכה] and in the lot, together with the angels of the face, without there being a mediator [מליץ] between [your holy ones...][60]

In the preceding context, the psalmist speaks of a remnant purified and cleansed of guilt, and taught (ירה) by God for his glory. This has not yet happened, though it is soon to happen (14.8). The reference to the lack of a mediator in 14.13 is potentially significant following this reference to future divine instruction, although several factors are hard to determine. First, the fragmentary state of the text allows for the possible reconstruction 'your holy ones,' but this is uncertain. Secondly, if 'holy ones' is indeed the correct reading, does it refer to humans or to angels, both of whom are mentioned in the preceding context? Thirdly, if it refers to the community, it is still difficult to say whether this is intended to describe the present state of the community or the condition that will obtain in the near future when God purifies his remnant. C. Barth rejects Johann Maier's restoration of the text (viz. 'No mediating interpreter is needed by the holy ones'), claiming that, 'the notion of revelation without a mediator...is alien to the Hodayoth.'[61] However, though 1QH[a] elsewhere recognizes the importance of those who mediate God's instruction, this text may envision a near future in which God will teach the community directly and without a mediator.[62] In light of the fragmentary text and ambiguity of the passage, however, this can only be considered a possibility.

---

[59] The role of the spirit in divine instruction within the OT has already been noted above in chapter 2.

[60] Reconstruction and translation from García Martínez and Tigchelaar, *Scrolls*, 1.175.

[61] Barth, 'ליץ,' *TDOT* 7.552.

[62] Mansoor, *Hymns*, 143 restores 'holy ones,' and interprets it to refer to the community, who require no intercessors on their behalf.

What is the content of divine instruction?

In the DSS, the content of divine instruction is variable: God teaches warfare,[63] he teaches 'in his covenant' (1QH[a] 15.10), his precepts (CD 3.8), all knowledge (1QS 11.17-18; cf. 4Q264 [4QSerekh ha-Yahad[j]] frg. 1.5), his path (4Q434 frg. 1ii.4), his truth (1QH[a] 15.26), his wonders (1QH[a] 18.4), his wonderful works (1QH[a] 19.4), and his mysteries (1QH[a] 20.20). I argued above that in 1QH[a] 10.17, God teaches the psalmist. But what is the *content* of God's teaching in this passage? Mansoor is probably wrong to take בינה as the beginning of a new sentence rather than the object of 'teach.'[64] למד in the Piel often has a specified content in the DSS, as it does in the only other use of למד in 1QH[a].[65] Moreover, in 4Q372 (4QApocryphon of Joseph[b]) frg. 3.5, we find the identical phrase למד בינה.[66] Therefore, it seems most likely that in 1QH[a] 10.17, God 'teaches understanding' to the psalmist.[67]

But what does this mean? The immediately following phrase states that, 'You placed in his heart to open the source of knowledge [מקור דעת] for all those who understand.' The 'source of knowledge' is a broad term indicating the place from which humans gain knowledge, and can refer to God himself (1QS 10.12; 11.3).[68] 10.13 states that the psalmist is a mediator of secret wonders (רזי פלא). The context indicates, then, that God has taught the psalmist understanding and secret wonders and knowledge.

Similar terminology is used in the Habakkuk Pesher. 1QpHab 2.8 claims that God has given understanding (בינה) in the heart of the priest so that he can interpret all the words of the prophets.[69] 1QpHab 7.4-5 suggests that God has made known to the Teacher of Righteousness 'all the mysteries [רזי] of the words of his servants, the prophets,' and these mysteries are said to be wonderful (פלא in 7.8). The similar terminology of 1QpHab 2.8; 7.4-5 and 1QH[a] 10.13, 17-18 suggests that the understanding taught to the psalmist by God in 1QH[a] 10.17 refers to insight into the meaning of the Scriptures.

This recalls our earlier suggestion that 'taught by God' in CD 20.4 may refer to the community's inspired interpretation of the Torah. Another text that points to the connection between divine instruction and the interpretation

---

[63] Cf. 1QM 14.6; 4Q372 frg. 2.4; 4Q491 frgs. 8-10i.4, in the biblical tradition of Ps 18.35 [ET 18.34]; 144.1; 2 Sam 22.35.

[64] Mansoor, *Hymns*, 107.

[65] As noted above, it is partially reconstructed in 15.10, but refers to instruction 'in the covenant.'

[66] Cf. the reference to 'learning understanding' (בינה and למד) in 4Q381 (4QNon-Canonical Psalms B) frgs. 76-77.13.

[67] Cf. Holm-Nielsen, *Hodayot*, 37.

[68] Cf. Leaney, *Rule*, 246-47.

[69] The text is admittedly fragmentary, but should probably be restored as:
הכוהן אשר נתן אל ב[לבו בינ]ה לפשור את כול... (cf. Horgan, *Pesharim*, 13, 25-26).

of the Law is 11Q5 24.8 (Syriac Psalm III). This is a prayer: 'Instruct me, YHWH, in your law, and teach me [למדני] your precepts.' It is quite clear that Qumran had a category of 'charismatic exegesis' typical of some strands of early Judaism, and that the community's interpretation of the Scriptures was perceived as divinely inspired.[70] The texts noted here indicate a link between divine instruction and this divinely revealed interpretation.

How is divine instruction given?

Finally, we may ask how divine instruction occurs in the DSS. Clearly, much of it comes through intermediaries. 1QM 10.2-4, 6-7 implies that Moses' teaching (למד) of the Law is a mediation of God's teaching. 4Q381 (4QNon-Canonical Psalms B) frg. 69.4 says that through God's spirit, 'prophets were given to you to teach you [שׂכל] and show [למד] you...' Here, prophets are seen as intermediaries of divine instruction. I have already noted above the teaching functions of the Instructor, the Examiner, and the Teacher of Righteousness, and below we will examine the teaching function of the eschatological Messiahs. All these figures mediate divine instruction. The idea of divine instruction at Qumran does not, then, seem to be in any necessary conflict with human teaching structures, which were plentiful and robust. However, we have noted above the possibility that 1QH[a] 14.12-13 envisions a future eschatological instruction that obviates the need for human instruction. If so, this appears to be in conflict with another Qumran text that envisions future education of children (1Q28a 1.6-9).[71]

Two texts link the spirit with instruction. In 1QS 4.21-22, examined already, it is the 'spirit of truth' who functions as the agent of divine instruction. As noted above, 4Q381 frg. 69.4 claims that it was through God's spirit (רוח) that prophets were given to instruct and teach the people. Other than these two texts, there are no links between the spirit and didactic terminology. This is surprising, since knowledge is said to come through the spirit (1QH[a] 5.24-25; 20.11-12). Moreover, the 'spirit of truth' in 1QS 4.1-8, which is the spirit of the 'sons of truth,' is a spirit of 'intelligence, understanding, potent wisdom...a spirit of knowledge in all the plans of action...'[72]

It seems that God's teaching of the psalmist in the *Hodayot* is direct, for there is no mention of an intermediary. Like the divine instruction of the biblical Psalms, God's teaching in the *Hodayot* is probably an inner illumination rather than an external, visible event. In many of the references

---

[70] Cf. Aune, 'Charismatic,' 126, and see below in chapter 6.

[71] I have noted this passage above.

[72] For an examination of *ruach* in the DSS, and its connection with the idea of revelation, cf. Deasley, 'Spirit,' 45-73.

to divine instruction in the DSS, there is no reference to how the divine instruction will occur. Rather, the emphasis is on the fact that it does, and on the status of the community as those who are 'taught by God.' In this respect, the DSS are similar to many biblical passages.

Conclusion

This study of divine instruction in the DSS has discovered several significant features. First, it is likely that the entire Qumran community saw itself as taught by God. Caution must be exercised in this claim because of the uncertainty regarding how representative CD is (see above in this chapter), and the fragmentary state of the other texts that appear to refer to disciples of God. In addition to the entire community being taught by God, certain individuals, such as the writer of the *Hodayot* (the Teacher of Righteousness?) were seen as specially taught by God. Secondly, divine instruction was thought to occur in the past (e.g. Sinai), present, and the future. It was likely understood as eschatological instruction, possibly in fulfillment of Isa 54.13.

Thirdly, the content of divine instruction was variable, ranging from warfare to insight into the meaning of the Scriptures. It is possible that there was a link between divine instruction and 'charismatic exegesis' at Qumran. Finally, the means of divine instruction was often unspecified, with the emphasis being simply upon the fact of divine instruction. However, certain individuals (e.g. Moses, the prophets, the Instructor, the Teacher of Righteousness, the Messiahs) were understood to mediate divine instruction. In most texts, there is no apparent tension between divine and human instruction. However, in 1QH^a 14.12-13, which deals with future divine instruction, there is a possible reference to the lack of a mediator.

3.2 Divine instruction in Philo of Alexandria

We turn now to Philo's development of the idea of divine instruction. Thematic investigations in Philo are complicated by his sometimes inconsistent handling of concepts and by the way in which his favorite ideas often overlap with one another.[73] This is the case for the present study, since references to divine instruction overlap with Philo's development of a Greek educational tradition, his concept of the 'self-taught' and 'self-learned' individual, his thinking on nature, and his description of ecstatic experience

---

[73] Cf. Birnbaum, 'Philo,' 539, 545; Borgen, *Bread*, 105.

and inward prompting. In this section, I note the overlap where it occurs, and also the areas in which Philo appears to be inconsistent.

Application of the method outlined in chapter 1 above yields about 100 instances in the Philonic corpus in which a reference to God is connected with didactic terminology.[74] Examination of these passages shows that Philo has a robust view of divine instruction. He compares God to a teacher,[75] refers to God *as* a teacher,[76] claims that God teaches,[77] and describes some individuals as students or disciples of God.[78] Sometimes Philo draws these ideas straight from the biblical text, as when he cites Isa 50.4 in *Her.* 25, or Prov 3.11-12 in *Congr.* 177. However, the main inspiration for Philo's references to divine instruction does not seem to be the biblical text, because often when he infers from biblical texts that God is a teacher, or that God teaches, the texts themselves do not demand such an inference. In *Her.* 17-19 Philo interprets Exod 19.19 ('Moses was talking to God, and God was answering him with a voice') as meaning that God taught Moses. Although this is a possible characterization (cf. Exod 4.12), didactic terminology is not used in the biblical text itself.[79]

Moreover, it is clear that in some cases Philo reads into biblical texts the notion of divine instruction based on associations of ideas he has developed elsewhere. This is particularly evident in his often-repeated interpretation of Gen 27.20. In the biblical text, Isaac asks Jacob how he found the wild game so quickly (ταχύ in the LXX), and Jacob replies that God the Lord delivered it to him. Philo draws on this text in *Sacr.* 64-65, apparently because he associates the haste of the Passover commandment (he cites Exod 12.11 in

---

[74] I have based my study on all uses of 20 didactic terms: διδάσκαλος, ὑφηγητής, παιδευτής (teacher); μαθητής, φοιτητής, γνώριμος (student, disciple); αὐτομαθής, αὐτοδίδακτος ('self-learned,' 'self-taught'); διδάσκω, παιδεύω (to teach, educate); διδασκαλία, δίδαγμα, διδαχή, παιδεία (lesson, instruction, teaching, education); διδακτικός (apt at teaching); διδακτός (taught); ἀδίδακτος (untaught); διδασκαλεῖον (teaching place, school); διδασκαλικός (of, for teaching); μανθάνω (learn). Cf. Birnbaum, 'Philo,' 536-40; Runia, 'Philo,' 193-95 for methodological reflection on thematic studies in Philo.

[75] *Opif.* 149; *Post.* 141-44; *Mut.* 270; *Mos.* 1.80.

[76] διδάσκαλος in *Sacr.* 65; *Her.* 19, 102; *Congr.* 114; ὑφηγητής in *Leg.* 3.102; *Post.* 16; *Her.* 19; *Congr.* 114; *Fug.* 169; *Somn.* 1.173.

[77] Cf. *Leg.* 2.85; 3.50; *Migr.* 42; *Mos.* 2.71, 141, 188-90. Philo often quotes Deut 8.5 ('like a man he shall train [παιδεύω] his son') to explain why the biblical texts use anthropomorphisms – it is for the purpose of *instruction* (e.g. *Deus* 54; *Conf.* 98; *Somn.* 1.237; *QG* 2.54a).

[78] E.g. μαθητής in *Sacr.* 7, 64, 79; *Post.* 136; *Mut.* 270; φοιτητής in *Sacr.* 79; γνώριμος in *Opif.* 149; *Sacr.* 79; *Somn.* 1.173; *Mos.* 1.80. Moses is said to have learned (μανθάνω) from God in *Det.* 86 (cf. *Fug.* 164; *Spec.* 1.42), as is Jacob in *Praem.* 44.

[79] Cf. the references to Gen 15.8-9 in *Her.* 100-102; Exod 25.40 in *Leg.* 3.102; Exod 33.13 in *Post.* 16.

paragraph 63) with the word 'quickly' in Gen 27.20. He infers from the use of ταχύ that, 'disciples [μαθηταί] of the only wise Being discover quickly what they seek.'[80] There is no indication in Gen 27.20 that God teaches disciples. Rather, Philo understands the biblical text to refer to 'disciples of God' because of his previous associations between 'disciples of God' and the phrases 'quickly' and 'that which God delivered.' This is clear from *Fug.* 166-69, where he associates the same two phrases in Gen 27.20 with the 'self-taught' individual who has God, not man, as his teacher.[81] Philo's association of speedy learning and divine instruction is part of a larger nexus of ideas formed from his personal observation and Greek educational ideas. Philo observes that some individuals naturally learn more easily and quickly than others.[82] He suggests, employing categories drawn from Greek educational theory, that these 'self-taught' individuals are taught by God. These ideas will be explored in more detail below.

Non-eschatological divine instruction

Although Philo demonstrates some eschatological expectations elsewhere in his writings, he never develops an eschatological understanding of God's teaching.[83] Divine instruction is always something that has happened in the past or happens in the present. While Philo draws upon several OT passages in developing his concept of divine instruction (e.g. Gen 27.20; Exod 19.19), he never mentions Jer 31.33-34, Isa 54.13, or the other prophetic promises of eschatological divine instruction noted above in chapter 2.[84] This clearly distinguishes him from the NT writings, as will become evident in chapters 4-9 of this thesis. Philo's use of Genesis and Exodus is not surprising, however, given the clear priority accorded to the Pentateuch in his writings, and the relative paucity of citations from the rest of the OT.[85]

Philo's adaptation of the Greek educational trinity

In many of his works, Philo develops an allegorical reading of the patriarchal trinity Abraham, Isaac, and Jacob,[86] even structuring three books of his

---

[80] In this respect, according to Philo, God's disciples imitate God, their Teacher, because God himself is swifter even than time (*Sacr.* 65-68).

[81] In *Fug.* 166-69, Gen 27.20 is taken even further out of context, since the one who learns quickly is associated with *Isaac*, not Jacob.

[82] Cf. *Deus* 92-98; *Ebr.* 119-20.

[83] For Philo's eschatological expectation, cf. *Praem.* 79-126, 162-72. See Mach, 'Lerntraditionen,' 123; Borgen, *Exegete*, 261-81.

[84] Cf. the data available in *Biblia Patristica*, 89. That Philo was familiar with Isa 50.4 is evident from the allusion in *Her.* 25, which is followed by a quotation from Exod 4.12.

[85] On this point, cf. Runia, 'Philo,' 189; Hay, 'Exegete,' 45.

[86] F. H. Colson describes the formula as one of Philo's 'leading ideas' (PLCL 6.x).

exposition of the Law of Moses around them.[87] Toward the beginning of the first of these three books, Philo sets out his allegorical reading of the three patriarchs (*Abr.* 47-55).[88] He establishes here a connection between Abraham and teaching (διδασκαλία), Isaac and nature (φύσις), and Jacob and practice (ἄσκησις). Each of the three patriarchs possesses all three qualities (since teaching, nature, and practice must work together in order to attain virtue), but each is named for the quality that predominates in him. The same formula appears in *De praemiis et poenis*, another of Philo's works expositing the Law of Moses, and again it plays a part in structuring the work.[89] In *Praem.* 64-65, Philo describes the soul that has received a good nature, good instruction, and exercise in the principles of virtue as possessing the 'triple excellence' of nature, learning, and practice.

Philo finds his allegorical reading of the patriarchal trinity useful in solving exegetical dilemmas. In *Somn.* 1.166-72, it explains why Abraham is said to be the father of *Jacob* (rather than the father of Isaac, as one would expect) in Gen 28.13 (solution: teaching and practice are more closely connected to each other than they are to nature). In *Mut.* 88, it explains why the names of Abraham and Jacob were changed, while Isaac's name was not changed (solution: the scholar and the practicer are more like one another than they are like the self-taught one).[90] Philo also mentions the allegory even when it holds no apparent exegetical value for the passage of Scripture he is treating (e.g. *Mos.* 1.76). The identification is so fixed that he can call Abraham the 'lover of learning' (*Congr.* 111) or refer to Jacob as the 'Practicer Jacob.'[91] His identification of Isaac as 'self-taught' is common enough that in *Conf.* 81 he refers only to the 'self-taught one' (αὐτοδίδακτος) and expects his reader to know he is referring to Isaac.[92]

This three-fold division of the patriarchs representing φύσις, διδασκαλία, and ἄσκησις is Philo's reworking of a Greek educational

---

[87] For a classification of Philo's expository writings, cf. Borgen, 'Philo,' 334-36. Only the book on Abraham has survived, but *Ios.* 1 indicates that there were also books on Isaac and Jacob.

[88] He is unclear about what exactly they represent: 'types of soul' that pursue the good (*Abr.* 52), the virtue that is acquired (*Abr.* 52, 54), or the actual pursuits of learning, nature, and practice (*Ios.* 1).

[89] Abraham is discussed in *Praem.* 28-30, Isaac in *Praem.* 31-35, and Jacob in *Praem.* 36-46.

[90] See also *Congr.* 34-38.

[91] E.g. *Sacr.* 5, 81; *Ebr.* 82; *Mut.* 85.

[92] Cf. *Congr.* 111; *Mut.* 137. Other individuals are said to be 'self-taught' (e.g. Adam in *Opif.* 148; *QG* 1.8; Moses in *Leg.* 3.135), but for Philo, Isaac is the example *par excellence* of the 'self-taught' one. Cf. e.g. *Sacr.* 6-7; *Det.* 30-31; *Deus* 4; *Plant.* 168-69.

tradition, seen in Plato and Aristotle, and even earlier.[93] In *Eth. eud.* 1.1.4-5, Aristotle considers how the good life is obtained: is happiness acquired by nature (φύσις), by study (μάθησις), or by a form of training (ἄσκησις)? Or does it come by none of these, but rather through, 'a sort of elevation of mind inspired by some divine power,' or by fortune (τύχη)? Aristotle answers that happiness comes from all of these, or by some or one of them.[94] In this educational tradition, nature, teaching, and practice are usually understood to work together within a person to produce moral excellence and right action. There is plentiful evidence of this formula in the ancient literature, and a few examples may be set out alongside Philo's patriarchal trinity:

Table 3. *The Greek educational trinity and Philo's patriarchal trinity*[95]

Pindar, *Ol.* Ode 9, 100-2[96]	δίδακτος	φυή	–
Xenophon, *Mem.* 3.9.1-3	δίδακτος, μάθησις	φυσικός, φύσις	μελέτη
Aristotle, *Eth. eud* 1.1.4-5	μάθησις	φύσις	ἄσκησις
Plutarch, *Lib. ed.* 2[97]	λόγος, μάθησις	φύσις	ἔθος, ἄσκησις
Sacr. 5-7	Ἀβραάμ	αὐτομαθής, Ἰσαάκ	ἀσκητής, Ἰακόβ
Mut. 12	διδασκαλία	τελειότητος[98]	ἄσκησις
Mut. 88	διδακτικός	αὐτοδίδακτος, αὐτομαθής	ἀσκητικός
Somn. 1.168	διδασκαλία	φύσις (αὐτήκοος καί αὐτομάθης)	ἀσκητικός, μελέτη
Abr. 52	διδασκαλία	φύσις	ἄσκησις
Ios. 1[99]	μάθησις	φύσις	ἄσκησις
Mos. 1.76	διδακτός	φυσικός	ἀσκητικός
Praem. 64	παίδευσις	φύσις	συνασκέω

These examples demonstrate that Philo's allegorical interpretation of the patriarchs Abraham, Isaac, and Jacob draws upon a widespread Greek

---

[93] On this tradition, cf. Völker, *Fortschritt*, 154-58; Bréhier, *Les Idées Philosophique*, 272-73; Borgen, *Bread*, 103; PLCL 2.488, §§5-7; 5.586, §12; 6.x; Colson, 'Education,' 160-61; Montefiore, 'Florilegium,' 516-19.

[94] Völker, *Fortschritt*, 154-55 points also to Plato, *Meno* 70a; Aristotle, *Pol.* 7.1332a; *Eth. nic.* 2.1103a; Diogenes Laërtius, *Lives of Eminent Philosophers* 5.18.

[95] This list is representative rather than exhaustive. Cf. Josephus, *C. Ap.* 2.171-72. Borgen, *Bread*, 103, n. 1 lists other passages in Philo where the formula appears.

[96] Cf. Pindar, *Nem.* Ode 3, line 40-42.

[97] I owe this reference to Borgen, *Bread*, 103.

[98] Here the Greek τελειότητος appears in place of the more common φύσις. Cf. PLCL 5.586 §12.

[99] These three terms (μάθησις, φύσις, ἄσκησις) appear together in *Somn.* 1.167, 169; *Praem.* 65.

educational tradition.[100] Given Philo's appreciation for the Greek encyclia, this is not unusual.[101]

Divine instruction, 'self-taught,' and natural gifting

For the purposes of this study, the most interesting feature of Philo's adaptation of the Greek educational trinity is the connection he draws between divine instruction and nature. Several passages indicate that, for Philo, being a 'student/disciple of God' can refer to being gifted by God with natural intelligence or ability. Tellingly, the 'self-taught' Isaac, who has God for his teacher (see below), is the member of the patriarchal trinity consistently associated with φύσις.[102] In *Praem.* 50, Philo associates Isaac with the joy of arriving at virtue through 'natural endowments': 'For good abilities and natural gifts [τά φύσεως δῶρα] are a matter for rejoicing.'[103] It is a matter of observation that some people naturally learn easily, quickly, and effortlessly, whereas others must labor slowly and diligently to learn from teachers or through practice.[104] Philo recognizes this, and suggests that the 'quick-learners' have *God* as their teacher.

This connection is evident in *Fug.* 166-72. Here, Philo develops several antitheses:

166 Self-learned and self-taught	Searchings and practicings and toilings
167 Nature	Practice
168 God-inspired ecstasy	Human will or purpose
169 Rapid	Slow
169 God as teacher	Man as teacher

In this passage, Philo considers those people who do not 'seek' and yet nevertheless 'find' (166).[105] He calls such a person a 'self-learned and self-

---

[100] Cf. Borgen, *Bread*, 104-5, who demonstrates parallels between *Mut.* 253-63 and Plutarch's *Moralia.*

[101] For Philo's appreciation of the Greek encyclia when used properly, cf. *Cher.* 71; *Congr.* 11-19; *Mos.* 1.23. See PLCL 1.xvi-xvii; Colson, 'Education,' 151-62; Mendelson, *Education*, 81-84.

[102] Cf. Mendelson, *Education*, 65, 106, n. 92.

[103] This may explain why Philo identifies Isaac, rather than Abraham or Jacob, as the one associated with natural ability: natural ability is a matter for 'rejoicing,' and Isaac's name means 'laughter.' For this suggestion, see the general introduction to PLCL 6 by F. H. Colson.

[104] Note the remarkable description of Moses in *Mos.* 1.21-24.

[105] *De fuga et inventione* follows upon *De congressu eruditionis gratia*, and exposits Genesis 16.6-12 (omitting 16.10). Philo focuses on the three words 'fled,' 'found,' and 'fountain.' His discussion of finding and seeking constitutes the second part of his treatise (119-75) and falls into four sections: not seeking and not finding, seeking and finding, not seeking and finding, seeking and not finding. Cf. PLCL 5.3-9.

taught wise man' (αὐτομαθὴς καὶ αὐτοδίδακτος σοφός in 166), the 'self-learned nature' (τὸ αὐτομαθὲς γένος in 168), and the 'self-learned ones' (τοῦ αὐτομαθοῦς in 168, 170), all of whom are identified with Isaac (167). Philo notes three characteristics of such people: they learn *quickly* (169), they learn from God (169), and they learn 'automatically' (170). The 'self-learned' and 'self-taught' are also identified as those who have God as their teacher (ὑφηγητήν in 169).[106] This identification between being taught by God and being 'self-taught' is found elsewhere in Philo (e.g. *Sacr.* 6-7, 78-79), although the two concepts should not be considered completely synonymous in Philo's thought.[107]

The emphasis upon nature in *Fug.* 166-72 is particularly noticeable. The self-taught, God-taught wise man (Isaac) is said throughout the passage to learn by nature.[108] In paragraph 169, Philo claims that this individual has God as his teacher. In paragraph 170, Philo explains how those who are naturally quick learners can be said to be taught by God. In noting his third mark of a 'self-learned' man, the 'automatic' way in which they learn, Philo quotes the Jubilee regulations of Lev 25.11: 'Ye shall not sow, nor shall ye reap its growths that come up of themselves.' Philo suggests that 'natural growths' do not need any treatment from humans since,

God sows them and by His art of husbandry brings to perfection, *as though they were self-grown, plants which are not self-grown* [ὡς ἂν αὐτόματα τὰ οὐκ αὐτόματα], save only so far as they had no need whatever of *human* attention [ἐπινοίας ἀνθρωπίνης] (170, my emphasis).

The implication is clear. Those who learn effortlessly, easily, and quickly (i.e. by nature) are 'self-taught' only in that they do not need a *human* teacher – in reality, it is God who is teaching and guiding them.[109] In other words, God works (i.e. teaches) through the natural gifting he has given certain people,

---

[106] A key mark of the 'self-learned' is thus summed up in the phrase from Gen 27.20 'that which God delivered' (ὃ παρέδωκε κύριος ὁ θεός).

[107] Montefiore, 'Florilegium,' 518 goes too far when he claims that 'self-taught' *means* 'taught by God.' More recently Roetzel, 'Theodidaktoi,' 328 lacks nuance in his identification of the 'self-taught' and the 'God-taught' in Philo. In *Plant.* 110; *Ebr.* 13, 60; *Decal.* 117; *Spec.* 2.240, there is no explicit connection between being 'self-taught' and being taught by God. There appears to be at least one passage in which 'self-learned' *cannot* be equivalent to being taught by God. Philo asserts in *Her.* 295 that in the second of the four stages of the soul, the soul is 'self-learned' (αὐτομαθής) in evil. Here there is a clear distinction between the two concepts, for Philo obviously does not suggest that God instructs the soul in evil.

[108] φύσει in 167, 168, 169, 170; ἐκ φύσεως in 171; φύσεως in 172; φύσις in 172.

[109] Cf. *Post.* 78; *Congr.* 36 for a similar point: the self-taught receive reason and knowledge from God.

just as he causes plants to grow that appear to be self-grown.[110] *Fug.* 166-71 emphasizes that the one who has God as a teacher does not need human instruction, so it is strange to find Philo apparently noting at the very end of the passage, in 172, that natural gifting from God *complements* human instruction rather than rendering it otiose:

> It is within the power of the teacher to lead us from one stage of progress to another; God only, Nature at its best [ὁ θεὸς μόνος, ἡ ἀρίστη φύσις], can produce in us the full completion (172).[111]

Perhaps the solution to this apparent discrepancy is that Philo sees human instruction as taking one a certain distance toward maturity, but then being eclipsed by divine instruction. In any case, *Fug.* 166-72 establishes a connection between those who have God as their teacher, those who are 'self-taught,' and those who are naturally gifted and therefore learn easily. We find a similar link between the 'self-taught' and φύσις in *Somn.* 1.160; *Abr.* 5-6. Moreover, according to Philo, *Adam* was αὐτομαθής and αὐτοδίδακτος (*Opif.* 148). Adam's 'native reasoning power in the soul' was 'still unalloyed,' as 'no infirmity or disease or evil affection' had yet entered (150). It is possible that for Philo the 'natural' state is one in which all are 'self-taught.' The entrance of 'infirmity or disease or evil affection' taints this, but some remain 'self-taught.'

Other means of divine instruction

Natural gifting does not exhaust the meaning of divine instruction in Philo's thought. God sometimes teaches individuals by speaking directly to them (e.g. Adam, Moses, Abraham, Jacob).[112] God can teach through an 'inspired ecstasy' (ἐνθέῳ μανίᾳ in *Fug.* 168) – an experience perhaps similar to the 'corybantic frenzy' Philo claims to have had many times, and which he describes in *Migr.* 29-35.[113] Moreover, God can teach through an internal voice or prompting. In *Praem.* 31-35 Philo discusses Isaac, who is 'self-

---

[110] Philo concludes from his reading of Lev 25.11 that the beginnings and endings of activities are automatic (αὐτόματον) in that they are accomplished by nature (φύσεως) and not by humans. He notes that it is the receptive nature (φύσις) within a student that allows for learning to begin and come to completion.

[111] Cf. the discussion of Borgen, *Bread*, 105-7 on *Mut.* 253-63. This passage is significant due to its sustained contrast between the self-taught nature (Sarah) and the lower instruction (Hagar).

[112] See e.g. *Leg.* 3.50 (Adam); *Leg.* 3.102; *Post.* 16; *Her.* 19 (Moses); *Her.* 102 (Abraham); *Sacr.* 64-65 (Jacob).

[113] Note the answer to the key question (Who is the heir?) in *Her.* 65, 68: it is the one who is filled with an ecstatic frenzy and comes out of himself (69). This 'frenzied' person is probably to be identified with the 'self-taught' individual in paragraph 65.

learned' (αὐτομαθής in 36). In paragraph 50, immediately after the passage on Isaac's natural gifting noted above, Philo suggests that,

> The mind exults in the facility of its apprehension and the felicity of the processes by which it discovers what it seeks without labour [ἀπόνως], as though [καθάπερ] dictated by an inward prompter [ἔνδοθεν ὑπηχοῦντος]. For to find the solution of difficulties quickly must bring joy.

Another reference to such inner prompting is found in *Legat.* 245. Philo says that the pagan viceroy of Syria, Petronius (207), was 'naturally kindly.' It seems he had some rudiments of the Jewish teaching either through early teaching or contact with the Jews,

> or else because his soul was so disposed, being drawn to things worthy of serious effort by a nature [φύσει] which listened to no voice nor dictation nor teaching but its own [αὐτηκόῳ καὶ αὐτοκελεύστῳ καὶ αὐτομαθεῖ]. But we find that to good men God whispers [ὑπηχεῖν] good decisions by which they will give and receive benefits, and this was true in his case.

In these two passages, the 'self-learned' individual receives inner direction from God himself.[114] This may be related to an 'inner voice' described by Philo in other passages. In *Cher.* 27-29, Philo mentions a voice in his own soul, 'which oftentimes is god-possessed and divines where it does not know.' In *Somn.* 2.252 he describes hearing the voice of 'the invisible spirit, the familiar secret tenant,' speaking to him and teaching things to him.[115] In *Mut.* 18, Philo, in the process of interpreting the Scriptures, claims that God's interpreting word (ὁ ὑποφήτης αὐτοῦ λόγος) will teach (διδάξει) him the correct interpretation of the Scriptures.[116]

Divine and human instruction

How does divine instruction relate to human instruction in Philo's thought? Do they complement one another, or does the former exclude the need for the latter? Philo appears to be inconsistent on this question. *Sacr.* 6-7, 78-79 suggests that while one may *begin* with human instruction, one must eventually leave human instruction behind when one has been taught by God. Paragraphs 6-7 contrast the 'self-learned' Isaac with Abraham and Isaac. We are told that Isaac was granted 'self-learned knowledge' (αὐτομαθοῦς ἐπιστήμης) and as such belongs to a select group:

---

[114] Cf. PLCL 5.601, §164: in Philo, ὑπήχει, 'seems to carry with it the thought of a voice heard inwardly and not audible in the ordinary sense.' It is sometimes used of the divine voice that speaks to the prophets (Colson cites *Mut.* 139).

[115] The verbs ὑφηγέομαι and ἀναδιδάσκω are used.

[116] Cf. Hay, 'Exegete,' 40-52, who notes passages in which Philo claims to be an inspired interpreter of the Scriptures.

Those who have advanced to perfection as pupils under a teacher have their place among many others; for those who learn by hearing and instruction are no small number, and these he calls a people. But those who have dispensed with the instruction of men [οἱ δὲ ἀνθρώπων μὲν ὑφηγήσεις ἀπολελοιπότες] and have become apt pupils of God [μαθηταὶ δὲ εὐφυεῖς θεοῦ] receive the free unlaboured knowledge and are translated into the genus of the imperishable and fully perfect.

Here, there is a strong contrast between being instructed by men and being a pupil of God, since being a pupil of God involves dispensing (ἀπολείπω) with human instruction.[117] The same contrast appears in *Sacr.* 78-79. Philo allows that one may acquire virtue by reading the ancient works of historians and poets that have been handed down (παραδεδώκασιν). But when we have received 'self-learned wisdom' (αὐτομαθοῦς σοφίας) and become 'spectators rather than hearers of knowledge,' we should no longer bother with human instruction. This point is repeated in 79. Philo suggests that the ancient writings may be usefully read,

Yet when God causes the young shoots of self-inspired wisdom [αὐτοδιδάκτου σοφίας] to spring up within the soul, the knowledge that comes from teaching [διδασκαλίας] must straightway be abolished and swept off. Ay, even of itself it will subside and ebb away. God's scholar [φοιτητήν], God's pupil [γνώριμον], God's disciple [μαθητήν], call him by whatever name you will, cannot any more suffer the guidance of men [θνητῶν ὑφηγήσεως].

Here again is a link between having 'self-learned knowledge' and 'self-taught wisdom,' and being a 'pupil/disciple of God,' and here again when one has received instruction from God, one abolishes and sweeps off the knowledge that comes from the instruction of men. In fact, it is said to 'subside and ebb away' of itself. Nevertheless, prior to the coming of this divine instruction one is encouraged to learn from books since, 'truly it is sweet to leave nothing unknown.'

The view expressed in *Sacr.* 6-7, 78-79, that divine instruction renders otiose human instruction, appears to be inconsistent with Philo's claim, noted above in *Abr.* 53 and *Praem.* 64-65, that nature, teaching, and practice exist *together and simultaneously* in humans. Several other passages also suggest that God, through nature, allows some to be more receptive to human instruction, and is therefore in some sense the source of encyclical knowledge.[118] The latter claim is in keeping with the Greek educational tradition from which Philo develops his allegory of the patriarchs. It seems that this is an instance in which Philo's indebtedness to Greek sources has perhaps led to inconsistency in his thought.[119] The inconsistency may reflect

---

[117] The verb ἀπολείπω has the sense of 'put aside, give up' (BDAG 115).

[118] Cf. *Fug.* 172; *Mut.* 211, and the discussion in Mendelson, *Education*, 38-40.

[119] Cf. Borgen, *Bread*, 105 for recognition of the inconsistency, and secondary literature on it.

Philo's two ways of thinking about divine instruction: when divine instruction is understood to come through natural gifting, it complements human practice and instruction rather than replacing them (although, see *Fug.* 166-72 above). When divine instruction is understood as a sudden impartation of knowledge or wisdom from God, it replaces human practice and instruction.[120] Along similar lines, Völker has demonstrated that Philo uses the term φύσις in various ways, and that this lends differing values to his educational trinity.[121]

Conclusion

This study of Philo's view of divine instruction, based on the passages in which God is closely connected with didactic terminology, has highlighted several significant features in Philo's thought. First, unlike the NT, Philo does not develop a concept of eschatological divine instruction. Secondly, his own observation combined with Greek educational ideas appears to be at least as important for his thinking on divine instruction as the biblical texts. His own ideas are sometimes read into the biblical texts instead of arising from them. Thirdly, for Philo, divine instruction comes through natural gifting and/or through direct divine speech or inward prompting. In the former instance, divine instruction often complements human instruction, while in the latter case, it renders human instruction unnecessary.

3.3 Divine instruction in Josephus

Josephus frequently uses didactic terminology.[122] The terminology sometimes refers to military training,[123] at other times to instruction in music,[124] a trade,[125] or education in general.[126] Only rarely does Josephus bring this terminology into close conjunction with a reference to God. In these instances, the didactic terminology is often used loosely and unreflectively.[127]

---

[120] Cf. Montefiore, 'Florilegium,' 518-19, who notes Philo's emphasis both on natural endowment and on sudden inspiration.

[121] Völker, *Fortschritt*, 155-56. I am indebted to Charles Anderson for pointing me to Völker's discussion.

[122] This section is based on an examination of all uses of 15 didactic terms in Josephus: διδακτός, διδασκαλία, διδασκαλικός, διδάσκαλος, διδάσκω, διδαχή, ἐκδιδάσκω, μάθημα, μάθησις, μαθητής, μανθάνω, παιδεία, παίδευμα, παίδευσις, παιδεύω.

[123] E.g. *B.J.* 2.577, 579; 5.268, 359, 460; 6.38.

[124] E.g. *Ant.* 7.305; 9.269.

[125] E.g. *Ant.* 18.314.

[126] E.g. *Ant.* 1.8, 10; 2.39; 16.203; 17.94; 18.206.

[127] E.g. διδασκαλία in *Ant.* 4.49.

Although God is said to teach (διδάσκω) Israel through adversity,[128] nowhere in Josephus' works is God referred to as a teacher (as in the OT and Philo).

The two most interesting texts in which didactic terminology is associated with God are *Ant.* 5.12; 17.159. In the former, Rahab claims to know, by signs 'taught by God' (σημείοις τοῖς ἐκ τοῦ θεοῦ διδαχθεῖσαν), that Israel would take her city and destroy its inhabitants. It is not clear what the signs are, but they may be the miracles performed on Israel's behalf, mentioned by Rahab in Joshua 2.10.[129]

In *Ant.* 17.159, Josephus addresses his Roman readership:

Nor is it at all surprising if we believe that it is less important to observe your decrees than the laws that Moses wrote as God prompted and taught him [διδαχῇ τοῦ θεοῦ], and left behind.[130]

In this passage, God's teaching of Moses underscores the importance of the Jewish laws, and therefore explains the Jews' belief that it is more important to keep their laws than those of the Romans. The idea that Moses was taught by God is a biblical one, and appears also in Philo, as we have seen above.[131]

The verb μανθάνω appears 213 times in Josephus' writings. While it can refer to formal education (e.g. *Ant.* 20.71), it more often refers simply to coming to know something that was not known before.[132] In this loose sense, God is said to cause someone to learn something.[133] Interestingly, when someone is said to learn 'from God' (παρὰ τοῦ θεοῦ), μανθάνω always refers to learning through direct communication with God, usually by a prophetic figure.[134] The prophetic emphasis of this use of the phrase is underscored in *C. Ap.* 1.37, where Josephus claims that the Scriptures were written by prophets who obtained their knowledge of past events through the 'inspiration which they learned from God' (τὴν ἐπίπνοιαν τὴν ἀπὸ τοῦ θεοῦ μαθόντων).

It appears that the idea of divine instruction is not very important to Josephus. Didactic terminology is not often combined with a reference to God. When it is, it seems usually to be used unreflectively in the loose sense of coming to know something (or God making something known), rather than

---

[128] *Ant.* 5.200.

[129] Cf. Marcus' suggestion in Josephus, LCL 5.6-7.

[130] Translation from Josephus, LCL 8.445. διδαχή here means 'the activity of teaching, teaching, instruction' (BDAG 241).

[131] Cf. e.g. Exod 4.12, 15; Philo, *Leg.* 3.102; *Post.* 16; *Her.* 19.

[132] *Ant.* 1.234; 3.20 are surprising, because in these texts God is said to learn! Cf. Isa 40.13-14.

[133] E.g. *Ant.* 5.60, 120, 216; 6.125; 8.45, 257.

[134] E.g. Samuel learns from God (μάθω παρὰ τοῦ θεοῦ) who will be given to Israel as king (*Ant.* 6.44). Cf. e.g. *Ant.* 4.4; 5.350; 6.65, 274.

formal instruction. Josephus does not develop an idea of eschatological divine instruction. Nor does he cite Isa 54.13 or Jer 31.31-34, the biblical passages to which the NT authors are most attracted in their development of this idea.[135]

3.4 Divine instruction in the Apocrypha

Only three of the thirteen books of the Apocrypha bring didactic terminology into close conjunction with a reference to God: Wisdom of Solomon, Sirach (Ecclesiasticus), and 2 Maccabees.[136] Most of the fifteen instances in which this combination occurs refer to the 'discipline' of the Lord, rather than to instruction *per se*, although these are of course closely related.[137] The writer of 2 Maccabees, after describing the violent persecution of Jews, beseeches his readers not to be discouraged by these calamities and not to think that they are for the destruction of the nation. Rather, they should recognize that they are intended to 'discipline [πρὸς παιδείαν] our people' (6.12), which is a sign of God's goodness. God forbears to punish the nations until their sins are full, but he never withdraws his mercy from Israel: 'Though [God] disciplines [παιδεύω] us with calamities, he does not forsake his own people' (6.16).[138]

Wisdom of Solomon also refers to God's discipline, as is common in the biblical wisdom literature (e.g. Prov 3.11-12).[139] In Wisdom of Solomon, God disciplines (παιδεύω) his people for their good (3.5) and as a father (11.9-10), not in the way he punishes the enemies of his people (12.22). God acted in the exodus so that his children would learn (μανθάνω) that his word preserves those who trust in him (16.26). His kindness in judging mercifully serves as an example to his children, and thereby teaches (διδάσκω) them (12.19).

Several passages in Sirach refer to divine instruction. Already in 1.27, along the lines of biblical wisdom (e.g. Prov 1.7), we find the assertion that the fear of the Lord is wisdom and instruction (παιδεία). God is merciful

---

[135] Cf. the partial index in Whiston, *Josephus*, 895-99, the index in Michel and Bauernfeind, *De Bello Judaico*, 122-27, and the indices in the available volumes of Mason, *Josephus, passim*.

[136] This section is based on an examination of all uses of the following 9 didactic terms in the Apocrypha (see the beginning of this chapter for definition of the corpus): γνώριμος, διδακτός, διδασκαλία, διδάσκαλος, διδάσκω, μανθάνω, παιδεία, παιδευτής, παιδεύω.

[137] Cf. e.g. Sir 30.1-3.

[138] Cf. also the similar use of παιδεία in 2 Macc 7.33 and παιδεύω in 2 Macc 10.4. Translations of the Apocrypha are taken from the RSV.

[139] On discipline in Proverbs, cf. Wegner, 'Discipline,' 715-32.

with all mankind because of the brevity of their lives (18.6-12), and his instruction demonstrates his compassion:

> The compassion of man is for his neighbor, but the compassion of the Lord is for all living beings. He rebukes [ἐλέγχω] and trains [παιδεύω] and teaches [διδάσκω] them, and turns them back, as a shepherd his flock. He has compassion on those who accept his discipline [παιδεία] and who are eager for his judgments (18.13-14).

In this passage, God teaches *all* living beings, not just Israel. In the context of 18.13-14, παιδεία can bear either the sense of 'discipline' or 'instruction.' It is a gift from God, intended for the good of those who receive it.

Finally, Sir 39.1-5 describes one who studies the Law, and 39.6-8 describes the Lord filling this one with a 'spirit of understanding,' so that he speaks wisdom. This spirit-filled interpreter of the Law will, 'reveal instruction in his teaching [αὐτὸς ἐκφανεῖ παιδείαν διδασκαλίας αὐτοῦ], and will glory in the law of the Lord's covenant.' Here, the teaching comes ultimately from God, as the 'spirit of wisdom' gifts the interpreter to understand what he is reading in the Law.

In conclusion, the idea of divine instruction does not feature heavily in the Apocrypha. When it does appear, the predominant emphasis is on the discipline of the Lord, in keeping with the biblical wisdom tradition. When God is said to teach (διδάσκω), it is a divine instruction of all mankind (Sir 18.13-14). There is no development of the concept of an eschatological divine instruction; rather, God's instruction and discipline occur in the past and the present.

3.5 Divine instruction in the OT Greek pseudepigrapha

Several passages in the OT Greek pseudepigrapha connect didactic terminology with a reference to God.[140] The most striking passage is *Pss. Sol.* 17.32, which will be discussed below in the next section. Much of the didactic terminology in the pseudepigrapha seems loose and unreflective. In *Apoc. Sedr.* 14.2, Sedrach and Michael ask the Lord to teach (διδάσκω) them how man may be saved, and in *3 Bar.* 13.5, Michael says, 'Wait until I learn [μανθάνω] from the Lord what is to happen.' These terms do not refer to formal education, but to coming to know something.

---

[140] This section is based upon an examination of all uses of the following 19 didactic terms in the OT Greek pseudepigrapha (see the beginning of this chapter for definition of the corpus): ἀδίδακτος, γνώριμος, δίδαγμα, διδακτός, διδασκαλία, διδάσκαλος, διδάσκω, διδαχή, κατηχέω, κατήχησις, μαθητής, μανθάνω, παιδεία, παίδευμα, παίδευσις, παιδεύτης, παιδεύω, συνετίζω, ὑφηγέομαι.

Most of the remaining passages associating God and didactic terminology in the OT Greek pseudepigrapha are found in *Psalms of Solomon*, and refer to the discipline of God.[141] Israel is under God's discipline, which is intended for their good (7.9; 8.26; 10.2, 3) and is different than his punishment of sinners (13.7). God disciplines Israel as a firstborn child, to divert them from sin.[142] One function of the future Lord Messiah in *Pss. Sol.* 17-18 is to offer discipline (see below).

Psalms of Solomon, then, envisions an eschatological divine instruction. The Lord Messiah will be taught by God and will discipline/instruct God's people (17.32). If this is an allusion to Isa 54.13 (see below), it is the only one in the OT pseudepigrapha.[143] While there are several allusions to Jer 31.31-34 in the OT pseudepigrapha,[144] none of these bring out the idea of eschatological divine instruction. It seems, then, that the OT Greek pseudepigrapha (with the exception of *Pss. Sol.* 17.32) do not draw upon the OT prophetic tradition of eschatological divine instruction.

3.6 The Jewish expectation of a God-taught messianic teacher

The purpose of this section is to explore the Jewish sources that indicate an expectation of a future messianic figure(s) who teaches and/or is himself taught by God. While limits of space do not permit a focus on related questions, such as the Jewish expectation of a messianic Torah[145] or the expectation of other, non-messianic teaching figures, these will be noted as they are raised in the primary texts. Caution must be exercised when speaking of a future messianic figure. A diversity of expectations is evident in the OT and early Jewish sources, and the term 'Messiah' is sometimes used and sometimes not. When used, it may refer to a presently reigning king, and not (at least not directly) to a future ideal son of David.[146] Despite these caveats, however, there are instances in which a future kingly, priestly, or prophetic figure, sometimes identified as 'Messiah,' is expected to teach or be taught by God, and these are the passages I will examine.[147]

---

[141] Cf. also *3 Bar.* 1.2; *Jos. Asen.* 11.18; *Apoc. Sedr.* 3.7-8; 4.1.

[142] See *Pss. Sol.* 13.9-10; 18.4; cf. 3.4; 7.3; 13.8; 14.1; 16.11, 13; and παιδευτής in 8.29.

[143] Cf. McLean, *Citations*, 95; Delamarter, *Index*, 29, 86.

[144] McLean, *Citations*, 102; Delamarter, *Index*, 30, 87.

[145] See Davies, *Torah, passim*; Davies, *Sermon*, 109-90; Chester, *Messiah*, 497-545.

[146] De Jonge, 'Messiah,' 787.

[147] Cf. Collins, *Scepter*, 1-19 for an overview of the recent scholarly discussion concerning Jewish messianic expectations, including the increasing recognition of the diversity of messianic ideas in the Jewish sources. Collins does not restrict his discussion of a 'Messiah' to figures that invariably bear the title משיח in the ancient sources, and I will follow this approach. See now the discussion of Chester, *Messiah*, 193-205.

A God-taught Messiah

At least some Jews expected a future royal figure who would be 'taught by God.' Already in the OT, we find the Lord's oath to David:

From the fruit of your body I will set upon your throne. If your sons will keep my covenant, and my testimonies which I will teach [למד/διδάσκω] them, their sons also will sit upon your throne forever (Ps 132.11b-12 [LXX Ps 131]).

The promise that David's heirs will sit on his throne is dependent upon their obedience to the covenant taught them by God. This idea is similar to the Deuteronomic stipulations concerning Israel's future king (Deut 17.18-20). As in Ps 132.11-12, the continuing reign of the king's descendants is an important concern in Deut 17. The purpose of the king's study of the Law is that he would learn (למד/μανθάνω) to fear the Lord, and not exalt himself over his countrymen, and that he and his sons would continue to rule Israel (cf. 2 Sam 7; Ps 89).

The idea of a God-taught Messiah is present in a text closer to the time of the NT, a text that may in fact address the concerns evidenced in Ps 132.11-12 and Deut 17.18-20. The first century B.C.E. *Psalms of Solomon*[148] describes the eschatological Lord Messiah[149] as 'taught by God' (διδακτὸς ὑπὸ θεοῦ):

...And he will be a righteous king over them, taught by God. There will be no unrighteousness among them in his days, for all shall be holy, and their king shall be the Lord Messiah. (For) he will not rely on horse and rider and bow, nor will he collect gold and silver for war. Nor will he build up hope in a multitude for a day of war. The Lord himself is his king, the hope of the one who has a strong hope in God (*Pss. Sol.* 17.32-34).[150]

The psalm begins and ends by affirming that God is king (17.1, 46) and recalls the divine promise to David that his descendants would continue to rule forever (17.4). The author claims that the ascendancy of the Hasmoneans, to whom God did not make a promise, is due to the sins of the people (17.5), and that the sins of the Hasmonean kings have resulted in their defeat at the hands of Pompey (17.6-10).[151] The ultimate solution to this problem of a sinful people and a sinful king is God's appointment of an eschatological Messiah, a son of David (17.21), who will rule over Israel. He will root out unrighteousness among the people (e.g. 17.27, 30, 32). Unlike the Hasmonean kings, who are described as sinners, he will be a 'righteous

---

[148] Wright, 'Solomon,' 640-41 suggests dating the *Psalms of Solomon* between 70 and 45 B.C.E. Atkinson, 'I Cried,' 211 also suggests a first century B.C.E. date.

[149] For the reading 'Lord Messiah,' cf. Wright, 'Solomon,' 667-68; Evans, 'Messianic,' 20-22. For a different reading, cf. De Jonge, 'Messiah,' 783.

[150] Translation from Wright, 'Solomon,' 667-68.

[151] For the probable identification of the 'sinners' as the Hasmonean rulers, cf. Wright, 'Solomon,' 665.

king, taught by God.' This description may well allude to Isa 54.13.[152]
Moreover, the description of the Lord Messiah may also be influenced by
Deut 17.[153] If so, the description of the Messiah as 'taught by God' likely
refers to his submission and obedience to the Law. In 17.37, the author
claims, drawing upon the language of Isa 11, that God made the Lord
Messiah 'powerful in the holy spirit and wise in the counsel of understanding,
with strength and righteousness.' This suggests that the divine instruction of
the Messiah is perhaps thought to be accomplished through the holy spirit of
God.[154]

This early expectation of a 'God-taught' Messiah may find a parallel in
4Q381 (4QNon-Canonical Psalms B), frg. 15.7-8. Here, the author claims
that 'I, your anointed, have understood…I have made known, and instruct
[שכל] for you instructed [שכל] me.'[155] If the 'anointed' one is understood as
a royal figure (cf. frgs. 31, 33), as is suggested by the close connections with
Ps 89, we have mention of God instructing an anointed king who then
instructs others.[156] While this is not necessarily a reference to an
eschatological messianic figure, the idea of kingly divine instruction is
reminiscent of *Pss. Sol.* 17.32 and the OT texts noted above, and Evans notes
that there is nothing to preclude an eschatological interpretation.[157] In both
Pss. Sol. 17 and 4Q381, then, the kingly figure is taught by God and teaches
others. Another parallel, though a much later one, is found in *Midr. Pss.* 21.4,
which describes the Messiah as a disciple of God.[158] There is therefore some
evidence, although not a great deal, for the belief that the Messiah, or more
generally a royal descendant of David, would be taught by God.

---

[152] See Evans, 'Messianic,' 21. This is presumably the text intended in McLean, *Citations*, 95.

[153] Cf. the allusion to Deut 17.16-17 in *Pss. Sol.* 17.33, not noted by Wright in the Charlesworth edition.

[154] See chapter 2, and above in this chapter, for the spirit as the means of divine instruction. However, it must be noted that while the influence of Isa 11 suggests a reference to *the* spirit (cf. Hengel, 'Messianic Teacher,' 96-98), 17.37 does not have a definite article before πνεῦμα.

[155] Translation from García Martínez and Tigchelaar, *Scrolls*, 2.757. There are other possible readings of these lines. For a different reading and translation, cf. Schuller, '4QNon-Canonical Psalms B,' 103.

[156] Cf. Zimmermann, *Messianische Texte*, 226; Chester, *Messiah*, 240-41. Cf. the discussion in Schuller, '4QNon-Canonical Psalms B,' 104 who suggests as one of several possibilities that the author identifies himself as משיח, and that the psalm is thus attributed to a king. 4Q161 frgs. 8-10, commenting on Isa 11.1-5, suggests that the Zakokite priests will instruct (ירה) the Branch of David (lines 17-25).

[157] Evans, *Jesus*, 139-40.

[158] See below for a citation of the midrash. Stemberger, *Talmud and Midrash*, 322-23 suggests that the Midrash on Psalms had an, 'extended period of development,' though most of the material dates to the Talmudic period.

A teaching Messiah

There is considerably more evidence for the Jewish expectation of a *teaching* Messiah.[159] Although a full discussion of the relevant Jewish texts is not possible here, several of the important passages will be noted, and these are dealt with more comprehensively in some of the secondary literature.[160] There are already hints of a teaching role for the Isaianic servant (Isa 42.1-4), who is described in terms similar to the shoot of David in Isa 11, and for whose 'Torah' the coastlands are said to wait.[161] The Jewish literature of the Second Temple period makes the Messiah's teaching role clearer. *Pss. Sol* 17-18, drawing on Isa 11, describes the Lord Messiah as one who will impart wisdom and instruction to the people. *Pss. Sol.* 17.42 claims that God will raise the future king of Israel (i.e. the Lord Messiah) over the house of Israel to instruct or discipline (παιδεύω) it. The context of this claim (e.g. 17.36-37, 43) suggests that παιδεύω in 17.42 refers to spoken instruction. The idea of discipline is clearer in 18.7, where it is claimed that the Lord Messiah will rule over the coming generation with a rod of discipline (ῥάβδος παιδείας).[162] While the Messiah in *Pss. Sol* 17-18 is described primarily as one who will judge the wicked,[163] his didactic role is nevertheless clearly present in this passage.

The expectation of a future teaching figure is also evident in the LXX and the Targum of Isaiah. LXX Isa 50.4 speaks of God giving the servant a tongue of instruction (παιδεία) to know when to speak a word (λόγος). This LXX translation (see the same reading in Philo, *Her.* 25) emphasizes the teaching role of the servant, differing from the MT's 'tongue of a disciple,' which refers to the servant as one who is himself taught. The combination of παιδεύω in *Pss. Sol.* 17.42 and the words (οἱ λόγοι) of the king in 17.43 may recall this similar combination of language in Isa 50.4.[164] As Riesner notes, *Pss. Sol.* 17.42 is even closer to an interpretive tradition found in the Targum of Isaiah 53.5.[165] While the LXX translates with παιδεία in closer

---

[159] *Contra* Yieh, *One Teacher*, 242-43, n. 10.

[160] Cf. Riesner, *Lehrer*, 304-330; Hengel, 'Messianic Teacher,' 73-117; Collins, 'Teacher,' 193-210; Collins, *Scepter*, 102-35; Zimmermann, *Messianische Texte, passim*; Chester, *Messiah*, 288-301, 329-63, 497-547.

[161] Cf. Riesner, *Lehrer*, 306-7.

[162] On *Pss. Sol.* 17, cf. Hengel, 'Messianic Teacher,' 96-98.

[163] So Chester, *Messiah*, 529.

[164] Cf. Riesner, *Lehrer*, 320.

[165] It is difficult to date the material in the Targum of Isaiah. Chilton, *Isaiah Targum*, xx-xxv suggests that the present Targum consists of 'interpretative levels' that emerged over the course of numerous generations, both Tannaitic and Amoraic.

dependence on the Hebrew מוּסָר, the Targum interprets מוּסָר (= 'discipline, training, exhortation') to refer to the teaching of the Messiah:[166]

And he will build the sanctuary which was profaned for our sins, handed over for our iniquities; and by his teaching (וּבְאָלְפָנֵיהּ) his peace will increase upon us, and in that we attach ourselves to his words our sins will be forgiven us.[167]

Several passages in the DSS may refer to the didactic role of a messianic figure. I have already discussed 4Q381, which likely refers to a royal figure teaching others, and is at least open to an eschatological interpretation.[168] CD 6.8-11 speaks of an individual who will arise at the end of days to 'teach justice.' John Collins has argued that this refers not to the Teacher of Righteousness, but to a future eschatological figure, perhaps a prophet like Moses, but more likely the Messiah of Aaron.[169] More recently, Zimmermann, in his comprehensive treatment of messianic texts in the DSS, agrees that the figure in CD 6.11 who will 'teach justice' is not the Teacher of Righteousness, but rather a future figure. Zimmermann suggests that this figure may combine priestly and prophetic roles, in analogy with the Teacher of Righteousness.[170] It must be said that the passage does not make clear whether the one who will 'teach justice' is specifically a messianic figure, but in any case, we seem to have here the expectation of an eschatological figure who will offer instruction.

Perhaps related to the eschatological figure in CD 6.11 is the 'Interpreter of the Law' in CD 7.18-20 and 4Q174 frg. 1i.10-13. While the 'Interpreter of the Law' in CD 6.7 is probably the Teacher of Righteousness,[171] the 'Interpreter of the Law' in 4Q174 frg. 1i.10-13 is clearly a future figure, and in CD 7.18-20 is probably also future, since in both passages, the 'Interpreter of the Law' is paired with a kingly messianic figure.[172] This pairing may be related to the tradition of an eschatological Messiah of Israel and a Messiah of Aaron, although this connection is not certain. In any case, Zimmermann suggests that the 'Interpreter of the Law' in CD 7.18-20 and 4Q174 frg. 1i.10-13 is to be seen as a priestly messianic figure, one who also incorporates prophetic traits.[173] Other Qumran texts, such as 4Q491c frg. 1.1-

---

[166] As Riesner, *Lehrer*, 315 notes, the Targum of Isa 52.13 (which identifies the servant as the Messiah) suggests that 53.5 is understood as referring to the Messiah.

[167] Chilton, *Isaiah Targum*, 104.

[168] Cf. Chester, *Messiah*, 267.

[169] Collins, 'Teacher,' 193-210; Collins, *Scepter*, 102-35. The DSS expect two future messianic figures, a Messiah of Aaron and a Messiah of Israel. Cf. VanderKam, 'Messianism,' 211-34.

[170] Zimmermann, *Messianische Texte*, 443.

[171] Zimmermann, *Messianische Texte*, 442-43.

[172] Zimmermann, *Messianische Texte*, 440.

[173] Note, however, the cautious approach of Chester, *Messiah*, 526-28.

17 (cf. 1Q28b 3-4; 4Q471b frgs. 1-3), indicate the possible expectation of a priestly Messiah who would bring incomparable teaching.[174] If Zimmermann is correct, the didactic function of the priestly Messiah as one who interprets the Law is underscored.[175]

4Q541 (4QApocryphon of Levi[b]) frg. 9i.2-3 may also refer to the teaching function of a priestly messianic figure:

And he will atone for all the children of his generation, and he will be sent to all the children of his [people]. His word is like the word of the heavens, and his teaching [וֹאלפונה], according to the will of God.

While the priestly figure in 4Q541 is never said to be 'anointed,' Zimmermann, in a careful discussion of 4Q541, suggests that there may be a connection with Essene messianic expectations.[176] Possible evidence for this is the atoning function of the priestly figure in 4Q541. This suggests that he may be the Messiah of Aaron, since the role of atoning is assigned to the Messiah figures in CD 14.19.[177] However, it must be admitted that this is not a decisive argument, and it is not possible to identify with certainty the figure in 4Q541 as messianic.[178] Even if the figure is not messianic, the passage remains of interest. Zimmermann has highlighted numerous points of connection between 4Q541 frg. 9i and *T. Levi* 18. While stopping short of positing literary dependence of one text upon the other, Zimmermann suggests a close connection between the priestly figure of 4Q541 frg. 9i and the 'new priest' of *T. Levi* 18.[179] This connection suggests the presence of a broader Jewish tradition of a priestly figure who teaches in the last days. In the end-time vision of *T. Levi* 18.2, 'all the words of the Lord' are revealed to the 'new priest,' and through him, the knowledge of the Lord is poured out on the earth (18.5, 9).[180]

A very fragmentary section of 11Q13 (11QMelchizedek) refers to a messenger anointed with the spirit, and seems to suggest that his task is to instruct (שׂכל) the afflicted in 'all the ages of the world' (2.18-20). It may be that the anointed messenger, spoken of in language that echoes Isa 61.1, is an eschatological prophetic figure, perhaps the 'prophet like Moses' of Deut 18.15-18.[181] If so, it is possible to speak here of a 'prophetic messiah.'[182]

---

[174] See the discussion in Chester, *Messiah*, 242-50. Cf. Zimmermann, *Messianische Texte*, 307-8.

[175] Cf. VanderKam, 'Messianism,' 233. For a listing of Qumran texts that likely refer to a priestly Messiah, cf. Chester, *Messiah*, 265.

[176] Zimmermann, *Messianische Texte*, 247-77.

[177] Collins, 'Teacher,' 208.

[178] See the points raised by Chester, *Messiah*, 258.

[179] Cf. Zimmermann, *Messianische Texte*, 271-72, 310. Cf. also Collins, *Scepter*, 88-9.

[180] Cf. Hengel, 'Messianic Teacher,' 98-99.

[181] Cf. Zimmermann, *Messianische Texte*, 410-12; Chester, *Messiah*, 259-61.

Other Qumran texts may refer to a prophetic messianic figure. 4Q521 frg. 2ii possibly describes a prophetic Messiah, to whom heaven and earth will listen.[183] The eschatological prophet of 1QS 9.9-11 and 4Q175, though not described as 'anointed,' is, as Chester has suggested, closely related to the prophetic Messiah.[184]

In the later rabbinic literature, the Messiah is also expected to be a teacher. *Midr. Pss.* 21.4 describes the Messiah as a student of God and a teacher of Torah:[185]

Glory and great worship shalt Thou lay upon him (Ps. 21:6) means that Thou, O God, layest a master's glory and a disciple's great worship upon the king Messiah.[186]

However, in numerous rabbinic texts *God* is expected to teach eschatologically, in accordance with the OT promises of eschatological divine instruction examined above in chapter 2. *Midr. Pss.* 21.1 appears to be R. Tanhuma's attempt to reconcile these expectations of divine instruction and instruction from the Messiah.[187] R. Tanhuma claims that the Messiah will teach the nations in the last days, while God himself will teach Israel (in fulfillment of Isa 54.13).[188]

The texts noted in this section suggest that there were early Jewish expectations of messianic figures who would be 'taught by God' and who would teach others. These figures are variously royal, priestly, or prophetic, and are related to other eschatological teaching figures (e.g. the 'new priest' of *T. Levi* 18) who are not specifically messianic. *Pss. Sol.* 17.32, 42-43 and *Midr. Pss.* 21.4 (and possibly 4Q381 frg. 15.7-8) are the clearest passages in which a messianic figure is described both as one taught by God and one who teaches others.[189]

---

[182] Chester, *Messiah*, 528-29.

[183] Cf. Chester, *Messiah*, 251-54, 528. See also possibly 4Q377 frg. 2ii.

[184] Chester, *Messiah*, 261, 268.

[185] Cf. Rengstorf, 'μανθάνω,' *TDNT* 4.403.

[186] Translation from Braude, *Midrash on Psalms*, 1.295-96.

[187] Cf. Riesner, *Lehrer*, 329.

[188] See also *Gen. Rab.* 98.9. Stemberger, *Talmud and Midrash*, 279 suggests that *Genesis Rabbah* had a final redaction in the first half of the fifth century.

[189] Keener, *John*, 1.686 suggests that 4Q491c frg. 1.9-10 may refer to the Messiah as one who is formally untaught but one who nevertheless teaches others, thus implying that he is taught by God. But the passage suggests that the speaker *has* been taught. Cf. the translation in Duhaime, 'Cave IV Fragments,' 153.

3.7 Conclusion

The writings examined above represent a broad swath of Jewish material, from Hellenistic diaspora Judaism to the sectarian community at Qumran, and much else in between. In some writings (i.e. DSS, Philo) the idea of divine instruction is more prevalent, while in others (i.e. Josephus, Apocrypha, Greek OT pseudepigrapha) it does not appear very often and does not appear significant. Our investigation of Philo showed that his development of the idea was indebted to Greek educational traditions, and did not draw heavily upon the OT. We found no development of an eschatological divine instruction in Philo. In contrast, the material in the DSS likely draws upon Isa 54.13, and the divine instruction of the community and of certain individuals (e.g. the psalmist of the *Hodayot*) was seen as an eschatological instruction. The expectation of an eschatological teaching Messiah in the DSS is paralleled in *Psalms of Solomon*, which also describes the Lord Messiah as 'taught by God,' possibly using the language of Isa 54.13. I conclude that in certain circles of Second Temple Judaism, although not all, there were expectations of end-time divine instruction, seen either as coming directly from God, or through messianic (or related) figures.

Chapter 4

Teaching and revelation in the Fourth Gospel

'...our Instructor [παιδαγωγός] is the holy God Jesus,
the Word, who is the guide of all humanity.
The loving God Himself is our Instructor.'

'For it was really the Lord that was the instructor of the ancient people by Moses; but He is
the instructor of the new people by Himself, face to face [πρόσωπον πρὸς πρόσωπον].'

Clement of Alexandria, *Paedagogus* 1.7, c. 200[1]

Having examined divine instruction in the OT and early Jewish literature, we may now turn to the Johannine corpus. This chapter begins by addressing the relationship between the Fourth Gospel and the Johannine letters. It then prepares the way for chapters 5-6 by comparing the language and concept of instruction in the Fourth Gospel with the synoptic gospels in order to identify what, if anything, is distinctive in the Fourth Gospel's portrayal of Jesus as a teacher and God as one who teaches.[2] Two questions are of primary importance: First, in what ways does the Fourth Gospel develop the common tradition regarding Jesus as teacher?[3] Secondly, are there distinctive contributions regarding God's teaching not found in the synoptics?

---

[1] Translation from *ANF* 2.223-24.

[2] This chapter is based on all uses of the following 8 didactic terms in the Fourth Gospel: δίδακτος, διδάσκαλος, διδάσκω, διδαχή, μαθητής, μανθάνω, ῥαββί/ῥαββουνί. Both διδάσκω and διδάσκαλος appear in the textually suspect passage 7.53-8.11, and I do not include these in the study. The Fourth Gospel clearly gives ῥαββί/ῥαββουνί a didactic connotation, verging on a titular use (1.38; 3.2; 20.16). I am unconvinced by the argument of Viviano, 'Rabbouni,' 207-18, esp. 209, that this is a late technical sense that is anachronistic in the Fourth Gospel. The evidence in Zimmerman, *Urchristlichen*, 69-91 suggests early didactic connotations for ῥαββί.

[3] The question of the relationship between the Fourth Gospel and the synoptic gospels has, of course, been long debated. The important work of P. Gardner-Smith in 1938 convinced many that the Fourth Gospel did not know or directly draw upon the synoptics, but in recent years this question has been re-opened, with a considerable number of scholars now arguing that the Fourth Gospel does draw directly upon the synoptics. On this latest direction, see Neirynck, 'John,' 73-106; Neirynck, 'John,' 3-62. My argument does not depend on resolving this debate. For the purposes of this discussion, I refer to 'common tradition' (understood as the early Christian traditions, whether oral or written, behind the

With regard to the first question, I will argue that the accomplishment of the fourth evangelist is to combine the didactic terminology of the common tradition with his own concept of revelation. According to the Fourth Gospel, Jesus' teaching (properly understood) is revelation. By 'revelation,' I mean, very broadly, communication from God.[4] This is a striking identification, because, as Samuel Byrskog has noted, 'learning' and 'revelation' normally belong to two different spheres. The latter derives from God and involves an experience of transcendent reality, while the former derives from human efforts to communicate these transcendent experiences to others.[5]

With regard to the second question, I will argue that the Fourth Gospel contains several references to the teaching of God and the Paraclete/Spirit not found in the common tradition. In other words, in the Fourth Gospel, revelation is distinctively described with didactic terminology. Taken together, these two points are significant. The identification of Jesus' teaching as *revelation* and the identification of divine revelation as *instruction*, presses the question of how precisely Jesus' teaching relates to God's teaching. That question is addressed in chapter 5. The prevalence of the idea of divine instruction also raises the question of how it functions in the Fourth Gospel. That question is addressed in chapter 6.

4.1 The Fourth Gospel and the Johannine letters

Similarities in theology, language, and style indicate a relationship between the Fourth Gospel and the Johannine letters,[6] and suggest that they arose within a common community.[7] However, Johannine scholarship as a whole remains undecided whether those similarities are best explained by positing common authorship[8] or authorship within a Johannine school.[9] Moreover, some who posit different authorship question whether the author of the Johannine letters had access to the Fourth Gospel, or even whether the Fourth Gospel was written prior to the letters.[10] In this study I assume neither

---

gospels) to explain the similarities between the Fourth Gospel and the synoptics, leaving open the question of direct dependence.

[4] Cf. the broad definition of Bockmuehl, *Revelation*, 2. The broad nature of my definition is suggested by the first century evidence. In early Jewish sources, revelation occurs in a number of ways, with varying content. Cf. Nickelsburg, 'Revelation,' 770-72, who distinguishes apocalyptic revelation from revelation at Qumran.

[5] Byrskog, 'Lernen,' 191.

[6] Cf. Painter, *1, 2, and 3 John*, 58.

[7] Cf. Smith, *Johannine Christianity*, 8, 21.

[8] E.g. Poythress, 'Johannine Authorship,' 350-69, esp. 365-66.

[9] E.g. Strecker, *Johannine Letters*, xxxv-xlii.

[10] E.g. Strecker, *Johannine Letters*, xl-xlii.

common authorship of the Fourth Gospel and Johannine letters, nor that the author of the letters[11] had access to the Fourth Gospel. My argument is therefore compatible both with theories of common authorship and of multiple authorship within a Johannine school.

Although my argument does not assume that the author of the letters had access to the Fourth Gospel in written form,[12] it is highly probable that he had access to the traditions behind the Fourth Gospel.[13] The differences between the Fourth Gospel and the letters in audience and setting suggest that these traditions are prior to the letters. While the Fourth Gospel speaks of the 'Jews' and appears to reflect a situation of conflict between Jews and Christians, the letters deal with ethical and theological problems within the Christian community.[14] Jewish-Christian debate over the meaning of the Scriptures is not at the fore; rather, debate with those who were formerly part of the community (1 John 2.19) occupies the attention of the writer.[15] Following Raymond Brown, I suggest that the focus of debate in the letters is the correct interpretation of Johannine tradition, rather than the Scriptures.[16] The author of the Johannine letters is concerned to interpret this tradition correctly over against his opponents. This shift in debate likely corresponds to an increasing separation of the Christian movement from the synagogue.

4.2 Comparing the Fourth Gospel and the synoptic gospels: what is distinctive about teaching in the Fourth Gospel?

Previous research: Pancaro, Hahn, and Untergassmair

A brief evaluation of several treatments of didactic terminology in the Fourth Gospel will set the context for the present investigation.[17] First, Severino

---

[11] Although it is unproven that the author of 1 John is also the author of 2-3 John (cf. Lieu, *Epistles*, 91; Kysar, *1, 2, 3 John*, 11-13), most scholars hold to common authorship of all three letters, e.g. Brooke, *Johannine Epistles*, lxxiv-lxxix; Painter, *1, 2, and 3 John*, 52; Johnson, *Writings*, 561-62.

[12] Lieu, 'Scripture,' 460 notes that the letters nowhere quote the Fourth Gospel.

[13] Cf. Brown, *Epistles of John*, 757-59.

[14] Cf. Smith, *First, Second, and Third John*, 11-12.

[15] Cf. Carson, 'John,' 256-57. Even if we accept the arguments of Lieu, 'Scripture,' 458-77 that there are OT allusions in 1 John (cf. Lieu, *Epistles*, 87-88), the OT texts are not the subject of debated interpretation or the ground of argument in 1 John as they are in the Fourth Gospel.

[16] Cf. Brown, *Community, passim*; Brown, *Epistles of John*, 69-115; Brown, 'Relationship,' 58.

[17] For surveys of the didactic terminology, cf. Pancaro, *Law*, 79-87; Rengstorf, 'διδάσκω,' *TDNT* 2.143-44; Rengstorf, 'διδάσκαλος,' *TDNT* 2.152-57; Brown, *Epistles of*

Pancaro argues that διδάσκω in the Fourth Gospel is a 'term of revelation,' and is therefore different than διδάσκω in the synoptics and Judaism.[18] Pancaro claims that in the Fourth Gospel, 'only Jesus may be called teacher,' and that while διδάσκαλος and ῥαββί are used in the synoptics 'in the ordinary sense,' such is not the case in the Fourth Gospel.[19] While Pancaro's recognition of the close link between teaching and revelation in the Fourth Gospel is appropriate, his direct identification of the two is unconvincing. As I will argue below, it does not adequately account for several passages in which teaching is clearly not intended to be understood as revelation (i.e. 3.10, 26; 7.35; 9.34). A more nuanced approach is necessary.

Secondly, Ferdinand Hahn deals with διδάσκαλος and ῥαββί in the Fourth Gospel and the synoptics as part of his well-known work on the titles of Jesus in Christology. He argues that an originally unreflective address διδάσκαλε/ῥαββί evolved over the course of time in the Christian communities into the titular ὁ διδάσκαλος, a Christological title that implied the ascription of authority to Jesus.[20] Hahn suggests that the Fourth Gospel, like the synoptic gospels, preserves examples of both the unreflective address (i.e. most uses of ῥαββί) and the Christologically-significant title (διδάσκαλος in 3.2; 11.27-28; 13.13-14; cf. the term ῥαββί in 3.2).[21]

Finally, Franz Georg Untergassmair has contributed an essay on 'Lernen bei Johannes,' a section of which he devotes to an analysis of the didactic terminology in the Fourth Gospel.[22] Untergassmair, closely following Hahn, concludes that ῥαββί is used in a largely unreflective sense in the Fourth Gospel, but that in John 3.2, the term is used with more significance.[23] Moreover, while the direct address διδάσκαλε (a translation for ῥαββί) plays 'no outstanding role,' 3.2 adumbrates a shift to the title ὁ διδάσκαλος that is clearly present in 13.13-14.[24]

Hahn and Untergassmair's recognition of both an unreflective and a Christologically-significant use of didactic terminology in the Fourth Gospel is helpful, but their distinction between address and title should not be overplayed. Hahn himself suggests that in 3.2, the address ῥαββί is

---

John, 359-60; Untergassmair, 'Lehrer,' 211-18; Van Der Watt, *Family*, 280-84; Kösten-berger, 'Rabbi,' 105-12; Hahn, *Titles*, 73-89.

[18] Pancaro, *Law*, 80-81 claims this is the key to understanding the Johannine use of didactic terminology.

[19] Pancaro, *Law*, 82, 85, n. 40.

[20] By 'unreflective,' Hahn means that the term does not carry Christological import, but is used in a normal sense, as it would be of any teacher.

[21] Hahn, *Titles*, 74, 78.

[22] Strangely, Untergassmair, 'Lehrer,' 211-33 does not include δίδακτος in his list of didactic terminology.

[23] Untergassmair, 'Lehrer,' 212-13.

[24] Untergassmair, 'Lehrer,' 214-15.

'somewhat more emphatic,' as is evident from the appended explanation.[25] This suggests that it is quite possible for the evangelist, in taking over the *originally* unreflective terms 'rabbi' and 'teacher' from the common tradition, to endow them with new Christological significance. This in turn suggests that it is incorrect to identify all instances of direct address as unreflective, and all titular usages as Christologically significant. As scholars have increasingly recognized, a 'title Christology' separated from attention to the narrative strategies of the NT authors is inadequate.[26] The gospel writers were fully capable of using previously known titles and filling them with new meaning through their narrative portrayals of Jesus.[27] Rather than focusing on 'teacher' as a Christological title, we must examine the narrative of the Fourth Gospel itself in order to understand what significance the evangelist attributes to Jesus' identity as a teacher.

Using the narrator/narrative distinction

In accounting for the didactic terminology of the Fourth Gospel, then, it is necessary to avoid Pancaro's over-simplification of the relationship between teaching and revelation. Moreover, while recognizing that Hahn and Untergassmair properly identify the presence of unreflective didactic terminology, a more useful distinction must be found than that between 'address' and 'title.' I suggest it is more helpful to distinguish between the tradition of Jesus as a teacher and the evangelist's reworking of that tradition. In order to utilize this distinction, I will employ a corresponding one that is a commonplace in literary theory. The distinction between a narrator and the story he narrates (of which the characters are one part), has already been applied fruitfully to the Fourth Gospel.[28] In any narrative, it is the distance between the narrator and his characters that allows for the narrator's use of devices such as misunderstanding and irony to instruct and persuade his readers, and the narrator of the Fourth Gospel uses these devices to great effect.[29] The prologue (1.1-18) demonstrates that he knows more about Jesus than do the characters in his narrative (with the exception of Jesus and the Beloved Disciple).

I suggest that the narrator/narrative distinction is directly relevant to understanding the use of didactic terminology. While most of the characters

---

[25] Hahn, *Titles*, 74.

[26] Cf. Keck, 'Renewal,' 368-70; Byrskog, 'Teacher,' 84, n. 3.

[27] Cf. Müller, 'Christology,' 163-65.

[28] Cf. the narrative structure outlined in Chatman, *Story*, 267. Chatman's model has been modified and applied to the Fourth Gospel by Culpepper, *Anatomy*, who provides an excellent treatment of the narrator of the Fourth Gospel (15-49). For the distinction between a narrator and the characters in his story, cf. Booth, *Fiction*, 156.

[29] Cf. Culpepper, *Anatomy*, 151-202, esp. 151-52.

in the narrative of the Fourth Gospel use διδάσκω and the rest of the
didactic terminology in a mundane and unreflective sense, the narrator's view
is that the terminology has Christological significance. Toward the beginning
of the Fourth Gospel, in 3.1-15, the narrator provides a hint to the discerning
reader that Jesus' teaching, properly understood, is not teaching in the normal
sense of the word, but is revelation. With the distinction between narrator and
narrative in place, I will examine the didactic terminology of the Fourth
Gospel. Although the terminology will be examined in three sections, my
argument will be cumulative, depending upon an analysis of all the didactic
terminology.

Jesus as διδάσκαλος and ῥαββί, and his followers as μαθηταί

In the Fourth Gospel, Jesus is often referred to as διδάσκαλος and ῥαββί by
characters within the narrative. As with the rest of the didactic terminology,
these terms refer almost exclusively to Jesus, who is the teacher *par
excellence* in the Fourth Gospel. All these references, both direct address and
non-vocative, identify Jesus as an ordinary teacher on the narrative level,
without carrying heavy Christological freight.[30] This unreflective use of the
terminology can be demonstrated by observing that, although διδάσκαλος
is concentrated upon Jesus, it is also used to refer to Nicodemus as 'the
teacher of Israel' (3.10).[31] Similarly, the term ῥαββί, though concentrated on
Jesus,[32] also refers to John the Baptist (3.26).[33] Furthermore, in the Fourth
Gospel, both disciples and non-disciples address Jesus as ῥαββί.[34] This
suggests that neither term is a special one reserved for the use of disciples
who have recognized Jesus' 'true' identity. Jesus is called 'rabbi' and
'teacher' because he fits within this common identity.

John 1.49 is a good example of the use of ῥαββί to refer unreflectively to
Jesus on the narrative level. In Nathaniel's address, 'Rabbi, you are the Son
of God; you are the King of Israel,' the vocative 'rabbi' is unemphatic, while

---

[30] διδάσκαλε, the form of direct address, is used of Jesus in 1.38; 20.16. The non-
vocative description of Jesus as a διδάσκαλος is used in 3.2; 11.28; 13.13-14 (with the
definite article in 11.28; 13.13-14). ῥαββί is always used in direct address.

[31] διδάσκαλος refers to Jesus in six of its seven occurrences: 1.38; 3.2; 11.28; 13.13-14;
20.16.

[32] ῥαββί refers to Jesus in seven of its eight occurrences: 1.38, 49; 3.2; 4.31; 6.25; 9.2;
11.8. The sole use of ῥαββουνί in the Fourth Gospel also refers to Jesus (20.16).

[33] Cf. the recognition in the Fourth Gospel that John the Baptist had disciples (see below).
The reference to John the Baptist as ῥαββί runs directly counter to Pancaro's argument that
in the Fourth Gospel only Jesus is said to be a teacher. It is clear from 1.38; 20.16 that 'rabbi'
means 'teacher.' Pancaro notes 3.26 (82, n. 25) and admits that it is an exception to his
argument (85, n. 44). On John as a διδάσκαλος with disciples, cf. Luke 3.12; 11.1.

[34] Disciples call Jesus ῥαββί in 1.38, 49; 4.31; 9.2; 11.8, and non-disciples in 3.2; 6.25.
Disciples call Jesus διδάσκαλος in 11.28 and a non-disciple (Nicodemus) in 3.2.

the two latter terms are important Christological affirmations.[35] Each of the other six uses of ῥαββί to refer to Jesus in the Fourth Gospel is equally unreflective. Similarly, the vocative διδάσκαλε functions as a normal address to a teacher (1.38; 20.16), and διδάσκαλος is used unreflectively of Jesus by Nicodemus and Martha (3.2; 11.28).[36]

This mundane use of didactic terminology on the narrative level of the Fourth Gospel is best explained by reliance upon the common tradition. This tradition probably arose from the fact that the historical Jesus actually was addressed and known as a teacher.[37] The four canonical gospels are the most important evidence for this, but it is also supported by the famous *Testimonium Flavianum*, in which Josephus refers to Jesus as a διδάσκαλος (*Ant.* 18.63-64). While the authenticity of this passage has been debated, a substantial number of recent scholars consider the received text at least partially authentic.[38] Another early reference to Jesus as a teacher (διδάσκαλος) occurs in Justin's *First Apology* 32. We may also note the later rabbinic references to Jesus' disciples in *b. 'Abod. Zar.* 16b-17a and *b. Sanh.* 43a, which imply that Jesus was seen as a (false) teacher by at least some later Jews.[39]

Each of the synoptic gospels took over the tradition of Jesus as teacher and rabbi in different ways, as evidenced by their varying uses of the didactic terminology.[40] Strikingly, Mark accords the terms διδάσκαλος and ῥαββί solely to Jesus.[41] Mark also has a higher proportion of didactic terminology overall than Matthew and Luke,[42] and most uses of διδάσκω and διδαχή

---

[35] Cf. Hahn, *Titles*, 74; Köstenberger, 'Rabbi,' 97-128.

[36] Untergassmair, 'Lehrer,' 213 suggests that 'rabbi' and 'teacher' in 3.2a are given importance by Nicodemus' association of these addresses with Jesus' signs in 3.2b. But this does not raise Jesus' identity as a teacher above that of other contemporary teachers, who also performed signs to vindicate their teaching. Cf. Schnackenburg, *St. John*, 1.366. Hahn, *Titles*, 78 suggests that the juxtaposition of the titles 'Christ' and 'Son of God' in 11.27 with ὁ διδάσκαλος in 11.28 makes it clear that 'the Teacher' is linked to the Christological idea of the Son of God. But this is not at all clear on the level of the narrative, which does not link the Christological affirmations and Martha's unreflective identification of Jesus as 'the Teacher.'

[37] Cf. Riesner, 'Teacher,' 185-210, esp. 185-88; France, 'Teaching,' 103; Normann, *Christos Didaskalos*, 178-79.

[38] E.g. Vermes, 'Josephus,' 2-10; Carleton Paget, 'Josephus,' 539-624; Whealey, *Josephus*, 41-43. Note the comments of Olson, 'Testimonium,' 306.

[39] Cf. Dodd, 'Teacher and Prophet,' 53-55.

[40] Cf. Phipps, *Rabbi Jesus*, 57-79, esp. 57-58.

[41] Mark uses διδάσκαλος 12 times, always referring to Jesus, both in direct address and non-vocative forms. Similarly, ῥαββί and ῥαββουνί always refer to Jesus. Viviano, 'Rabbouni,' 207-18 argues that Mark 9.5 preserves an early, non-didactic use of ῥαββί/ῥαββουνί. Cf. Byrskog, *Teacher*, 285 for critique.

[42] Cf. Byrskog, 'Lernen,' 194.

come in Mark's editorial 'seams,' indicating that the theme of Jesus as a teacher is a significant one.[43] R. T. France, pointing especially to the programmatic pericope 1.21-28, has argued that in Mark, Jesus' identity as a teacher is understood as part of his messianic identity.[44] This may well be. However, the fact that Jesus is addressed as 'teacher' and 'rabbi' indiscriminately – by disciples and non-disciples alike – demonstrates that Jesus is viewed as a normal teacher, albeit a particularly authoritative one, by those who are not disciples.[45]

Luke uses διδάσκαλος of Jesus, but omits ῥαββί because of his Hellenistic readership.[46] He also uses the term ἐπιστάτης seven times (it occurs nowhere else in the NT), always in direct address to Jesus, and sometimes as a replacement for the Markan διδάσκαλος or ῥαββί.[47] Glombitza has argued that Luke nowhere has disciples address Jesus as διδάσκαλε, and instead uses the vocative ἐπιστάτα, which has a non-didactic sense, because he wants to communicate that Jesus was *not* a teacher, i.e. the head of a philosophical school.[48] Riesner suggests that the lack of address to Jesus as διδάσκαλε by disciples indicates that for Luke, Jesus was far superior to any teacher.[49] However, neither of these views accounts for 21.7, which is most likely spoken by disciples.[50] It is better to recognize that in Luke, Jesus is addressed as διδάσκαλε by both disciples and non-disciples.[51] This suggests, as John Nolland notes, that for Luke, it is an 'objective description…without prejudice to the personal attitude toward [Jesus] of the one who uses the title…'[52]

---

[43] Cf. France, 'Teaching,' 103-4; Byrskog, 'Lernen,' 194.

[44] France, 'Teaching,' 106-12.

[45] In Mark, Jesus is referred to as διδάσκαλος by disciples (4.38; 9.38; 10.35; 13.1), non-disciples (5.35; 9.17; 10.17, 20; 12.14, 19, 32), and himself (14.14); as ῥαββί by Peter (9.5; 11.21) and Judas (14.45); as ῥαββουνί by a non-disciple, Bartimaeus (10.51). Cf. Hahn, *Titles*, 74.

[46] Cf. Oepke, 'ἐπιστάτης,' *TDNT* 2.622-23. Luke uses διδάσκαλος of Jesus 13 times (7.40; 8.49; 9.38; 10.25; 11.45; 12.13; 18.18; 19.39; 20.21, 28, 39; 21.7; 22.11), once of John the Baptist (3.12), once of the teachers in the Temple (2.46), and twice in a general statement about disciples and teachers (6.40).

[47] In 8.24; 9.49, ἐπιστάτης replaces the Markan διδάσκαλε; in 9.33 it replaces the Markan ῥαββί.

[48] Glombitza, 'Titel,' 275-78.

[49] Riesner, 'Teacher,' 187.

[50] 21.7 creates problems for Green, *Luke*, 733-34. Glombitza's argument also fails to account for 22.11.

[51] In Luke, Jesus is referred to as διδάσκαλος by disciples (21.7), non-disciples (7.40; 8.49; 9.38; 10.25; 11.45; 12.13; 18.18; 19.39; 20.21, 28, 39); and himself (22.11).

[52] Nolland, *Luke*, 1.355. Cf. also Rengstorf 'διδάσκαλος,' *TDNT* 2.152-53.

Matthew applies the terms διδάσκαλος and ῥαββί both to Jesus and to others.[53] What is most distinctive about Matthew's use of the terminology, however, is *who* refers to Jesus with these terms. In Matthew, Jesus is usually called διδάσκαλος by non-disciples,[54] and is only called ῥαββί by Judas (26.25, 49). Matthew's redaction of the Markan material[55] shows an interest in removing didactic terminology from the lips of disciples.[56] Some scholars have suggested that, for Matthew, those who truly know Jesus' identity consider him more than a teacher.[57] In my opinion, this is not quite right: rather, both Matthew and the Fourth Gospel invite their readers to understand Jesus as an eschatological (and divine?) teacher (see chapters 5 and 9 below).[58]

All three of the synoptic gospels therefore demonstrate the presence of a normal, unreflective use of didactic terminology applied to Jesus, one which finds its basis in historical fact, even while Matthew (and possibly Mark) brings Jesus' identity as a teacher into association with his messianic identity.[59] Luke is the clearest instance of using the terminology in a non-Christological, 'objective' way. It is this unreflective use of the didactic terminology that I propose is functioning on the narrative level of the Fourth Gospel.

Finally, the term μαθητής appears 78 times in the Fourth Gospel. In the majority of cases, μαθητής refers to Jesus' disciples, who carry out the duties of normal disciples.[60] It is also used of John the Baptist's disciples (1.35, 37; 3.25), and in the Pharisees' claim that they are 'disciples of Moses' (9.28). This again agrees with the synoptic usage,[61] further suggesting that the

---

[53] Matthew uses διδάσκαλος of Jesus 10 times, and twice in a general statement about disciples and teachers (10.24-25); ῥαββί is twice used of Jesus (26.25, 49) and twice of others (23.7-8).

[54] Matt 8.19; 9.11; 12.38; 17.24; 19.16; 22.16, 24, 36 – but cf. 23.8; 26.18, where he refers to himself as 'teacher.' Moreover, the reference in Matt 8.21 to 'another of the disciples' may indicate that the scribe who calls Jesus 'Teacher' in 8.19 is considered a 'disciple.'

[55] I am here of course assuming the two-source hypothesis.

[56] Cf. Hahn, *Titles*, 74. Matt 17.4 changes Peter's reference to Jesus as ῥαββί (Mark 9.5) to κύριε. In Matt 21.20, the ῥαββί of Mark 11.21 is entirely omitted. διδάσκαλος in Mark is changed to κύριε in Matt 8.25 (spoken by the disciples); 17.15 (spoken by a non-disciple). Cf. Byrskog, 'Lernen,' 198.

[57] Cf. Kingsbury, *Matthew*, 92-93.

[58] In my view, the formulations of Byrskog, 'Teacher,' 92-93; Byrskog, 'Lernen,' 197-201; Lincoln, 'Teachers,' 103-25, esp. 122-23 are more satisfactory.

[59] For Matthew, cf. Matt 23.10. For Mark, cf. France, 'Teaching,' 106-12, noted above.

[60] Cf. Culpepper, *Anatomy*, 116; Köstenberger, 'Rabbi,' 119-24.

[61] Matthew uses μαθητής 72 times: it refers to John the Baptist's disciples, the disciples of the Pharisees, disciples in general, and Jesus' disciples. Mark uses μαθητής 46 times: it refers to John the Baptist's disciples, the disciples of the Pharisees, and the disciples of Jesus.

didactic terminology of the Fourth Gospel, when used by the characters within the story, does not have major Christological import but is used unreflectively of Jesus and his followers.

Thus far we have seen that the characters within the narrative of the Fourth Gospel use ῥαββί, διδάσκαλος, and μαθητής in an unreflective manner without Christological significance. It seems likely that the fourth evangelist has taken over his characterization of Jesus as a teacher and rabbi with disciples, as well as his reference to John the Baptist as a rabbi with disciples, from the common tradition.

However, there is some evidence that the evangelist himself considers Jesus a teacher – and not in an unreflective, 'objective' sense as do the characters within the narrative. To employ our narrator/narrative distinction, we may ask where the narrator (not a character within his story) identifies Jesus as a teacher. This should include any instances in which Jesus identifies himself as a teacher, for Culpepper has demonstrated remarkable similarities between Jesus and the narrator throughout the Fourth Gospel, and especially in the discourse of chapters 14-17.[62]

A clear instance of Jesus' self-identification as a teacher is in 13.13-14, in which Jesus affirms that the disciples properly call him διδάσκαλος and κύριος.[63] These verses appear only in the Fourth Gospel, so it seems that the evangelist has not simply taken them over from common tradition.[64] Moreover, Jesus' self-identification as a teacher in 13.13-14 is placed prominently at the beginning of the farewell discourse (chaps 13-16). Importantly, Jesus' identity as teacher serves as the basis for the disciples' imitation of him (13.14-15), a theme repeated in the following chapters (13.34; 15.10, 12; 17.21). This suggests that Jesus addresses his disciples as their teacher throughout the entire section. However, while 13.13-14 demonstrates that the idea of Jesus as διδάσκαλος is significant to the narrator, it does not prove that he sees a more significant Christological meaning in the term than the characters in his narrative. Jesus simply affirms that the disciples are correct to call him διδάσκαλος.

In order to demonstrate that the Fourth Gospel reflects a development beyond the unreflective references to Jesus as a διδάσκαλος in the common tradition, I turn to 3.1-15. Here it is again important to recall the distinction

---

Luke uses μαθητής 37 times: it refers to John the Baptist's disciples, the disciples of the Pharisees, disciples in general, and Jesus' disciples.

[62] Cf. Culpepper, *Anatomy*, 34-43.

[63] It is not clear whether the reversal of the order of these terms in 13.14 is significant or merely stylistic. Cf. Brown, *John*, 2.553.

[64] 13.16, which is similar to the sayings regarding the relationships of teachers/disciples and masters/slaves in Matt 10.24-25; Luke 6.40, may reflect a common oral tradition. It is probably not directly dependent upon Matthew or Luke. Cf. Dodd, 'Parallels,' 75-86, esp. 75-78.

between the characters in a narrative and the narrator himself. In 3.1-15, Nicodemus, a 'man of the Pharisees,' recognizes Jesus as a 'rabbi' and 'teacher come from God' (ἀπὸ θεοῦ ἐλήλυθας διδάσκαλος). This is not unlike the Pharisees' recognition of Jesus as a διδάσκαλος in the synoptics.[65]

In saying that Jesus is a teacher who has come 'from God' (ἀπὸ θεοῦ), Nicodemus means simply that Jesus is approved by God.[66] However, the narrator, as he does elsewhere, allows Jesus' interlocutor to speak better than he knows.[67] In suggesting that Jesus comes 'from God,' Nicodemus unwittingly affirms Jesus' heavenly origin, a theme at the heart of the gospel and one known already to the reader of the prologue.[68] In the rest of the dialogue, Jesus emphasizes his heavenly origin (e.g. 3.11-13, cf. 3.31).[69] Therefore, although the term διδάσκαλος is used unreflectively by Nicodemus on the narrative level, the narrator endows the term with new significance.

That the narrator intentionally emphasizes Jesus' identity as a *teacher* 'come from God' is evident from the contrast developed in these verses between Jesus, a 'teacher come from God,' and Nicodemus, the 'teacher of Israel' (3.10). Although Nicodemus is recognized by Jesus as a teacher, the narrator portrays Jesus as a superior teacher, one 'from above' who can therefore speak earthly and heavenly things (3.12). This certainly goes beyond the portrayal of Jesus as a teacher in Luke. It also pushes beyond the messianic categories of Matthew and Mark. Here, Jesus' identity as a teacher is explicitly connected to his origin from God in language never used in the synoptics: 'a teacher come from God.' He is, in the Fourth Gospel, a heavenly teacher in a sense different from that found in the synoptics.

Importantly, the only two instances in the Fourth Gospel in which individuals other than Jesus are referred to as teacher (Nicodemus) or rabbi (John the Baptist) occur in John 3.10, 26. In both cases, Jesus is explicitly contrasted with Nicomedus and John, precisely because he is the one who has come 'from God' and 'from above.' Jesus speaks heavenly things because,

---

[65] E.g. Matt 9.11; 12.38; Luke 19.39. However, Nicodemus' affirmation that Jesus is a teacher *from God* is undoubtedly more generous than the view of the Pharisees as it is portrayed in the synoptics.

[66] Cf. Brown, *John*, 1.138. Note the phrase ἐξ οὐρανοῦ in Luke 20.4-5.

[67] The clearest example of this in the Fourth Gospel is 11.49-52, where the narrator sees more significance in Caiaphas' words than does Caiaphas himself. For other examples, cf. Culpepper, *Anatomy*, 176-77.

[68] See ἀπὸ θεοῦ ἐξῆλθεν in 13.3; ἀπὸ θεοῦ ἐξῆλθες in 16.30; cf. 1.9; 3.31; 6.46; 16.27-28.

[69] Cf. Neyrey, 'John III,' 115-27.

unlike Nicodemus and John, he is from heaven.[70] The point is that, while both Nicodemus and John are indeed teachers of a normal sort (*contra* Pancaro, the evangelist does not deny them this status), Jesus alone is a teacher who has come from the presence of God.

I conclude that the evangelist has taken over from the common tradition the language of Jesus as a teacher and rabbi with disciples. On the level of the narrative, these words are unreflective, as seen in Nathaniel's confession (1.49). However, 13.13-14 demonstrates that Jesus' identity as a teacher is important to the narrator, and 3.1-15 goes beyond anything found in the synoptic gospels. This latter text pushes Jesus' identity as a teacher to a new level, and sets all the other texts in the Fourth Gospel humming with potential significance. Even if, on the level of the narrative, Jesus is addressed as a normal teacher and rabbi, the reader is perhaps entitled to see in these addresses a deeper significance – Jesus as a teacher who has come from God. The effect is a subtle yet powerful one.

My argument in this section runs counter to the suggestion of Raymond Brown that the 'almost exclusive' concentration of the terms 'rabbi' and 'teacher' in John 1-12, and the disciples' address of Jesus as 'lord' in John 13-21, suggests that the evangelist portrays a 'growth of understanding on the disciples' part.'[71] Brown's thesis does not account for John 13.13-15 or for 20.16, in which Mary Magdalene addresses the post-resurrection Jesus as ῥαββουνί. Andreas Köstenberger argues that the Fourth Gospel confines the address of Jesus as rabbi to Jesus' earthly ministry, and suggests that the Farewell Discourse portrays the exalted Jesus as transcending the identity of ῥαββί.[72] However, Köstenberger also fails to explain 20.16. On my reading of the Fourth Gospel, the evangelist does not show that the disciples grow to see Jesus as more than a teacher, or that the resurrected Jesus transcends the role of teacher. Rather, the evangelist invites his reader to see Jesus as the *heavenly* teacher.

Those who teach (διδάσκω) in the Fourth Gospel

The verb διδάσκω is used nine times in the Fourth Gospel: Jesus teaches, as do the Father (8.28), the Spirit (14.26), and the man born blind (9.34). As in the previous section, my goal is to determine how the Fourth Gospel is similar to, and different from, the synoptic usage of διδάσκω. I will suggest

---

[70] Although John the Baptist, like Jesus, is sent 'from God' (1.6), John 3.31 suggests that this does not refer to heavenly origins but to prophetic commissioning. In 1.6, παρά + genitive indicates agency rather than source. Cf. Wallace, *Greek Grammar*, 378. When παρά and ἀπό are used of Jesus, they probably do indicate source, given the Johannine theme of Jesus' heavenly origins and his coming into the world.

[71] Brown, *John*, 1.75.

[72] Köstenberger, 'Rabbi,' 107-8.

that Jesus' teaching is, for the narrator, synonymous with revelation in the sense defined above (i.e. 'communication from God'). We will begin with the six instances in which Jesus is said to teach, and then discuss the other three uses of διδάσκω.[73]

As with the terms διδάσκαλος, ῥαββί, and μαθητής, the description of Jesus teaching is clearly a part the common tradition. Mark 10.1 indicates that it was Jesus' custom to teach, and Jesus is the subject of the vast majority of uses of διδάσκω in the synoptic gospels.[74] In Acts 1.1, the author characterizes his first account as being about all that Jesus began to do (ποιεῖν) and teach (διδάσκειν). The Fourth Gospel's portrayal of Jesus teaching, is then, at least on the face of it, in agreement with the common tradition. However, our distinction between the narrator and the characters in his narrative again proves helpful here.

It is not correct to say without qualification, as Pancaro does, that the teaching of Jesus *is* revelation, because it clearly does not mean this on the narrative level in some passages.[75] In 7.35, the Jews ask if Jesus will teach the diaspora. In 9.34, the man born blind is asked by the Pharisees if he will teach them. In these passages, διδάσκω maintains a normal sense and, on the level of the narrative, does not refer to revelation. On the other hand, when the narrator suggests that Jesus teaches (6.59; 7.14, 28; 8.20) and when Jesus himself states that he has taught (18.20), the broader context of the Fourth Gospel suggests that 'teach' actually does mean 'reveal.' Already in the prologue, the narrator has claimed that Jesus has 'come into' the world and explained (ἐξηγέομαι) God (1.9, 18), and Jesus claims that he can speak 'heavenly things' because he has descended from heaven (3.11-13). The narrator's melding of Jesus' teaching with his revelatory work suggests that the Jews in 7.35, like Nicodemus in 3.2, may speak better than they know.

---

[73] Jesus is the grammatical subject of διδάσκω in John 6.59; 7.14, 28, 35; 8.20; 18.20.

[74] διδάσκω is used 14 times in Matthew: 10 times Jesus teaches, and in the other four uses, others are said to teach (in 28.15 the sense is, uniquely, 'instruct'). διδάσκω is used 17 times in Mark: 15 times with Jesus as its subject, once with the apostles, and once with others. διδάσκω is used 17 times in Luke: 15 times with Jesus as its subject, once with the Holy Spirit, and once with John the Baptist.

[75] According to Pancaro, *Law*, 80, the revelational character of διδάσκω in the Fourth Gospel accounts for its frequent parallelism with λαλέω, which is also a term of revelation. This explanation is unconvincing. The juxtaposition of Jesus 'teaching' and 'saying' is frequent in the Fourth Gospel, but this is more likely because 'say and teach' is a common idiom: cf. Job 8.10; Prov 4.4; 1QM 10.2. The combination of λαλέω and διδάσκω is present in numerous Jewish and Christian, non-revelatory contexts (LXX Deut 11.19; Acts 4.1-2; 5.20-21; 18.25), as is the combination of λέγω and διδάσκω (*T. Reu.* 5.3; Matt 5.2; Mark 4.2; 9.31; 11.17; 12.35; Luke 20.21; cf. Mark 12.38; Acts 4.18). The Fourth Gospel uses λαλέω and διδάσκω together (8.20; 18.20), but also combines λέγω and διδάσκω (6.59; 7.28), and λέγω is clearly not a 'term of revelation.'

An important question concerning the use of διδάσκω for Jesus' teaching in the Fourth Gospel is whether the term maintains its Jewish sense of teaching Torah. According to Pancaro, Jesus' teaching in the Fourth Gospel is different from teaching in the synoptics and Judaism in its relationship to the Torah. Jesus' teaching is not an expounding of the Scriptures' teaching, as it is in the synoptics, nor is it given mainly to explain the Torah or to reveal its hidden meaning, as is the teaching of Qumran. According to Pancaro, Jesus' teaching, while presented in terms familiar to Jewish thought, is *contrasted* with the Law of Moses.[76] Jesus' teaching is new revelation that supersedes and replaces the Law.[77] Rather than offering an interpretation of the Law, Jesus claims that the Law points to himself.[78]

I suggest that the content of Jesus' teaching in the Fourth Gospel is not as different from the synoptic gospels and wider Judaism as Pancaro has proposed. It is true that in 7.28-29, Jesus' teaching is self-referential and makes no explicit reference to the Scriptures. This might suggest that his teaching is new revelation, and not teaching in the Jewish sense of the term (i.e. an exposition of the Scriptures). However, in three other passages, Jesus' teaching appears to be an interpretation of the Scriptures. We will see this below in chapter 6, in exegeses of John 6.31-58 and 7.14-19. It also seems to be the case in 8.12-20, where Jesus interprets the Law and thereby demonstrates that his witness and that of the Father are valid (this is identified as teaching in 8.20).[79] While the content of Jesus' teaching in the Fourth Gospel is ultimately his own person, then, this at least sometimes draws upon an exposition of the Scriptures.[80] That Jesus' teaching concerns the meaning of the Torah does not conflict with the narrator's equation of teaching and revelation, because, as I noted above, revelation in first century Judaism was broad enough to include revealed interpretation of the Scriptures. The important *difference* between the Johannine Jesus' teaching and normal Jewish teaching is that the Johannine Jesus uses the Law apologetically rather than as an ethical norm (see chapter 6).

We may now examine the remaining uses of διδάσκω in the Fourth Gospel. I have already noted that in 9.34, the man born blind is asked if he will teach the Pharisees. It is 8.28 and 14.26 that are of particular interest here. In 8.28, Jesus claims that, 'I do nothing from myself, but I speak these things as the Father taught [ἐδίδαξεν] me.' This use of didactic terminology

---

[76] Pancaro, *Law*, 83-84.

[77] Pancaro, *Law*, 116.

[78] Pancaro, *Law*, 100-101.

[79] Cf. 13.18; 15.25.

[80] Two passages (7.35; 18.20) do not specify the content of Jesus' teaching, but this does not prove a uniquely Johannine 'empty' teaching that contrasts with the Torah. It is common in the synoptic gospels, and the rest of the NT, for the content of teaching to be unspecified (e.g. Matt 13.54). Cf. Rengstorf, 'διδάσκω,' *TDNT* 2.141.

to describe the Father's relationship with the Son is without precedent in the synoptic gospels (διδάσκω is used this way only here in the Fourth Gospel). In 14.26, Jesus promises his disciples that the Holy Spirit/Paraclete will 'teach [διδάξει] you all things and remind you of all things that I have spoken to you.' This is also distinctive. The only reference in the synoptic gospels to the Holy Spirit teaching is Luke 12.12, where Jesus reassures the disciples that when they stand on trial before 'synagogues and rulers and authorities' the Holy Spirit will teach (διδάξει) them what they should say.[81] The reference in John 14.26 is therefore not wholly unique, but it differs significantly from the Lucan passage in the extent of what will be taught, and has been worked into a major motif in the Fourth Gospel.

I conclude that the Fourth Gospel's reference to the Father teaching the Son (8.28) is different than anything found in the synoptics, as is the idea that the Spirit will teach the disciples all things (14.26). Both uses of didactic terminology are by definition revelation on our broad definition of revelation as 'communication from God.' However, some uses of διδάσκω in the Fourth Gospel clearly do not refer to revelation (7.35; 9.34). The narrator's references to Jesus teaching, while they appear on the surface similar to the common tradition preserved in the synoptics, must be understood within the context of the Fourth Gospel as referring to Jesus' revelation.

The other didactic terminology

We may now consider the remaining didactic terminology in the Fourth Gospel: διδακτός, διδαχή, and μανθάνω. The use of διδακτός in 6.45a is distinctive: the word is never used in the synoptics, nor is there any reference in the synoptic gospels to believers being 'taught by God.'[82] The use of μανθάνω in 6.45b and 7.15 is also important: in the latter text it is used 'as a technical term for academic study of Scripture,'[83] while in the former, the idea is that one can learn directly from God. The language of 'learning from God' is without precedent in the synoptics, which speak of learning from a fig tree (Matt 24.32; Mark 13.28) and from Jesus (Matt 11.29; cf. Matt 9.13), but never of learning from God.

Finally, διδαχή appears in John 7.16, 17; 18.19. In 18.19, it refers to Jesus' teaching. This usage is similar to the synoptics, which speak of the διδαχή of Jesus, as well as the διδαχή of the religious leaders.[84] However, 7.16, 17 are distinct from the synoptic gospels in their affirmation that Jesus' διδαχή is the διδαχή of God. Although the synoptics emphasize the

---

[81] Cf. Karrer, 'Lehrende,' 19. The parallels in Matt 10.19-20; Mark 13.11 (cf. Luke 21.14-15) refer to the 'Spirit of the Father' and the 'Holy Spirit,' but do not use διδάσκω.

[82] Cf. 1 Thess 4.9; 1 Cor 2.13 (see chapter 8).

[83] Rengstorf, 'μανθάνω,' *TDNT* 4.408.

[84] Jesus: Matt 7.28; Mark 1.22, 27; Luke 4.32. Religious leaders: Matt 16.12.

amazement of the crowds at the remarkable authority of Jesus' teaching (Matt 7.28-29; Mark 1.22, 27; Luke 4.32), they nowhere explicitly affirm that Jesus' διδαχή comes from God.

The significance of divine instruction

The purpose of this section has been to discover how the Fourth Gospel differs from the synoptics in its use of didactic terminology. We have found significant similarities and yet several striking differences. In particular, we have discovered a group of texts without exact parallel in the common tradition: the claims in 6.45ab; 7.16-17; 8.28; 14.26 are distinctive to the Fourth Gospel. Moreover, even when the fourth evangelist has likely drawn upon common tradition in his presentation of Jesus as a διδάσκαλος and ῥαββί, he has endowed this tradition with new significance by allowing Nicodemus unwittingly to affirm Jesus as a 'teacher come from God' (3.2). When Jesus teaches (διδάσκω), this is understood as revelation from God. As Byrskog has suggested, in the Fourth Gospel, Jesus' διδαχή explodes didactic categories, because it is finally understood as revelation.[85] Byrskog suggests that the same fusing of teaching and revelation occurs in the synoptic gospels.[86] I agree that, particularly in Matthew, the line between teaching and revelation sometimes grows thin.[87] However, in my judgment, the clarity and comprehensiveness with which the Fourth Gospel brings into relationship the traditional didactic terminology and a thoroughly developed idea of revelation sets it apart from the synoptic gospels.

The theme of *divine* instruction is an important one in the Fourth Gospel. The texts mentioned here are not random, disconnected references – rather, they cast Jesus' instruction in a new light and raise the question of how Jesus' teaching is related to God's teaching. The coherence and intentionality of the evangelist's references to God's instruction and Jesus' instruction is demonstrated in part by the clustering of didactic terminology in chaps 6-8, which hardly seems accidental.[88] Furthermore, in John 18.19-20, the focus of the high priest's inquiry concerns Jesus' μαθηταί and διδαχή. This differs from the synoptic accounts of the trial, which focus upon the messiahship of Jesus and the accusation of blasphemy.[89] In response to the high priest, Jesus

---

[85] Byrskog, 'Lernen,' 202. Cf. Karrer, 'Lehrende,' 19; Van Der Watt, *Family*, 279.

[86] Byrskog, 'Lernen,' 202, 206-7.

[87] E.g. Matt 11.27-29.

[88] Cf. Pancaro, *Law*, 79. Of six instances in which Jesus is said to teach, five occur in chaps 6-8. The other (18.20) refers back to chaps 6-8. This is paralleled by the clustering of other didactic terminology in the same chapters: διδακτός in 6.45a; μανθάνω in 6.45b, 7.15; διδαχή in 7.16, 17; διδάσκω in 8.28. διδαχή in 18.19 refers to Jesus' teaching in chaps 6-8.

[89] Cf. Barrett, *John*, 527-28.

sums up his ministry as one of 'speaking openly' to the world, always teaching (διδάσκω) in synagogues and in the Temple where all the Jews come together (18.20).[90] This recalls Jesus' teaching in the synagogue at Capernaum (6.59) and in the Temple at the Feast of Booths in chapters 7-8 (7.14, 28; 8.20).[91]

While the didactic terminology is clustered in chapters 6-8, divine instruction in the Fourth Gospel extends over a huge sweep of time: from before human history (8.28b) and into the future (14.26). The Father's instruction of Jesus, as I will argue below, occurred at least in part in Jesus' pre-existence (7.14-18; 8.28b),[92] while God's instruction of his people is understood as the eschatological fulfillment of Isaiah's promise (6.45). Using the categories of narrative time set out by Culpepper, we can say that divine instruction in the Fourth Gospel extends from the 'pre-historical past' into the 'historical future' of the Johannine community.[93]

The importance of the language of instruction has frequently been overlooked in Johannine studies. This may be due, at least in part, to the influence of Rudolf Bultmann, who famously summarized the central theological motif of the Fourth Gospel: 'Jesus as the Revealer of God *reveals nothing but that he is the Revealer.*'[94] What is interesting here is Bultmann's language of 'revelation,' since words for 'reveal' are scarce in the Fourth Gospel. Bultmann constantly refers to Jesus as the Revealer. The Fourth Gospel never does: instead, it refers to him as a 'teacher' and 'rabbi.' The evangelist never uses ἀποκάλυψις, and ἀποκαλύπτω appears only in 12.38, in a citation of Isa 53.1, mentioning the revealing of God's arm.[95] Q 10.22, the so-called 'meteorite fallen from the Johannine sky,'[96] speaks of the Son revealing [ἀποκαλύπτω] the Father, and Q 10.21 speaks of the Father

---

[90] Cf. Mark 14.49; Matt 26.55.

[91] In the Fourth Gospel, Jesus' teaching always occurs in the Temple or synagogue. This differs from the synoptics, which describe Jesus teaching in these locations but also in other places (e.g. Matt 11.1; Mark 2.13; 4.1; Luke 5.3; 23.5). Cf. Pancaro, *Law*, 79, 84.

[92] In my judgment, it is justifiable to speak of Jesus' pre-existence in the Fourth Gospel. In the prologue, the Word is said to have been with God in the beginning (1.1) and the 'true light' is said to come into the world (1.9). These figures are identified with Jesus both in the Prologue itself, and by the relationship between the Prologue and the entire Fourth Gospel. Cf. Dunn, *Christology*, 239-45, 249-50. Moreover, the Son of Man 'descended from heaven' (3.13), and Jesus himself is said to come 'from above' and 'from heaven' (3.31), and to have 'come forth from the Father' and 'into the world' (16.27-28).

[93] Cf. Culpepper, *Anatomy*, 53-75.

[94] Bultmann, *Theology*, 2.66.

[95] Ashton, *Understanding*, 515 wrongly claims that ἀποκαλύπτω is not used in the Fourth Gospel, but rightly notes the dearth of terminology for 'revelation.' Cerfaux, 'Jean,' 147 also notes the ubiquity of the concept and the lack of terminology. Other terminology is used: e.g. ἀναγγέλω, γνωρίζω, φανερόω. Cf. Louw, 'Narrator,' 32-40.

[96] The expression is that of K. Hase, cited in Sabbe, 'Logion,' 366.

revealing things to people.[97] This is what the Fourth Gospel *should* say, but does not. Instead, the Father teaches (6.45ab; 8.28) and is known to those whom the Son teaches (chapters 6-8).

Bultmann uses the language of revelation because of his conviction that the Fourth Gospel draws on Gnostic redeemer myths. Although his hypothesis of Gnostic origins has been largely dismissed in Johannine scholarship,[98] the language of revelation is still used by many scholars. This may in turn reflect the belief that apocalyptic backgrounds influence the Johannine imagery of Jesus 'seeing,' 'hearing,' and 'being sent.' However, when we take the Fourth Gospel on its own terms, it is evident that Jesus is presented as the eschatological teacher who brings divine instruction from God. If, as I have suggested above, διδάσκω means 'reveal' when Jesus, the Paraclete, and God are its grammatical subjects, why has the evangelist chosen to use didactic terminology rather than the language of revelation?

In the remainder of this chapter, I will suggest that some of the didactic terminology is drawn from the OT. In chapter 5, I will argue that it ideally suits the evangelist's Christology. In chapter 6, I will argue that it functions polemically and as a means of self-legitimation.

4.3 From where does the evangelist derive the language and concept of divine instruction?

Having demonstrated in section 2 that the theme of divine instruction is particularly emphasized and developed in the Fourth Gospel, I will seek to establish in this section the sources of this theme. The clearest source is in 6.45-46, where a citation formula in 6.45a introduces an OT citation. Sources for the idea of divine instruction in 7.14-18; 8.28b; 14.26 are more difficult to discern, since no OT texts are cited in these passages. However, I will consider some possible sources below.

The OT citation in John 6.45a

There is currently widespread agreement that Isa 54.13 is the sole OT text cited in John 6.45a. Comparison of the John 6.45a citation and the various text-forms of Isa 54.13 indicates clear similarities, with some differences.

---

[97] Cf. Robinson, Hoffman, and Kloppenborg, *Q*, 192. On this saying, cf. Allison, 'Key,' 477-85; Denaux, 'Q-Logion,' 163-99; Sabbe, 'Logion,' 363-71; Hunter, 'Crux Criticorum,' 241-49.

[98] Cf. Brown, *John*, 116-26.

Table 1. *Isa 54.13 and John 6.45a*

John 6.45a	καὶ ἔσονται[99] πάντες διδακτοὶ θεοῦ
LXX Isa 54.13[100]	(θήσω)...καὶ πάντας τοὺς υἱούς σου διδακτοὺς θεοῦ
MT Isa 54.13	וְכָל־בָּנַיִךְ לִמּוּדֵי יְהוָה
1QIsaᵃ 54.13[101]	וכול בניך למודי יהוה
Targum of Isaiah[102]	וכל בנך[104] יהון[103] אלפין באוריתא דיהוה

When Georg Richter, in 1972, surveyed scholarly opinion concerning the
source of the citation, he noted a considerable number of views in addition to
the majority view that Isa 54.13 was the source of the citation, and concluded
that no view had won unanimous consent.[105] However, 20 years later, in
1992, Bruce Schuchard could write that, 'Recently...few scholars have
argued for a passage other than Isa 54.13 as John's referent.'[106] In the
intervening years since Schuchard's study, the scholarly consensus that Isa
54.13 is the sole OT text cited in John 6.45a has been confirmed in
commentaries and monographs.[107]

Minor dissent from this consensus comes from a few scholars who suggest
tentatively that Jer 31.34, in addition to Isa 54.13, may be the source of
6.45a.[108] This is not a new suggestion, as is evident from Richter's survey of
the literature.[109] It would seem at first to find some support in the citation
formula of 6.45a, ἔστιν γεγραμμένον ἐν τοῖς προφήταις, with its
reference to the 'prophets' (plural). However, references to the 'prophets' in
the NT and early Jewish literature often refer to the OT prophetic writings
considered as a whole, and are sometimes used in this sense to introduce a

---

[99] See Witmer, 'Citation,' 136 for my argument that καὶ ἔσονται is part of the OT
citation.

[100] Ziegler, *Isaias*, 326. There are no textual variants in the LXX of Isa 54.13a.

[101] Parry and Qimron, *Isaiah Scroll*, 90-91.

[102] Stenning, *Targum of Isaiah*, 184-85: 'And all thy children shall be learning the law of
the Lord...'

[103] As noted in chapter 2, יהון is present in two manuscripts, but omitted in the other
witnesses.

[104] Sperber, *Latter Prophets*, 110 notes the variant בניך in some manuscripts, but
preserves בנך.

[105] Richter, *Johannesevangelium*, 250-54.

[106] Cf. Schuchard, *Scripture*, 50.

[107] E.g. Ridderbos, *John*, 232; Köstenberger, *John*, 214; Wengst, *Johannesevangelium*,
1.244-45; Moloney, *John*, 218, 220; Keener, *John*, 1.685-86; Obermann, *Erfüllung*, 151.

[108] Cf. Schnackenburg, *St. John* 2.50-51. Morris, *John*, 329, after suggesting that both Isa
54.13 and Jer 31.34 may be in view, declares himself in favor of Isa 54.13 as the source of
the citation.

[109] See also Martin Luther's *Lectures on Hebrews* (*LW* 29.198).

particular prophetic passage.[110] Therefore, the reference to the 'prophets' cannot be taken as support for the view that Jer 31.34 is a source of the citation.[111] Rather, that question must be determined by comparing Jer 31.34 with John 6.45a.

The most significant verbal similarity between Jer 31.34 and John 6.45a is the use of 'all,' which receives emphasis in both passages.[112] In John 6.45a, 'all' are taught by God, and in Jer 31.34, 'all' will know God. Although both texts use didactic terminology, the terms are used differently: in Jer 31.34, individuals will not need to teach (διδάξωσιν) one another, while in John 6.45a, all will be taught (διδακτοί) by God. The presence of πάντες and διδακτοί in John 6.45a is more convincingly explained by the influence of Isa 54.13. It is best, given the lack of much verbal similarity between John 6.45a and Jer 31.34, to suggest that Jer 31.34 is not the source of the evangelist's citation, although it likely forms part of the broader conceptual background.[113] That background has been highlighted above in chapters 2-3, which examined the OT and early Jewish expectations of eschatological divine instruction.

I conclude that the current scholarly consensus (i.e. that Isa 54.13 is the sole source of the evangelist's citation) is correct. But what of the obvious *differences* between the citation in John 6.45a and the Hebrew or Greek of Isa 54.13? Some scholars suggest that these differences are attributable to the evangelist's use of Jewish or Christian traditions, or to a faulty memory. I have argued elsewhere that this is unlikely, and that the differences (noted below) are more likely attributable to intentional redaction of a written (or accurately memorized) textual tradition.[114] In my opinion, it is not possible to be certain whether the evangelist has drawn upon a Greek or Hebrew text in 6.45a.[115] Nevertheless, attention to the ways in which the citation differs from both the Greek and Hebrew of Isa 54.13 provides valuable insight into the

---

[110] Cf. Menken, 'Old Testament Quotation,' 165-67 for examples in Hellenistic Judaism and early Christianity; Richter, *Johannesevangelium*, 247, n. 305 for examples in rabbinic literature.

[111] Nor can it necessarily be taken to indicate vagueness with regard to the source of the citation, *contra* Noack, *Johanneischen Tradition*, 75-76; Reim, *Studien*, 182-83.

[112] It is emphasized in Jer 31.34 by the appended phrase 'from the least of them to the greatest of them.' For its emphasis in John 6.45a, see chapter 6 below.

[113] Cf. Barrett, *John*, 296; Pancaro, *Law*, 282, 329.

[114] See Witmer, 'Citation,' 134-38. On the conscious adaptation of OT texts by NT authors, cf. Stanley, 'Social Environment,' 18-27.

[115] So also Freed, *Quotations*, 118. The majority of scholars think the evangelist cites a Greek text: cf. Menken, *Quotations*, 77; Obermann, *Erfüllung*, 166; Swancutt, 'Hungers,' 230-34; Wengst, *Johannesevangelium*, 1.244; Barrett, *John*, 296. Some argue for a Hebrew text: cf. Burney, *Aramaic Origin*, 118; Borgen, *Bread*, 84, n. 1. The most compelling argument for a Greek text is the use of θεοῦ in 6.45a, since the Hebrew is יהוה. However, this is not decisive. Cf. Schuchard, *Scripture*, 52.

ways in which he develops the idea of divine instruction. When we compare
the texts, two significant differences are prominent: the omission of 'your
sons,' and the use of ἔσονται.[116] I will comment upon the former difference
in chapter 6 – here, we may address the latter difference.

Table 2. *The evangelist's redaction*[117]

John 6.45a	καὶ ἔσονται πάντες	διδακτοὶ θεοῦ
LXX Isa 54.13	καὶ	πάντας τοὺς υἱούς σου διδακτοὺς θεοῦ
MT/ 1QIsaᵃ Isa 54.13	וכול בניך למודי יהוה	

The use of ἔσονται in the citation reflects quite closely the sense of both the
Hebrew and Greek texts of Isa 54.13. Although neither includes a verb, the
Hebrew likely assumes a future tense of היה,[118] and the Greek clause
depends on the future tense verb θήσω. While the addition of ἔσονται is
therefore not a radical change in meaning, its use emphasizes the
eschatological nature of the Isaianic promise by making the verb explicit and
using the future tense.[119] This is a valuable insight. As we discovered in our
study of divine instruction in the OT and early Jewish literature, the idea of
divine instruction is non-eschatological in much of the OT and in Philo. In
the prophetic literature, divine instruction is given an eschatological
emphasis, and this is picked up in *Pss. Sol.* 17, the DSS, and the later rabbinic
literature.

Our redactional analysis of 6.45a suggests that the Fourth Gospel also
emphasizes the eschatological nature of divine instruction. This emphasis
must be understood within the larger context of the nature of the eschatology
of the Fourth Gospel. In his three-volume work on Johannine eschatology,
Jörg Frey has persuasively argued that the Fourth Gospel's eschatology is not
purely present.[120] This of course differs from the view of many previous
scholars (most famously, Bultmann) that the Fourth Gospel's eschatology is
fully realized.[121] As Frey suggests, this view often relied on literary critical

---

[116] *Contra* Lindars, *Apologetic*, 270 who claims Isa 54.13 is quoted loosely 'for no
apparent reason.'

[117] Differences between John 6.45a and the OT texts are underlined.

[118] See above in chapter 2, and cf. the Targum of Isaiah.

[119] Cf. Obermann, *Erfüllung*, 158; Williams, 'Isaiah,' 106-8. The eschatological emphasis
of John 6.45a renders unlikely some of the OT texts suggested as a background by Freed,
Quotations, 18. Cf. Richter, *Johannesevangelium*, 249, n. 314.

[120] See Frey, *Eschatologie I, Eschatologie II, Eschatologie III*. Volume 1 contains a
thorough survey of research on Johannine eschatology from Reimarus to the present. Cf. also
Frey, 'Eschatology,' 47-82 for a convenient summary of Frey's three-volume work.

[121] Cf. Bultmann, 'Eschatologie,' 134-52. See also Kammler, *Christologie und
Eschatologie, passim*, esp. 212-25, for a recent attempt to interpret the eschatology of the
Fourth Gospel, and particularly 5.17-30, as fully realized.

theories that are methodologically faulty.[122] A number of passages in the final form of the Fourth Gospel refer to the eschatological future, e.g. 5.28-29; 6.39, 40, 44, 54; 12.48; 14.2-3; 17.24; 21.22.[123] However, there are also numerous passages that refer to realized eschatology (e.g. 3.16, 18, 36; 5.24). Due to the author's Christological convictions, this present eschatology receives the dominant emphasis in the Fourth Gospel: because Jesus is given by the Father the ability to judge and to give life, one's eschatological destiny is decided by the encounter with him in the present. But this does not require the elimination of a future eschatological act.[124] The key point made by Frey is that the Fourth Gospel includes both present and future eschatology, sometimes even very closely together (e.g. 3.36; 5.24-29).[125]

With this larger context in place, we may ask whether the evangelist conceives of the promise of eschatological divine instruction in Isa 54.13 as being fulfilled in the present, or in the eschatological future, or perhaps in both. Although there are references in the immediate context to the eschatological future (6.39, 40, 44, 54), the interpretation of the OT citation in 6.45b-46 indicates that, in keeping with his heavily realized eschatology, the evangelist sees Isaiah's promises as presently fulfilled (I will argue in chapter 5 that the evangelist sees this fulfillment as coming through Jesus). If the evangelist conceives of a future eschatological period in which God will even more directly instruct his people, he makes no mention of it.

Other sources of the concept of divine instruction

Are there discernible sources for Jesus' claim in 14.26 that the Spirit will teach the disciples all things? Certainly there are precedents in both Jewish and Christian writings for the idea that the Spirit teaches people. The didactic function of the spirit in the LXX and at Qumran was noted in chapters 2-3 above, and in section 2 of this chapter, I pointed to the Spirit's teaching in Luke 12.12. Below, I will discuss the reference in 1 John 2.27 to the anointing which teaches all things (chapter 7) and Paul's development of the idea that the Spirit teaches believers (chapter 8). These NT references, however, are probably independent of John 14.26 or, in the case of 1 John 2.27, part of the same community tradition as John 14.26, rather than its source.

Brown suggests that John 14.26; 16.13 are a 'divided echo' of Ps 25.5.[126] There may be something to Brown's suggestion, as the common vocabulary indicates. If so, then the Holy Spirit/Paraclete does in the Fourth Gospel what

---

[122] Frey, 'Eschatology,' 50.

[123] Cf. De Jonge, 'Eschatology,' 481-87.

[124] Cf. Frey, 'Eschatology,' 75-76, 82; De Jonge, 'Eschatology,' 483-84.

[125] Frey, 'Eschatology,' 58-61 notes that this is also the case in the Johannine Epistles.

[126] Brown, *John*, 2.650.

the psalmist asks God to do for him in LXX Ps 24.5. Possible sources for the idea of divine instruction in John 7.14-19; 8.28 are not readily discernible, and these passages will receive closer attention in chapters 5-6.

4.4 Conclusion

The purpose of this chapter has been to prepare the way for the following two chapters by examining closely the didactic terminology of the Fourth Gospel. This investigation has demonstrated that the Fourth Gospel joins traditional descriptions of Jesus as a teacher with a developed theology of revelation, and develops the notion of divine instruction to a degree not found in the synoptic gospels. In developing this idea, the Fourth Gospel has been influenced by OT ideas of eschatological divine instruction, particularly the prophecy of Isa 54.13. As noted at the beginning of this chapter, these findings raise the question of how Jesus' teaching relates to God's teaching, and how the idea of divine instruction functions in the Fourth Gospel. These questions will be addressed, respectively, in chapters 5-6.

Chapter 5

The teaching of Jesus and the teaching of God

'...he here rebukes those who in Ex. 20:19 said: "Let not the Lord speak to us, lest perchance we die, but you speak to us, and we will hear." O stupid prayer! Not like this for me, Lord, not like this! But speak Thou, for Thy servant hears (1 Sam. 3:10). I will hear not what Moses but what the Lord says to me, since He will surely speak peace to His people, and the Lord can do no other than speak peace. And therefore I will rejoice, namely, because of the Lord's speaking. Therefore note here that when the Lord speaks without intermediary, He speaks most effectively. This is what the prophet asks for. And here is where the church makes its boast. For thus He promised, John 6:45: "They will all be taught by God," and, Jer. 31:33: "I will give My law into their hearts."'

Martin Luther, *First Psalm Lectures* 60.6, 1513[1]

This chapter proceeds from the conviction that the theological dimension of Jesus' identity and authority as a teacher, in both the Fourth Gospel and the synoptic gospels, has not been addressed adequately. Writing in 1954, Erich Fascher complained of a lack of secondary literature on Jesus as a teacher.[2] This is no longer the case: in the years since Fascher's article, a huge volume of literature has appeared on the subject.[3] However, much of it focuses on the didactic techniques of Jesus' teaching rather than the Christological importance of his identity as a teacher.[4] Some recent work has helpfully examined Jesus' teaching in terms of his messianic identity, but there has been no adequate discussion of the theological dimension. That dimension of Jesus' didactic identity in the Fourth Gospel is precisely the question raised

---

[1] Translation from *LW* 10.293.

[2] Fascher, 'Jesus der Lehrer,' 325-26.

[3] I have interacted with some of this literature in chapter 4. For Jesus as teacher in Mark, cf. Robbins, *Jesus the Teacher, passim*; Stein, 'Seam,' 90-94; Meye, *Discipleship, passim*; Meye, 'Messianic Didache,' 57-68; Scholtissek, *Vollmacht*, 119-25. For Jesus as teacher in Matthew, cf. Byrskog, *Teacher, passim*; Byrskog, 'Teacher,' 83-100; Yieh, *One Teacher, passim*; Saggin, 'Magister,' 205-13. For Jesus as teacher in Luke, cf. Bachmann, *Tempel*, 261-89; Glombitza, 'Titel,' 275-78. More generally, cf. Karrer, 'Lehrende,' 1-20; Riesner, *Lehrer, passim*; Riesner, 'Teacher,' 185-210; Perkins, *Jesus as Teacher, passim*; Normann, *Christos Didaskalos, passim*; Morgenstern, 'Teacher,' 1-7; Hengel, *Charismatic Leader*, 38-83; Herzog, *Prophet and Teacher, passim*; Curtis, *Teacher, passim*; Dillon, *Teacher, passim*. For further bibliography, cf. Byrskog, *Teacher*, 202; Dillon, *Teacher*, 194-209.

[4] E.g. Perkins' otherwise excellent volume never raises the issue of Christology.

by chapter 4 of this study. Furthermore, chapters 2-3, which represent the only comprehensive investigation of divine instruction in the OT and Jewish literature, place us in a unique position to shed fresh light on the question.

Two features of my discussion in chapters 2-3 provide the basis for the argument of this chapter. First, in chapter 2, I suggested that while most of the OT prophetic texts dealing with divine instruction do not demand that God's eschatological instruction will be direct and without human intermediaries, they all open this up as a viable interpretive possibility. My discussion of the prophetic literature in chapter 2 drew on categories developed through an examination of the biblical accounts concerning Sinai. In my discussion of divine instruction at Sinai, I noted a clear distinction between direct divine instruction and mediated divine instruction. Further, I demonstrated in chapters 2-3 that some early Jewish interpreters understood Sinai as divine instruction, and distinguished between direct and mediated divine instruction there.

Secondly, I concluded that the prophetic emphasis falls on the fact of divine eschatological instruction rather than how that instruction will occur. This means that even if the prophetic hope is interpreted as direct divine instruction, it is still unclear how that will be accomplished. The possible allusions to Isa 54.13 in *Pss. Sol.* 17.32 and CD 20.4 also leave the means of divine instruction quite vague. This lack of clarity in Isa 54.13 and the prophetic expectation allows for the possibility of various understandings of its fulfillment.

Both these points – the distinction between direct and mediated divine instruction at Sinai and in the prophetic vision of eschatological divine instruction, and the lack of clarity about how divine instruction will take place – are immediately relevant to an understanding of the theological dimension of Jesus' identity as a teacher in the Fourth Gospel. My argument in this chapter is two-fold. First, the evangelist understood Isa 54.13 as a prophecy of direct, unmediated divine instruction, analogous to the direct divine instruction at Sinai. Secondly, the lack of clarity in Isa 54.13 regarding the means of divine instruction allowed the evangelist to interpret it as fulfilled through the teaching of Jesus and the Holy Spirit/Paraclete.

5.1 Possible models for Jesus as teacher:
Messiah, Servant, Prophet

Before arguing that the evangelist sees Jesus' teaching as direct divine instruction, it is first necessary to show that he does not portray Jesus' teaching in terms of OT and Jewish intermediary figures. As I will argue below, the two most important elements of the evangelist's description of

Jesus' identity as a teacher are that Jesus himself is taught by God, and that he teaches others. Therefore, in looking for intermediary figures the evangelist might potentially have employed in his portrayal of Jesus, I will consider other 'God-taught' teachers.

Jesus as the God-taught, teaching Messiah?

I demonstrated above in chapter 3 that some Jews expected the Messiah to be taught by God, and even more expected a teaching Messiah. *Pss. Sol.* 17.32, 42-43 and *Midr. Pss.* 21.4 are the clearest passages in which the Messiah is described as a teacher who is himself taught by God. It is possible that the evangelist took over this particular messianic tradition, or that he combined both messianic expectations from early Jewish tradition and ascribed them to Jesus, whom he clearly believed to be the Messiah[5] and the offspring of David.[6] However, while the Fourth Gospel portrays Jesus as the Messiah and as a teacher, it nowhere explicitly portrays Jesus as one who fulfills an expected role of messianic teacher. The Jewish leaders and the crowds expect the Christ to baptize (1.25) and perform signs (7.31), but there is no indication that they expect him to teach. The closest conjunction of 'Messiah' and 'teacher' occurs in 11.27-28, but, as I argued in chapter 4, this does not indicate that Martha perceives Jesus as the messianic teacher. While it is possible that the Jewish expectation of a God-taught, teaching Messiah has informed the evangelist's description of Jesus as teacher (cf. Matt 23.8-10), I conclude that the evangelist has not made that connection explicit.

Jesus as the God-taught, teaching Servant?

The Servant in Isa 50.4 is described as one who is taught by God, and who teaches others,[7] and it is possible that the evangelist understands Jesus' identity as a teacher in these terms. As we saw in chapter 3, the Servant of Isa 50.4 functioned as an exemplar for the author of the *Hodayot*. Moreover, there is some evidence to suggest that the evangelist, who has been influenced by Isaiah in the writing of the Fourth Gospel,[8] portrays Jesus as the Servant figure from Isa 40-66.[9] Although Jesus is never referred to as 'the Servant' in the Fourth Gospel, we encounter the repeated claim that on the cross he will be lifted up (3.14-15; 8.28; 12.32-34) and glorified (12.23;

---

[5] Cf. John 1.41; 4.25-26, 29; 7.26-27, 31, 41-42; 9.22; 10.24; 11.27; 12.34; 17.3; 20.31.

[6] Cf. 7.42. However, for the evangelist, Jesus' human origin is less important than his heavenly origin. See Barrett, *John*, 330-31.

[7] Cf. the Targum of Isa 50.4 and 53.5, and see above in chapter 3.

[8] Cf. Young, 'Isaiah,' 215-33; Williams, 'Isaiah,' 101-16.

[9] Cf. Bauckham, *God Crucified*, 63-68; Carson, 'John,' 250; Evans, 'Obduracy,' 221-36; Moo, *Narratives*, 163, 171.

13.31-32). This probably alludes to LXX Isa 52.13, which says that the Servant will be lifted up and glorified.[10] Again, however, while it is possible that the evangelist understands the didactic identity of Jesus in terms of the Servant, there are no explicit pointers in this direction in the Fourth Gospel.

Jesus as the God-taught, teaching prophet like Moses?

In the OT and Jewish literature, Moses is portrayed as one who is taught by God and teaches others.[11] Moses is in fact one of Philo's main examples of the kind of person whom God teaches so that he may teach others (*Her.* 17-19). This recalls the evidence of the Pentateuch itself (particularly Deuteronomy), in which God speaks directly to Moses, who then teaches the Law to Israel (see chapter 2). Deut 18.14-22 suggests that the future prophet like Moses (18.15) will be raised up for the same purpose: to act as an intermediary (18.16). The prophet will speak everything God commands (18.18) and only what God commands (18.20), so that his words will be God's words (18.19).

Does the evangelist portray Jesus as a teacher in terms of the prophet like Moses? 'The prophet' (with definite article and in the singular) is mentioned four times in the Fourth Gospel: John the Baptist denies that he is the prophet (1.21, 25), and some of the people in the crowd believe that Jesus is the prophet (6.14; 7.40). The prophet may also be in the background of John 4.25, in which the Samaritan woman suggests that when the Messiah comes, he will 'announce to us all things [ἅπαντα]' (cf. 4.29). This possibly echoes the language of Deut 18.18, which claims that the prophet to come will speak 'all' that God commands him.[12] Moreover, Wayne Meeks has argued that Deut 13.2-6; 18.18-22 are in view in John 7.14-24. If this is the case, Jesus claims to be the true prophet like Moses, the one who speaks the words of God, while the crowd wishes to kill him because they believe he is a false prophet.[13]

However, Meeks' thesis does not explain the didactic terminology of 7.14-19, because such terminology is not used of the prophet in Deut 18. The prophet like Moses, unlike Moses, is never said to teach, nor is he said to be

---

[10] Bauckham, *God Crucified*, 63-68.

[11] See above in chapters 2-3. Cf. Josephus, *Ant.* 17.159; Philo, *Det.* 86; *Fug.* 164; *Mos.* 2.71; *Spec.* 1.42. See also *Exod. Rab.* 2.6 (cited in Meeks, *Prophet-King*, 213); *b. Ber.* 63b.

[12] Samaritans expected an end-time prophetic figure called the *Taheb*, who would fulfill the promise of Deut 18.18 and 'reveal the truth.' Cf. *Memar Markah* 4.12 (likely third or fourth century). See Dexinger, 'Samaritan,' 266-92, esp. 272-76; Macdonald, *Samaritans*, 362-71; Meeks, *Prophet-King*, 250-54. The Samaritan interest in the mediatorial role of the prophet is reflected in the conflation of Exod 20.18-21, Deut 5.24-31; 18.18-22 in the Samaritan Pentateuch. Cf. Bowman, *Samaritan*, 16-25.

[13] Cf. Meeks, *Prophet-King*, 42-57.

'taught by God.' Further, if we read the reference to Jesus' διδαχή in 7.14-19 within the larger didactic storyline of his divine instruction in the Fourth Gospel (see below), the prophet like Moses is not an adequate exemplar. He never learns from God by *imitatio* and is not said to become like God (cf. John 5.17-30), nor is the father/son language used of his relationship with God.

Conclusion

I conclude from this survey of OT intermediary figures that while the Messiah, the Servant, and the prophet like Moses are used by the evangelist in the Fourth Gospel to explain Jesus' identity, the evangelist does not clearly employ them in his portrayal of Jesus as a teacher. Jesus' didactic identity must therefore be understood along other lines. My argument is that Jesus' teaching is understood primarily in terms of *direct* divine instruction rather than in terms of intermediary figures.

5.2 Direct divine instruction in Isaiah 54.13

John 6.45-46 is the most important text for understanding how the Fourth Gospel relates the idea of divine instruction to Jesus as a teacher. I argued above in chapter 4 that 6.45a is a citation of the promise of divine eschatological instruction in Isa 54.13. This raises the question of whether the evangelist interpreted Isa 54.13 as referring to direct divine instruction, like some later Jewish interpreters, or to mediated divine instruction (like other Jewish interpreters).

In order to answer this question, it is helpful to observe that 6.45a is explained in 6.45b-46, first with a restatement of the OT citation (6.45b), and then with a qualification (6.46).[14]

Table 1. *John 6.45b-6.46 as an explanation of 6.45a*

6.45a	ἔστιν γεγραμμένον ἐν τοῖς προφήταις· καὶ ἔσονται πάντες διδακτοὶ θεοῦ
6.45b	πᾶς ὁ ἀκούσας παρὰ τοῦ πατρὸς καὶ μαθὼν ἔρχεται πρὸς ἐμέ.
6.46	οὐχ ὅτι τὸν πατέρα ἑώρακέν τις εἰ μὴ ὁ ὢν παρὰ τοῦ θεοῦ, οὗτος ἑώρακεν τὸν πατέρα.

---

[14] This suggests that 6.45-46 is a unity, and therefore undermines the unconvincing attempt of Theobald, 'Gezogen,' 315-41, esp. 321 to isolate an original dominical saying. It also suggests that the evangelist interprets θεοῦ in the OT citation as designating the agent, rather than the content, of the teaching, since 6.45b speaks of hearing and learning from (not about) the Father. Cf. BDF §183.

Although the relationship between 6.45a and what follows is syntactically ambiguous due to the asyndeton at the beginning of 6.45b,[15] several factors suggest that 6.45b-46 explains 6.45a. First, there are other instances in the Fourth Gospel, and even in the immediate context, in which an explanation follows an OT citation (6.31-33; 7.37-39). Secondly, Peder Borgen has demonstrated the use of participial statements (like those in 6.45b) by Philo and the Palestinian *midrashim* to explain OT citations.[16] Borgen has also shown that statements of reservation and clarification similar to 6.46 appear in Philo and the Palestinian *midrashim*.[17] Finally, the correlative didactic terminology in 6.45a and 6.45b-46 supports this interpretation. The OT citation focuses on the activity of the teacher (i.e. God), while the explanation in 6.45b focuses on the hearing and learning of the pupil (i.e. those who come to Jesus).[18] This discussion suggests that the evangelist's interpretation of Isa 54.13 may be clarified by understanding 6.45b-46.

It is therefore significant that the references to hearing, learning, and seeing in 6.45b-46 allude to the biblical accounts of Sinai.[19] As we saw in chapters 2-3, OT and early Jewish accounts of Sinai contain references to what was seen and heard.[20] Even more impressively, the biblical accounts of Sinai combine the language of instruction with references to hearing and seeing. As noted in chapter 2, Moses reminds Israel in Deut 4.36 that God let them hear his voice to instruct (יסר; παιδεύω) them, and that he let them see his fire and hear his words. Deut 4.10, 12 is even more relevant. It asserts that the people heard and learned (μανθάνω) from God, but denies that they saw God.[21] In this passage, Moses' command to the people to remember when they 'stood before the Lord your God at Horeb' emphasizes their direct hearing and learning from the Lord. In Deut 4.12-13, the hearing of God's voice speaking the ten words is direct and unmediated. In the ensuing narrative, the fact that Israel did not see the Lord when he spoke to them from the midst of the fire is emphasized: this is why Israel must not make any graven images (4.15-24).

---

[15] Manuscripts A Θ Ψ f¹ 𝔐 q sy^{c.p.h} add an οὖν in 6.45b in order to clarify the connection.

[16] Borgen, *Bread*, 70-71.

[17] Borgen, *Bread*, 84-85. See also Bultmann, *John*, 232. Cf. John 7.22; 1 John 4.10.

[18] For a similar emphasis first on teacher and then on pupil, cf. the fifth century *Pesiq. Rab Kah.* 12.21.1: 'In this world I gave you the Torah, and individuals work hard at it, but in the world to come, I shall personally teach [אני מלמדה] it to *all* Israel, and they will study it [למידין] and not forget.' Translation from Neusner, *Pesiqta deRab Kahana*, 2.21.

[19] Cf. Keener, *John*, 1.686; Borgen, *Bread*, 150-51; Borgen, 'Agent,' 90; Schnackenburg, *St. John*, 2.52; Thompson, *God*, 110.

[20] E.g. LXX Exod 20.18; Philo, *Decal.* 32-35, 46-49.

[21] In Jewish sources, there are varying opinions as to whether or not the people saw God at Sinai. Cf. Thompson, *God*, 111-13.

The similarity with John 6.45b-46 is clear: in both texts, people hear and learn from God, but are denied a vision of him. The denial that anyone has seen God appears also in John 1.18 and 5.37, both of which allude to the biblical accounts of Sinai.[22] I conclude that the Isa 54.13 citation in John 6.45a is explained in 6.45b-46 by means of an allusion to the direct, unmediated divine instruction that occurred at Sinai before Moses was appointed an intermediary. This strongly suggests that the evangelist interpreted Isa 54.13 to promise direct, unmediated divine instruction.

The correlation of God's direct instruction at Sinai and his direct, eschatological instruction is not unique to the Fourth Gospel. A strikingly similar comparison is drawn in the midrash on Song of Songs. Stemberger dates this work to the middle of the sixth century, but claims that it contains much older material:[23]

> R. Judah said: When Israel heard the words, *I am the Lord thy God*, the knowledge of the Torah was fixed in their heart and they learnt and forgot not. They came to Moses and said, 'Our master, Moses, do thou become an intermediary between us, as it says, "*Speak thou with us, and we will hear*"...*now therefore why should we die* (Ex. xx,16; Deut. v, 22). What profit is there in our perishing?' They then became liable to forget what they learnt. They said: Just as Moses, being flesh and blood, is transitory, so his teaching is transitory. Forthwith they came a second time to Moses and said: 'Our master, Moses, would that God might be revealed to us a second time! Would that He would kiss us WITH THE KISSES OF HIS LIPS! Would that He would fix the knowledge of the Torah in our hearts as it was!' He replied to them: 'This cannot be now, but it will be in the days to come,' as it says, *I will put My law in their inward parts and in their heart will I write it* (Jer. xxxi, 33). (*Cant. Rab.* 1.2.4)[24]

In this passage, the directness of God's relationship with the people is the point of similarity between his words at Sinai and his eschatological work in Jer 31.33. Moses' intermediary teaching is perceived as inadequate. In the eschatological future, God will again teach without an intermediary.[25]

In two Christian sources, the inadequacy of Moses' intermediary teaching at Sinai is contrasted with the directness of God's eschatological instruction. Writing roughly one hundred years after the Fourth Gospel, Clement of Alexandria claims that, unlike Moses' instruction, Jesus' teaching was the direct and unmediated teaching of God (*Paedagogus* 1.7).[26] Clement refers to

---

[22] Cf. Dahl, 'Johannine Church,' 133; Meeks, *Prophet-King*, 299-300; Thompson, *God*, 110.

[23] Stemberger, *Talmud and Midrash*, 315.

[24] Translation from Freedman and Simon, *Songs*, 25-26.

[25] Cf. TanB *Yitro* Exod 5.13 (S. Buber Recension), which contrasts the giving of the Law at Sinai with the future divine instruction described in Isa 54.13; Jer 31.33. For English translation, see Townsend, *Tanhuma*, 106. Many scholars date Tanhuma to the first half of the ninth century (cf. Stemberger, *Talmud and Midrash*, 305). Cf. *Pesiq. Rab Kah.* 12.21.1.

[26] See the epigraph at the beginning of chapter 4.

Jesus as 'the holy God,' and claims that the Lord is the instructor of his new people 'by Himself, face to face' (cf. Deut 5.4). This passage pointedly raises the question of whether the Fourth Gospel itself might have interpreted Jesus' teaching as the direct, unmediated divine instruction prophesied in Isa 54.13. I will address this question in the next section.

Much later in the history of interpretation, Martin Luther, in his lectures on the Psalms, also contrasts the intermediary role of Moses at Sinai with the eschatological divine instruction prophesied in Jer 31.33 and fulfilled in John 6.45 (see the epigraph at the beginning of this chapter). After stating that the request of Israel at Sinai for an intermediary (Exod 20.19) was a 'stupid prayer,' Luther claims that, 'when the Lord speaks without intermediary, He speaks most effectively.' The boast of the church, according to Luther, is that it enjoys this direct divine instruction.

5.3 The teaching of Jesus as the fulfillment of Isaiah 54.13

The quotation from Clement of Alexandria in the previous section raises the question of whether the evangelist understands Jesus' teaching as the direct divine instruction prophesied in Isa 54.13. As I concluded in chapters 2-3, there is a distinct lack of clarity in Isa 54.13 and other prophetic texts concerning exactly how eschatological divine instruction will be given. This vagueness allowed the evangelist to interpret Isa 54.13 as fulfilled in the teaching of Jesus. However, the evangelist surprisingly indicates this fulfillment of direct divine instruction by implying that Jesus functions in an *intermediary* role.

6.46 is the clearest indication of this tension. As we saw above, the claim that some have heard and learned from the Father is qualified in 6.46: no one has ever seen the Father. As in the first instance of direct divine instruction (Sinai), so here: although Isa 54.13 is coming to fulfillment, a vision of God is denied. The evangelist's striking addition to this Sinai allusion is the exception clause in 6.46: εἰ μὴ ὁ ὢν παρὰ τοῦ θεοῦ, οὗτος ἑώρακεν τὸν πατέρα. This clearly refers to Jesus,[27] whose vision of God distinguishes him from all other humans, including Moses. Although Moses spoke with God face to face (Exod 33.11), he was not permitted to see God face to face (Exod 33.18-23).[28]

The evangelist's reference to Jesus' vision of the Father suggests a unique intimacy. In the prologue of the Fourth Gospel, this intimacy of the Son with the Father is closely connected with the claim that the Son has made the

---

[27] Cf. Thompson, *God*, 110.

[28] Cf. Thompson, *God*, 110-17; Ridderbos, *John*, 58-59.

Father known (1.18). The evangelist's claim in 6.46 that only Jesus has seen the Father therefore implies that to come to a full knowledge of the Father, all others must come through Jesus. This is a claim consistent with the Fourth Gospel as a whole, and establishes Jesus as a kind of intermediary between the Father and others.[29] By implication, the 'hearing and learning' from the Father in 6.45b occurs as one hears and learns from Jesus: God teaches through the teaching of Jesus (cf. 6.59).[30] This creates something of a paradox in 6.45-46. In the oft-quoted words of Hugo Odeberg, 'no one can come to the Son, without having received the teaching from the Father; no one can hear and learn from the Father except through the Son.'[31] In Barrett's words, the 'process is circular.'[32]

The tension in John 6.45-46

The previous two sections have highlighted an important tension in John 6.45-46. The allusion to Sinai in 6.45b suggests that Jesus' teaching is seen as the direct instruction of God prophesied in Isa 54.13. However, the emphasis on Jesus' unique vision of the Father in 6.46 suggests that Jesus mediates divine instruction. This tension is in fact at the heart of the evangelist's Christology. In order to understand and resolve it, we must examine an important and yet neglected theme: Jesus' own instruction from the Father. I will argue that this theme explains how the evangelist describes Jesus' teaching as mediated divine instruction, but ultimately understands it as the direct divine instruction prophesied in Isa 54.13.

5.4 Jesus as the one taught by God *par excellence*

Samuel Byrskog has used the phrase 'didactic storyline' to refer to the way in which Matthew defines Jesus as a teacher in the course of his narrative.[33] The phrase applies equally well to the Fourth Gospel. As I argued above in

---

[29] Cf. Barrett, *John*, 296; Carson, *John*, 294; Martin Luther, *Sermon on the Gospel of St. John, Chapters 6-8* (*LW* 23.88-99, esp. 88-89).

[30] Cf. Bultmann, *John*, 232; Schnackenburg, *St. John*, 2.50-52; Köstenberger, *John*, 214; Moloney, *John*, 218; Ridderbos, *John*, 234. *Contra* Theobald, 'Gezogen,' 335, who suggests that the aorist tense of ὁ ἀκούσας and μαθών in 6.45b indicates a temporal distinction between the Father's instruction and coming to Jesus, with the former antecedent to the latter. Cf. Pancaro, *Law*, 282-83. The aorist participles in 6.45b are substantival and probably generic, involving a gnomic idea without a time reference. Cf. Wallace, *Greek Grammar*, 615, n. 8.

[31] Odeberg, *Fourth Gospel*, 257-58.

[32] Barrett, *John*, 296.

[33] Byrskog, 'Teacher,' 94-97.

chapter 4, the references to divine instruction in the Fourth Gospel are not random, disconnected references. Rather, they function to produce a coherent didactic storyline. One important aim of this storyline is to lead the reader of the Fourth Gospel to the conclusion that the teaching of Jesus is the teaching of God. Within this storyline, the evangelist develops the idea that Jesus himself is taught by God. In chapter 4, I noted Nicodemus' reference to Jesus as a 'teacher come from God' (3.2). This already suggests that Jesus' teaching has its source in the Father. The evangelist expands on this idea in chapters 5, 6, 7, and 8, as well as several other passages that do not use specifically didactic terminology. In the present section, I will examine these passages in order to highlight the uniquely Johannine idea that Jesus is 'taught by God.'

Jesus learns from and imitates his Father (John 5.17-30)

For our purposes, the key verses in this passage are 5.19-20:

Truly, truly I say to you, the son is not able to do anything from himself except what he sees (βλέπω) the father doing; for whatever things this one does, these things also the son is doing in the same way (ὁμοίως). For the father loves (φιλέω) the son and shows all things which he is doing to him...

Several factors suggest that the common motif of a father teaching his son is used as an analogy for the description of the Father and Son in 5.17-30.[34] First, in both the Jewish and Greco-Roman milieux, the father had a primary role in the education of his children.[35] Moreover, in some cases, ancient teachers were called 'father' by their students.[36] The language of Father/Son is prominent in 5.17-30,[37] and this language opens the way for an analogy

---

[34] Dodd, 'Parable,' 30-40 and Gaechter, 'Form,' 65-68 independently suggested that the 'parable' of a son learning a craft from his father stands behind 5.19-20. Brown, *John*, 1.218 thinks the idea is plausible. Carson, *John*, 250 rightly questions the existence of an originally independent parable, because 'the son' is a 'standard Christological expression.' Better is Carson's suggestion that the idea of sons learning from fathers is presupposed.

[35] Cf. Van Der Watt, *Family*, 266-74; Barclay, 'Family,' 66-80; Townsend, 'Ancient Education,' 139-63, esp. 154; Dodd, 'Parable,' 30-40; van Tilborg, *Imaginative Love*, 28-30; Estes, *Hear*, 94. Cf. the wisdom texts cited below (e.g. Prov 4.1-5; 23.26), and see also 4 Macc 18.6-19 (I am thankful to Hans-Josef Klauck for this reference). The fact that fathers *and mothers* teach children in Proverbs suggests that the references to fathers teaching sons should be taken literally, rather than as metaphors for teacher and pupil. Cf. Waltke, *Proverbs*, 1.62-63.

[36] For Sumerian schoolteachers, cf. Waltke, *Proverbs*, 1.62. For rabbinic practice, cf. Byrskog, *Teacher*, 53; Schrenk, 'πατήρ,' *TDNT* 5.977-78, 991; Garland, *Intention*, 59; Schürer, *History*, 2.326-27.

[37] The reaction of the Jews in 5.18 also highlights the importance of Jesus' claim that God is his Father.

with human fathers (or teachers) who train their sons (or students).[38] Secondly, the references to the Son seeing what the Father does (5.19) and hearing the Father (5.30) are similar to the language of hearing, learning from, and seeing the Father in the didactic context of 6.45-46.[39] Thirdly, the idea of *imitatio* is clearly present in 5.19-20: whatever Jesus sees the father doing, he does likewise (ὁμοίως). This is emphasized throughout the passage, particularly through the 'just as...so also' constructions in 5.21, 26:

5.21: For just as the Father [ὥσπερ γὰρ ὁ πατήρ] raises the dead and gives life, so also the Son [οὕτως καὶ ὁ υἱὸς] gives life to whomever he desires.

5.26: For just as the Father [ὥσπερ γὰρ ὁ πατήρ] has life in himself, so also he has given to the Son [οὕτως καὶ τῷ υἱῷ] to have life in himself.

The idea of *imitatio* is common in didactic contexts in Jewish and Christian writings. In Prov 23.26, a son is to learn by watching his father's ways (σοὶ ὀφθαλμοὶ ἐμὰς ὁδοὺς τηρείτωσαν). Sir 30.3-4 links the idea of a father teaching his son with the idea that the son imitates his father and thus becomes like him:

He who teaches his son (ὁ διδάσκων τὸν υἱὸν αὐτοῦ) will make his enemies envious, and will glory in him in the presence of friends. The father may die, and yet he is not dead, for he has left behind him one like himself (ὅμοιον γὰρ αὐτῷ κατέλιπεν μετ᾽ αὐτόν)...

A similar thought is evident in a wholly different sphere. Dio Chrysostom, in his *De Homero et Socrate*, argues that Socrates was a pupil of Homer:

For whoever really follows any one surely knows what that person was like, and by imitating his acts and words (μιμούμενος τὰ ἔργα καὶ τοὺς λόγους) he tries as best he can to make himself like him (ὅμοιον). But that is precisely, it seems, what the pupil (μαθητής) does – by imitating his teacher (μιμούμενος τὸν διδάσκαλον) and paying heed to him he tries to acquire his art (Or. 55.4-5).[40]

Dio Chrysostom goes on to demonstrate his claim that Socrates was a disciple of Homer by showing numerous points of resemblance between the two.[41]

Several passages in Philo also attest to the educational tradition of imitating one's teacher. Philo describes Joshua as the 'student and imitator' (ὁ φοιτητὴς αὐτοῦ καὶ μιμητής) of Moses (*Virt.* 66), and speaks of imitating (μιμέω) the perfection of one's teacher (διδάσκαλος) (*Sacr.* 65).[42]

---

[38] Van Der Watt, *Family*, 272, n. 574. On the use of analogy in this passage, cf. page 278 in Van Der Watt's monograph. The analogy in John 5 is an implicit one; it is nowhere explicitly stated that as a human father teaches his son, so the Father teaches his Son.

[39] See below. Cf. Dodd, 'Parable,' 39, n.1.

[40] Translation from Dio Chrysostom, LCL 4.385. Cf. Gerhardsson, *Memory*, 183.

[41] Cf. Quintilian, *Inst.* 2.8.1-2. On imitation among the sophists and their pupils, cf. Winter, *Corinth*, 32-36.

[42] This is connected to the imitation of God in paragraph 68.

I noted above in chapter 3 that Philo adopts the Greek educational tradition concerning those who acquire virtue by teaching, practice, or nature. In *Congr.* 69-70, Philo notes that the characteristic mark of the 'learner' (i.e. Abraham) is to, 'listen to a voice and to words.' On the other hand, the one who acquires the good through practice (i.e. Jacob) does not listen, but observes and imitates (μιμέομαι) the life of the one from whom he learns.

As I noted in chapter 4, the idea of imitating a teacher is explicit in John 13.13-15, where Jesus as the διδάσκαλος gives his disciples an example (ὑπόδειγμα) to follow.[43] Accordingly, throughout the remainder of the discourse in John 13-17, reference is made to the disciples' likeness to their teacher (13.34; 15.10, 12; 17.21). A similar idea is evident in Luke 6.40: '…everyone, after he has been fully trained, will be like his teacher [ἔσται ὡς ὁ διδάσκαλος αὐτοῦ].'

The widespread nature of this educational tradition of hearing, seeing, and imitating is suggested by its use not only in the wisdom literature, Dio Chrysostom, Philo, and the NT, but also in the later rabbinic literature. This literature stresses the importance of learning from one's master by listening to him,[44] and also by observing and imitating his actions. Disciples were to learn Torah by imitating the example of their master, who embodied Torah.[45] Robert Kirschner's examination of the formula 'fix a halakhah' has demonstrated that rabbinic masters were conscious of their status as *exemplars* for both their disciples and a wider public. Not only what a master said, but what he did, could be understood as normative and thus the source of halakhah.[46]

Finally, the reason (note the γάρ in 5.20) the Son does what the Father does is that the Father loves (φιλέω) the Son, and therefore, 'shows all things which he doing to him.' This constellation of ideas (i.e. the love of the Father for the Son, his teaching by example) is similar to Sir 30.1-5, partially cited above. In the Sirach passage, the father who loves (ἀγαπάω) his son disciplines (παιδεύω) and teaches (διδάσκω) him, and leaves behind him one 'like himself.'[47] I conclude that in 5.17-30, the didactic relationship of a father and son is used analogically to explain the relationship of Jesus to his Father. It appears from some of the verb tenses in 5.17-30 that Jesus'

---

[43] Cf. Van Der Watt, *Family*, 279.

[44] Cf. Rengstorf, 'μαθητής,' *TDNT* 4.435 for discussion of the rabbinic תלמיד as a listener.

[45] Cf. Aberbach, 'Master,' 5; Stemberger, *Talmud and Midrash*, 13; Westerholm, *Jesus*, 31; Wilkins, *Disciple*, 122-23; Gerhardsson, *Memory*, 183-87; Neusner, 'Phenomenon,' 72-77; Neusner, *History of the Jews III*, 130-49; Neusner, *History of the Jews IV*, 295-309; Neusner, *History of the Jews V*, 146-68; Wenthe, 'Rabbi-Disciple,' 173.

[46] Kirschner, 'Imitatio,' 70-79. Examples abound of the importance of imitation in the master-disciple relationship: e.g. *m. Sukkah* 3.9; *b. Ber.* 23a, 24a, 38b, 62a; *b. Sabb.* 40-41.

[47] Cf. Dodd, 'Parable,' 38.

education by the Father is an ongoing process.[48] Because 5.17-30 is the first of the references to Jesus' instruction from the Father on the Fourth Gospel's didactic storyline, the passages that follow should be read in light of it.

Hearing, learning, and seeing the Father (John 6.45-46)

I suggested in section 2 that the language of hearing, learning, and seeing in 6.45b-46 alludes to the biblical accounts of Sinai. Here we may note a complementary background: the language also fits within an educational milieu. This is unsurprising, since Sinai was considered the example *par excellence* of instruction. That one must hear in order to learn was assumed in the ancient world,[49] and it is therefore normal that ἀκούω and μανθάνω are used together in 6.45b. They are found together in Jewish didactic contexts,[50] as are ἀκούω and διδάσκω.[51] In the wisdom literature, commands to 'hear instruction' are frequent,[52] and in Prov 5.13, the disobedient son admits that, 'I have not listened to the voice of my teachers nor inclined my ear to my instructors!'

In the wisdom literature, the sense of hearing was to be supplemented with the sense of sight, in order to learn more effectively by imitating the example of one's teacher.[53] This is also the case in Philo, who recognizes that both senses (hearing, seeing) are important for learning (*Post.* 137; *Congr.* 20), but suggests that sight is superior for gaining knowledge.[54] Some NT passages also indicate the importance of both hearing and seeing for learning. In Phil 4.9, Paul uses a combination of terms similar to John 6.45-46:

The things you learned (ἐμάθετε) and received (παρελάβετε) and heard (ἠκούσατε) and saw (εἴδετε) in me, do these things...

The above texts demonstrate that the language of hearing and seeing is found in Jewish and Christian contexts that speak of learning and being taught. The qualification in John 6.46 and its relation to 6.45ab may therefore be understood within this didactic context. The implicit claim of these verses is

---

[48] Note the present and future tenses of δείκνυμι in 5.20, and the present tense of ἀκούω in 5.30. Cf. Van Der Watt, *Family*, 277, n. 603.

[49] E.g. Isa 50.4. Hearing a teacher's words did not guarantee that one learned, of course. Cf. Philo, *Congr.* 64-68. John 6.45b specifies that those who come to Jesus are the ones who hear from the Father *and learn*. Cf. Bultmann, *John*, 232.

[50] Cf. Wis 6.1; Sir 16.24. Cf. Meye, *Discipleship*, 49-50 for ἀκούω in didactic contexts in Mark.

[51] Cf. LXX Deut 4.1; Job 33.33; Ps 33.12; Prov 5.13; Jer 39.33. Cf. Eph 4.21.

[52] Cf. Prov 1.8; 4.1; 19.20; cf. Sir 23.7. More generally, the call to listen occurs in e.g. Prov 4.10, 20; 5.1, 7; 7.24; 8.32; 22.17; 23.12, 19, 22; Sir 3.1; 6.23, 33; 31.22.

[53] Cf. Prov 23.26; Sir 30.3-4, cited above.

[54] Cf. *Sacr.* 78-79.

that Jesus is the only one who has learned from the Father[55] both by hearing and by seeing, and is therefore the one who has been 'taught by God' *par excellence*. If this is indeed the implication of 6.45-46, we might expect to find the language of hearing, learning, and 'being taught,' which is applied in 6.45ab to all who are drawn by the Father, also applied to Jesus in the Fourth Gospel. This is precisely what we find.

Table 2. *Parallels between those 'drawn' in 6.44-46 and Jesus*

Believers	Jesus
'They will all be taught [διδακτοί] by God' (6.45a)	Just as the Father taught (ἐδίδαξέν) me, these things I am speaking (8.28)
–	My teaching (διδαχή) is not mine, but his who sent me (7.16, cf. 7.17)
Everyone who has heard from the Father (ὁ ἀκούσας παρὰ τοῦ πατρός)... (6.45b)	The things I heard from him (ἤκουσα παρ' αὐτοῦ) I am speaking to the world (8.26)
–	I told you the truth, which I heard from God (ἤκουσα παρὰ τοῦ θεοῦ) (8.40)
–	All the things I heard from my Father (ἤκουσα παρὰ τοῦ πατρός μου) I made known to you (15.15)
...and learned (καὶ μαθών) (6.45b)	How is this one educated, having never learned (μὴ μεμαθηκώς)? (7.15)

These considerations suggest that 6.45-46 refers above all to Jesus (but also to his followers, see chapter 6) as 'taught by God.' 5.17-30 and 6.45-46 employ a similar combination of terminology and ideas. Both passages refer to Jesus learning through hearing and seeing, and importantly, both passages refer to God as 'Father.'[56] It seems likely that 6.45-46, like 5.17-30, employs the idea of normal father/son education analogically in order to describe the didactic relationship of Jesus and his Father.

Jesus' διδαχή comes from God, who sent him (John 7.14-19)

John 7.14 describes Jesus teaching (διδάσκω) in the Temple. I will argue below in chapter 6 that the Jews' comment in 7.15 calls into question Jesus' ability to teach, because of his lack of formal education. If this reading is correct, we would expect Jesus' response to concern his education. This is in fact what we find. Two constructions are used in 7.16-17 to link the term διδαχή with God. First, in 7.16, Jesus claims that ἡ ἐμὴ διδαχὴ οὐκ ἔστιν ἐμὴ ἀλλὰ τοῦ πέμψαντός με. The genitive τοῦ πέμψαντος, together

---

[55] The prepositional phrase παρὰ τοῦ πατρός precedes καὶ μαθών, but as Keener, *John*, 1.686 notes, word sequence interference is common in Greek. Cf. BDF §472-473. Therefore, 6.45b refers to hearing *and* learning from the Father.

[56] 'Son' is used in 5.17-30, but not in 6.45-46. However, the issue of Jesus' parentage is prominent in 6.42, so his references to God as 'Father' in 6.44-46 may be emphatic.

with the 'not-but' construction, associates the διδαχή very closely with 'the one who sent me.' Secondly, in 7.17, Jesus asserts that if one is willing to do God's will, he will know that Jesus' teaching is ἐκ τοῦ θεοῦ. This clarifies the ambiguous genitive in 7.16: the idea in both verses is that the teaching comes from God (genitive of source).

Therefore, the purpose of Jesus' denials in 7.16-17 is not to distance himself from his teaching, but to emphasize that the teaching has not originated from himself but from God. This is further emphasized by the reference to God as 'the one who sent me' (7.16, 18). The teaching has come from God because it is spoken by one sent from God.[57] This explains why God is not referred to in 7.14-19 as Jesus' Father, as he is in 5.17-30; 6.45-46; 8.28. At this point on the didactic storyline, the source of Jesus' teaching, and Jesus' mission to proclaim that teaching, is emphasized by reference to God as 'the one who sent me.' When Jesus speaks (λαλέω), he is passing on the διδαχή God has given him. 7.14-19 does not explicitly claim that God teaches Jesus, but it implies that this is the case.

Jesus was taught by the Father (John 8.28b)

8.28b allows for two possible readings. First, διδάσκω may have the non-didactic sense 'instruct, tell,' similar to Matt 28.15, where soldiers take money from the priests and do as they were told (ἐδιδάχθησαν) by the priests. This clearly implies no didactic relationship between the priests and soldiers.[58] Some commentators favor this reading.[59] Secondly, another plausible reading is that 8.28b makes explicit what was already implied in 7.14-17. This reading suggests that 8.28b does imply a didactic relationship between Jesus and the Father.[60] 8.28b does not simply claim that the Father told Jesus what to say; it asserts that Jesus has learned from the Father and then has perfectly conveyed what he learned.[61]

Although there is a difference between these two readings,[62] many commentators do not even raise the question.[63] Perhaps the importance of 8.28a has detracted attention from the second half of the verse.[64] I suggest that the latter reading is more likely, for three reasons. First, the non-didactic meaning of διδάσκω appears nowhere else in the Fourth Gospel, and would

---

[57] Cf. 3.34.

[58] This reading of 8.28b parallels 12.49.

[59] E.g. Bultmann, *John*, 353; Witherington, *Wisdom*, 176.

[60] Cf. Pancaro, *Law*, 109, 198.

[61] On this reading, 8.28b is more closely parallel to 12.50.

[62] Cf. Pancaro, *Law*, 413.

[63] E.g. Moloney, Ridderbos, Wengst, Brown, Carson, Beasley-Murray.

[64] E.g. Schnackenburg, *St. John*, 2.202-3 offers a full discussion of 8.28a but barely mentions the Father teaching in 8.28b. Barrett, *John*, 344 provides no discussion of 8.28b.

therefore be unusual here. Secondly, the claim in 8.28b that Jesus does nothing 'from himself,' but speaks just as the Father taught him, recalls the great authority of the teacher over his pupil in Jewish didactic relationships.[65] Finally, 8.28b should be read as part of the Fourth Gospel's didactic storyline rather than as an isolated verse. Jesus refers to God in this passage as 'Father' (cf. 5.17-30; 6.45-56) and 'the one who sent me' (cf. 7.14-18): both are terms that appear previously on the didactic storyline. The mention of intimacy and affection between the Father and Son (8.29) recalls the intimacy expressed in 5.20, and follows most naturally upon a reference to a teaching relationship.[66] The similarity of 8.28b with 7.14-17, which appears in the immediate context and uses similar language (λαλέω + didactic terminology), also suggests that 8.28b refers to the Father teaching Jesus rather than simply telling him what to say. The meaning of 8.28b, then, is that the Father taught the Son; Jesus learns from his Father, as sons learn from their fathers.

The didactic framework for other passages in the Fourth Gospel

The passages I have examined suggest that the evangelist conceives of the relationship between Jesus and the Father as analogous to the didactic relationship of a human father and son, or teacher and pupil.[67] Several other descriptions of Jesus and the Father in the Fourth Gospel may also employ this analogy, although they do not use didactic terminology. For example, the educational milieu of teachers and students may stand behind Jesus' witnessing (μαρτυρέω) to what he has seen and heard (John 3.11, 32). Birger Gerhardsson suggests that in the rabbinic literature, the language of seeing and hearing, 'has as a rule a distinctly legal character. The pupil/traditionist tells what he has seen and heard.'[68] Legal terminology is sometimes used. At Yabneh, traditionists come forward as witnesses and 'bear witness' to the older halakhah.[69] First century evidence for the role of a pupil in witnessing to his teacher appears in Philo, *Aet.* 16:

...this view of Plato's meaning has the testimony [μαρτυρεῖ] of Aristotle, who had too much respect for philosophy to falsify anything. A teacher can have no more trustworthy witness than a disciple... [οὐδεὶς ὑφηγητῇ γνωρίμου μαρτυρεῖν].

---

[65] Cf. Rengstorf, 'διδάσκω,' *TDNT* 2.137, 143.

[66] Cf. Keener, *John*, 1.745; Wach, 'Master and Disciple,' 1-21. John 8.29 says that Jesus always does the things that are pleasing (ἀρέστος) to the Father. This is a common motif in the wisdom literature, where wise sons are said to make their fathers (and mothers) rejoice (εὐφραίνω). Cf. Prov. 10.1; 15.20; 23.15-16, 24-25; 27.11; 29.3; Sir 25.7; 30.1, 5; cf. Prov 17.21; Sir 16.1-2.

[67] As noted, 7.14-19 is the only one of these passages that refers to 'God' instead of the 'Father.'

[68] Gerhardsson, *Memory*, 183.

[69] Gerhardsson, *Memory*, 183-84. For examples, cf. *m. 'Ed.* 1.3; 2.1.

Another possible use of the analogy with teachers and pupils is the Fourth Gospel's claim that the basis of Jesus' ability to speak the words of God is his profound unity and intimacy with the Father, both in his pre-existence and in the present (1.18; 3.34-35; 7.18; 8.28; 14.10).[70] This may recall the Jewish teacher/student relationship, which involved intimacy and instruction over time. The one who learned did not merely receive information, but was profoundly shaped by the one who taught him, and this intimacy was the context of instruction.

In my judgment, an analogical use of teacher/pupil relationships more convincingly explains some Johannine descriptions of the Father and Son than apocalyptic or Gnostic backgrounds. I have shown above that references to hearing and seeing are combined in Jewish and Christian sources, and in John 5.17-30; 6.45-46, with the language and concept of education. This indicates that the other references throughout the Fourth Gospel to Jesus hearing and seeing (e.g. 3.11, 32; 5.19; 8.26, 38, 40; 15.15) may also be part of the evangelist's analogy with the educational realities of his day. As a human son learns from his father by hearing and seeing, so Jesus learns by hearing and seeing things from his Father.

This proposal differs from other explanations of the same passages. Bultmann argued that they were influenced by the Gnostic redeemer myth.[71] Pancaro argues, *contra* Bultmann, that the evangelist's claim that Jesus speaks the 'truth' he has heard and seen comes not from Gnosticism, but from Jewish apocalyptic literature.[72] However, it seems to me that, for two reasons, my suggestion is superior to the explanations of Pancaro and Bultmann. First, it takes seriously the didactic context of Jesus' hearing and seeing in 5.17-30 and 6.45-46, especially the motif of *imitatio* in 5.17-30. To my knowledge, this motif does not figure in the Gnostic redeemer myth or in apocalyptic texts. Secondly, Jesus' sayings about what he has seen and heard use the language of Father and Son.[73] This is not explicable by appealing to Gnostic or apocalyptic backgrounds, but, as we saw in 5.17-30, it makes sense within the context of a father/son teaching relationship. In the Fourth Gospel, Jesus hears the Father, just as the son in Proverbs is commanded to hear his father.[74] Because Jesus sees and imitates his Father, to see Jesus is to see his Father (12.45; 14.9; cf. Sir 30.4).

---

[70] Cf. Louw, 'Narrator,' 38.

[71] Bultmann, *Theology*, 61-62.

[72] Pancaro, *Law*, 204-6. Pancaro cites Ignace de la Potterie's study approvingly, but fails to mention that for de la Potterie, both apocalyptic and wisdom literature explain the Fourth Gospel's use of the expression 'truth.' Cf. de la Potterie, 'Truth,' 68-70.

[73] Cf. 5.19; 8.26-27, 38; 15.15. 8.40 is only an apparent exception ('the truth which I heard from God'), because it comes in a discussion about fathers, where Jesus is claiming that God is his father. The context of 3.11, 32 refers both to God and the Father (3.33-36).

[74] Prov 4.1, 10, 20-21; 5.1-2, 7.

The analogical use of didactic relationships is also superior to other suggested backgrounds. In the Fourth Gospel, the Father has given Jesus a commandment (ἐντολή) what to speak and to say, and Jesus speaks just as the Father spoke (εἶπον) to him (12.49-50). Jesus receives commandments (ἐντολή) from the Father, and keeps them (15.10). Jesus gives to his disciples the words (ῥῆμα, λόγος) his Father gave to him (14.10, 24; 17.8, 14; cf. 3.34). Wayne Meeks proposes that John 3.34; 12.47-50; 14.10; 17.8 allude to the prophet like Moses of Deut 18.18.[75] While some of the verbal similarities between these passages and Deut 18.18 are impressive, Meeks (like Bultmann and Pancaro) does not adequately account for the Father/Son language of these passages. In contrast, several passages in the wisdom literature use similar terminology, and deal specifically with the didactic relationship between a father and son. In Proverbs, a father gives commandments (ἐντολή, νόμος) and words (λόγος) to his son, and urges his son to keep them.[76] Similarly, parents give teaching to their sons (cf. John 7.14-15)[77] and teach (διδάσκω, παιδεύω) their sons (cf. John 8.28).[78]

Jesus as distinct from other learners

I have argued in this section that Jesus is portrayed as the one who learns from his Father *par excellence* in the Fourth Gospel. Although both Jesus and his followers learn from the Father, Jesus is separated from all other learners by the fact that he alone has seen the Father (6.46). This suggests an intimacy that no one else possesses. He is also separated from other learners by *when* he learns from God. In 8.28b, Jesus claims to speak (λαλέω) as the Father taught (ἐδίδαξεν) him. The verb tenses suggest that Jesus was taught by the Father in the past (aorist tense) and now speaks (present tense) what he learned from the Father.[79]

If Jesus was taught by the Father in the past, according to the evangelist, when did that instruction occur? During Jesus' childhood? Through study of Torah as a young man? The proximity between teaching and sending language in 7.16; 14.24; and 8.28-29 is suggestive in this respect.[80] The idea

---

[75] Meeks, *Prophet-King*, 45-46.

[76] Prov 2.1-2; 6.20, 23; 7.1-2. Cf. Wis 6.9-11, 25.

[77] Prov 1.8; 3.1.

[78] Cf. Prov 4.4; 31.1.

[79] Teaching is by its nature a continuous process, and the use of the aorist tense in 8.28b does not, of course, suggest otherwise. The aorist in 8.28b is constative, viewing the action as a whole, and therefore does not indicate whether the action is durative or momentary. Cf. BDF §332. In the LXX, διδάσκω is used in the aorist tense more often than in the imperfect. When used in the aorist, it nevertheless refers to an ongoing process: e.g. Deut 31.22.

[80] 14.24 does not use didactic terminology but is similar to the other two passages conceptually.

in each of these passages is that the word/teaching does not come from Jesus, but from God, who gave it to Jesus and then sent him with it. The implication is that Jesus was instructed by the Father before he came into the world.[81] However, 5.17-30 seems to suggest, as I have noted above, that Jesus' education from the Father continues on into the present.[82]

I argued in chapter 4 that the evangelist's redaction of Isa 54.13 in 6.45a highlights the eschatological nature of the divine instruction of Jesus' followers. If my argument in this section is correct, then the Father's teaching of Jesus might better be termed 'protological.' The instruction of Jesus took place above, before he was sent, as well as during his mission. The instruction of Jesus is therefore temporally and spatially distinguished from the instruction of all others in the Fourth Gospel.

5.5 Jesus as taught by God, and his teaching as *direct* divine instruction

The purpose of this exploration of the neglected theme of Jesus' own instruction from the Father has been to explain the tension evident within John 6.45-46: while Jesus' teaching is seen as the direct instruction of God, and thus reminiscent of Sinai and a fulfillment of Isa 54.13, it is also described as a mediation of God's teaching. We are now in a position to resolve this tension.

The evangelist does not develop the theme of Jesus as the one who learns from his Father in order to suggest that Jesus passed from ignorance to knowledge at some point. Such a position is impossible to defend in light of the Fourth Gospel's portrayal of Jesus. In this gospel, his supernatural knowledge is stressed more than in any other.[83] Jesus did not arrive at this knowledge by being taught by God: already in 1.1-18, Jesus is identified as God, and said to have been with God in the beginning.

Rather, the evangelist's description of Jesus as the Son who is taught by his Father is ultimately intended to convey Jesus' total transparency to the Father. Just as a son who becomes like the father who teaches him (Sir 30.3-4), and a student who becomes like his teacher (Luke 6.40; Dio Chrysostom, *Hom. Socr.* 4-5), so Jesus, because he perfectly learns from (and imitates) his

---

[81] Culpepper, *Anatomy*, 57 rightly designates 8.28 as a pre-historical external analepsis. Bultmann, *Theology*, 62 wrongly downplays the importance of the verb tenses.

[82] Cf. Van Der Watt, *Family*, 276-77.

[83] Although this theme is not unique to the Fourth Gospel (e.g. Mark 2.8), it is developed into a major motif surpassing anything in the synoptic gospels. Cf. John 2.24-25; 4.17-19, 29, 39; 5.6; 6.6; 11.4; 13.1, 3, 21; 14.29; 16.4; 18.4. It is, in fact, Jesus' supernatural knowledge that leads the disciples to the awareness and confession that Jesus came from God (16.30).

Father, perfectly reflects the Father who sent him. To see Jesus is to see the Father (12.45; 14.9), even though the evangelist also claims that no one has seen God (1.18; 6.46). The analogy of father/teacher and son/pupil is therefore employed in order to convey that Jesus' teaching is the promised direct eschatological teaching of God. Jesus' teaching in the Fourth Gospel is the word of God in a sense distinct from, and higher than, that of Moses' words. Although Jesus mediates God's teaching, his mediation is so perfect that it becomes totally transparent to God's teaching. Because Jesus teaches only what he has seen and heard with the Father, and because he submits totally to the authority of the one who teaches him (8.28), his teaching is the direct, unmediated word of God, and therefore the fulfillment of Isa 54.13. Because he learns perfectly from the Father, his teaching is God's teaching. This is in fact the paradox of the Fourth Gospel's 'Christology from below': Jesus' claim to be one with God is the result of his perfect and absolute submission to the Father.[84] Jesus is the one perfectly obedient to the Father, and it is because of this perfect obedience that he can claim to represent God perfectly.[85]

5.6 The teaching of the Holy Spirit/Paraclete

I have argued that divine instruction comes through Jesus. However, it is likely that to be 'taught by God' in John 6.45 also has an internal aspect.[86] In addition to Jesus' teaching, divine instruction seems to be an inward teaching by which an individual is drawn to Jesus. This is indicated by the parallel between the 'drawing' of 6.44, and the teaching and learning of 6.45ab.[87] That teaching in the Fourth Gospel can be understood as an internal event is clear from the reference to the Holy Spirit/Paraclete teaching all things (14.26).[88]

John 14.26 is in fact a significant passage for discerning how the evangelist understands divine instruction. Here, the Paraclete and Holy Spirit are clearly identified.[89] The future tense of the verbs in 14.26 is notable; the Spirit's activity is said to be (from Jesus' perspective) in the future.[90] As

---

[84] Cf. Smith, *John*, 135, 246-47.

[85] Smith, *John*, 211-14, 245. See also Cowan, 'Subordination,' 115-35.

[86] Cf. Barrett, *John*, 296; Brown, *John*, 1.277; Carson, *John*, 293-94.

[87] Cf. Wengst, *Johannesevangelium*, 1.245; Barrett, *John*, 296; Carson, *John*, 293.

[88] Cf. Luke 12.12; 1 Cor 2.13; 1 Thess 4.9; 1 John 2.20, 27.

[89] Cf. Burge, *Anointed Community*, 142; Brown, *John*, 2.650, 1140.

[90] In fact, the references to the παράκλητος in the Fourth Gospel suggest that he will come after Jesus has gone away (14.16, 26; 15.26; 16.7). Similarly, the Spirit is given when Jesus is glorified (7.39; 16.13; 20.22; although cf. 14.17).

Schnackenburg suggests, 14.26 is directly connected with 14.25. Jesus speaks to the disciples while abiding with them (14.25), but cannot clarify everything in his limited discourse. Therefore, he promises them the future teaching of the Holy Spirit/Paraclete (14.26).[91] In light of the many clear parallels between the Paraclete and Jesus in the Fourth Gospel,[92] this suggests that the Holy Spirit (here the grammatical subject of διδάσκω) continues the didactic role of Jesus.[93] If my argument in this chapter is correct (i.e. that Jesus' teaching is understood by the evangelist as direct divine instruction) then the teaching of the Paraclete, as the continuation of Jesus' teaching, must also be understood as the fulfillment of the promise of eschatological divine instruction. This is not wholly without precedent. Chapters 2-4 of this thesis have demonstrated a connection between divine instruction and the Spirit in Jewish and Christian writings.

5.7 Conclusion

Chapter 4 raised the question of how Jesus' teaching relates to God's teaching in the Fourth Gospel. I have sought to understand this relationship in the present chapter. I began by arguing that the evangelist does not clearly employ the Messiah, Servant, or prophet like Moses in developing Jesus' didactic identity. I then suggested, employing the categories of direct/mediated divine instruction developed in chapters 2-3, that the evangelist understands Jesus' didactic identity primarily in terms of divine instruction. My two-fold argument was that the evangelist reads Isa 54.13 as a prophecy of direct divine instruction, and that he sees Jesus as fulfilling that prophecy. The didactic storyline of the Fourth Gospel suggests that in order to portray the didactic relationship between Jesus and the Father, the evangelist develops an analogy based on the relationship of a father and son. The ultimate purpose of the analogy is to indicate that Jesus learns so perfectly from the Father that he becomes transparent to God. Therefore, when people hear Jesus' teaching, they receive direct divine instruction. I concluded the chapter by suggesting that the teaching of the Holy Spirit/Paraclete, because it is understood as the continuation of Jesus' teaching, is also regarded as the fulfillment of the promise of eschatological divine instruction.

---

[91] Schnackenburg, *St. John*, 3.83.
[92] Cf. Burge, *Anointed Community*, 137-47; Brown, *John*, 2.1140-41.
[93] Cf. T. Brown, *Spirit*, 208.

Chapter 6

The function of divine instruction

> '...It is absolutely certain that one cannot enter into the [meaning of] Scripture by study or
> innate intelligence. Therefore your first task is to begin with prayer...'
>
> '...For there is no one who can teach the divine words except he who is their author, as he
> says, "They shall all be taught by God." You must therefore completely despair of your own
> diligence and intelligence and rely solely on the infusion of the Spirit.'
>
> Martin Luther, *letter to George Spalatin*, 1518[1]

In this chapter, I ask how divine instruction functions in the Fourth Gospel. The question of function is inseparable from that of content, and here the findings of chapters 2-3 shed fresh light on the Fourth Gospel. Chapter 2 demonstrated that, while the content of divine instruction in the OT is variable, including warfare and agriculture, an association with the Mosaic Law is noticeable.[2] Importantly, an examination of Ps 119 suggested that divine instruction there may refer in at least some instances to a revelation of the meaning of a previously given Torah. It was also noted that Isa 54.13 does not specify the content of divine instruction.

Chapter 3 found that, in keeping with the OT, the content of divine instruction in early Jewish literature is variable. A connection with the Mosaic Law was again noticeable.[3] I suggested that in CD 20.4, the claim to be 'taught by God' may be a claim that God has revealed to the community the correct interpretation of the Law (cf. 11Q5 24.8). I argued that divine instruction in 1QH^a 10.17 may refer to divinely given insight into the meaning of the prophetic writings. Finally, I noted Philo's claim in *Mut.* 18 that God's 'interpreting word' would teach (διδάσκω) him the correct interpretation of the Scriptures, and the description of a spirit-inspired interpreter and teacher of the Law in Sir 39.1-8.

No comparable investigation of the content of divine instruction in the OT and Jewish literature exists in the secondary literature, and chapters 2-3 open up a significant and unexplored interpretive possibility in the Fourth Gospel.

---

[1] Translation from *LW* 48.53-54.

[2] E.g. Exod 24.12; Deut 4.36; Jer 31.33-34; perhaps Isa 2.2-4; Mic 4.1-3.

[3] E.g. Josephus, *Ant.* 17.159.

They demonstrate that in the OT and early Jewish literature, the claim to have received divine instruction was sometimes a claim to have God-given insight into the Scriptures (sometimes more narrowly focused on the Mosaic Law).[4] My thesis in this chapter is that, similarly, in several passages in the Fourth Gospel, divine instruction is a claim to God-given insight into the Scriptures.[5] Some claims to divine instruction in the Fourth Gospel are comparable to the early Jewish phenomenon of charismatic exegesis.

The fourth evangelist's interpretation of Isa 54.13 is different from CD 20.4 and the rabbinic literature, in which the promised instruction of Isa 54.13 leads to Torah observance.[6] Such an interpretation was not possible for the fourth evangelist: while his view of the Mosaic Law is basically positive (it is seen as authentic revelation that witnesses to Jesus), it does not continue to function as an ethical norm, and is surpassed in the revelation brought by Jesus.[7] Rather, the evangelist employs the concept of divine instruction to legitimate his apologetic, Christological reading of the Scriptures, and as a polemic against those who disagree with this reading.[8] My thesis suggests that the claim of divine instruction would have been a powerful one in the context of a church-synagogue split. Moreover, it may well have been integral to the writing of the Fourth Gospel itself, functioning to legitimate the evangelist's own Christological interpretation of the OT.

6.1 Jesus and his disciples as 'taught by God'

In this section, I examine three passages in which divine instruction appears to be a claim to the revealed exegesis of the Scriptures.[9] Two of these

---

[4] Cf. Ps 119; 1QH^a 10.17; CD 20.4; Philo, *Mut.* 18; Sir 39.1-8.

[5] This is suggested in passing by Borgen, *Bread*, 150; Juel, 'Social Dimensions,' 550; Juel, *Messianic Exegesis*, 57, but never developed. By 'the Scriptures,' I intend the entire OT (cf. John 5.39).

[6] Rabbinic interpreters of Isa 54.13 claimed that the Lord would teach the Law in the last days. Cf. *Pesiq. Rab Kah.* 12.21.1; *Gen. Rab.* 95.3; *Deut. Rab.* 6.14; *Midr. Pss.* 21.1; TanB *Wayyiggash*, Gen 11.12 (S. Buber Recension); TanB *Yitro*, Exod 5.13 (S. Buber Recension); *Yal.* 2.317. This tradition is to be distinguished from another that understands Isa 54.13 as referring to the study of Torah (*Exod. Rab.* 38.3; *b. Ber.* 64a).

[7] Cf. Pancaro, *Law*, 528; Clark-Soles, *Scripture*, 324; Edwards, 'Grace,' 3-15, esp. 10.

[8] For the polemical and self-legitimating function of divine instruction in other literature, see my discussion of CD 20 in chapter 3. Note also the frequent patristic claim that Christian wisdom, because it is taught by God, is superior to Greek wisdom: e.g. Clement, *Strom.* 1.20; 2.11; Theophilus, *Autol.* 2.8-9, 33; Tatian, *Oratio ad Graecos* 29.1-2. Cf. Martin Luther, *To the Christian Nobility* (*LW* 44.134-35); *Misuse of the Mass* (*LW* 36.138-39, 151).

[9] My argument is not that every instance of divine instruction in the Fourth Gospel is a claim of revealed exegesis. The content of divine instruction is not always specified (8.28), and in some cases appears to be something else entirely (5.17-30).

passages concern Jesus (3.1-15; 7.14-19) and one, his followers (6.44-46). In all three passages, divine instruction functions polemically and to legitimate an interpretation of the Scriptures. Notably, all three passages appear in the first part of the Fourth Gospel (1.1-12.50), during Jesus' public ministry, in contexts in which Jesus engages in conversation or confrontation with Jewish teachers. This helps to explain the didactic terminology.[10]

Jesus as the heavenly teacher (John 3.1-15)

The conversation between Jesus and Nicodemus begins with Nicodemus addressing Jesus as 'Rabbi,' and his acknowledgment that 'you have come from God as a teacher' (3.2). This suggests that the context is not as polemical as it will become in chapters 7-8. Nevertheless, Jesus' acknowledgement that Nicodemus is 'the teacher of Israel' (3.10) develops a clear contrast between two teachers. The point of John 3 is that Jesus is an incomparably superior teacher.[11]

Nicodemus' misunderstanding of Jesus' reference to being born from above (ἄνωθεν) leads to his question in 3.4 ('how can one be born when he is old?') and Jesus' response in 3.5-8. Importantly, Jesus suggests that Nicodemus should not be surprised at what he says (3.7) and implies that Nicodemus, because he is the teacher of Israel, should know the things of which Jesus is speaking (3.10). These are earthly things, and *a fortiori*, how will Nicodemus believe the heavenly things of which Jesus speaks if he has not believed the earthly things (3.12)?[12] The earthly things of which Jesus speaks in 3.5-8 are the necessity of being born of water and the Spirit if one is to enter the Kingdom of God (3.5). Nicodemus should know that being born from above (3.7) and of the Spirit (3.8) is a necessary requirement for entering the Kingdom. These earthly things are contrasted with the heavenly things, which include Jesus' coming from, and going to, heaven via the lifting up of the cross (3.13-15).

For our purposes, it is important to ask why Jesus thinks Nicodemus, as the teacher of Israel, should know that one must be born from the Spirit and water in order to enter the Kingdom of God. The answer is probably that the elements of this idea appear in OT prophetic texts, in passages such as Ezek 36.25-27; 37.5, 14.[13] Jesus, as a 'teacher come from God,' is able to understand the eschatological import of the Scriptures, whereas 'the teacher of Israel' does not understand the Scriptures he is responsible for teaching to

---

[10] Cf. Schnackenburg, *St. John*, 2.132.

[11] Cf. Smith, *John*, 96, and see my discussion above in chapter 4.

[12] Meeks, 'Sectarianism,' 53-54 suggests that 3.12 is a typical cliché intended to put a slow learner in his place. However, the reference in 3.13 to Jesus ascending into heaven suggests otherwise.

[13] Cf. Carson, *John*, 191-98; Köstenberger, *John*, 124.

others. Furthermore, Jesus understands the heavenly things of his origin and destination, of which the Scriptures also speak (6.31-58). The rest of the Fourth Gospel demonstrates that the religious leaders understand neither earthly nor heavenly things, nor do they understand their own Scriptures. Although the claim that Jesus has been taught by God is not yet explicit in John 3, it is clear that Jesus has gained his insight from God, and is a *teacher* come from God (3.11, 32, 34).

Jesus' education and knowledge of the Scriptures (John 7.14-19)

7.14-19 narrates Jesus' teaching (7.14), the Jews' response (7.15), and Jesus' counter-response (7.16-19). The conflict between Jesus and the Jews continues throughout chapters 7-8, escalating until the Jews attempt to stone him, and he leaves the Temple (8.59). In this section, I focus on 7.14-19.

7.14 Ἤδη δὲ τῆς ἑορτῆς μεσούσης ἀνέβη Ἰησοῦς εἰς τὸ ἱερὸν καὶ ἐδίδασκεν.
7.15a ἐθαύμαζον οὖν οἱ Ἰουδαῖοι λέγοντες·
7.15b πῶς οὗτος γράμματα οἶδεν μὴ μεμαθηκώς;

In 7.14, Jesus enters the Temple and begins to teach. Although the Temple was a normal place in which to teach,[14] Jesus' teaching occasions astonishment from the Jews in 7.15a.[15] Comparison of 7.15 with 7.26, 32 suggests that the Jews are the educated, ruling elite, and not the crowd (ὁ ὄχλος) mentioned in 7.20.[16] The adverbial participle λέγοντες indicates that the Jews' astonishment is expressed by their question in 7.15b: πῶς οὗτος γράμματα οἶδεν μὴ μεμαθηκώς. There are two main options for how to interpret this question.[17]

First, πῶς may express astonishment that Jesus 'knows γράμματα' despite his lack of formal education. On this view, which is held by a significant number of scholars, the Jews marvel at Jesus' knowledge of γράμματα: it is amazing to them that he can know γράμματα even though he has not learned.[18] The perfect participle μεμαθηκώς is thus understood as

---

[14] E.g. Matt 26.55; Luke 2.46; 21.37. Cf. Schrage, 'συναγώγη,' *TDNT* 7.822; Rengstorf, 'διδάσκω,' *TDNT* 2.139.

[15] The rearrangement of Bultmann, *John*, 273 in which 7.15-24 follows 5.19-47, is unnecessary, since the reference to Jesus teaching (7.14) sufficiently introduces 7.15-24. Cf. Barrett, *John*, 317. For rearrangements of the section, cf. Schnackenburg, *St. John*, 2.130-31; Bernard, *John*, 1.xix-xx.

[16] 7.12-13 establishes a distinction between the Jews and the multitude. The identity of the Jews in the Fourth Gospel is, of course, debated. For one plausible thesis, cf. Motyer, 'Salvation of Israel,' 96.

[17] Cf. BDAG 900-901 for nuances of πῶς used in a direct question.

[18] Cf. e.g. Carson, *John*, 311; Lightfoot, *St. John*, 178; Bernard, *John*, 1.259; Barrett, *John*, 317; Witherington, *Wisdom*, 171-72; Köstenberger, *John*, 232; Keener, *John*, 1.712; BDAG 901.

concessive to the main verb οἶδεν. A paraphrase of 7.15 on this interpretation might be:

Therefore the Jews were marveling (at Jesus' incredible knowledge), saying, 'How is it that this one knows γράμματα, even though he has not learned?'

This interpretation, although common and certainly possible,[19] is somewhat problematic. An admission from the Jews that Jesus actually does know γράμματα sits uncomfortably within the context of John 7-8, where the Jews are portrayed as opposed to Jesus.[20] In addition, οὗτος in 7.15b ('how does *this one* know γράμματα?') may indicate a contemptuous, rather than merely surprised, response.[21]

I suggest, in light of these considerations, that πῶς more likely indicates doubt that Jesus does 'know γράμματα.'[22] The participle μεμαθηκώς is therefore causal: Jesus cannot know γράμματα because he has not learned. The use of πῶς to express doubt or impossibility is not uncommon in the Fourth Gospel and the rest of the NT.[23] It is used this way in 5.44a:

5.44a πῶς δύνασθε ὑμεῖς πιστεῦσαι δόξαν παρὰ ἀλλήλων λαμβάνοντες
7.15b πῶς οὗτος γράμματα οἶδεν   μὴ μεμαθηκώς

In 5.44a, Jesus calls into question the Jews' ability to believe: 'how are you able to believe, receiving glory from one another?' Here, the πῶς indicates doubt, and the participle λαμβάνοντες is causal, giving the ground of this doubt. Jesus does not ask in amazed wonder how the Jews are able to believe *despite* receiving glory from one another. Rather, the question casts doubt on their ability to believe by calling attention to the fact that they are receiving glory from one another. Similarly, in 7.15b the Jews' question casts doubt on the possibility that Jesus knows γράμματα, due to his lack of learning.

This understanding of πῶς in 7.15b suggests that the astonishment (θαυμάζω) in 7.15a is a surprised disapproval at Jesus' audacity in teaching rather than a marveling at his extraordinary knowledge. This interpretation is within the semantic range of θαυμάζω, which is not necessarily a positive

---

[19] Cf. Acts 4.13, on which, see Kraus, 'Uneducated,' 434-49.

[20] 7.1, 13, 32, 47-52; 8.22, 40, 48, 52, 59; although see also 8.30-31.

[21] Cf. Barrett, *John*, 317. For the contemptuous use of the demonstrative pronoun, cf. possibly 6.52; 7.27, 35; 18.30, 40; 19.12, although 7.31 suggests that it is not necessarily scornful.

[22] Cf. Schnackenburg, *St. John*, 2.131-32; Moloney, *John*, 242; possibly Beasley-Murray, *John*, 108.

[23] E.g. Matt 12.26, 34; John 3.12; 5.47; 6.52; Rom 6.2. Cf. LXX Gen 44.8; Exod 6.30; 2 Kgs 18.24. In most cases where πῶς indicates doubt or impossibility, either a future verb or a form of δύναμαι is used, e.g. Matt 12.26, 34; John 5.44a (see below). However, 1 John 3.17 demonstrates that πῶς with a simple present tense verb can express doubt or impossibility (cf. LXX Job 21.34).

word, and can indicate disapproval depending on context.[24] This is the case in 7.21, where those who are surprised at Jesus' healing miracle are also angry with him because of it.[25]

On this reading of 7.15b, the Jews imply by their question that Jesus does not know γράμματα. A paraphrase of 7.15b on this interpretation might be:

Therefore the Jews were astonished (at Jesus' audacity in teaching publicly), saying, 'This one cannot possibly know γράμματα, because he has not learned!'

In order to understand the Jews' claim more clearly, it is necessary to understand the phrase γράμματα οἶδεν and the participial phrase μὴ μεμαθηκώς. First, what is the meaning of γράμματα in 7.15b? When used without an article and in combination with verbs like ἐπίστασθαι or εἰδέναι, it often refers to primary learning, particularly reading.[26] This is not unexpected, since γράμματα often refers to letters of the alphabet (Gal 6.11). One who does not know letters is unable to read.[27] However, it is unlikely that γράμματα οἶδεν in 7.15b refers to primary education or to basic literacy. Both primary education[28] and literacy[29] were widespread enough in first century Judaism that it is unlikely they would occasion denial (or surprise) from the Jews in the narrative.[30]

---

[24] Cf. e.g. Mark 6.6; Luke 11.38; BDAG 444. See Wengst, *Johannesevangelium*, 1.276; Bultmann, *John*, 273; Pancaro, *Law*, 88.

[25] Cf. Beasley-Murray, *John*, 108.

[26] Cf. BDAG 206; *T. Levi* 13.2. In the בֵּית סֵפֶר, where primary education took place, students were taught to read but not to write. The latter was a professional skill, and less widespread than reading ability. Cf. Safrai, 'Education,' 952.

[27] Cf. LXX Isa 29.11-12.

[28] Primary schools are attested in the first century C.E. Cf. Schürer, *History*, 2.419 on *b. B. Bat.* 21a, and Hengel, *Judaism*, 1.81-83, who pushes this even earlier. Scholars differ on how early the primary school became widespread. Safrai, 'Education,' 948 probably goes too far in claiming that schools existed in every town in the first century. Note Neusner's methodological critique of Safrai in Wenthe, 'Rabbi-Disciple,' 153. It seems safest to conclude with Stemberger, *Talmud and Midrash*, 9 and Townsend, 'Education,' 316 that primary schools became the norm only in the second century. Even so, primary education occurred also in the home. One reason for the relatively late rise of primary schools in Judaism, compared to Hellenistic culture, may have been the Jewish emphasis on education in the home (cf. Townsend, 'Ancient Education,' 154) on the basis of OT commands such as Deut 6.7; 11.19 (cf. Barclay, 'Family,' 68-72). Cf. *Sipre* on Deuteronomy 46; Philo, *Legat.* 115, 210; Josephus, *C. Ap.* 1.60; 2.178, 204. On Jewish education generally, cf. Lemaire, 'Education,' 305-12.

[29] Although there is not a great deal of evidence as to the extent of literacy among average Jews in the first century, what evidence there is suggests that the ability to read was more widespread than some have thought. Cf. Millard, *Reading and Writing*, 157-58, 166-68, 179-82, whose examination of the archaeological evidence from Herodian Palestine is more persuasive than the unconvincing approach of Thatcher, 'Literacy,' 123-42, esp. 127-28.

[30] Cf. Schnackenburg, *St. John*, 2.131-32.

It is more likely that γράμματα οἶδεν has the broader sense of 'being educated.'[31] Bultmann suggests that the lack of a definite article before γράμματα precludes a one-to-one translation: 'How can this man understand the Scriptures?'[32] However, Bultmann is correct to note that since Jewish instruction was instruction in the Scriptures, 'to be educated' and 'to know the Scriptures' come to mean the same thing.[33] With this proviso, I can accept Schnackenburg's translation of γράμματα οἶδεν as 'know (the) Scriptures.'[34] Two other factors suggest that knowledge of the Scriptures is in view in 7.15b. First, the only other use of γράμματα in the Fourth Gospel is Jesus' reference to the γράμματα of Moses in 5.47, there clearly a reference to the Scriptures. Secondly, if Jesus' authority to interpret the Scriptures is in view in 7.14-18, this explains his otherwise abrupt claim in 7.19 that the Jews do not keep the Law: the Jews attack Jesus' knowledge of the Scriptures, and Jesus replies by charging that they themselves do not keep the Law.

If γράμματα οἶδεν refers to knowledge of the Scriptures, this suggests that the content of Jesus' teaching (διδάσκω) in 7.14 is the Scriptures. It also indicates that the claim that Jesus has not learned (μὴ μεμαθηκώς) refers to formal education of some kind,[35] rather than to realizing something through experience or practice.[36] Further, the reference is probably not to the primary education of the בית ספר, since simple literacy is not in view. The most likely reference is to Jesus' lack of formal education as the disciple of a recognized teacher.[37] Something like this sense of μανθάνω is attested elsewhere in Greek sources.[38]

In summary, my exegesis of 7.15ab suggests the following paraphrase:

This man cannot know the Scriptures, for he has not received instruction under a recognized master. It is unacceptable that he is teaching in the Temple!

John 7.15 is therefore an attempt by the Jewish leaders to delegitimate Jesus by highlighting his lack of formal education. Because he is not formally

---

[31] γράμματα can refer to higher learning: cf. BDAG 206; Acts 26.24.

[32] For γράμματα with the definite article referring to the Scriptures, cf. 2 Tim 3.15 (uncertain textually); Rom 2.27; 7.6. Cf. BDAG 205-6.

[33] Bultmann, *John*, 273.

[34] Schnackenburg, *St. John*, 2.129, 131-32. Cf. Neyrey, 'Trials,' 111.

[35] BDAG 615. Rengstorf, 'μανθάνω,' *TDNT* 4.408, understands it here as a technical term for the academic study of Scripture.

[36] E.g. Phil 4.11; Heb 5.8.

[37] Cf. Brown, *John*, 1.316; Schnackenburg, *St. John*, 2.131-32; Bernard, *John*, 259.

[38] Cf. the Moscow MS of the *Martyrdom of Polycarp* 22.2 (Holmes, *Apostolic Fathers*, 245). The author of the *Martyrdom* notes that Irenaeus claimed to have 'learned' (μανθάνω) from Polycarp, and earlier we are told that Irenaeus was a 'disciple' (μαθήτης) of Polycarp. Cf. BDAG 615.

educated, he is not qualified to teach the Scriptures publicly.[39] My reading is supported by that of Jerome Neyrey, whose contribution is to set the challenge and riposte of 7.14-19 within the honor-shame world of the first century, in which one's education, or lack thereof, was a source of honor or shame.[40] This reading of 7.14-19 suggests similarities with the scornful response of the Pharisees to the man born blind: 'You were born entirely in sins, and are you teaching [διδάσκεις] us?' (9.34). The implication of that question is, of course, that the man born blind has no right to teach the Pharisees because he was born in his sins. The question assumes a social hierarchy, defined in terms of education and knowledge of the Law, also evident in the division between the 'rulers and Pharisees' and ὁ ὄχλος, which does not know the Law (7.49).[41] In both 7.15 and 9.34, the religious leaders seek to delegitimate the teaching of one who does not belong to their educated elite.

The Jews' use of μανθάνω in 7.15b may be an instance of Johannine irony, intended for the perceptive reader. They suggest that Jesus is not a qualified teacher because he has not learned (μανθάνω). The only other use of μανθάνω in the Fourth Gospel is in 6.45, which speaks of individuals (and preeminently Jesus, as I argued in chapter 5) hearing and learning from God.[42] Ironically, therefore, the Jews point to the answer to their own question. Jesus is qualified to teach in the Temple because he does know the Scriptures, and he knows the Scriptures because he has learned them directly from God. This is in fact the substance of Jesus' reply. 7.16-19 is clearly spoken by Jesus in response to 7.15.[43] Because the issue raised by the Jews in 7.15 is Jesus' lack of formal education, his emphasis upon the source of his διδαχή should be understood as a counter-claim concerning his education. Jesus claims that his διδαχή ultimately has God as its source. His response in 7.16-17 is a claim to be taught directly by God (cf. 8.28).

Moreover, because the context of Jesus' claims about God's διδαχή is the debate about whether he knows the Scriptures (7.15), the most natural reading of the passage is that the διδαχή concerns the meaning of the Scriptures. Schnackenburg suggests that the evangelist gives διδαχή a 'new meaning' divorced from a reference to the Scriptures, but he gives no reasons for this claim other than to say that Jesus is directly proclaiming God's word and instructions.[44] However, this by no means precludes a reference to the

---

[39] See Origen, *Cels.* 1.29 for early Christian recognition of Jesus' lack of formal education.

[40] Neyrey, 'Trials,' 111, 119-20.

[41] Cf. Barrett, *John*, 332.

[42] Cf. Clark-Soles, *Scripture*, 250-51.

[43] Note the οὖν and the verb ἀποκρίνομαι in 7.16.

[44] Schnackenburg, *St. John*, 2.132.

Scriptures. As I suggested in chapter 4, the idea of revelation in first century Judaism is broad enough to allow for a reference to the Scriptures (i.e. revealed interpretation). Schnackenburg's interpretation pays insufficient attention to the context of 7.16-17. I conclude that in 7.14-19, divine instruction functions to legitimate Jesus' knowledge and teaching of the Scriptures. Moreover, the polemical implication of the passage is that the Jews are *not* taught by God, and do not understand their own Scriptures.

Jesus' disciples are taught by God (John 6.45)

Several considerations suggest that the evangelist understands Isa 54.13 to refer to the revealed interpretation of the Scriptures. First, 6.45b speaks of learning (μανθάνω) from the Father. As I observed above, the only other use of μανθάνω in the Fourth Gospel is in 7.15. In my discussion of that verse, I noted Rengstorf's suggestion that μανθάνω is used as a technical term for the academic study of the Scriptures.[45] This reflects similar usage in the OT and Jewish literature. Although one can learn many things, the Scriptures (primarily the Torah) are the preeminent object of teaching and study.[46] The point of the explanation in 6.45b, then, is that one learns the meaning of the Scriptures from God.

Secondly, there is a close parallel between 5.37-47 and 6.44-46:[47]

Table 1. *Comparison of John 5 and John 6*

You have not heard his voice (5.37)	Everyone who has heard from the Father (6.45)
You have not seen his form (5.37)	Not that anyone has seen the Father (6.46)
You search the Scriptures (5.39), but do not believe Moses (5.46) or his writings (5.47)	Everyone who has been 'taught by God' (6.45a), who has heard and learned from the Father (6.45b)...
You do not come to Jesus (5.40)	...is coming to Me (6.45b)

In John 5.39-47, Jesus claims that the Scriptures bear witness of him and that Moses wrote of him. In John 6.32-58, he demonstrates that this is so.[48] The contrast between those who do not believe the Scriptures in 5.39-47 and those who learn from the Father in 6.45b indicates that learning (μανθάνω) refers to understanding the Christological significance of the Scriptures.

Thirdly, in chapter 5, I suggested that the drawing (ἑλκύω) of 6.44b is parallel to the divine instruction of 6.45ab. In a substantial discussion of ἑλκύω, Michael Theobald has shown that in later rabbinic texts the verb 'to

---

[45] Cf. Matt 9.13.
[46] Cf. Rengstorf, 'μανθάνω,' *TDNT* 4.401-4; Rengstorf, 'διδάσκω,' *TDNT* 2.137-38.
[47] Cf. Borgen, *Bread*, 151.
[48] Cf. Borgen, 'John 6,' 111-13.

draw' is used for God drawing people through Torah and oral tradition.[49] While the rabbinic texts Theobald cites must be used cautiously (they date to about the third century), they indicate the possibility that in John 6.44-46, God draws people to Jesus by revealing to them the meaning of the Scriptures.[50]

Finally and most convincingly, the claim that Jesus' followers are 'taught by God' is set in the context of a *pesher*-like, exegetical discussion that occurs in the Capernaum synagogue (6.31-58).[51] Demonstration of this exegetical context, and the similarities with *pesher* exegesis, requires discussion of the structure of John 6 and an identification of the organizing center of Jesus' teaching (6.59). To begin, we may rule out two possibilities. First, Wayne Meeks' suggestion of an *inclusio* between 6.27 and 6.58, with the saying of Jesus in 6.27 functioning as the starting point of a midrashic exposition, does not sufficiently recognize the differences in terminology between 6.27 and 6.58, and the closer verbal links between 6.31 and 6.58.[52] Therefore, while Meeks rightly highlights the introduction of the theme of 'life' in 6.27, his suggestion is unconvincing.

More recently, Paul Anderson has argued that the 'words and works' of Jesus in 6.1-24 constitute the 'haggadic text' of Jesus' sermon in 6.25-66, with 6.27 serving as the main exhortation of the entire discourse.[53] However, while 6.25-66 sheds light on the significance of the feeding miracle in 6.1-14, Anderson's claim that 6.1-24 is interpreted in 6.25-66 is unconvincing. The repeated references to the 'fathers' who ate manna and died in the wilderness (6.31, 49, 58) indicate that the focus of attention in 6.32-58 is the OT text in 6.31b, not Jesus' feeding miracle in 6.1-14.

A more plausible suggestion is that Jesus' authoritative claim 'I am the bread of life' in 6.35a, the first of four such declarations in John 6, is the

---

[49] Theobald, 'Gezogen,' 324-26, 335. Cf. Schlatter, *Der Evangelist Johannes*, 176. Cf. *Mek.* on Exod 16.31; 18.7-8.

[50] As noted above in chapter 5, Theobald's own reading of 6.44-46 is unconvincing.

[51] In arguing this, I build on the seminal work of Peder Borgen (see below). Together with an increasing number of Johannine scholars, I consider 6.51-58 an integral part of John 6. Cf. Culpepper, *Readings*, *passim*, esp. 253; *contra* Brown, *John*, 1.284-94. For the unity of John 6, cf. Crossan, 'John 6,' 4.

[52] Cf. Meeks, 'Sectarianism,' 58, n. 50. John 6.27 refers to food (βρῶσις), while 6.58 refers to bread (ἄρτος). The similarities between 6.31, 58 point toward an *inclusio* there. Meeks does not adequately take into account Borgen's argument that 6.32-58 expounds the words from the citation in 6.31. Cf. Borgen, 'Debates,' 40 for a response to Meeks.

[53] Anderson, *Christology*, 52-61; Anderson, 'Bread,' 2. Anderson bases his argument on the observation that the Jewish sources use the manna tradition as a 'rhetorical trump' within the context of a larger argument rather than as the proem text of an exposition. But this is not decisive, since he admits that the manna motif is the main text in *Exod. Rab.* Cf. Anderson, *Christology*, 58-60. Attention to John 6 itself must decide the question of where the 'center' of the passage lies.

center and basis of the entire discourse, and that 6.35 as a whole provides the structure for the rest of Jesus' speech. This position has been well argued recently by several scholars, particularly Michael Theobald.[54] If 6.35 is the center and basis of the entire discourse, then Jesus' teaching seems unconnected to the Scriptures, perhaps even contrasted with them, because it is essentially a self-referential claim.[55] However, this reading is inadequate. Its main error is that it fails to read Jesus' 'I am' claim in 6.35 contextually. When read within the context of 6.31-58, Jesus' claim 'I am the bread of life' (6.35) is properly seen as his interpretation of the OT citation in 6.31: 'He gave them bread out of heaven to eat.'[56] In an authoritative interpretive move, Jesus identifies himself as the bread spoken of in the OT citation.[57]

Table 2. *The logic of John 6.31b-35*

6.31b: <u>ἄρτον</u> ἐκ τοῦ οὐρανοῦ ἔδωκεν αὐτοῖς φαγεῖν (LXX Ps 77.24)
6.32:   ἀμὴν ἀμὴν λέγω ὑμῖν introduces Jesus' authoritative interpretation:

οὐ...   **...ἀλλ'**
     not Moses,   *but* my Father
     not δέδωκεν (נָתַן – perfect tense),   *but* δίδωσιν (נֹתֵן – present ptcp)
     not bread understood as manna,   *but* true <u>ἄρτον</u> = Jesus

6.33:   FOR (γάρ) the '<u>ἄρτος</u> of God' is ὁ καταβαίνων ἐκ τοῦ οὐρανοῦ καὶ   ζωὴν διδοὺς τῷ κόσμῳ
6.34:   (misunderstanding): 'Give us this <u>ἄρτον</u> forever'
6.35a: (clarification of 6.33): ἐγώ εἰμι ὁ <u>ἄρτος</u> τῆς ζωῆς

6.32-33 provides the clearest evidence that Jesus is interpreting the OT citation in 6.31. Michael Theobald suggests that the ἀμὴν ἀμὴν λέγω ὑμῖν in 6.32 sets Jesus' own word over against the Scripture citation, and notes the similarity with the antitheses of Matthew 5. However, even if Theobald is correct in his interpretation of the Matthean antitheses, and this is open to

---

[54] Cf. Theobald, 'Schriftzitate,' 327-66; Theobald, *Herrenworte*, 245-58; Painter, 'Jesus,' 79-80; Hakola, *Identity*, 162-63. See also Beutler, 'Structure,' 115-27; Zumstein, 'Schriftrezeption,' 130-31.

[55] Cf. Hakola, *Identity*, 162-66, esp. 163.

[56] Words from the OT citation are underlined, following the example of Borgen, *Bread*, *passim*.

[57] Bultmann's complex rearrangement of 6.27-51a, in which 6.35 comes before 6.30-33, prevented him from seeing that 6.35 interprets 6.31. Cf. Bultmann, *John*, 221.

question,[58] he ignores the clear difference between the antitheses and John 6.32. In 6.32, the language of antithesis is not between the OT citation and Jesus' words, but between the correct and incorrect interpretations of the OT citation.[59] Therefore, ἀμὴν ἀμὴν λέγω ὑμῖν indicates the authoritative nature of Jesus' interpretation of the OT.[60]

The οὐ...ἀλλ' structure of 6.32 establishes both how the OT citation is not to be read, and how it should be read, but the crucial move that explains the authoritative reading advanced by Jesus is the assertion of 6.33 (note the γάρ). In 6.33, Jesus declares that the ἄρτος of the OT citation[61] is ὁ καταβαίνων ἐκ τοῦ οὐρανοῦ καὶ ζωὴν διδοὺς τῷ κόσμῳ. Within the context of the discourse and the larger context of the Fourth Gospel, this is a reference to Jesus himself, since the manna is said *not* to have given life to those who ate it (6.49, 58), and the Son of Man has been identified already in 3.13 as 'the one who descended from heaven.'[62]

However, as many commentators have noted, ὁ καταβαίνων is ambiguous: is it '*he* who comes down' (i.e. Jesus) or '*that* which comes down' (i.e. masculine participle, referring to the masculine 'bread')?[63] The crowd misses Jesus' claim that the bread is a person, and asks Jesus to give them the bread of which he has spoken (6.34). Jesus clarifies by identifying himself as the bread from the OT citation (6.35a)[64] and drawing out the implications of that fact (6.35b).

If this reading of 6.31-35 is correct, the arguments of Painter and Theobald that 6.35 is the center and basis of the entire discourse are mistaken. Rather, ἐγώ εἰμι (in 6.35, 41, 48, 51) is an identification formula demonstrating that Jesus is the bread of the OT citation, and clarifying the ambiguous ὁ καταβαίνων of 6.33. The use of ἐγώ εἰμι as an identification formula finds support from parallel formulae in the Fourth Gospel and in other Jewish literature. In a published study, I have noted these parallel formulae (as well

---

[58] Cf. Stanton, *New People*, 80, 301-3.

[59] *Contra* Theobald, 'Schriftzitate,' 346, n. 77; Hakola, *Identity*, 166.

[60] Cf. Borgen, *Bread*, 64.

[61] Now called the 'bread of God,' because Jesus has asserted that it is given by 'my Father' (6.31).

[62] Theobald, 'Schriftzitate,' 339-40 rightly argues (*contra* Borgen) that καταβαίνων is not taken from the haggadic tradition. It does not appear in connection with the manna tradition in Philo, as Borgen himself notes. Cf. Borgen, *Bread*, 21, 66-67. Rather, it is a direct reference to the Son of Man (3.13). The repeated references to the bread that descends (καταβαίνω) from heaven (6.41, 42, 50, 51, 58) build upon Jesus' identification of the bread and the Son of Man (6.33).

[63] Cf. Pancaro, *Law*, 463-64.

[64] The genitive 'of life' is used due to Jesus' claim that the bread of God 'gives life' to the world (6.33).

as the uniqueness of the 'I am' formula).[65] The formula ἐγώ εἰμι is certainly more than an identification formula, given all the overtones of ἐγώ εἰμι in the Fourth Gospel, but here it does identify Jesus as the bread of the OT citation.[66] In his full-scale study of the ἐγώ εἰμι-sayings in the Fourth Gospel, David Ball agrees that 'I am' functions as an identification formula in John 6, and extends this insight to argue that ἐγώ εἰμι + a predicate in the Fourth Gospel consistently refers to an Old Testament image.[67]

From the identification established in 6.33-35a (ἄρτος = Jesus), the Scriptural exegesis in 6.32 makes sense. First, Jesus says, 'Not Moses, but my Father...' Moses is not the subject of the verb ἔδωκεν in the Scripture citation, because the true referent of the word 'bread' is not the manna, but Jesus (and Moses does not give Jesus). Evidently, the crowd assumes that the subject of the verb in the OT citation is Moses. This is due to two errors: first, they think the verse refers primarily to the giving of the manna, and, secondly, they think Moses gave the manna. Maarten Menken has shown that in a number of Jewish sources, Moses-centered piety tended toward deification of Moses, and has plausibly argued that this accounts for the crowd's apparent ascription of the manna miracle to Moses.[68] Jesus corrects the crowd's reading of the Scriptures by interpreting the subject of ἔδωκεν as 'my Father.' Importantly, he corrects the crowd not by debating who gave the manna (Moses or God), but by suggesting that the OT text does not refer primarily to the manna at all. This is evident in what follows.

Secondly, if the bread of the citation refers to Jesus, then the verb should be read in the present tense, because Jesus himself is present: not 'gave,' but 'gives.' This is likely an instance of the *al tiqreh* formula found in the *midrashim*, Philo, and the DSS. As Borgen has suggested, the Scripture text is interpreted philologically: 'do not read δέδωκεν (נָתַן – perfect tense), but δίδωσιν (נוֹתֵן – present participle).'[69] Jesus' correction of both the subject and tense of the verb shows that he is not concerned with the question of who gave Israel manna in the desert but rather with the question of who currently gives the bread as he (not the crowd) understands it in the Scripture citation.[70] Because the bread is Jesus, the question is not who gave the manna, but rather

---

[65] Witmer, 'Approaches,' 313-28. Cf. Borgen, *Bread*, 72-73; Neugebauer, 'Miszelle,' 130.

[66] Cf. Borgen, *Bread*, 73, 78.

[67] Ball, *I Am*, 67-79, 259-60.

[68] Cf. Menken, *Quotations*, 54-65; Schuchard, *Scripture*, 43.

[69] Borgen, *Bread*, 62-64. *Contra* Hakola, *Identity*, 165-66; Theobald, 'Schriftzitate,' 346, n. 76, the presence of the method requires neither the exact terminology (cf. Brooke, *Exegesis at Qumran*, 280-81, 288-89), nor the readers' awareness. See John 12.40 for another possible instance of changing Hebrew vocalizations. Cf. Menken, *Quotations*, 110.

[70] Phillips, 'John 6,' 41 misses this point.

who presently gives Jesus.[71] This contemporizing of the OT text is also accomplished by Jesus' use of ὑμῖν in 6.32 (the OT citation has αὐτοῖς).[72]

Finally, what the Father gives is said to be the true 'bread from heaven.' The adjective ἀληθινός, used elsewhere of Jesus in the Fourth Gospel (1.9; 15.1), indicates that the bread of the OT citation refers to Jesus. Some scholars suggest that we have here a typology between the manna and Jesus.[73] However, while John 3.14 uses the language of typology to compare Jesus with the serpent, this is different from the οὐ...ἀλλ' structure of 6.32, which suggests that the true meaning of the OT citation does not concern Moses or the manna. Jesus' claim in 6.32-35, and the rest of the discourse, is that the true meaning of the OT citation concerns the eschatological event of his own descent from heaven.[74]

I conclude that in John 6.31-58, Jesus teaches (6.59) by advancing an interpretation of the OT citation in 6.31. The best articulation of this view remains Peder Borgen's well-known 1965 monograph *Bread from Heaven*,[75] in which Borgen argues that 6.32-48 interprets the first part of the OT citation ('He gave them bread out of heaven'), and 6.49-58 interprets the second part of the citation ('to eat').[76] This method of sequential exposition of an OT text is present in Philo and midrashic literature, as Borgen has shown.[77] While parts of Borgen's thesis are unconvincing,[78] I agree with his claim that John 6.32-58 is an interpretation of the OT citation.[79]

However, I would suggest that certain aspects of Jesus' biblical interpretation in 6.32-58 are closer to the Qumran *pesharim* than to the Philonic and midrashic examples Borgen offers.[80] In my previous study, I demonstrated similarities between John 6.31-58 and the *pesharim* in

---

[71] Cf. John 3.16: *God* gives his Son.

[72] I follow Borgen's suggestion that in 6.36, Jesus explains his use of ὑμῖν in 6.32: 'But I said "you" because you have seen me and do not believe.' Borgen, *Bread*, 74-75.

[73] Cf. Barrett, *John*, 290; Martyn, *History*, 128; Carson, *John*, 287. Against this, see Theobald, 'Schriftzitate,' 347, n. 81.

[74] Despite numerous disagreements with Theobald's understanding of this passage, there are also similarities in our readings. Theobald has brought out nicely Jesus' identification of the 'true' sense of the 'bread' as a reference to himself (Theobald, 'Schriftzitate,' 345-57).

[75] Cf. the positive reviews of Schnackenburg, 'Bread,'143-45; Martyn, 'Bread,' 244-45; Lindars, 'Bread,' 192-94. For critique, cf. Menken, *Quotations*, 50-51.

[76] Cf. Barrett, *John*, 284.

[77] Cf. Borgen, *Bread*, 34-35.

[78] E.g. most scholars agree that LXX Ps 77.24 is cited in 6.31. Cf. Menken, *Quotations*, 49-54; Schuchard, *Scripture*, 34-38; Obermann, *Erfüllung*, 132-36; Zumstein, 'Schriftrezeption,' 125. See also Geiger, 'Aufruf,' 449-64. This consensus undermines Borgen's theory of a homiletical pattern.

[79] Cf. Borgen, 'Debates,' 39; Borgen, 'Observations,' 232-40.

[80] Cf. Finkel, *Teacher*, 158-59 for identification of Jesus' teaching as a 'pesher-homily.'

lemmatic structure and identification formulae.[81] A further similarity is the authority of Jesus' interpretation. He offers an eschatological identification of the bread in the OT citation: it is himself. This opens up an understanding of the true meaning of the text, one not accessible without the identification 'bread = Jesus.'[82] The eschatological identification of the bread with himself, and the urgency of decision this should create in his hearers, is similar to *pesher* exegesis.[83] This urgency does not argue against the idea that Jesus interprets the Scriptures, as Martyn thinks; rather, it presents similarities with the eschatological urgency and immediacy of the *pesharim*.

This discussion demonstrates that Jesus' exchange with the crowd (6.24) and the Jews (6.41, 52) concerns the interpretation of the Scriptures. This exegetical debate about the identity of Jesus is the context of 6.45. The question raised by the Jews in 6.41-42 is how Jesus can be the 'bread from heaven' in the OT citation if his earthly origins are known. Jesus' reply in 6.44-46 therefore concerns a proper understanding of the Scriptures.[84] His response to the grumbling regarding his claim to be the 'bread' of the OT citation is to assert that no one is able to come to him unless the Father draws and teaches him.[85] Therefore, there is no point in grumbling, and the Jews should stop doing so (6.43). In this context, it seems likely that divine instruction refers to the revealed interpretation of the Scriptures. The similarities of 6.32-58 with *pesher* exegesis increase this likelihood, since similar claims are present in the *pesharim*.[86] This is a powerful polemical and self-legitimating claim: the reason that the Jews do not understand the Scriptures is that they are not able to, because they are not 'taught by God.' Jesus' followers, on the other hand, are 'taught by God,' and can understand that the Scriptures point to him.

In 7.14-19, divine instruction functions to legitimate Jesus in the face of accusations that he is uneducated. Does 6.45 similarly address a perceived lack of education among his followers? It is not possible to be certain. However, the Jews' question in 9.34 indicates that Jesus' disciples may, like Jesus himself, be marginalized because of their lack of education.

---

[81] Witmer, 'Approaches,' 313-28.

[82] Cf. the description of *pesher* exegesis in Dimant, 'Pesharim,' 249.

[83] Martyn, *History*, 128 captures well the urgency of Jesus' words.

[84] Cf. Borgen, *Bread*, 150-51.

[85] Note the use of δύναται in 6.44.

[86] Cf. 1QH^a 10.13, 17-18; 1QpHab 2.8; 7.4-5. See below in section 2.

6.2 'Taught by God' and charismatic exegesis

Having argued that the claim to be 'taught by God' is in several Johannine passages a claim to possess the divinely revealed interpretation of the Scriptures, I will now briefly examine the phenomenon of charismatic exegesis in early Judaism.[87] My suggestion in this section is that the claim of the Fourth Gospel that Jesus and his followers are 'taught by God' fits within the framework of charismatic exegesis. David Aune has suggested that charismatic exegesis is not identifiable by form, content, or function, but is essentially:

...a *hermeneutical ideology* that provides divine legitimation for a particular understanding of a sacred text which is shared with others who understand the text differently.[88]

The *sine qua non* of charismatic exegesis is, 'the implicit or explicit claim that the interpretation itself has been divinely revealed.'[89]

An early development of this idea may be seen in Ps 119.18, in which divine aid is required to understand the wonderful things (נפלאות) in the Law.[90] The idea of divinely revealed exegesis was widespread in early Judaism.[91] Hengel has argued that Zealot prophecy in the first century involved the charismatic interpretation of the Scriptures,[92] and Josephus' *B. J.* 3.351-54 demonstrates that Josephus understood himself to possess divinely given insight into dreams and the Scriptures.[93] In *2 Bar.* 4.1-7, God reveals the meaning of Isa 49.16 to Baruch.[94] In *Cher.* 27-29; *Mut.* 18; *Somn.* 2.252; *Spec.* 3.1-6, Philo claims to have inspired exegetical insights.[95]

For our purposes, the most interesting instance of charismatic exegesis is at Qumran.[96] Two passages from 1QpHab are important. 1QpHab 2.8 speaks of,

...the priest into whose heart God gave understanding to interpret all the words of his servants the prophets...[97]

---

[87] On the phrase 'charismatic exegesis,' cf. Aune, 'Charismatic,' 126.

[88] Aune, 'Charismatic,' 149. Cf. Mach, 'Implications,' 173.

[89] Aune, 'Charismatic,' 126.

[90] Cf. Fishbane, *Biblical Interpretation*, 539-41; Fishbane, 'Revelation,' 350; Aune, 'Charismatic,' 130. See chapter 2.

[91] Cf. Bockmuehl, *Revelation*, 13-14, 27-31, 44-45; Instone-Brewer, *Techniques*, 212, 222-25.

[92] Cf. Hengel, *Zealots*, 233-45.

[93] Cf. Aune, 'Charismatic,' 138-39; Levison, *Spirit*, 202-4.

[94] Mach, 'Implications,' 168-69.

[95] Cf. Levison, *Spirit*, 190-94; Hay, 'Exegete,' 40-52; Wan, 'Charismatic Exegesis,' 54-82. See chapter 3.

[96] On revelation and the study of Scripture at Qumran, cf. Betz, *Offenbarung, passim.*

1QpHab 7.1-5 claims that Hab 2.2 refers to the Teacher of Righteousness,

> to whom God has made known [הודיעו] all the mysteries [רזי] of the words of his servants, the prophets.

Both texts suggest that divine insight into the prophetic writings has been given to an individual within the community.[98] I noted above in chapter 3 that 1QHᵃ 10.13, 17-18, which speaks of divine instruction, has terminological parallels with these passages. Also interesting are several texts in 1QS claiming that the community's interpretation of the Scriptures is divinely revealed (1.9; 5.8-10; 9.13). Aune draws attention to 1QS 8.15, which suggests that revelation of the meaning of the Scriptures is an ongoing process:

> This is the study of the law wh[i]ch he commanded through the hand of Moses, in order to act in compliance with all that has been revealed from time to time [כבול הנגלה עת בעת].[99]

Although only a brief sketch of charismatic exegesis is provided here, three points may be noted. First, charismatic exegesis involves the claim that a particular interpretation of the Scriptures has been divinely revealed. I have argued in section 1 that this is the claim of John 3.1-15; 6.44-46; 7.14-19. Secondly, the widespread presence of charismatic exegesis in early Jewish sources, and its possible presence in other early Christian communities, suggests that it might plausibly be present in the Fourth Gospel.[100] Thirdly, Aune claims that charismatic exegesis is a 'hermeneutical ideology' providing divine legitimation for one reading of a text rather than another. I have suggested that this is the function of divine instruction in the Fourth Gospel. A key part of Aune's definition is that the sacred text is shared with others who understand it differently. If the text is not shared, it provides no legitimation.

This prompts the question, who are the 'others' with whom the Scriptures are shared in the Fourth Gospel? Two answers are possible. The claim to be 'taught by God' plausibly functions both at an early, intra-Jewish level and at a later, Christian (church) v. Jewish (synagogue) level. 1QHᵃ 10.17 and CD 20.4-6, discussed above, provide an example of the former. In these texts,

---

[97] For this reconstruction of the text, cf. Horgan, *Pesharim*, 25-26. Martínez García and Tigchelaar, *Scrolls*, 1.13 reconstruct the text differently, but the parallel between 1QpHab 2.8 and 1QHᵃ 6.8 favors Horgan's reconstruction. Cf. Brownlee, *Habakkuk*, 57.

[98] Aune, 'Charismatic,' 136 claims that 4QpPsᵃ 4.27 also ascribes divine insight to the Teacher of Righteousness, but the text is too fragmentary to be sure.

[99] I have here adapted the translation of Martínez García and Tigchelaar, *Scrolls*, 1.89. But see Levison, *Spirit*, 200, who notes the ambiguity of the Hebrew, which could mean 'age to age' and thus refer to revelation in the course of Israel's history.

[100] Cf. Aune, 'Charismatic,' 143-48.

divine instruction allows the Qumran community to know God's mysteries and be faithful to the covenant in a way that the larger Jewish community cannot be.[101] This suggests that the evangelist might plausibly have intended John 3, 6, and 7 to reflect an early first-century *Sitz im Leben*. However, this is not the only relevant setting for the claim to be 'taught by God.' I will suggest in what follows that it is relevant to the later church/synagogue situation.

6.3 The Johannine community as taught by God

There are several indications in the Fourth Gospel that the Johannine community itself is taught by God. First, 6.45ab claims that in order to come to Jesus, one must be 'taught by God.' As those who have come to Jesus, the entire community can presumably count itself as taught by God. This is the case even though some are likely Gentiles,[102] because the evangelist's redaction of the OT citation in 6.45a suggests that both Jews and Gentiles are taught by God. As I noted in chapter 4, 'your sons' in Isa 54.13 (both the Hebrew and Greek texts) is omitted in the citation. As many scholars have observed, this omission broadens the Isaianic promise of divine instruction, addressed to Israel in its original context, to include Gentile believers.[103] The evangelist's emphasis on Gentile inclusion throughout the Fourth Gospel strengthens the likelihood that this is his intention.[104]

Secondly, the exchange between Jesus and the Jews in John 7 may point in this direction. After Jesus speaks of his departure, the Jews confer among themselves:

He is not intending to go to the dispersion among the Greeks [διασπορὰν τῶν Ἑλλήνων] to teach the Greeks [διδάσκειν τοὺς Ἕλληνας], is he? (7.35)

With typical Johannine irony, the Jews unknowingly speak the truth. In his glorification, Jesus will draw all men (including Gentiles) to himself (12.32), and will teach the Gentiles.[105] The 'drawing' and 'teaching' of the Gentiles

---

[101] Cf. Betz, *Offenbarung*, 59.

[102] Cf. Keener, *John*, 1.158-59.

[103] E.g. Menken, *Quotations*, 75-77; Schuchard, *Scripture*, 56; Freed, *Quotations*, 19-20; Obermann, *Erfüllung*, 158-59; Schnackenburg, *St. John*, 2.51. The rabbis note the universal nature of divine instruction implied by the כל of Isa 54.13, but interpret this to refer to all *Israel* (*Pesiq. Rab Kah.* 12.21.1; TanB *Yitro*, Exod 5.13 [S. Buber Recension]).

[104] E.g. 1.29; 3.16-17; 4.42; 6.33, 51; 7.35; 8.12; 9.5; 10.16; 11.51-52; 12.32, 47. The use of πάντες in 6.45a does not imply an unqualified universalism. Cf. Menken, *Quotations*, 76.

[105] Cf. Barrett, *John*, 325. However, it is possible that Ἕλλην refers here to diaspora Jews rather than to Gentiles, e.g. Ridderbos, *John*, 271-72. Commentators disagree on this question.

occurs *after* the glorification of Jesus, and this points to a time beyond the narrative itself, i.e. to the time of the Johannine community. Finally, the disciples addressed in 14.26 are probably to be understood in a secondary sense as representative of the future community of believers, who will also be taught by the Spirit (cf. 1 John 2.20, 27).[106] These three points suggest that the promise of divine instruction is extended beyond the narrative to include the believing reader/hearer of the Fourth Gospel.[107]

If the Johannine community did understand itself as 'taught by God,' how was this heard and received?[108] Answers to this question must be suggested with appropriate caution. Most of this chapter has dealt with the narrative of the Fourth Gospel itself, because I am skeptical about reconstructing a history of the Johannine community from the narrative, which is intended to tell us primarily about the life of Jesus and his immediate disciples.[109] The 'Jews' should not be read merely as a cipher for the synagogue, because the evangelist distinguishes between the time before and after Jesus' glorification and resurrection.[110]

Nevertheless, although it is not possible to know much about the community, the unique theology, language, and style of the Fourth Gospel and the Johannine letters suggest that they were written to and within a distinct community.[111] It is likely that by the time of the writing of the Fourth Gospel, this community had experienced some kind of rift, whether local or widespread, with the Jewish synagogue. If the Fourth Gospel was written to a Christian community already expelled from the Jewish synagogue, the claim that Christians were 'taught by God' and thus uniquely enabled to understand the Jewish Scriptures as pointing to Jesus would have had a powerfully self-legitimating function.[112] Aune's description of 'charismatic exegesis' is apropros:

---

[106] Cf. Schnackenburg, *St. John*, 3.84; Lagrange, *Saint Jean*, 424-25. See esp. 14.16; 17.20.

[107] Cf. Culpepper, *Johannine School*, 274-75.

[108] Cf. Schnelle, *New Testament Writings*, 482.

[109] The methodological dangers of reconstructing the Johannine community from the Fourth Gospel are increasingly recognized in Johannine scholarship. See Klauck, 'Community,' 82-90; Kysar, 'Community,' 65-81; Bauckham, *Gospels, passim*; Mitchell, 'Counter-evidence,' 36-79, esp. 37. For a penetrating critique of the two-level hypothesis, cf. Hägerland, 'Two-Level,' 309-22.

[110] Cf. 2.17, 22; 7.39; 8.28; 12.16. Hengel, 'Eye-witness,' 71 points also to 17.20-21; 20.29. On the post-Easter perspective of the Fourth Gospel, cf. Hoegen-Rohls, *Der nachösterliche Johannes, passim*.

[111] See chapter 4.

[112] Pancaro, *Law*, 507-8, 525, 530 helpfully brings out the significance of the Johannine apologetic for the church-synagogue rift, although he goes too far in speaking of the 'Jamnian' school giving rise to a 'normative' and 'monolithic' Judaism (495).

...[the divinely revealed interpretation] often exhibits a marked sectarian orientation, and the thrust of the interpolated or interpreted text serves to reinforce or legitimate the group's particular view of the present or program for the future.[113]

In her recent study of the social function of the Scriptures in the Johannine community, Clark-Soles has highlighted the role of the Scriptures in the debate with the synagogue.[114] However, she fails to recognize the more fundamental insight that the claim of divine instruction in the Fourth Gospel functions to legitimate the community's *interpretation* of the Scriptures over against the synagogue.

My proposal is strengthened by noting that the Johannine claim to be 'taught by God' constitutes an early development in continuity with Christian writings of a slightly later date. Justin's *First Apology* emphasizes that the Jews fail to understand the Scriptures, while Christians recognize their fulfillment in Christ (31). In his *Dialogue with Trypho*, composed perhaps around 155 C.E., Justin claims that the Jews do not understand the sense of the Scriptures they read (14.2; 29.2). Justin accuses the Jews of being self-deceived (32.5), ignorant of the Scriptures, and lacking in understanding of their Christological meaning (9.1; 34.1-7; 43.8; 53.1-6; 68.3-4). He suggests that God has hidden from the Jews the ability to discern the meaning of his words in the Scriptures (55.3).[115] Stephen Wilson claims that the crucial arguments in Justin's *Dialogue*,

...turn on the meaning of a common scripture. Both participants accept that to win the argument would be largely a hermeneutical victory. The authority of the scriptures is a presupposition, which is assumed but not discussed....[116]

A belief in the 'hidden meaning' of the Scriptures, which Christians grasp but Jews miss, is evident in *Barnabas*, likely written in the first half of the second century. The author claims that the ability of Christians to understand the Scriptures is a gift from God.[117] Similarly, Origen's *Cels.* 2.4-6, written in the early third century, asserts that only Christians have a true understanding of the Law. They treat the Law with greater honor than the Jews, who read it superficially.[118]

These examples demonstrate the claim of some early Christians that they understood the meaning of the Jewish Scriptures, while the Jews missed their Christological significance. My exegesis of John 3.1-15; 6.31-58; 7.14-19 has

---

[113] Aune, 'Charismatic,' 150. On the sectarian nature of the Johannine community in relation to Judaism, cf. Esler, *First Christians*, 84-90.

[114] Clark-Soles, *Scripture*, 322.

[115] I owe the Justin references in this paragraph to Lieu, *Image and Reality*, 124-29 and Wilson, *Related Strangers*, 270-71.

[116] Wilson, *Related Strangers*, 270, cf. 267, 284.

[117] *Barn.* 6.8-10; 10.9, 12.

[118] I owe this reference to Wilson, *Related Strangers*, 281.

demonstrated that similar claims are made in the Fourth Gospel, and that these claims are supported by the assertion that Jesus and the Johannine community are 'taught by God.' The evangelist's claim is not simply that Jesus and his followers understand the meaning of the Scriptures. It is also that the Jewish leaders, with all their educational advantages, do not understand them (5.39-47).

6.4 The teaching of the Spirit and the writing of the Fourth Gospel

John 14.25-26 is unlike the passages examined in section 1 above. It does not appear within the public, polemical context of John 1-12, but is spoken by Jesus in the context of his last great discourse, in John 13-17. Two observations are relevant to our study. First, the primary recipients of the promise of the Paraclete's teaching in 14.26 are the original disciples. I indicated above that in some sense the disciples of chapters 14-16 are representative of the future community of believers. However, in 14.26 the Johannine community is only secondarily in view. The main purpose of 14.26 is to demonstrate to readers of the Fourth Gospel how the original disciples came to an accurate understanding of Jesus' life and teaching after his glorification and resurrection. This is decisively indicated by the recurring theme of the disciples' post-resurrection memory of Jesus in 2.17, 22; 12.16, passages which are linked to 14.26 by the references to remembering.[119]

The uniform emphasis in 2.17, 22; 12.16 upon the Scriptures[120] suggests a second point; that the promised teaching of the Paraclete/Spirit in 14.26 is (in part) a promise to the original disciples that the Spirit will reveal to them the Christological meaning of the Scriptures.[121] The teaching of the Spirit clearly recalls Jesus' teaching,[122] which, as we have seen above, is understood in some passages to be an interpretation of the Scriptures (e.g. 6.59; 7.16-17), so this suggestion is plausible. It is the Christogical significance of the Scriptures that is finally understood through the work of the Spirit/Paraclete. É. Cothenet and others have highlighted precisely this aspect of the work of the Spirit/Paraclete in the Fourth Gospel.[123] John 20.9 offers confirmation of this suggestion. The 'not yet' of 20.9 suggests that the disciples' original

---

[119] Cf. Carson, *John*, 505.

[120] Cf. Ps 69.10 in 2.17; Zech 9.9 in 12.15-16. Perhaps the general OT prediction of God's vindication of the Messiah is in view in 2.22 (cf. Barrett, *John*, 201).

[121] Cf. Origen's reading of John 16.12-13 in *Cels.* 2.2. This focus on the Scriptures is missed by Schnelle, 'Geisttheologe,' 17-31.

[122] Cf. Schnackenburg, *St. John*, 3.83.

[123] Cothenet, 'Témoignage,' 367-80, esp. 372. Cf. Obermann, *Erfüllung*, 390-408; Stuhlmacher, 'Remembering,' 63; Burge, *Anointed Community*, 212.

incomprehension of the Christological reference of the Scriptures is eventually replaced by insight. This motif is extended to Jesus' word in 2.22, which links the disciples' post-resurrection understanding of Jesus' word and the Scriptures. In light of the fact that the Fourth Gospel grants Jesus' words equal (and greater) status with the Scriptures (2.22; 18.9, 32),[124] the promised teaching of the Spirit/Paraclete should probably be understood to consist of the revelation of the meaning of both the Scriptures and Jesus' own words.

If the proper interpretation of the Scriptures is in view in 14.26, this is of great significance. The original disciples are promised continued divine instruction so that they can perceive the way in which the Scriptures point to Jesus. Even after Jesus has departed, the disciples will be helped to continue on rightly discerning the Christological meaning of the Scriptures.[125] This legitimates the *evangelist's* interpretation of the story of Jesus and his use of the OT throughout the Fourth Gospel. The evangelist can assert that Isaiah spoke of Jesus (12.37-41), because he is taught by the Spirit (14.26).[126] His abundant apologetic use of the OT through citations and allusions[127] is legitimated by the divine instruction of the Spirit.

6.5 Conclusion

I have argued in this chapter that, according to the evangelist, Isaiah's promise of eschatological divine instruction is fulfilled as God teaches the true (Christological) meaning of the Scriptures.[128] This divinely taught interpretation of the Scriptures is given first to Jesus as the student of God *par excellence*, and comes to Jesus' disciples through Jesus (6.46) and the Spirit (14.26). The Johannine claim is analogous to the widespread phenomenon of charismatic exegesis, particularly as that phenomenon manifests itself in the Qumran *pesharim*. The claim of divine instruction

---

[124] Cf. Stuhlmacher, 'Remembering,' 64.

[125] There is debate concerning whether or not the Paraclete provides new revelation beyond Jesus' teaching. Cf. T. Brown, *Spirit*, 209; Brown, *John*, 2.650; Kothgasser, 'Offenbarung,' 586-98. In my view, the Spirit grants new insights to the original disciples, but these are in continuity with Jesus' revelation. Cf. Burge, *Anointed Community*, 211-17.

[126] Cf. Stuhlmacher, 'Remembering,' 63.

[127] For secondary literature on the use of the OT in the Fourth Gospel, cf. Witmer, 'Citation,' 134-35.

[128] The Johannine passages I have examined in the present chapter emphasize this aspect of the fulfillment of Isa 54.13. However, it is likely that the evangelist sees Isa 54.13 as fulfilled in *all* the words of Jesus, not just his interpretation of the Scriptures. As noted above, in the Fourth Gospel, Jesus' words ultimately have greater status than the Scriptures. Moreover, even when Jesus interprets the Scriptures, he claims that they point beyond themselves to him (e.g. John 5.39-40).

legitimates the uneducated Jesus and his uneducated followers over against the educated Jewish leaders. Moreover, it was likely heard in the Johannine community as a claim that they understood the Jewish Scriptures better than the synagogue. In this respect, it represents an early development of a polemic common in the Christian literature of the second and third centuries. Finally, I have suggested that the promise of the Spirit's instruction legitimates the Christological exegesis of the Fourth Gospel itself.

Chapter 7

The anointing that teaches all things

'Therefore said he, that with the budding rod
Did rule the Iewes, All shalbe taught of God...

Now once a weeke vpon the Sabbath day,
It is enough to doo our small deuotion,
And then to follow any merrie motion...

By that he ended had his ghostly sermon,
The Foxe was well induc'd to be a Parson;
And of the Priest eftsoones gan to enquire,
How to a Benefice he might aspire.'

Edmund Spencer, *Prosopopoia, or Mother Hubberds Tale*, 1591[1]

In this chapter, I examine the idea of divine instruction in the Johannine letters.[2] As in chapters 5-6, I am interested in how the author has interpreted the promise of divine instruction, and in how the concept functions. However, the question of greatest interest is how divine instruction affects human teaching.

7.1 Didactic terminology in the Johannine letters

Didactic terminology in the letters is infrequent compared to the Fourth Gospel: διδάσκω is used three times in 1 John 2.27, while διδαχή appears twice in 2 John 9 and once in 2 John 10. The only instance in which this terminology is brought into close conjunction with a reference to God is 1 John 2.27, where the 'anointing' is a reference to the Spirit (see below). Also unlike the Fourth Gospel, in neither 1 John 2.27 nor 2 John 9-10 does the didactic terminology obviously relate to the Scriptures. Rather, it is related to proper affirmations about Jesus. In 1 John 2.20, 27 the teaching of the

---

[1] de Selincourt and Smith, *Poetical Works of Spenser*, 499-500. I owe this reference to Edwards, *John*, 77.

[2] See chapter 4 for my discussion of the relationship between the Fourth Gospel and the Johannine letters.

'anointing' concerns the person of Jesus.[3] In 2 John 9-10, the διδαχή is opposed to the deceivers who do not acknowledge Jesus Christ as coming in the flesh. As I suggested in chapter 4, this difference between the Fourth Gospel and the Johannine letters likely reflects their different milieux.

A clear similarity with the Fourth Gospel is that the didactic terminology of the letters is focused upon Jesus. Jesus and the 'anointing' are the only mentioned sources of teaching. While humans are said to bear (φέρω) the διδαχή of Christ (2 John 10), no one, including the author himself, is said to teach. 1 John 2.27 probably refers to the teaching of the earthly Jesus,[4] and Jesus is likely the source of the 'anointing' that teaches all things (2.20, 27).[5] The genitive Χριστοῦ in 2 John 9 (διδαχῇ τοῦ Χριστοῦ) is probably subjective ('Christ's teaching'),[6] although it may also be objective ('the teaching concerning Christ'). This emphasis of the letters on Jesus as the source of teaching raises the possibility that didactic terminology in the letters, as in the Fourth Gospel, expresses the concept of revelation. I will return to this point below in section 5, because it offers a fresh way forward in the interpretation of 1 John 2.20, 27. A final point is that 2 John 9 manifests a 'conserving' approach toward teaching, warning that everyone who goes ahead (προάγω) and does not remain in the 'teaching of Christ' (διδαχῇ τοῦ Χριστοῦ) does not have God.[7]

7.2 An allusion to Jeremiah 31.34 in 1 John 2.20, 27

As noted above in chapter 1, I am interested in this study in all references to divine instruction, but particularly in allusions to Isa 54.13 and Jer 31.34 [LXX Jer 38.34], which promise eschatological divine instruction. A comparison of 1 John 2.20, 27 and LXX Jer 38.34 reveals several verbal and conceptual parallels.

Table 1. *LXX Jer 38.34 and 1 John 2.20, 27*

LXX Jer 38.34	καὶ <u>οὐ μὴ διδάξωσιν ἕκαστος τὸν πολίτην αὐτοῦ καὶ ἕκαστος τὸν ἀδελφὸν αὐτοῦ</u> λέγων γνῶθι τὸν κύριον ὅτι <u>πάντες εἰδήσουσίν</u> με ἀπὸ μικροῦ αὐτῶν καὶ ἕως μεγάλου αὐτῶν...
1 John 2.20b	καὶ <u>οἴδατε πάντες</u>
1 John 2.27b	καὶ <u>οὐ χρείαν ἔχετε ἵνα τις διδάσκῃ ὑμᾶς</u>

---

[3] It fortifies believers against the deceivers (2.26) who deny that Jesus is the Christ (2.22).

[4] See below for argument that Jesus is the subject of ἐδίδαξεν.

[5] See below.

[6] Cf. Brown, *Epistles of John*, 674-75.

[7] Cf. 1 John 2.14, 24.

The presence of an allusion to LXX Jer 38.34 is suggested by three considerations. First, the combination of πᾶς + οἶδα (third person plural in LXX Jer 38.34, second person plural in 1 John 2.20b) in both passages is noteworthy. Secondly, the lack of human instruction under Jeremiah's new covenant is closely parallel to the lack of need for instruction in 2.27b, and the verb διδάσκω is used in both passages. Finally, I will argue below that the reading πάντες is the most probable one for 2.20b. If this is correct, an allusion to LXX Jer 38.34 explains the choice of the nominative πάντες and the lack of grammatical object for οἴδατε, which is a deviation from Johannine style. If the expression οἴδατε πάντες functions in 1 John 2.20b as a marker pointing back to LXX Jer 38.34, the object of knowledge is not so important as the status of the community as those who 'know' in accordance with the new covenant prophecy.[8]

I conclude on the basis of these considerations that an allusion to Jer 31.34 is likely. Carson is perhaps overly confident when he claims that 'it is hard not to detect a link' between the two passages, and that the connection is 'rather obvious.'[9] However, a significant number of scholars agree that an allusion to Jer 31.34 is present.[10] This is further supported by the possibility of an allusion to Jer 31.33-34 only a few verses earlier, in 1 John 2.12-14.[11] Because it combines didactic terminology with a reference to God and alludes to Jer 31.34, 1 John 2.27 is of significant interest for this study. I will ask how the author of the letters understood the fulfillment of the promise of divine instruction in Jer 31.33-34, what effect he understood divine instruction to have upon human teaching, and how divine instruction functions in the letters.

7.3 The χρῖσμα in 1 John 2.20, 27

It is of great importance for our study to establish the meaning of the 'anointing' (χρῖσμα) in 1 John 2.20, 27. If the 'anointing' refers to the Spirit, we have a striking and important reference to divine instruction. If the 'anointing' refers to something else (e.g. the word of God), we must conclude that the theme of divine instruction is not explicitly developed in the

---

[8] Cf. Couture, 'Teaching Function,' 45.

[9] Carson, 'No Need,' 274.

[10] In addition to Carson and Couture, cf. e.g. Westcott, *Epistles*, 79; Brown, *Epistles of John*, 349, 370, 375; Beutler, *Johannesbriefe*, 75; Stuhlmacher, 'Remembering,' 63. Kennedy, 'Covenant,' 23-26 argues that 1 John draws on a 'covenant-conception,' but strangely does not mention 2.20-27. Boismard, 'La connaissance,' 365-91 also fails to mention the influence of Jer 31.34 on 1 John 2.27.

[11] Cf. Marshall, *Epistles*, 138; Couture, 'Teaching Function,' 45-47.

Johannine letters. Before addressing the meaning of the 'anointing,' it is first necessary to establish the text and structure of the two verses in which the term appears.

Establishing the text of 1 John 2.20

The most significant textual question in 2.20 is whether we should read the nominative πάντες ('and you are all knowing') or the accusative πάντα ('and you are knowing all things'). As Raymond Brown has rightly noted, the external support for the readings is too close to decide between the two.[12] The case must therefore be decided on the basis of internal evidence. David Black has argued that the reading πάντα is original. According to Black, the correspondence between 2.20 and 2.27 suggests that the accusative πάντα in 2.20 is more likely, since 2.27 has περὶ πάντων. Moreover, if the nominative πάντες is original, the verb οἶδα must be used absolutely, but this is never the case elsewhere in the Fourth Gospel and Johannine letters. Finally, Black suggests that the parallels in John 14.26 (ἐκεῖνος ὑμᾶς διδάξει πάντα) and 16.30 (οἶδας πάντα) point toward the accusative πάντα as the more natural Johannine expression in 1 John 2.20.[13]

The main weakness of Black's argument is that he offers no explanation for how the reading πάντες originated if πάντα was original. It is more likely that πάντες was original, and then changed by a copyist to πάντα in order to conform to Johannine style.[14] Although πάντες with an absolute use of οἶδα is not typically Johannine, three factors explain the abnormal style. First, as I have already suggested, the author may use the nominative πάντες under the influence of LXX Jer 38.34 (πάντες εἰδήσουσίν με). Secondly, if the 'antichrists' of 2.18-29 are claiming to have a special knowledge of truth limited to themselves, the nominative πάντες may emphasize the knowledge of the *whole* community.[15] Finally, a nominative πάντες in 2.20 contrasts nicely with the nominative πάντες in 2.19.[16] I conclude, together with the majority of commentators, that πάντες is the original reading:

2.20a καὶ ὑμεῖς χρῖσμα ἔχετε ἀπὸ τοῦ ἁγίου
2.20b καὶ οἴδατε πάντες

Establishing the text and structure of 1 John 2.27

Although 2.27 contains numerous variant readings, the printed text of the NA-27 almost certainly preserves the original readings in each case. As

---

[12] Brown, *Epistles of John*, 348; cf. Breck, 'Function,' 205; Le Fort, *Les Structures*, 32.
[13] Black, 'Argument,' 205-8.
[14] Cf. Smalley, *1,2,3 John*, 91-92; Painter, *1, 2, and 3 John*, 199.
[15] Cf. Brown, *Epistles of John*, 348-49; Dodd, *Epistles*, 53.
[16] Cf. Klauck, *Johannesbrief*, 156; Schnackenburg, *Epistles*, 143.

Raymond Brown has demonstrated, the variants are intentional scribal emendations, meant to correct the considerable grammatical and lexical obscurity of the verse.[17] External and internal evidence points toward the readings preserved in the NA-27.

Table 2. *The structure and grammar of 1 John 2.27*

2.27a καὶ ὑμεῖς τὸ χρῖσμα ὃ ἐλάβετε ἀπ᾽ αὐτοῦ, **μένει** ἐν ὑμῖν
2.27b καὶ <u>οὐ</u> χρείαν **ἔχετε** ἵνα τις διδάσκῃ ὑμᾶς,
2.27c <u>ἀλλ᾽</u>
ὡς τὸ αὐτοῦ χρῖσμα διδάσκει ὑμᾶς περὶ πάντων
2.27d   καὶ ἀληθές ἐστιν
2.27e   καὶ οὐκ ἔστιν ψεῦδος,
2.27f   καὶ καθὼς ἐδίδαξεν ὑμᾶς,
2.27g **μένετε** ἐν αὐτῷ.

With this text, the grammar of the verse is difficult, but not impossible to construe. The sentence has three main verbs (μένει, ἔχετε, μένετε) and is built around an οὐ... ἀλλ᾽ construction: the χρῖσμα remains in the community (2.27a) and as a result, the members of the community do not have a need for anyone to teach them (2.27b), but rather they are remaining in Jesus (2.27g).[18] Recognition of the οὐ...ἀλλ᾽ structure in 2.27 suggests that since the verb ἔχετε is indicative, μένετε is also indicative.[19] Furthermore, 2.27c-f should be understood as a two-fold causal ground for the assertion in 2.27g that the community is remaining in Jesus:[20] *inasmuch as/because* (ὡς) the anointing teaches the community concerning all things and *inasmuch as/because* (καθώς) Jesus taught the community,[21] they are remaining in Jesus.[22] 2.27d-e is a parenthetical expansion, emphasizing the trustworthiness of the χρῖσμα. This interpretation of 1 John 2.27 can be paraphrased:

---

[17] Brown, *Epistles of John*, 360.

[18] My grammatical analysis is very similar to that of Malatesta, *Interiority*, 223.

[19] For commentators on either side of the question of whether μένετε is indicative or imperative, cf. Strecker, *Johannine Letters*, 76. There are several οὐ...ἀλλ᾽ constructions in 1 John (e.g. 2.2, 7, 16, 21; 4.10, 18; 5.6, 18) and two μή...ἀλλ᾽ constructions (3.18; 4.1). None of these pair an indicative with an imperative. Nor do the similar constructions in the Fourth Gospel and 2 John.

[20] The repetition of 'remain in him' in 2.28, where it clearly refers to Jesus, suggests that the αὐτῷ in 2.27g is also Jesus. Cf. Calvin, *1, 2, & 3 John*, 49.

[21] καὶ καθὼς ἐδίδαξεν ὑμᾶς probably refers to the teaching of Jesus, because the phrase is unnecessarily redundant if 'the anointing' is the subject of ἐδίδαξεν. Furthermore, this explains the shift from the present tense διδάσκει in 2.27c to the aorist ἐδίδαξεν in 2.27f, and renders unnecessary the complicated and grammatically problematic reading of Brown, *Epistles of John*, 360-61.

[22] Both ὡς and καθώς can be used causally. For causal uses of ὡς, cf. Matt 6.12; Acts 28.19; 2 Pet 1.3 (BDAG 1105). ὡς is possibly causal in John 2.9; 4.1; 6.16; 11.6, 20, 29, 33;

And you, the χρῖσμα which you received from Jesus is remaining in you, and as a result, you do not have a need for anyone to teach you, but rather you are remaining in Jesus, inasmuch as Jesus' χρῖσμα is teaching you concerning all things – and is true and is not a lie – and inasmuch as Jesus taught you.

Identifying the 'anointing'

The proper identification of χρῖσμα in 1 John 2.20, 27 is a source of much debate. A number of scholars have argued that it refers to 'what you have heard from the beginning' (2.24), that is, the word of God, or the teaching of the community.[23] The strongest argument for this view is the parallel between 2.24a and 2.27a.[24]

Table 3. *1 John 2.24a and 2.27a*

2.24a	ὑμεῖς ὃ ἠκούσατε ἀπ᾽ ἀρχῆς,	ἐν ὑμῖν μενέτω
2.27a	καὶ ὑμεῖς τὸ χρῖσμα ὃ ἐλάβετε ἀπ᾽ αὐτοῦ,	μένει ἐν ὑμῖν

However, several considerations call into question this identification of the 'anointing' with what was heard from the beginning. First, although the language of 'abiding in you' is used of both the χρῖσμα and 'what you heard from the beginning,' many things in 1 John are said to 'abide in' the believer. One of these is 'the word of God' (2.14), but the list also includes 'God's seed' (3.9), 'eternal life' (3.15), 'the love of God' (3.17), and 'God' (3.24; 4.13-16).[25] It is clear that 'eternal life' and 'the love of God' are not to be aligned with the 'anointing' in the sense that they *are* the 'anointing.' This should caution against identifying the χρῖσμα and 'what you heard from the beginning' on the basis of this parallel.

Secondly, there is a difference between 2.24 and 2.27; the former is a command, while the latter is a statement of fact. This suggests that the χρῖσμα should perhaps be distinguished from 'what you heard from the beginning.' The main point of 2.18-27 is the command in 2.24 to, 'let that abide in you which you heard from the beginning,' and everything else in the passage functions to support this main point. 2.20 and 2.27 are affirmations that the community already has the χρῖσμα, and that the χρῖσμα *does* abide

---

18.6. καθώς is causal in John 17.2; Rom 1.28; 1 Cor 1.6; 5.7; Eph 1.4; 4.32; Phil 1.7 (BDAG 494).

[23] Reitzenstein, *Mystery-Religions*, 505-6; Dodd, *Epistles*, 63; Houlden, *Epistles*, 79; Lieu, *Epistles*, 28-31; Beutler, *Johannesbriefe*, 73; T. Brown, *Spirit*, 241. Prete, 'L'unzione,' 211-14 notes some of the main arguments for this position.

[24] Cf. T. Brown, *Spirit*, 241; de la Potterie and Lyonnet, *Spirit*, 107.

[25] T. Brown rightly notes that nowhere in 1 John is the Spirit said to 'abide' in the faithful; rather, the Spirit is said to constitute proof of *God's* abiding in believers (3.24; 4.13).

in them. This community possession of the χρῖσμα grounds the author's command for the community to let the original message remain in them.[26]

Thirdly, identification of the χρῖσμα as 'what you heard from the beginning' fails to explain convincingly the language of 'anointing.' Why is the word of God referred to as χρῖσμα? C. H. Dodd argues that the term χρῖσμα is borrowed from the opponents who have withdrawn from the community, and that it refers to initiation into supernatural knowledge; he then concludes that since all Christians underwent baptism, χρῖσμα refers to the Word of God communicated to catechumens and confessed in baptism.[27] I. de la Potterie points to the language of 'anointing by faith' in Clement of Alexandria, and refers also to second century pre-baptismal anointings.[28] However, both hypotheses are tenuous, relying as they do on later evidence, and (in Dodd's case) the speculation that the author draws his language from the opponents.

Finally, a significant and often overlooked problem with identifying the χρῖσμα as the teaching of the community is the claim in 2.27 that 'his anointing' teaches (διδάσκω) the community. In chapter 4 of this thesis, we saw that the Fourth Gospel uses διδάσκω nine times, always with a personal subject. Its other two uses in 2.27 take personal subjects.[29] In the Fourth Gospel, διδάσκω is never used with an impersonal subject, and in the rest of the NT it is used only one time with an impersonal subject.[30] It would therefore be unusual for the writer of 1 John to state that 'what you heard from the beginning' teaches the community; that is not the way διδάσκω is used in the Johannine, or indeed the early Christian, tradition.[31]

---

[26] Cf. Burge, *Anointed Community*, 175. Michl, 'Geist,' 144-45, n. 21 rightly concludes that the author of 1 John distinguishes between 'what you heard from the beginning' (2.24) and the 'anointing' (2.20, 27), but unconvincingly argues for this by suggesting that the author ascribes differing effects to them. According to Michl, the effect of the abiding of 'what you heard from the beginning' is an abiding in the Son and in the Father (2.24), while the effect of the abiding of the 'anointing' is knowledge of the truth (2.20). Michl fails to note that the effect of the 'anointing' in 2.27 is an 'abiding in him' (2.27g).

[27] Dodd, *Epistles*, 58-64.

[28] de la Potterie and Lyonnet, *Spirit*, 117-35.

[29] The first use of the verb in 2.27 has τίς as its subject, while the implied subject of the third use of the verb in 2.27 is probably Jesus himself, as I argued above.

[30] Cf. 1 Cor 11.14, where nature (ἡ φύσις) teaches. διδάσκω is used 96 times in the NT (excluding John 8.2, which is not original).

[31] Thus, Marshall, *Epistles*, 154 is wrong to assert that, 'the thought of teaching by the "anointing" (v. 27) fits in nicely with the identification of the anointing as the Word of God.' On the didactic language as an argument for the Spirit, cf. also Schnackenburg, *Epistles*, 141, n. 39; Hiebert, '1 John,' 83. Importantly, de la Potterie and Lyonnet, *Spirit*, 115, n. 66 acknowledge the force of this argument against views that exclude the role of the Spirit in 1 John 2.27. T. Brown's view appears intentionally to exclude the role of the Spirit: 'All in all,

This point raises an important methodological issue. Tricia Brown suggests that it is methodologically unsound to use the parallels in John 14.16-17, 26 (where the Spirit-Paraclete abides and teaches) as direct evidence that the 'anointing' in 1 John 2.20, 27 is the Spirit.[32] In response, I would argue that even if we grant that the Fourth Gospel and 1 John were written by different individuals, and that the parallels between the Fourth Gospel and 1 John do not function as *direct* evidence for reliance of the latter upon the former, it is nevertheless appropriate to note parallels between the two works, and to hypothesize that, at the very least, their writers had access to common traditions, ways of thinking, and verbal expressions.

Much work has been done in recent years on the importance of 'in-group' language in the Pauline communities, and in particular the importance of such language for reinforcing group identity.[33] I suggested above in chapter 4 that the Fourth Gospel and the Johannine letters belong to a single community. If this is correct, we should expect similar verbal expressions, even if we do not postulate direct literary dependence between the Johannine letters and the Fourth Gospel.[34] I suggest that these similar expressions can be used, with due caution, in matters of interpretation.[35]

There are several clear verbal parallels between 1 John 2.27 and the Fourth Gospel, though most of these are not probative in identifying the referent of the 'anointing.' In John 14.17, Jesus promises his disciples that the 'Spirit of truth' will abide with them and will be in them (παρ' ὑμῖν μένει καὶ ἐν ὑμῖν ἔσται). This language is almost identical to the claim in 1 John 2.27 that the 'anointing' will 'remain in you' (μένει ἐν ὑμῖν). However, as noted above, the Johannine writings refer to many things that 'remain in' the believer, so this parallel does not offer a definitive argument for identifying the 'anointing' as the Spirit/Paraclete. If we look in the Fourth Gospel for parallels to the language of receiving (λαμβάνω) the anointing in 1 John 2.27, we find references to receiving the Spirit (John 7.39; 20.22, cf. 14.17),

---

evidence suggests that the anointing that the community is told abides in them, denotes the "word", *not* the spirit' (241, my emphasis).

[32] T. Brown, *Spirit*, 240. See also Lieu, *Epistles*, 30. Klauck, 'Gemeinde,' 214 reads 1 John 2.27 as a direct remembrance of the teaching of the Paraclete in John 14-16.

[33] Cf. e.g. Meeks, *Urban Christians*, 93-94; Meeks, 'Apocalyptic Language,' 687-705; Barclay, 'Social Dialect,' 157-67.

[34] T. Brown, *Spirit*, 20-21, acknowledges the linguistic and stylistic similarities between the Fourth Gospel and the 1 John.

[35] T. Brown, *Spirit*, 252-53 herself sets out something like this approach as methodologically sound. She limits herself to looking for 'general Johannine traditions,' but offers no reason why verbal expressions could not also have been common within the Johannine community.

but also to receiving Jesus' words (John 12.48; 17.8).[36] Again, this is not a definitive argument in either direction.

I argued above that the use of διδάσκω in 1 John 2.27 constitutes a serious difficulty for the view that the χρῖσμα is equivalent to the word that was heard from the beginning (2.24). However, there *is* precedent both in the Johannine tradition (John 14.26) and in the broader Christian tradition (Luke 12.12) for asserting that the Spirit teaches.[37] Comparison of John 14.26 and 1 John 2.27 demonstrates a similar use of the didactic terminology:

Table 4. *Comparison of John 14.26 and 1 John 2.27*

John 14.26	ἐκεῖνος ὑμᾶς	διδάξει	πάντα
1 John 2.27 ἀλλ' ὡς τὸ αὐτοῦ χρῖσμα		διδάσκει ὑμᾶς περὶ πάντων	

This common use of the didactic terminology points toward an identification of the χρῖσμα with the Holy Spirit, a view that enjoys the support of the majority of contemporary scholars, and was held already by a range of earlier interpreters, including Augustine, Cyril of Jerusalem, Bede, and Calvin.[38] In its favor we may note, in addition to the Johannine language of the Spirit teaching, the connection between the Spirit and 'anointing' language in both the OT and NT.[39]

Against this view, Tricia Brown argues that, given the common OT connection between anointing and the Spirit, the fact that 1 John claims a χρῖσμα for the community without reference to the Spirit 'could signal a *deliberate avoidance* of spirit on [the author's] part.'[40] Similarly, Judith Lieu suggests that since the author of 1 John uses the term 'spirit' elsewhere, it would be strange for him to use a different term in 2.20, 27 for the same reality.[41] Both arguments are unconvincing. In response to Brown, we may note that if the author of 1 John wanted to avoid reference to the Spirit, it would have been far more effective to avoid the use of a word associated with the Spirit. To use such a word would be confusing and counter-productive if his intention was to avoid a reference to the Spirit. In response to Lieu, we

---

[36] Cf. de la Potterie and Lyonnet, *Spirit*, 101.

[37] The original hand of Sinaiticus actually reads 'just as his Spirit teaches you all things' in 1 John 2.27, recalling John 14.26. Cf. de la Potterie and Lyonnet, *Spirit*, 103; Breck, 'Function,' 190-91.

[38] Cf. Calvin, *1, 2, & 3 John*, 44. For a list of proponents of this view, cf. Brown, *Epistles of John*, 345; Prete, 'L'unzione,' 215. Among modern scholars who identify the χρῖσμα as the Spirit are Westcott, *Epistles*, 73; Le Fort, *Les Structures*, 32; Bultmann, *Epistles*, 37; Schnackenburg, *Epistles*, 141; Stott, *Letters*, 111-12, 114-15; Grundmann, 'χρίω,' *TDNT* 9.572; Brown, *Epistles of John*, 345-47; Burge, *Anointed Community*, 174-75; Burge, *Letters*, 128; Klauck, *Johannesbrief*, 157.

[39] E.g. 1 Sam 16.13; Isa 61.1; Luke 4.18; Acts 10.38; 2 Cor 1.21-22. Cf. Hesse, 'χρίω,' *TDNT* 9.503.

[40] T. Brown, *Spirit*, 241, 244, italics original.

[41] Lieu, *Epistles*, 29.

need simply observe that on her view as well, the author uses a different term (i.e. χρῖσμα) to refer to something expressed with other terminology elsewhere (i.e. what was 'heard from the beginning' in 2.24). Her argument is therefore not decisive.

Brown and Lieu helpfully raise the question of why the term χρῖσμα is used in 1 John 2.20, 27. If the author is referring to the Spirit, why does he employ an unusual word[42] instead of simply using πνεῦμα? I suggest that χρῖσμα is used for two reasons. First, the use of χρῖσμα creates a word-play that contrasts the community with the ἀντίχριστοι of 2.18-19, 22,[43] and identifies the community with the Χριστός of 2.22.[44] The deceivers are opposed to the anointed one (the Christ), while the community has an anointing from the Christ. Secondly, the use of χρῖσμα highlights the separateness and holiness of the community by using a word associated with the setting apart of a chosen individual.[45]

A number of scholars have argued for a mediating position, i.e. that the χρῖσμα refers to the word of God made active by the Spirit.[46] The most often cited formulation of this view is that of de la Potterie:

…the anointing is indeed *God's word*, not as it is preached externally in the community, but as it is received by faith into men's hearts and remains active, *thanks to the work of the Spirit.*[47]

This view manages to avoid some of the arguments set forth above against the view that the χρῖσμα refers to the teaching of the community and not to the Spirit. However, it does not satisfactorily deal with the argument that in the Johannine corpus, διδάσκω always has a personal subject, for it still identifies χρῖσμα (at least primarily) as 'God's word.' Moreover, it melds the word and Spirit, whereas the author of 1 John seems to distinguish the two in 2.18-27.

I began this section by noting the importance of determining the proper referent of the χρῖσμα in 1 John 2.20, 27. I conclude, on the basis of contextual and lexical considerations, that the most likely referent is the Spirit. The claim that the Spirit (χρῖσμα) teaches the community is therefore

---

[42] χρῖσμα is used only here in the NT. Cf. Prete, 'L'unzione,' 204.

[43] This contrast is also indicated by the emphatic position of καὶ ὑμεῖς in 2.20, 27.

[44] Cf. Klauck, *Johannesbrief*, 156. ἀντίχριστος is clearly intended to contrast with ὁ Χριστός in 2.22. *Contra* Schnackenburg, *Epistles*, 141, the two contrasts (with Christ, and with the community) are not mutually exclusive.

[45] Cf. Brooke, *Johannine Epistles*, 55-56.

[46] Cf. Malatesta, *Interiority*, 204; Smalley, *1,2,3 John*, 106-7 (who thinks the *primary* reference is to the Spirit); Marshall, *Epistles*, 155; Painter, *1, 2, and 3 John*, 198, 209; Couture, *Teaching Function*, 55; Strecker, *Johannine Letters*, 64-65 (although he is somewhat unclear).

[47] de la Potterie and Lyonnet, *Spirit*, 114-15.

a claim to divine instruction. The word πνεῦμα is used twelve times in 1 John.[48] In 3.24 and 4.13, the πνεῦμα is identified as God's own Spirit, which he has given to believers,[49] while in 4.2 the Spirit is described as the 'Spirit of God' (τὸ πνεῦμα τοῦ θεοῦ). The Spirit in these texts is likely understood as the presence of God.[50]

7.4 The teaching of God, the teaching of Jesus, and the teaching of the Spirit

The above discussion raises the question of how the writer of the letters interprets the eschatological divine instruction of Jer 31.33-34. In that passage, God places his Law within his people and writes it on their heart. As a result of this divine eschatological work, all God's people will know him, and human teachers will be unnecessary. The author of 1 John claims this status for the Christian community in 2.20, 27. But he re-interprets the divine instruction of Jer 31.33-34 in light of the teaching of Jesus and the teaching of the Spirit. As I have argued, the χρῖσμα of 2.20, 27 is the Spirit. Therefore, for the author of 1 John, the promise of Jer 31.33-34 is fulfilled in the Christian community through the teaching of the Spirit. Moreover, three factors suggest that the author closely connects the teaching of the Spirit with the teaching of Jesus.

First, the teaching of the Spirit is aligned with the past teaching of Jesus in 2.27c-f (see section 3). Secondly, the 'holy one' who gives the anointing is probably Jesus. In 2.20, the recipients are said to have the χρῖσμα 'from the holy one' (ἀπὸ τοῦ ἁγίου). Although 'the holy one' could be a reference to the Father,[51] the more likely referent is Jesus, on the basis of Johannine and early Christian usage.[52] In 2.27, where the anointing is said to be that 'which you received from him' (ὃ ἐλάβετε ἀπ' αὐτοῦ), and 'his anointing' (τὸ αὐτοῦ χρῖσμα), the context following 2.27 refers both to Jesus and God.[53]

---

[48] It does not occur in 2 or 3 John.

[49] Cf. Brown, *Epistles of John*, 465.

[50] Cf. Burge, *Anointed Community*, 173-74.

[51] This ambiguity is not unusual in 1 John, in which it is frequently difficult to determine whether pronouns refer to the Father or to Jesus.

[52] Cf. John 6.69. See also Mark 1.24; Luke 4.34; Acts 3.14; 4.27, 30; Rev 3.7. While Jesus refers to God as 'Holy Father' (πάτερ ἅγιε) in John 17.11, the adjective is not used substantively there.

[53] The use of παρουσία in 2.28 suggests that Jesus is in view, since the word almost always refers to the coming of Jesus in early Christian tradition. The claim in 2.29 that 'he is righteous' is inconclusive, since in 1 John both God (1.9) and Jesus (2.1) are called righteous. The reference to being 'born from him' in 2.29 is probably a reference to God; cf. 1 John 3.9; 4.7; 5.1, 4, 18; cf. John 1.13.

Although we must recognize that the giver of the χρῖσμα is not clearly identified (is it perhaps intentionally ambiguous?[54]), the most likely option is Jesus. This is the majority view among scholars.[55] Thirdly, I suggested in section 3 that the author refers to the Spirit with the unusual term χρῖσμα in order to identify the community with the χριστός of 2.22. Because the Spirit is given by 'Jesus the Christ,' he teaches in accordance with the teaching of Jesus. The reference to Jesus as ὁ χριστός raises the possibility that the Jewish expectation of the messianic teacher (see chapter 3) is in the background here.

These considerations suggest that 1 John 2.20, 27 interprets Jer 31.33-34 by means of a reference to the Spirit and to Jesus, the Christ. We saw above in chapter 5 that the author of the Fourth Gospel does very much the same thing, interpreting Isa 54.13 in light of Jesus and the Spirit/Paraclete (John 6.45-46; 14.26).

7.5 Does the teaching of the χρῖσμα affect teaching structures in the Johannine community?

In this section, my purpose is to inquire whether an understanding of the Spirit as one who teaches (1 John 2.27) had an impact upon teaching and governing structures in the Johannine community. This question is brought sharply into focus by 1 John 2.27b: καὶ οὐ χρείαν ἔχετε ἵνα τις διδάσκῃ ὑμᾶς. What is the meaning of this provocative claim, and what is its relation (if any) to Johannine ecclesiology? On an initial reading, 2.27b appears to claim that the teaching of the anointing-Spirit renders all human teaching unnecessary. This is indicated by the fact that 2.27b ('you have no need for anyone to teach you') follows as the result of 2.27a (the possession of the anointing). It is also indicated by the οὐ...ἀλλ' construction of 2.27b and 2.27c, which contrasts human instruction with the instruction of the anointing (2.27c) and of Jesus (2.27f).

Numerous commentators have remarked upon the apparent inconsistency of the comment in 1 John 2.27b, since it appears in a heavily didactic letter.[56] Unsurprisingly, the verse has attracted the attention of many scholars and generated a variety of interpretations regarding how 2.27b relates to the Johannine ecclesiology. Some have argued that 2.27b evidences a causal relationship between the Johannine view of the Spirit as teacher, and the lack of teaching and authority structures in the Johannine community. In order

---

[54] Cf. Brown, *Epistles of John*, 348; Grundmann, 'χρίω,' *TDNT* 9.572.

[55] Cf. Brown, *Epistles of John*, 348.

[56] E.g. Smalley, *1,2,3 John*, 125.

properly to evaluate the various interpretations of 2.27b, and the possible relationship of this verse to Johannine ecclesiology, we must first address the complicated question of Johannine ecclesiology.

Johannine ecclesiology

More than one question is involved here. We must ask, first, whether the Johannine corpus conceives of a 'church' at all, or whether it promotes a completely individualistic version of Christianity. Secondly, if there *is* a Johannine conception of the church, a community of believers, does it include a hierarchical structure with teaching offices? There is little or no consensus on these questions.[57]

On one end of the spectrum is Rudolf Schnackenburg, who, while recognizing that ἡ ἐκκλησία is not used in the Fourth Gospel or 1 John, argues that the idea of the Church is indispensable to Johannine theology.[58] In the Fourth Gospel, Jesus' gaze is fixed on the future Church, as evidenced by the corporate imagery of the flock in John 10, and the imagery of the vine and branches in John 15. Schnackenburg also notes the commissioning of Peter in John 21.[59] He concludes that in the churches of the Johannine communities 'liturgical and sacramental life was flourishing,'[60] and that a strong interest was felt for mission.[61] Stephen Smalley also affirms that the concern of the Fourth Gospel and the Johannine letters is corporate, although he notes a shift in ecclesiology between the Fourth Gospel and the letters; as the community begins to divide, the focus in the letters shifts from the wider Church to the local Johannine community.[62]

On the other end of the spectrum are Rudolf Bultmann, Ernst Käsemann, Eduard Schweizer and C. F. D. Moule, who stress the individualism of the Fourth Gospel and its lack of ecclesial concern.[63] Schweizer suggests that in the Johannine vision (both the Fourth Gospel and the letters), there is no church order comparable to the rest of the New Testament. Individual believers do not need other believers: 'They are all equal, perfect units living side by side. One seed grows beside another, one branch beside another, one sheep feeds beside the other.' According to Schweizer, in the Johannine communities, there 'is no church order at all.'[64] Käsemann also argues that

---

[57] Note the wide range of positions in O'Grady, 'Ecclesiology,' 36-44.

[58] Schnackenburg, *Church*, 103-4.

[59] He recognizes that chapter 21 may be an addition, but suggests that it nevertheless belongs to the evangelist's tradition.

[60] Schnackenburg, *Church*, 111.

[61] See Schnackenburg, *St. John*, 1.162-64.

[62] Smalley, 'Community,' 95-104.

[63] Moule, 'Individualism,' 171-91, esp. 182-85.

[64] Schweizer, 'Church,' 236-37. Cf. Schweizer, *Order*, 124.

the Johannine community has 'let the apostolate, the ministry and its organization melt into the background.'[65] What unites the Johannine church is not tradition or organization, but the Word and the Spirit.[66] Bultmann suggests that the Church is only indirectly dealt with in the Fourth Gospel, and that (due largely to the Gnostic influence upon the Fourth Gospel) no particular interest is shown in cult or organization.[67]

In between these ends of the spectrum is a range of positions. J. L. D'Aragon, while appreciating the emphasis on individualism suggested by Schweizer and Bultmann, argues that there are sacramental developments in the Fourth Gospel, and some idea of church office (in chapter 21). D'Aragon also notes the Johannine development of the idea of the unity of believers with Jesus, the Father, and one another as their distinctive mark.[68] Pierre Le Fort argues that there is ecclesiastical authority in the community, but that such authority is subordinated to christology.[69]

Raymond Brown is the most influential scholar in this middle ground. As we will see below, he holds that the Spirit *relativizes* the teaching office in the Johannine community. Nevertheless, he resists the view of Schweizer that there was no church structure in the Johannine community. In his discussion of Johannine ecclesiology, Brown engages the frequent arguments from silence advanced by those who advocate a total lack of ecclesiology in the Fourth Gospel. Brown rightly notes that some things may receive no mention in John, not because the author disagrees with them, but rather because they are presupposed.[70] Brown also suggests that the Johannine emphasis on the individual relationship with Jesus does not negate the emphasis on community and unity, and notes the idea of church order (John 20.23; 21.15-17) and mission (4.35-38; 13.20).

What are we to make of this wide range of opinion? The comments of D. Moody Smith are helpful. While suggesting that Schweizer's description of Johannine ecclesiology is a 'reasonable inference' from the text, Smith notes that it is not the only possible inference, and that, 'Exegesis will lend some support to more than one interpretation...'[71] Smith cautions that, 'a residual element of uncertainty remains when one extrapolates from the implications and omissions of a document that does not deal explicitly with ecclesiology a doctrine of the church.'[72]

[65] Käsemann, *Testament*, 31.
[66] Cf. O'Grady, 'Ecclesiology,' 39.
[67] Bultmann, *Theology*, 2.91-92.
[68] For this summary of D'Aragon's position, cf. O'Grady, 'Ecclesiology,' 39-40.
[69] Le Fort, *Les Structures*, *passim*. I owe this summary to Brown, 'Review,' 454-56.
[70] Cf. Brown, *John*, 1.cv-cxi; O'Grady, 'Individualism,' 229.
[71] Smith, *Johannine Christianity*, 3.
[72] Smith, *Johannine Christianity*, 2.

While it seems we can safely posit that the Johannine writings are not solely individualistic and do have a conception of the Christian community, it is difficult to know how many teaching and authority structures there actually were in the Johannine community. The term ὁ πρεσβύτερος is used in 2 John 1 and 3 John 1, but this may be a term of respect rather than an established office.[73] The 'we' of 1 John 1.1-4; 4.6 does not require the presence of a group of authoritative teachers.[74] The commissioning of Peter in John 21 may be important, but we cannot infer from it a fully developed hierarchical structure.

It is important, then, to recognize the difficulty of establishing a causal relationship between the idea of the Spirit/Paraclete as teacher (1 John 2.27; cf. John 14.26) and the Johannine ecclesiology. In order to demonstrate that the Johannine view of the Spirit as teacher resulted in a lack of teaching structures and hierarchy in the Johannine community, one would first need to demonstrate that there *was* a lack of teaching structure and hierarchy. But it is difficult or impossible to establish with certainty the Johannine ecclesiology from the texts available to us, and 1 John 2.27 cannot bear that weight by itself.

Interpretations of 1 John 2.27b

It is helpful to consider the various interpretations of 1 John 2.27b on a continuum; from those scholars who see here a radical statement of anti-hierarchicalism and no teaching authority in the community, to those who see no necessary conflict with the presence of established teaching authorities in the Johannine community.[75] Here, I distinguish six positions, recognizing that some may be partially compatible with others.

Table 5. *Summary of views on 1 John 2.27b*

Views that take 2.27b as rendering obsolete or relativizing some or all kinds of human teaching				Views that do not take 2.27b as rendering obsolete any human teaching	
#1	#2	#3	#4	#5	#6
No human teaching: Schweizer, Büchsel; Rensberger	Relativizing human teaching: Brown, Burge	No 'mediating' teachers: Carson, Westcott	No false teachers: Bultmann, Houlden, Smalley, Burge, Hiebert	*Sensum fidelium*: Calvin, Michl, Stott?	Two-fold teaching: Augustine, Malatesta, Schnacken-burg, Marshall

---

[73] Cf. Klauck, 'Gemeinde,' 207, although Donfried, 'Authority,' 325-33 makes a case that ὁ πρεσβύτερος refers to a teacher and ecclesiastical officer.

[74] Cf. Brown, *Epistles of John*, 94-97.

[75] Strecker, *Johannine Letters*, 76-77 is unclear on how 2.27 should be interpreted with regard to human teaching.

(1) This view has two variations. E. Schweizer claims that 1 John 2.20, 27 is the 'most radical statement' of the Johannine view of the church:

> Here there is no longer any kind of special ministry, but only the direct union with God through the Spirit who comes to every individual; here there are neither offices nor even different charismata; here there is only the witness of the Spirit himself.[76]

Schweizer sees no teaching authority at all in the Johannine community, a situation perhaps somewhat similar to the one mischievously envisioned in Edmund Spencer's *Prosopopoia* (see the epigraph at the beginning of this chapter). A similar view is held by F. Büchsel.[77] Schweizer seems to suggest that this is not only the ideal vision of 1 John 2.27, but actually reflects the reality of the Johannine community. David Rensberger argues, like Schweizer, that the author promotes the vision of a church without teachers.[78] However, unlike Schweizer, Rensberger suggests that the author nonetheless continues to function as a teacher.[79]

The advantage of Schweizer and Rensberger's hypotheses is that they both take 2.27 very seriously, particularly the claim οὐ χρείαν ἔχετε ἵνα τις διδάσκῃ ὑμᾶς. However, they are both problematic. Schweizer's work relies on a questionable overall reconstruction of Johannine ecclesiology (see above), and opens the author of the letter to the charge of inconsistency; while saying that no teaching should occur, he appears to be doing just that in 1 John itself. This latter problem is heightened in the case of Rensberger. It is of course possible that Rensberger's charge of blatant inconsistency is correct. However, such inconsistency would be obvious to the letter's recipients and would undermine the rhetorical effectiveness of the letter. It is unlikely that an otherwise careful author would make this mistake.

(2) Raymond Brown advocates a position close to that of Schweizer. He speaks of a 'lack of organized teaching authority' in the Johannine community, and of 'the author's vision of a Christianity without human teachers,'[80] and claims that 1 John renders otiose the function or office of teaching.[81] This all sounds like Schweizer. Nevertheless, in some places Brown prefers to speak of the teaching of the Spirit/Paraclete as 'relativizing' institutions and offices rather than abolishing them altogether.[82] Brown suggests that the Paraclete as the authoritative teacher and the possession of

---

[76] Schweizer, *Order*, 127. Cf. Schweizer, 'Church,' 238-40.

[77] Büchsel, *Johannesbriefe*, 42.

[78] Rensberger, *John*, 83, claims that the author puts forward a 'nearly anarchic concept of the church.'

[79] Rensberger, *John*, 83.

[80] Brown, *Epistles of John*, 375.

[81] Brown, *Epistles of John*, 93.

[82] See the important statements in Brown, *Community*, 87 and Brown, *Epistles of John*, 94.

the Paraclete by every believer, 'would have *relativized* the teaching office of any church official.'[83] Brown's claim that 1 John renders otiose the function or office of teaching seems inconsistent with his claim that the teaching office is only relativized. In any case, Brown clearly does not agree with Schweizer's picture of a radically egalitarian and individualistic community.

On Brown's reconstruction, the 'we' of the Johannine school thought of themselves as witnesses (not teachers), who were vehicles of the one teacher, the Paraclete.[84] In his view, the amalgamation of the Johannine church with the larger church, 'must have been at the price of the Johannine acceptance of authoritative church teaching structure, probably because their own principle of the Paraclete as the teacher had not provided sufficient defense against the secessionists.'[85] Gary Burge follows Brown in claiming that the Paraclete relativizes the authority of any single teacher.[86] Brown's reconstruction of the Johannine community, from a pre-Gospel phase to the period after the writing of the letters, is an exciting and imaginative *tour de force*.[87] One of the recurring themes of his reconstruction is precisely this feature of the community; that the teaching of the Paraclete has relativized its teaching and authority structures. However, it must be asked whether Brown's view, like that of Schweizer and Rensberger, exposes the author of 1 John to the charge of inconsistency, since for all intents and purposes he is teaching through his writing of the letter, even if he does not refer to his activity as teaching. This leads directly to the next position to be discussed.

(3) In a recent essay, D. A. Carson suggests that Raymond Brown's view that 1 John 2.20, 27 renders all teaching otiose leads to inconsistency on the part of the author of 1 John, since the author is clearly teaching in 1 John itself. Carson argues that 1 John 2.20, 27 indeed renders teaching unnecessary in the Johannine community, but that the 'anointing' renders obsolete a particular *kind* of teacher, not all teachers in general.[88] Carson's thesis emphasizes the allusion to Jer 31.34 (LXX 38.34) in 1 John 2.20, 27, and argues that this background causes the writer's argument to take on a 'new specificity.' Because Jer 31.34 suggests that not teachers *per se*, but *intermediary* teachers, will no longer be needed under the new covenant,

---

[83] Brown, *Community*, 141, my italics.

[84] Brown, *Epistles of John*, 96. Although Dodd, *Epistles*, 63 interprets the 'anointing' as the Word, he also sees a relativizing of teaching roles; although human teaching can be helpful in developing the implications of the gospel, it is not necessary.

[85] Brown, *Community*, 24.

[86] Burge, *Anointed Community*, 173, cf. page 40. In his recent commentary, however, Burge takes 2.27 as a polemic against false teachers, apparently differing from his earlier view. See below.

[87] See also Brown, 'Ecclesiology,' 379-93.

[88] Carson, 'No Need,' 269-80. This position is perhaps adumbrated in Westcott, *Epistles*, 79.

Carson understands 1 John 2.27 to mean, 'You do not need anyone to teach you in a mediating sort of way.'[89] Teaching that 'expound[s] the truth that is in the domain of the entire church and accessible to the entire church' is not what is intended in 2.27.[90] This is immediately relevant to the situation underlying 1 John, since the 'protognostics' were likely claiming a special knowledge that would have elevated them to the role of 'mediating teachers.'[91]

Carson's view has the two-fold advantage of taking 2.27 seriously (his hypothesis recognizes that οὐ χρείαν ἔχετε actually carries force) and excusing the author of 1 John from the charge of inconsistency (by limiting the kind of teaching obviated to intermediary teachers, rather than teaching in general). However, the weakness of Carson's theory is that it does not demonstrate that the idea of intermediary teaching is present in 2.27. It must be asked whether the distinction of teacher/intermediary teacher is really present in Jer 31.34, and if so, whether the author of 1 John picks up on, and develops, this distinction.

(4) Carson's thesis focuses on intermediary teachers, of which the false teachers, the 'protognostics,' are one kind. A similar view (one that has been long held) is that only the false teachers, i.e. the opponents of the community, are in view in 2.27. Only they are banned, not all teaching or teachers in general. This view is held by Bultmann,[92] Houlden,[93] Smalley,[94] Burge,[95] and Hiebert.[96] Again, like Carson's thesis, this view has the multiple advantages of taking 2.27 seriously, while at the same time avoiding authorial inconsistency.[97] The main difficulty faced by this interpretation is that 2.27 does not explicitly limit itself to the false teachers – it claims that 'you have no need for anyone [τις] to teach you.'[98] It might be argued that contextually, the false teachers are very much in view, but the fact remains that the author of 1 John does not explicitly limit the referent of τις to the false teachers.

(5) Over against the first four views, which posit a disallowing or relativizing of some or all human teaching, the next two views see no

---

[89] Carson, 'No Need,' 279.

[90] Carson, 'No Need,' 280.

[91] However, Carson thinks that 2.27b refers to more than just the false teachers.

[92] Bultmann, *Epistles*, 41, although he also thinks it could refer to the author himself.

[93] Houlden, *Epistles*, 82.

[94] Smalley, *1,2,3 John*, 125, who also notes that 2.27 is probably cast in extreme form to emphasize the effect of the 'anointing,' and that in the early church, teachers themselves had to be taught by the chrism of the Spirit.

[95] Burge, *Letters*, 132.

[96] Hiebert, '1 John,' 90.

[97] The criticism of this view by Schnackenburg, *Epistles*, 149 misses the point and is rightly rejected by Carson, 'No Need,' 276, n. 19.

[98] Cf. Carson, 'No Need,' 277.

disallowing of human instruction in 2.27. John Calvin, in fact, reacted sharply against the view that human teaching was rendered obsolete in 1 John 2: 'It is absurd, then, for fanatics to seize on this passage to exclude outward ministry from the church.'[99] Calvin suggested in his commentary on the Johannine letters that 1 John 2.27 is intended, not to exclude an outward teaching ministry of the church, but to emphasize that the influence of the Spirit means that the recipients of the letter already understand what is being written to them.[100] The author of 1 John makes this claim, 'so that he might add more authority to his doctrine...'[101] J. Michl argues along somewhat similar lines that 2.27 refers to the *sensus fidelium* (to use later terminology) possessed by Christians; through the work of the Spirit, Christians know what they should believe.[102] The main problem with these interpretations is that they do not take seriously enough the claim in 2.27b that 'you have no need for anyone to teach you.' Neither Calvin nor Michl offer a convincing explanation of this phrase, nor do they sufficiently recognize the contrast established in 2.27bc between the teaching of the 'anointing' and human teaching.

(6) A similar view can be found already in Augustine, who spoke of a 'two-fold teaching':

There is here, my brothers, a great mystery on which to meditate: the sound of my voice strikes your ears, but the real Teacher is within. Do not think that one learns anything from another human being. We can draw your attention by the sound of our voice; but if within there is not the One who instructs, the noise of our words is in vain.[103]

Augustine is followed in more recent times by Malatesta,[104] Schnackenburg,[105] and Marshall.[106] Malatesta suggests that the author of 1 John, 'cannot mean that there is no place at all for human teachers,' since he himself has written a letter to instruct the community, and attaches importance to the role of witnesses and preachers.[107] Instead, in Malatesta's view, 2.27 is intended to highlight that God, not humans, is the '*ultimate origin of all truth*' (my emphasis). This view, like the previous one, fails to offer a convincing explanation of 2.27b. Moreover, it posits a 'two-fold' teaching not clearly present in 1 John itself. 2.27 seems to contrast divine and

---

[99] Calvin, *1, 2, & 3 John*, 48.

[100] Stott, *Letters*, 118-20 is not perfectly clear, but seems to hold a view similar to that of Calvin.

[101] Calvin, *1, 2, & 3 John*, 49.

[102] Michl, 'Geist,' 142-51, following Paulinus of Nola.

[103] Cited in Brown, *Epistles of John*, 376.

[104] Malatesta, *Interiority*, 222-23.

[105] Schnackenburg, *Epistles*, 149.

[106] Marshall, *Epistles*, 163, following Schnackenburg.

[107] Malatesta, *Interiority*, 222.

human instruction, rather than placing them together as complementary influences.

The χρῖσμα and teaching: critical assessment, and a way forward

What are we to make of the views noted above? A convincing explanation of 1 John 2.27 must take seriously the contrast between divine and human teaching, in which the former renders unnecessary the latter. This consideration suggests the inadequacy of views 5 and 6. At the same time, a convincing explanation of 2.27 will account for the apparently didactic nature of the Johannine letters, and our necessary lack of certainty regarding the teaching and authority structures of the Johannine community. It will also recognize the unlikelihood that the author is transparently inconsistent, thus undermining the persuasiveness of his letter. These considerations weigh strongly against the positions of Schweizer and Rensberger (view 1), and against the stronger formulations of Brown's position (view 2).

This leaves us with views 3 or 4. In considering view 4, we note that the context of 1 John 2.27b suggests that it refers *at least* to the false teachers – however, the pertinent question is whether it refers *only* to the false teachers. Two factors suggest a broader reference. First, as noted above, the τὶς in 2.27b is general and unspecific. Secondly, I argued above that an allusion to Jer 31.34 in 1 John 2.20, 27 is likely. If this is correct, the author of 1 John probably refers not only to the teaching of the antichrists, but more broadly to human instruction. Therefore, while view 4 is doubtless correct as far as it goes, it is inadequate because it is overly specific.

The most promising approach toward understanding 1 John 2.27b seems therefore to be focusing attention on the meaning of διδάσκω, rather than limiting the referent of τὶς. The main problem with most of the views summarized above is in fact that they assume they understand what 'teaching' means.

Carson (view 3) properly focuses on the meaning of διδάσκω, arguing that the allusion to Jer 31.34 narrows the kind of teaching rendered obsolete to intermediary teaching. This is correct, but not in the way Carson suggests. Carson proposes that Jer 31.34 declares obsolete prophets, priests, and kings with a 'special endowment of the Spirit.' Our discussion of Jer 31.31-34 in chapter 2 suggested, to the contrary, that *all* teachers – including parents and scribes – are rendered unnecessary in Jeremiah's eschatological vision. However, I suggested that Jer 31.31-34 may employ the Sinai distinction of direct/mediated divine instruction. In this case, all these teachers are understood as intermediaries of divine instruction (cf. my discussion of teaching in Deuteronomy, in chapter 2). Jeremiah's claim is that in the eschatological future, as at Sinai, God's instruction will be direct and unmediated.

In order to understand how the author of the Johannine letters interprets this Jeremianic promise, we must ask what διδάσκω (and the other didactic terminology) means for him. It is here that the results of our study of the Fourth Gospel's didactic terminology (chapter 4) can shed fresh light on the problem. I concluded in chapter 4 that the unique accomplishment of the fourth evangelist is to combine traditional didactic terminology with his own concept of revelation. In the Fourth Gospel, Jesus' teaching *properly understood* is revelation. In chapter 5, we saw, moreover, that Jesus' teaching is in fact understood by the evangelist as the direct, unmediated instruction of God. I suggest that this understanding of the didactic terminology may be present in the Johannine letters. We observed in section 1 above that Jesus is the sole source of teaching in the letters: humans can 'bear' this teaching (2 John 10) but are never themselves said to teach. If, for the author of the letters as for the author of the Fourth Gospel, διδάσκω properly understood refers to the kind of direct 'communication from God' brought decisively by Jesus, *this* is what he claims is not needed from other humans. This is directly relevant to the situation of 1 John if the 'antichrists' are claiming special revelation from God.

On this reading, the author of 1 John declares all human teaching (understood as the kind of direct revelation from God that occurred through Jesus) obsolete on the basis of the Jer 31.34 promise, and does not consider himself to be teaching through his writing of the letter. This line of interpretation is confirmed by 1 John 2.21, in which the writer states that he is not writing to inform the community of a truth they do not know, but to remind them of a truth they already know. He perceives his function to be reminding them of what they have already heard from the beginning (2.24); that is, of what Jesus taught them (2.27f). Teaching is left to Jesus (2.27f) and the χρῖσμα (2.27c).

My thesis is compatible with Brown's suggestion that the writer of the letters thinks of himself as a witness rather than a teacher. However, while the author of the letters does not count his writings as teaching in the sense of the revelation brought uniquely through Jesus, they clearly involve a substantial degree of authority, persuasion, and reminder. This is perfectly understandable on the author's understanding of teaching. The charge of inconsistency (e.g. Rensberger) is incorrect if the author's use of the didactic terminology is properly understood.

On my interpretation, it is quite possible that didactic and leadership structures existed in the community, although always considered under the authority of the teaching/revelation of Jesus and the 'anointing.' Schweizer's view of a radically egalitarian community is unproven and unlikely. As noted, Brown seems inconsistent on this point. Given the nature of the letter itself as one that involves authority and persuasion, it seems better to speak of a relativizing of authority structures rather than a radically egalitarian, chaotic community.

Although we can infer some basic probabilities about the community situation from the letter, it is one thing to understand 1 John, and another thing altogether to reconstruct from it an entire community's didactic and authority structures. 1 John 2.27b negates the need for human teaching in the Johannine community, but it is not clear how this vision played out in the community. Perhaps it involved teaching structures similar to other early Christian communities, but self-consciously subordinated to the teaching of Jesus and the χρῖσμα. We do not know for sure.

7.6 The function of divine instruction in the Johannine letters

The idea of divine instruction is used in 1 John 2.20, 27 in a polemical and self-legitimating manner. The status of the community as those who receive the Jeremianic promise of divine instruction distinguishes them sharply from the antichrists and deceivers (2.18-19, 26),[108] and clearly implies that the latter group is not taught by the χρῖσμα.[109] Interestingly, then, the concept of divine instruction retains its polemical edge from the Fourth Gospel to the Johannine letters, but cuts against a different enemy in the letters. In the Fourth Gospel, Jesus and his disciples are 'taught by God' and the Jews are not; in the letters, the faithful community is 'taught by the anointing,' and the former community members who have gone out are not. The debate has shifted from a Jewish-Christian one to one that concerns the proper interpretation of the Johannine tradition.

7.7 Conclusion

In this chapter, I have argued that the 'anointing' of 1 John 2.20, 27 is a reference to the Spirit, and that 2.27 therefore refers to divine instruction. In seeking to understand the effect of divine instruction on human instruction in 2.27, I evaluated a range of scholarly opinions and suggested that it is plausible that some didactic structures existed in the Johannine community, but that if teaching did occur, it was understood as subordinated to the authoritative teaching/revelation of Jesus and the χρῖσμα.

---

[108] I have already noted the emphatic καὶ ὑμεῖς of 2.20 and 2.27.

[109] Cf. my discussion of CD 20.4 in chapter 3 above.

Chapter 8

God-taught to love

'For this is comely before God and before men, that we should remember the poor, and be
lovers of the brethren and of strangers...for ye know the words which have been spoken
concerning the love of the brotherhood and the love of strangers because this same thing is
pleasant and agreeable to you: because ye are all taught of God; powerfully are the words
spoken to all those who do them.'

Pseudo-Clement, Epistulae de virginitate 1.12[1]

In this chapter, I examine the idea of divine instruction in the seven
undisputed Pauline letters.[2] Only a few passages bring didactic terminology
into close combination with a reference to God: 1 Thess 4.9; 1 Cor 2.13; Gal
1.11-12.[3] Of these, the former two may be influenced by Isa 54.13. I have
argued in a published study that the neologism θεοδίδακτος in 1 Thess 4.9
draws upon Isa 54.13. In my judgment, this can be established with a
reasonable degree of certainty.[4]

Few scholars have considered the possibility that 1 Cor 2.13 echoes Isa
54.13, and indeed this is more uncertain.[5] Nevertheless, several factors
suggest that Isa 54.13 may be in the background of Paul's claim that, 'we
speak not in words taught by human wisdom, but taught by the Spirit
[διδακτοῖς πνεύματος]...' 1 Cor 2.13 is Paul's sole use of διδακτός in
his extant letters, and an allusion to Isa 54.13 explains his choice of a *hapax
legomenon*. Paul does employ διδακτός in his neologism θεοδίδακτος in 1
Thess 4.9, and I have argued that this alludes to Isa 54.13, which contains the

---

[1] Translation from *ANF* 8.60. The editors of *ANF* note that the reference to being 'taught
of God' may be a later addition.

[2] This chapter is based on an examination of all uses of the following 10 didactic terms:
δίδακτος, διδασκαλία, διδάσκαλος, διδάσκω, διδαχή, θεοδίδακτος, κατηχέω,
μανθάνω, παιδευτής, παιδεύω.

[3] Cf. Eph 4.20-21; 2 Tim 3.16; Tit 2.10-12. In 1 Cor 11.32, παιδεύω has more punitive
than didactic connotations, and will not be discussed.

[4] Cf. Witmer, 'Neologism,' 239-50.

[5] Cf. Rigaux, *Thessaloniciens*, 517; Derrett, 'Midrash,' 376. Schuchard, *Scripture*, 47
suggests that 1 Cor 2.13 concerns God's eschatological instruction. Schrage, *Korinther*,
1.261 argues against an allusion to Isa 54.13; Jer 31.34.

only use of διδακτός in the OT.[6] Moreover, Paul draws upon Isaiah several times in 1 Cor 1-3 in order to develop his theme of eschatological, divine wisdom.[7] Isa 54.13, with its emphasis on divine instruction in the last days, is a natural passage upon which to draw.

I conclude that Paul likely draws upon Isa 54.13 in 1 Thess 4.9, and possibly in 1 Cor 2.13. Due to the brevity of this chapter, I will focus on the more certain reference to Isa 54.13 in 1 Thess 4.9, referring only briefly to 1 Cor 2.13; Gal 1.11-12. The questions that guided our study of the Johannine writings (chapters 4-7) will be asked: 1. How does the author interpret the promise of divine instruction? 2. What is the content and function of divine instruction? 3. How does it affect human teaching?

8.1 Paul's understanding of eschatological divine instruction

There is a wide range of proposals for the meaning of θεοδίδακτοι in 1 Thess 4.9. The majority view in modern scholarship is that it refers exclusively to the internal instruction of the Spirit.[8] Ellingworth and Nida see a reference to instruction through the Spirit or experience,[9] while Gaventa construes it as referring to God's love for the Thessalonians, the apostles' modeling of love at the founding mission, and the gift of the Spirit.[10] Some have suggested that θεοδίδακτοι refers to the Christian preaching accepted by the Spirit,[11] or to Paul's apostolic instruction.[12] Zachariae suggests that it refers to instruction through prophets (cf. 1 Thess 5.20),[13] and Spicq, that it refers to the day of Christian initiation when, as newly baptized believers, the

---

[6] Note also that in *Pss. Sol.* 17.32, διδακτός likely draws upon Isa 54.13, and in John 6.45, it is part of a citation of Isa 54.13. Cf. above in chapters 3-4.

[7] Cf. 1 Cor 1.19; 2.9, 16. Cf. Williams, *Wisdom, passim.*

[8] See Lünemann, *Thessalonians*, 118; Denney, *Thessalonians*, 153; von Dobschütz, *Thessalonicher-Briefe*, 177; Milligan, *Thessalonians*, 52; Frame, *Thessalonians*, 158; Bicknell, *Thessalonians*, 40; Neil, *Thessalonians*, 85; Moore, *Thessalonians*, 65; Marshall, *Thessalonians*, 115; Wanamaker, *Thessalonians*, 160-61; Morris, *Thessalonians*, 128-29; Stott, *Thessalonians*, 89; Richard, *Thessalonians*, 210, 216-17. Already in 1551, John Calvin anticipated this view: Calvin, *Thessalonians*, 46. Several commentators suggest that the divine instruction is internal, but do not specify that it is the teaching of God's Spirit: Lightfoot, *Epistles*, 59; Plummer, *Thessalonians*, 65; Whiteley, *Thessalonians*, 65.

[9] Ellingworth and Nida, *Thessalonians*, 87.

[10] Gaventa, *Thessalonians*, 57.

[11] Cf. Rigaux, *Thessaloniciens*, 518.

[12] E.g. Holtz, *Thessalonicher*, 175; Weatherly, *Thessalonians*, 142; Malherbe, *Thessalonians*, 244; Green, *Thessalonians*, 205; Beale, *Thessalonians*, 124-25.

[13] Gotthilf Traugott Zachariae, *Paraphrastische Erklärung der Briefe Pauli an die Galater, Ephes., Phil., Col., und Thess.*, Göttingen, 1771. Cited in Lünemann, *Thessalonians*, 118.

Thessalonians were instructed to love others.[14] Koester and Roetzel argue that θεοδίδακτοι is coined by Paul to engage with the contemporary Hellenistic-Jewish concept (represented by Philo) of being 'self-taught' (αὐτοδίδακτος).[15] Malherbe suggests that it is an implicit critique of Epicurean claims to be 'self-taught.'[16] Kloppenborg thinks it refers to the example of the divine twins Castor and Polydeuces (Pollux) with respect to φιλαδελφία.[17]

I have argued elsewhere that the suggestions of Koester, Roetzel, Malherbe, and Kloppenborg are unlikely.[18] Several of the other hypotheses are equally unconvincing. Ellingworth and Nida's thesis that Paul refers to the Thessalonians' experience is implausible given the eschatological tone of the allusion to Isa 54.13. C. Spicq's conjecture that baptismal catechesis is in view encounters several difficulties. Not only are there are no contextual indications that Paul is referring to catechesis, but there is no evidence that catechesis was understood as being 'taught by God.'[19] Spicq's suggestion is based on his claim that φιλαδελφία and ἀγάπη were 'two essential articles of early catechesis.' But catechesis was not the only way in which Christians were instructed to love: such instruction was a significant part of Paul's ministry in person and through letter. Also unconvincing is Zachariae's suggestion that Paul refers to the activity of prophets within the community. It is unlikely that Paul would equate prophetic activity and the teaching of God without qualification. His admonitions in 1 Thess 5.19-22; 1 Cor 14.29-33 reflect a more circumspect attitude.

The range of scholarly opinion on the meaning of θεοδίδακτοι highlights a characteristic of the text not often noted by scholars: Paul himself does not clearly define θεοδίδακτοι. Although introducing a provocative concept with a new word, and implicitly claiming the fulfillment of Isa 54.13, Paul does not explain himself. This lack of concern to clarify θεοδίδακτοι is matched by Paul's 'one-off' use of the term: it appears in 1 Thess 4.9 and not again.

A partial explanation may be that Paul's main purpose in 4.9-12 is not to discuss how love is produced but to rejoice *that* it is produced and urge its increase. This is signaled in several ways. First, θεοδίδακτοι grounds (γάρ) Paul's claim that the Thessalonians have no need for anyone to write them concerning brotherly love. Paul's main concern, as suggested by the topic heading περὶ δὲ τῆς φιλαδελφίας (4.9), is to address love in the

---

[14] Spicq, *Agape*, 18.

[15] Koester, 'Experiment,' 33-44; Roetzel, 'Theodidaktoi,' 324-31.

[16] Malherbe, 'Exhortation,' 253; Malherbe, *Thessalonians*, 244-45.

[17] Kloppenborg, 'Rhetorical Engagement,' 265-89.

[18] Cf. Witmer, 'Neologism,' 239-43.

[19] Cf. Best, *Thessalonians*, 173.

Thessalonian community. Secondly, the εἰς τό + infinitive construction in
4.9 indicates that Paul is mainly interested in the purpose, result, or content of
divine instruction, rather than divine instruction itself. The ground clause of
4.10a focuses on the result: Paul notes that the Thessalonians are practicing
(ποιεῖτε) love to all the brothers in all Macedonia. Finally, Paul's
exhortation in 4.10b-12 to abound in love focuses on the practical forms love
should take (4.11) and the reasons for increasing in it (4.12). The means by
which love is produced is not revisited after 4.9. These factors suggest that
perhaps Paul chooses not to explain θεοδίδακτοι because it is not his main
concern in 4.9-12. This goes some way toward an explanation but does not
wholly satisfy. Even though divine instruction is a subsidiary topic in 4.9-12,
we might expect Paul to offer some explanation of his claim that a prophetic
promise is being fulfilled, particularly because the idea of divine instruction
does not appear frequently in his letters.

The lack of explanation is understandable if, with Best, we presume that
Paul intends θεοδίδακτοι only in a general sense to emphasize the divine
origin of the command to love.[20] If this is correct, Paul's point is a general
one requiring no clarification. Similarly, Collins' view that Paul's vagueness
is due to the undeveloped nature of his thought in 1 Thessalonians provides
an adequate explanation for the lack of clarity.[21] It is only later, in Galatians
and Romans, that Paul identifies love as the gift of the Spirit of God. In 1
Thessalonians, Paul does not specify how God teaches because he has not yet
worked that out in his own thinking. However, the views of Best and Collins
are unpersuasive. I will suggest below that Paul does connect the Spirit with
divine instruction in 1 Thess 4.9. In this case, Paul's thought is not as
undeveloped as Collins supposes. Moreover, if Paul interprets Isa 54.13 as
fulfilled by Jesus and the Spirit (see below), θεοδίδακτοι is not as
unspecific as Best suggests.

In my judgment, a more convincing explanation for Paul's lack of
clarification is that he supposes the meaning of θεοδίδακτοι obvious enough
that an explanation is unnecessary. Perhaps the claim that believers are
'taught by God' was part of Paul's instruction at the founding mission, or was
discussed during Timothy's visit (3.2). In this case, Paul's willingness to
allude to it in passing and without clarification is understandable. The
suggestions of Collins and Best, while unconvincing, are helpful: they
counsel caution lest Paul's interpreter be more confident about the meaning
of θεοδίδακτοι than 1 Thessalonians allows. Paul does not explicitly clarify
his meaning, so we must look for hints of how he understands the term.

---

[20] Best, *Thessalonians*, 173.
[21] Collins, 'First Reflections,' 349.

Divine instruction and the Spirit

Several factors indicate that Paul has the Spirit in mind as at least one means by which the Thessalonians are 'taught by God.' First, the preceding context refers to the Holy Spirit (4.8).[22] Although περὶ δε (4.9) indicates the beginning of a new section, 4.1-8 and 4.9-12 are closely connected.[23] Importantly, 4.8 draws upon the language of Ezek 36.27; 37.6, 14.[24] Paul's redaction of Ezekiel is noteworthy. He changes Ezekiel's δώσω to a present participle διδόντα in order to emphasize the ongoing work of the Spirit in the lives of the Thessalonians[25] and the present fulfillment of the eschatological promise of Ezekiel 36-37.[26] In keeping with the emphasis on holiness throughout 4.1-8, Paul emphasizes that the Spirit is holy by placing τὸ ἅγιον in an unusual position (it is the *Holy* Spirit who produces the requisite ἁγιασμός).[27] The influence of Ezek 36-37 in 4.8, and Isa 54.13 in 4.9, suggests that Paul reads the two prophetic promises in light of one another.[28]

Secondly, the only other use of διδακτός in Paul's letters is in 1 Cor 2.13, where he identifies the Spirit as the one who teaches. This passage is different than 1 Thess 4.9, because it is the apostles (not the entire community) who are 'taught by the Spirit,' and the content of the teaching is the wisdom of salvation through the cross (not love).[29] Nevertheless, the Spirit's teaching in 1 Cor 2.6-16 is seen as *eschatological* divine instruction, as in 1 Thess 4.9.[30] The didactic role of the Spirit in 1 Cor 2.13 increases the probability that in 1 Thess 4.9, Paul has the Spirit in view.

Finally, the result of divine instruction is love. While it is not possible to be certain whether the construction εἰς τό + infinitive in 4.9 expresses the

---

[22] Cf. Frame, *Thessalonians*, 158; Marshall, *Thessalonians*, 115; Wanamaker, *Thessalonians*, 160-61.

[23] This is evident from Paul's earlier prayer (3.11-13) and from the similar structures of the two sections. Cf. Ellingworth and Nida, *Thessalonians*, 85-86.

[24] Cf. Collins, 'Church,' 292; Deidun, *Covenant*, 19.

[25] Cf. Fee, *Presence*, 52-53; Lightfoot, *Epistles*, 58; Ellingworth and Nida, *Thessalonians*, 84; Morris, *Thessalonians*, 126-27; Weatherly, *Thessalonians*, 140; Malherbe, *Thessalonians*, 235. *Contra* Best, *Thessalonians*, 170; Marshall, *Thessalonians*, 114.

[26] Cf. Deidun, *Covenant*, 33.

[27] Cf. Lightfoot, *Epistles*, 58-59; Morris, *Thessalonians*, 126.

[28] Cf. *Deut. Rab.* 6.14, which cites Isa 54.13; Joel 3.1 [ET 2.28]; Ezek 36.26 together. Stemberger, *Talmud and Midrash*, 308 suggests that *Deut. Rab.* was composed between 450-800 C.E.

[29] Cf. Fee, *Corinthians*, 112-14.

[30] Cf. Fee, *Corinthians*, 100; Thiselton, *Corinthians*, 165; Gaffin, 'Reflections,' 103-24, esp. 109-11.

purpose, result, or content of divine instruction,[31] 4.10 indicates that divine instruction has resulted in love. In his other letters, Paul considers the Spirit to be the means by which love is produced in believers (Rom 5.5; 15.30; Gal 5.5-6, 22).[32] Best argues that the teaching of 1 Thess 4.9 cannot be internal because, 'when Paul writes of internal testimony he thinks of the Spirit...'[33] This argument assumes that θεοδίδακτοι does not refer to the Spirit. But this ignores the arguments advanced above, as well as Paul's identification of the Spirit and God in his other letters.[34] I conclude that Paul sees Isa 54.13 as fulfilled through the influence of the Spirit.

Divine instruction and Jesus

In addition, there are indications that the teaching of Jesus fulfills Isa 54.13. As suggested above, there is a close connection between being 'taught by God' and love (φιλαδελφία, ἀγαπάω). It is therefore interesting that the expression 'to love one another' was widespread in early Christianity, possibly originating from the words of Jesus (John 13.34; 15.12, 17).[35] Paul does not often quote the words of Jesus (cf. 1 Thess 4.15), but it is possible that he refers here to Jesus' teaching.[36] Accordingly, several scholars have argued that in 1 Thess 4.9, he considers the teaching of the earthly Jesus to be the fulfillment of the promise of eschatological *divine* instruction.[37] However, even if we assume that the love commands of the Fourth Gospel are attributable to the historical Jesus, a Pauline allusion to the words of Jesus in 1 Thess 4.9 is by no means certain, so this suggestion cannot be confirmed.

More interesting is the close parallel between Paul's prayer-wish in 3.12 that the Lord would cause the love of the Thessalonians to increase and abound, and his exhortation in 4.9-12:[38]

---

[31] In 1 Thessalonians, εἰς τό + infinitive indicates result (2.16), purpose (3.2, 5, 13), and content (2.12; 3.10). Scholars have differed on how to interpret the construction in 4.9. For purpose, cf. Hogg and Vine, *Thessalonians*, 122-23. For purpose or result, cf. Best, *Thessalonians*, 173. For content, cf. Robertson, *Grammar*, 1072; Frame, *Thessalonians*, 158.

[32] Cf. Fitzmyer, *Romans*, 725. Cf. Dibelius and Conzelmann, *Pastoral Epistles*, 98-99 on 2 Tim 1.7.

[33] Cf. Best, *Thessalonians*, 173.

[34] Cf. 1 Cor 2.11, 14; 3.16; 6.11.

[35] Cf. Rom 13.8; 1 Pet 1.22; 1 John 3.11, 23; 4.7, 12; 2 John 5; cf. Gal 5.13; Heb 10.24. On the possibility that Rom 13.8 draws upon Jesus tradition, cf. Thompson, *Christ*, 123-25.

[36] Tuckett, 'Tradition,' 160-82 limits his study to synoptic tradition and does not consider this possibility.

[37] Cf. Tambyah, 'Suggestion,' 527-28; Beale, *Thessalonians*, 124-25; Bruce, *Thessalonians*, 90; Williams, *Thessalonians*, 76.

[38] Cf. Beale, *Thessalonians*, 124.

Table 1. *Parallels between 1 Thess 3.12 and 4.9-12*

1 Thess 3.12	1 Thess 4.9-12
And may the Lord (ὁ κύριος)	You are God-taught (θεοδίδακτοι)
cause you to increase and abound (πλεονάσαι καὶ περισσεῦσαι)	But we urge you to excel still more (περισσεύειν μᾶλλον)
in love (τῇ ἀγάπῃ)	You are God-taught to love (εἰς τὸ ἀγαπᾶν)
for one another (εἰς ἀλλήλους)	one another (ἀλλήλους), for you are practicing it toward all the brothers (εἰς πάντας τοὺς ἀδελφούς)
and for all (καὶ εἰς πάντας)[39]	Work with your hands, so that you may behave properly toward outsiders (τοὺς ἔξω)

For our purposes, the important parallel is the first one in the table above. In 3.12, Paul's prayer-wish is that the Lord would produce love in the Thessalonians. Paul refers to the 'Lord Jesus' in 3.11, 13, so ὁ κύριος in 3.12 must refer to Jesus.[40] This is remarkable, in light of Paul's claim in 4.9-10 that *God* teaches the Thessalonians to love one another. Claiming that God produces love, Paul prays to the risen Jesus to do just that.[41] This 'functional overlap' between God and Christ is present elsewhere in Paul's letters.[42] It suggests that Paul may include the risen Christ within the meaning of θεός in his compound θεοδίδακτοι.

8.2 The content and function of divine instruction

As noted above, the εἰς τό + infinitive construction in 4.9 could signify content, purpose, or result. If the first of these, divine instruction has specific content: the command to love one another. Alternatively, if εἰς τό + infinitive indicates the purpose or result of divine instruction, that instruction may be understood as an inner enabling for love. In favor of this latter possibility is the allusion to Ezek 36.27; 37.6, 14 in 1 Thess 4.8. If divine instruction is understood as moral enabling, this is clearly different than the Johannine writings. There, divine instruction is often cognitive, communicating knowledge (i.e. insight into the Scriptures or the Johannine tradition).

What is the function of Paul's claim that the Thessalonians are 'taught by God'? Wanamaker suggests that it functions as a warrant for mutual love among the Thessalonians, comparable to 'this is the will of God' (4.3).[43]

---

[39] 'Unto all' (3.12) likely refers to unbelievers, and so is parallel to 'those outside' (4.12). Cf. Bruce, *Thessalonians*, 72.

[40] Cf. Malherbe, *Thessalonians*, 212.

[41] Paul prays to Jesus in 2 Cor 12.8; 2 Thess 3.3, 5, 16. Cf. Malherbe, *Thessalonians*, 212.

[42] Cf. Kreitzer, *Jesus and God*, 156-58.

[43] Cf. Wanamaker, *Thessalonians*, 161.

While this may be true to some degree, Paul's emphasis in 4.9-10 is clearly on encouragement, since he praises the Thessalonians for what they are *already* doing. The evidence of the letter suggests that the community needed encouragement. It was a young group facing persecution (1.6; 2.14; 3.3-4), challenged with a major change in lifestyle (4.1-8), and discouraged and confused by the sudden death of some members (4.13-18).[44] By calling the Thessalonians θεοδίδακτοι, Paul encourages them in several ways.[45]

Paul's θεοδίδακτοι encourages the Thessalonians by communicating that they are God's people. By drawing upon Ezek 36.27; 37.6, 14 and Isa 54.13 in 1 Thess 4.8-9, Paul asserts that the young, predominantly Gentile community of believers (1.9; 2.14) is experiencing the fulfillment of OT prophetic promises. This is in keeping with Paul's practice in the rest of 1 Thessalonians,[46] and suggests that the Thessalonians are part of God's people.[47] This is also implied in 1 Thess 4.1-8. The Thessalonians, living in a world of widespread sexual promiscuity in which they had likely participated before their conversions,[48] are called to live according to Jewish sexual practices.[49] This standard of holiness is to set them apart from the Gentiles, 'who do not know God' (4.5).[50] In fact, Paul separates the Christian community from outsiders by the criterion of who knows God and who does not.[51] I argued in chapter 6 that the fourth evangelist's redaction of Isa 54.13 demonstrates that he consciously expands Isaiah's promise to include Gentiles. Paul does the same thing in 1 Thess 4.9.

Paul's claim that the letter's recipients are 'taught by God' is related to another feature of 1 Thessalonians: its many references to what the Thessalonians know.[52] θεοδίδακτοι has a parallel in 5.1-2, in which the Thessalonians have no need for anything to be written them (cf. 4.9) since they already know that the day of the Lord will come like a thief in the night. This parallel between θεοδίδακτοι and 'knowledge' suggests that the two may have similar rhetorical functions. Malherbe notes that Paul's references

---

[44] Cf. Nicholl, *Hope to Despair*, 183-85.

[45] Note also my suggestion in Witmer, 'Neologism,' 248-49 that Paul's *coinage* of θεοδίδακτοι may have been part of his epistolary strategy of strengthening the identity of the Thessalonian community.

[46] Language descriptive of Israel is applied to the Thessalonian Gentiles. Compare 1 Thess 1.4 with LXX Deut. 10.15; Isa 41.8; 44.2; 48.12-16; Hos 11.1. Compare 1 Thess 1.9; 2.12 with Isa 41.8-9.

[47] Weima, 'Walk,' 98-119, esp. 102.

[48] Cf. Weima, 'Walk,' 104-6.

[49] Hodgson, 'Holiness Tradition,' 199-215; Carras, 'Jewish Ethics,' 314.

[50] Cf. LXX Ps 78.6 (ET 79.6); Isa 44.18; 45.20; 2 Thess 1.8. Cf. Meeks, *Urban Christians*, 227.

[51] Cf. Gal 4.8-9; 1 Thess 4.12. Cf. Meeks, *Urban Christians*, 94-96.

[52] Cf. 1.5; 2.1-2, 5, 9, 11; 3.3-4; 4.2; 5.2. Cf. Plevnik, 'Presuppositions,' 53-54; Malherbe, 'Exhortation,' 240; Malbon, 'Write,' 58-59.

to knowledge introduce *topoi* on the moral life,[53] but this is probably not their only function. Plevnik suggests that Paul's frequent references to his instruction at the founding mission function to, 'affirm the believers in their young faith amidst trials.'[54] Plevnik does not expand on this observation, but it is a good one. The references to knowledge are encouraging to the young community because they emphasize how much the community already knows. Likewise, Paul's claim that the community is 'taught by God' emphasizes God's prior, and ongoing, instruction. There is more for them to learn (4.13), but there is much they know already.

Finally, the Thessalonians may have heard Paul's claim as encouraging in yet another way. The status of teachers and pupils was bound together in the first-century world. A teacher's reputation could be boosted by the accomplishments of his students,[55] who were concerned to enhance his status.[56] Conversely, the status of a student benefited from a good education and a respected teacher.[57] Malina and Neyrey have noted the importance of education in contributing to one's status in the ancient world.[58] They point to the discussions of Cicero, *Inv.* 1.35 and Quintilian, *Inst.* 5.10.24-29, which mention education as an indicator of one's character. These passages suggest that being educated and securing a particular instructor might contribute to one's reputation.[59]

Perhaps in 1 Thess 4.9, Paul seeks to encourage the Thessalonians by reminding them that their teacher is *God*. Malina and Neyrey suggest that Paul elevates his own status in Galatians 1 by claiming to be taught by God.[60] In Gal 1.12, Paul asserts that he did not receive his gospel from men (παρὰ ἀνθρώπου) and was not taught it (ἐδιδάχθην). Rather, he received it through a revelation of Jesus Christ (δι᾽ ἀποκαλύψεως).[61] By eschewing human instruction and claiming direct divine instruction Paul claims that his teacher is none less than God, and this reflects well upon him. θεοδίδακτοι in 1 Thess 4.9 may function similarly.

---

[53] Malherbe, 'Exhortation,' 240.

[54] Plevnik, 'Presuppositions,' 59.

[55] Quintilian, *Inst.* 1.2.16; Philo, *Congr.* 127. See Winter, *Philo*, 91-92.

[56] Cf. Winter, *Corinth*, 38-40; Winter, 'Entries,' 62.

[57] Cf. Acts 22.3.

[58] Cf. Malina and Neyrey, *Portraits*, 41-43, 70; Townsend, 'Ancient Education,' 150-51; Borgen, *Bread*, 124-27.

[59] Cf. Philo, *Leg.* 3.167. See Winter, *Philo*, 93.

[60] Malina and Neyrey, *Portraits*, 41-43.

[61] Cf. the similar οὐκ...οὐδὲ...ἀλλά construction of Gal 1.1. Cf. Longenecker, *Galatians*, 23-24.

8.3 How does divine instruction affect human teaching?

In chapter 2, I suggested that the lack of clarity in Isa 54.13 allows for varying interpretations: it may be seen as promising direct divine instruction, but it does not specify that this is the case. Jer 31.34, on the other hand, explicitly denies the presence of human teachers in the last days. In chapter 5, I argued that the fourth evangelist interpreted Isa 54.13 as promising direct divine instruction, and that he understood this promise as fulfilled in the teaching of Jesus and the Spirit. In chapter 7, I argued that the author of the Johannine letters interpreted Jer 31.34 as fulfilled through Jesus and the Spirit, and so declared that no human teaching (understood as the unique, direct revelation brought by Jesus) was necessary in the community.

This raises the question of how *Paul* interprets Isa 54.13, and whether he alludes to Jer 31.34. As a few commentators have noted, 1 Thess 4.9 bears some resemblance to 1 John 2.20, 27.[62] In 1 John 2.27, the phrase οὐ χρείαν ἔχετε denies the need for human teaching, and is grounded by the claim that the community is taught by the Spirit. In 1 Thess 4.9, οὐ χρείαν ἔχετε denies the need for anyone to write concerning brotherly love, and is grounded by the claim that the community is taught by God. Does this suggest that Paul understands Isa 54.13 to promise direct divine instruction that removes the need for human (apostolic) instruction?

A significant number of scholars have argued that 'taught by God' is meant to *contrast* with apostolic instruction, and that divine instruction makes apostolic instruction unnecessary.[63] This view is stated forcefully by Olshausen in his 1840 commentary on Thessalonians: 'where *God* teaches, there, the apostle says, *I* may be silent.[64] Among recent scholars, it has been most clearly articulated by Koester.[65] This view suggests that Paul (like the fourth evangelist) interprets Isa 54.13 as promising direct divine instruction, without intermediaries.

However, it accounts neither for 1 Thessalonians as a whole, nor the rest of the Pauline letters. After claiming that the Thessalonians have no need for anyone to write them concerning love (4.9), Paul goes on to do just that (4.11-12).[66] In fact, in both the founding mission (2.8-9; 3.12; 4.9-12) and 1

---

[62] Cf. Hogg and Vine, *Thessalonians*, 122; Plummer, *Thessalonians*, 65; Stott, *Letters*, 89.

[63] Cf. Calvin, *Thessalonians*, 46; Stott, *Thessalonians*, 89; Marshall, *Thessalonians*, 115; Milligan, *Thessalonians*, 52; Frame, *Thessalonians*, 158; Plummer, *Thessalonians*, 64; Bicknell, *Thessalonians*, 40; Neil, *Thessalonians*, 85; Rigaux, *Thessaloniciens*, 517.

[64] Cited in Lünemann, *Thessalonians*, 118.

[65] Koester, 'Experiment,' 39.

[66] Moore, *Thessalonians*, 66 rightly notes that 4.11-12 shows, 'the way in which brotherly love must express itself.' 2.8-9 has already established a close connection between love and physical labor, and 4.10b-12 is all one sentence. *Contra* Lünemann, *Thessalonians*, 120-22.

Thessalonians itself (3.11-13; 5.8, 12-13), love is a major part of Paul's exhortation. This is also the case in other Pauline letters (e.g. Rom 13.8-14; 1 Cor 13; Gal 5). Moreover, in 1 Thessalonians, Paul never contrasts his apostolic preaching with God's word. Instead, he asserts that his preaching is the word of God (2.13; 4.3, 8).[67]

Rather than contrasting divine and apostolic instruction, οὐ χρείαν ἔχετε is probably an example of *paralipsis*, or *praeteritio*,[68] a rhetorical device in which a writer 'pretends to pass over something which he in fact mentions.'[69] This is clearly what Paul does. By noting that the Thessalonians have no need to be instructed in brotherly love, Paul encourages his readers while simultaneously introducing a short exhortation on precisely this topic. The same formula appears a few verses later (5.1) and functions the same way. Paul's rhetorical move is not unusual. It was a 'paraenetic commonplace' in the first century to note that advice given was a reminder of what was known already, not new information.[70]

This discussion suggests that divine instruction in 1 Thess 4.9 does not contrast with apostolic instruction. This suggests, in turn, that Paul's reading of Isa 54.13 is not of direct, unmediated instruction. Unlike 1 John 2.20, 27, Paul does *not* allude to Jer 31.34 with the expression οὐ χρείαν ἔχετε (4.9; 5.1).[71] Paul's claim is not that the Thessalonians need no one to 'teach' them (cf. Jer 31.34; 1 John 2.27), but that they need no one to 'write' to them. Moreover, Paul appears to conceive of eschatological divine instruction as fully compatible with human instruction. Paul himself had a didactic role among the Thessalonians: this is implied by his self-characterization as a father exhorting his children (1 Thess 2.11).[72] This is similar to Paul's activity in other churches. In 1 Cor 4.14-21, Paul claims to be the Corinthians' father, calls for them to imitate him, and says that he has sent Timothy to remind them of his way, just as he teaches (διδάσκω)

---

[67] Note the emphatic καθώς ἐστιν ἀληθῶς in 2.13, and Paul's references to the 'gospel of God' (2.2, 8, 9) and the 'gospel of Christ' (3.2). Cf. Malherbe, 'Exhortation,' 254, n. 69.

[68] Cf. Lünemann, *Thessalonians*, 117; Alford, *Thessalonians*, 271; Ellicott, *Thessalonians*, 57; Ellingworth and Nida, *Thessalonians*, 86; Wanamaker, *Thessalonians*, 159; Richard, *Thessalonians*, 210; Malherbe, *Thessalonians*, 243-44; Gaventa, *Thessalonians*, 56.

[69] BDF §495. Although BDF §495 is often cited by commentators, it is not as often noted that BDF itself does not understand 1 Thess 4.9 as an example of *paralipsis*. For a definition of *praeteritio*, cf. Lausberg, *Literary Rhetoric*, 393: it is 'the announcement of the intention to leave certain things out.'

[70] Cf. Olson, 'Confidence,' 282-95, esp. 291-93; Stowers, *Letter Writing*, 103-4. I owe the Stowers reference to Wanamaker, *Thessalonians*, 159. Cf. Cicero, *Fam.* 1.4.3 (mentioned in Malherbe, *Thessalonians*, 244). On the common disavowal of the need for further instruction, cf. Malherbe, *Moral Exhortation*, 125.

[71] *Contra* Deidun, *Covenant*, 20, whose argument relies on uncritical use of late rabbinic texts.

[72] Cf. Burke, *Family Matters*, 142-45.

everywhere in every church.[73] In addition, Paul clearly endorses the presence of teachers and teaching within his communities.[74] All these factors suggest that Paul did not understand Isa 54.13 as promising direct divine instruction.

Interestingly, in the two passages in which Paul refers to his own divine education (Gal 1.12; 1 Cor 2.13), there is a clear contrast between divine and human instruction. He denies that he has received human instruction, and instead claims divine instruction (revelation). This probably reflects Paul's awareness of the uniqueness of his own situation. He had received a direct, apocalyptic revelation from God, and was the founder and source of a Christian tradition.[75]

8.4 Conclusion

I argued in chapters 4-5 that the fourth evangelist interprets Isa 54.13 in light of the teaching of Jesus and the Spirit. This chapter has argued that Paul likely does the same thing in 1 Thess 4.9. If 1 Cor 2.13 is influenced by Isa 54.13 (I suggested that this is possible, though by no means certain), it is another instance in which Paul interprets Isaiah's promised divine instruction as fulfilled through the teaching of the Spirit. However, despite Paul's similar re-interpretation of divine instruction in terms of Jesus and the Spirit, there are differences from the Johannine writings. In 1 Thessalonians, divine instruction has a different content and function. It is focused on love for others, and functions primarily in 1 Thessalonians as an encouragement to the community. In addition, Paul does not interpret Isa 54.13 as promising direct, unmediated divine instruction. For Paul, divine instruction is compatible with continuing human teaching.

---

[73] Cf. Belleville, 'Imitate Me,' 120-42, esp. 121-24. Sanders, 'Imitating,' 363 wrongly plays off instruction against Paul's paternal relationship.

[74] Cf. Rom 12.7; 1 Cor 12.28-29; 14.6, 19, 26; Gal 6.6.

[75] On tradition and apocalyptic in Gal 1 and Paul, cf. Martyn, *Galatians*, 148-51; Betz, *Galatians*, 62-66.

Chapter 9

One is your teacher

*'Let him that teaches, although he be one of the laity, yet, if he be skilful in the word and
grave in his manners, teach; for "they shall be all taught of God."'*

Apostolic Constitutions 8.32, fourth century[1]

'Today...we all are priests, and Is. 54:13 is now fulfilled...and Jer. 31:34.'

Martin Luther, *Works on the First Twenty-two Psalms*, 1519-1521[2]

In this chapter, I examine the idea of divine instruction in Matthew.[3] The
passage of greatest interest is 23.8-10, which emphasizes Jesus' identity as
teacher in close conjunction with a statement about God.[4] It may also draw
upon Jer 31.33-34, as many scholars have noted.[5] This is suggested initially
by the conceptual similarity of Jer 31.34 and Matt 23.8-10: in both passages,
a unique didactic authority (Jesus or God) appears to render unnecessary (or
relativize) other teaching. It is further suggested by the unusual use of
ἀδελφοί in 23.8c. Because 23.8b claims that 'one is your διδάσκαλος,' we
would expect μαθηταί instead of ἀδελφοί in 23.8c. The presence of
ἀδελφοί is explained if Matthew has Jer 31.34 in mind, since LXX Jer 38.34
claims that in the future, a man will not need to teach his *brother*
(ἀδελφόν).[6]

---

[1] Translation from *ANF* 7.495.

[2] Translation from *LW* 14.341.

[3] This chapter is based on examination of all uses of the following seven didactic terms:
διδασκαλία; διδάσκαλος; διδάσκω; διδαχή; μαθητής; μανθάνω; ῥαββί.

[4] This is the only passage in Matthew that links didactic terminology with a reference to
God.

[5] E.g. Jeremias, *Theology*, 169; Schniewind, *Matthäus*, 228-29; Garland, *Intention*, 61, n.
102; Hagner, *Matthew*, 2.661; Schweizer, *Matthäus*, 281.

[6] Cf. Schweizer, *Matthäus*, 281; Derrett, 'Midrash,' 377-78. The influence of Jer 31.34
more convincingly explains the use of ἀδελφοί than theories that 23.8c is displaced from
23.9, or that ἀδελφοί is used from the desire to universalize beyond the original disciples
(Davies and Allison, *Matthew*, 3.276). The latter theory explains why Matthew does not use
the term μαθηταί, but not why he uses the term ἀδελφοί. Cf. also the unconvincing

I find unconvincing Derrett's elaborate attempt to demonstrate that Matt 23.8-10 is the reworking and application to Jesus of an original Jewish midrash on Jer 31.33-34 and Isa 54.13. Derrett suggests that the pre-Matthean midrash expounded 'rav' in Isa 54.13 to mean teacher, patron, and preceptor (referring to God), and that Matthew applies it to Jesus.[7] Derrett's case is overly ingenious, and his putative midrash is built on an interpretation of Isa 54.13 alien to the Hebrew text and the LXX. While Derrett's thesis fails to convince, it is nevertheless possible that Isa 54.13, together with Jer 31.34, stands behind Matt 23.8-10. The claim of Isa 54.13 that 'all will be taught [διδακτός] by God' is closer to the claim that 'one is your teacher [διδάσκαλος]' than is Jer 31.34, and it is possible that Matthew has read the two prophetic promises together.[8]

The purpose of this chapter is to offer a close reading of Matt 23.8-10, in order to understand the categories with which Matthew understands Jesus as teacher, the function of the Matthean Jesus' claim that he is the one teacher, and the way in which Jesus' identity as 'the one teacher' affects human instruction.

9.1 Matthew's understanding of eschatological divine instruction

In chapter 5, I suggested that fresh light could be shed on the Fourth Gospel's Christology, and particularly upon its understanding of Jesus as teacher, by showing that Jesus is understood to fulfill the promise of eschatological divine instruction. In this section, I suggest something similar for Matthew's gospel. The discussion in chapters 2-3 of God (and the Messiah) as teacher in the OT and early Judaism provides important categories for understanding Matt 23.8-10.

In chapter 4, I noted that in Matthew, only Judas refers to Jesus as rabbi (26.25, 49), and that Jesus is usually referred to as διδάσκαλος by non-disciples. Kingsbury concludes from this that 'rabbi' and 'teacher' are for Matthew only terms of human respect, and not Christological titles.[9] Patte goes further, suggesting that perhaps 'teacher' is not an appropriate designation for Jesus.[10] While Kingsbury rightly emphasizes that it is Jesus the Messiah, the Son of God, who teaches (see below), he undervalues the

---

explanation of Davies, 'Bar Abbas,' 260-62. The term 'brother' is significant in Matthew. Cf. Hoet, *Omnes, passim*; Tuckett, 'Review,' 508-9.

[7] Cf. Derrett, 'Midrash,' 372-86.

[8] Cf. Knowles, *Jeremiah*, 209-12; Vivianio, 'Social World,' 14; Davies and Allison, *Matthew*, 3.276.

[9] Kingsbury, *Matthew*, 92-93.

[10] Patte, *Matthew*, 330.

importance of 23.8-10; 26.18, in which Jesus refers to himself as a teacher ('the' teacher in 26.18).[11] Matthew's narrative as a whole, not just a title, shows that Jesus' teaching is a crucial part of his identity.[12] *Contra* Kingsbury, Matthew does not dismiss 'teacher' as a mere term of respect. Rather, he seeks to define what kind of teacher Jesus is. Byrskog perceptively observes two paradoxical tendencies in Matthew. On the one hand, Jesus as teacher is exalted, and on the other, didactic addresses by true disciples are avoided.[13] This does not suggest that Matthew downplays Jesus' identity as teacher. Rather, it suggests that Matthew portrays Jesus as a teacher unlike any other teacher.[14] As many have noted, Matt 23.8-10 defines Jesus' teaching identity in messianic terms. I will argue that it pushes beyond this to portray Jesus the teacher as the Son of God. Jesus' teaching is divine instruction.

We may begin by noting that 23.8-10 has a triadic structure,[15] with each part roughly parallel to the other.[16]

Table 1. *The structure of Matt 23.8-10*

23.8a	ὑμεῖς δὲ μὴ κληθῆτε ῥαββί·
23.8b	εἷς γάρ ἐστιν ὑμῶν ὁ διδάσκαλος,
23.8c	πάντες δὲ ὑμεῖς ἀδελφοί ἐστε.
23.9a	καὶ πατέρα μὴ καλέσητε ὑμῶν ἐπὶ τῆς γῆς,
23.9b	εἷς γάρ ἐστιν ὑμῶν ὁ πατὴρ ὁ οὐράνιος.
23.10a	μηδὲ κληθῆτε καθηγηταί,
23.10b	ὅτι καθηγητὴς ὑμῶν ἐστιν εἷς ὁ Χριστός.

This triadic structure is more convincing that Michaels' suggestion of a bi-partite structure (23.8-9, 10-12).[17] Michaels suggests that the active verb of 23.9 indicates that it is not parallel to 23.8 and 23.10. This conclusion is unwarranted, as the parallelism need not be exact (even Michaels' proposed bi-partite structure is not exactly parallel). Moreover, on Michaels' reading, 23.9 is a call to Jesus' disciples not to rely on being Jewish,[18] but this does

---

[11] Cf. Byrskog, 'Teacher,' 95.

[12] Cf. Lincoln, 'Teachers,' 122-24.

[13] Byrskog, 'Lernen,' 199.

[14] Cf. Byrskog, 'Teacher,' 92. Byrskog argues that Matthew breaks the 'semantic synonymity' of ῥαββί and διδάσκαλος, giving the former term only negative connotations (97). This is possible, but in light of the parallel between the two terms in 23.8ab, I think it unlikely (cf. John 1.38; 3.2; 20.16).

[15] Cf. Luz, *Matthew*, 97. Matthew's frequent use of triadic structures is demonstrated by Davies and Allison, *Matthew*, 1.61-72.

[16] The most significant differences are the presence of 23.8c and the active verb in 23.9a.

[17] Michaels, 'Prophecy,' 305-10.

[18] Cf. Townsend, 'Matthew,' 56-59.

not fit the context of 23.1-12, which is about humility toward others rather than not relying on one's ethnicity.

Reading 23.8-10 as a triad, there are three prohibitions (23.8a, 9a, 10a) grounded by four assertions (23.8bc, 9b, 10b). These prohibitions and assertions center on four terms, all of which have didactic connotations. The two terms in 23.8ab (ῥαββί, διδάσκαλος) both refer to teachers (cf. John 1.38; 3.2). Similarly, πατήρ is a term used for Jewish teachers.[19] The lack of evidence in Jewish sources for 'father' used as an address to a teacher[20] has suggested to some that it refers in Matt 23.9 to teachers from previous generations.[21] However, that interpretation does not fit the context, which emphasizes humility. It is probably better to recognize that Matt 23.9 implies the use of 'father' as a form of address.[22] In the wisdom tradition, instructors were known as 'father,' and there is at least some rabbinic evidence for 'father' used in direct address to a teacher.[23]

The meaning of καθηγητής is the most difficult to ascertain, in part because its only use in the NT is in 23.10.[24] In Greek literature, the word-group was used to refer to (among other things) founders of schools, leaders, guides, or teachers.[25] On the view that it is basically synonymous with ῥαββί in 23.8, καθηγητής is often considered a 'translation' or interpretation for Gentile readers.[26] However, some have proposed that it bears a meaning distinct from ῥαββί. Winter argues that it means 'tutor,'[27] while Luz suggests it is a broader term used in order to preclude not only the specific titles of 23.8-9 but any designation that would differentiate leaders and subordinates in the community.[28] Many others suggest that a Semitic original lies behind καθηγητής.[29] We need not decide this question here. For our purposes it is important to note that in this context, καθηγητής, like the other three terms, clearly has a didactic meaning.[30]

---

[19] Cf. Byrskog, *Teacher*, 53; Schrenk, 'πατήρ,' *TDNT* 5.977-78; Garland, *Intention*, 59; Schürer, *History*, 2.326-27. Cf. 2 Kgs 2.12. Forestell, *Targumic Traditions*, 78 notes that the Targum on 2 Kgs 2.12 changes 'my father' to 'my rabbi.' Cited in Wilkins, *Disciple*, 59.

[20] Cf. Dalman, *Words*, 339.

[21] Cf. Carson, 'Matthew,' 475. Barbour, 'Titles,' 139 notes this as a possibility.

[22] Cf. Dalman, *Words*, 338.

[23] Cf. Davies and Allison, *Matthew*, 3.276-77.

[24] Cf. Saggin, 'Magister,' 209.

[25] Cf. LSJ 852; BDAG 490.

[26] E.g. Dalman, *Words*, 340; Michaels, 'Prophecy,' 307; Garland, *Intention*, 60.

[27] Winter, 'Messiah,' 152-57. Cf. Byrskog, *Teacher*, 289-90.

[28] Luz, *Matthäus*, 3.308.

[29] Cf. Riesner, *Lehrer*, 263-64; Vivianio, 'Social World,' 12-13; Derrett, 'Midrash,' 380-81; Spicq, 'Allusion,' 387-96; Barbour, 'Titles,' 141. This view is criticized by Byrskog, *Teacher*, 287-90.

[30] Cf. *EDNT* 2.222.

In this section, I am most interested in the four assertions (23.8bc, 9b, 10b), and particularly the identity of the 'teacher' (διδάσκαλος) in 23.8b. While the 'father' (πατήρ) of 23.9 is clearly God,[31] and the 'teacher' (καθηγητής) of 23.10 is 'the Christ,' the 'teacher' (διδάσκαλος) of 23.8 is not explicitly identified. This allows for an identification as God (if 23.8 is read with 23.9) or Christ (if read with 23.10).[32] A number of scholars understand διδάσκαλος to refer to God, either in a pre-Matthean tradition or in its Matthean form. This is certainly possible: as we saw in chapters 2-3, God is identified as a teacher in the OT and in early Jewish literature. Bousset, followed by Bultmann, argues that 23.8-9 was an original doublet referring to God, to which 23.10 was later added. Jeremias arrives (apparently independently) at the same view.[33] Similarly, Schweizer suggests that 23.8-9 derives from a dominical saying referring to God. After Easter, the saying is re-interpreted through the addition of 23.10.[34]

The Bousset-Bultmann-Jeremias-Schweizer hypothesis suggests that when Matthew (or a later redactor) sought to express Jesus' identity as teacher, he took over the highest possible model, namely a tradition concerning God as teacher. This is also the implication of Derrett's view, summarized above. If correct, these suggestions have major implications for understanding Matthew's portrayal of Jesus as teacher: God as the one teacher in pre-Matthean tradition becomes *Jesus* the one teacher in Matthew's gospel. However, I have already noted above that Derrett's view is unlikely. The Bousset-Bultmann-Jeremias-Schweizer hypothesis is at best an intriguing, and unproven, possibility. It is based on the theory that 23.8-9 is an original doublet, and 23.10 a later addition. But there is no external evidence that 23.10 is a later addition to the Matthean text,[35] nor is there evidence that Matthew himself expanded upon an original doublet in 23.8-9. Riesner argues, to the contrary, for two separate dominical sayings, one in 23.8, and the other 23.9-10.[36] If this is correct, or if an original triadic structure is supposed, the hypothesis is undermined.

Patte argues that 23.8b in its Matthean context refers to God.[37] However, several factors suggest that in its present context, ὁ διδάσκαλος refers to

---

[31] Cf. Matt 5.48; 6.14, 26, 32; 15.13; 18.35.

[32] Cf. Zimmerman, *Urchristlichen*, 166. The suggestion of Alford, *Four Gospels*, 227-28 that 23.8 refers to the Spirit is unconvincing, given the context (so, rightly, Davies and Allison, *Matthew*, 3.276).

[33] Bousset, *Kyrios Christos*, 36, n. 13; Bultmann, *Synoptic Tradition*, 144; Jeremias, *Theology*, 169.

[34] Schweizer, *Matthäus*, 281-82.

[35] Cf. Byrskog, *Teacher*, 287.

[36] Riesner, *Lehrer*, 259-64.

[37] Patte, *Matthew*, 322.

Jesus.[38] First, Jesus is referred to as 'teacher' throughout Matthew's gospel, and is frequently said to 'teach.'[39] Secondly, 23.1 states that Jesus is speaking to the multitudes and his disciples (τοῖς μαθηταῖς αὐτοῦ). Together with the explicit linking of teacher/disciple terminology in 10.24-25; 26.18, this suggests that the διδάσκαλος in 23.8 is Jesus. Finally, 23.8, 10 have passive verbs, and are therefore more closely parallel with each other than with 23.9. If this is the case, 23.8b, 9b, 10b forms an A-B-A pattern: two statements about Jesus as the 'one' teacher on either side of a claim that God is the 'one' father. As noted above, πατήρ in this context has a didactic connotation. Jesus' didactic identity is connected with God's own didactic identity.

A further feature of the text makes this close connection even more interesting: the language of 23.8-10 (εἷς ἐστιν...εἷς ἐστιν...ἐστιν εἷς) echoes the language of the Shema.[40] That such an echo was intended and heard is supported by abundant evidence that the Shema was widely known and used in the Judaism of the first century[41] and in other early Christian writings.[42] Even more to the point, Matt 19.17 contains a probable allusion to the Shema,[43] and Matt 22.37 cites Deut 6.5. If an echo of the Shema is present in 23.8-10, Jesus is named as the 'one teacher' of the Christian community employing the very language used to affirm the oneness of God in the common, daily practice of first century Judaism.[44]

These features of the text suggest that Matt 23.8-10 accords Jesus a remarkable degree of authority in his role as teacher. It is important for our purposes to ascertain within which categories Matthew understands Jesus as teacher. Clearly, he appeals to Jesus' identity as the Messiah. The term ὁ Χριστός in 23.10, which many scholars suggest is a Matthean addition,[45] indicates that Jesus' role as διδάσκαλος and καθηγητής is linked with his identity as Messiah.[46] We saw above in chapter 3 that there was already an expectation in early Judaism of a teaching Messiah.[47] Matt 23.10 suggests

---

[38] Cf. Hagner, *Matthew*, 2.661.

[39] Cf. Michaels, 'Prophecy,' 310.

[40] Cf. Davies and Allison, *Matthew*, 3.277; Hagner, *Matthew*, 2.661; Luz, *Matthew*, 107.

[41] Cf. Instone-Brewer, *Prayer*, 41-52; Schürer, *History*, 2.455; Reif, *Judaism*, 83; Sanders, *Jewish Law*, 68-69. *Contra* Foster, 'Shema,' 321-31. Of the many Mishnaic references to the Shema, note especially the connection between the Shema and the Temple in *m. Tamid* 4.3-5.1; *m. Ta'an.* 4.3. Cf. Josephus, *Ant.* 4.212; possibly 1QS 10.10.

[42] Cf. Marcus, 'Authority,' 196-211, esp. 199-200; Verseput, 'Prayers,' 177-91. Birger Gerhardsson has written on the influence of the Shema on the NT in numerous publications over the years. Cf. e.g. Gerhardsson, 'Early Christianity,' 275-93.

[43] Cf. Byrskog, *Teacher*, 301-2; Davies and Allison, *Matthew*, 3.42.

[44] Cf. Becker, *Kathedra*, 203-4; Byrskog, *Teacher*, 300-302; Karrer, 'Lehrende,' 17-18.

[45] E.g. Riesner, *Lehrer*, 262.

[46] Cf. Gaston, 'Messiah,' 38-39; Kingsbury, *Matthew*, 93.

[47] *Contra* Yieh, *One Teacher*, 242, n. 10.

that Matthew may have drawn upon this tradition: Jesus is the authoritative teacher because he is the Messiah.

However, I suggest that Matt 23.8-10 may advance beyond messianic categories. In 23.8-10, Matthew accords authority to Jesus' teaching primarily by relating Jesus as teacher to God as father/teacher. As we have seen, statements about Jesus as teacher are placed in close conjunction with a similar statement about God, the language of the Shema is used, and there is possible ambiguity as to the identity of the διδάσκαλος in 23.8.[48] This close unity between Jesus and God is highly significant. While Matthew could have made primary reference to other categories in order to describe Jesus as teacher, the main category he in fact utilizes is *God*.[49] But how does this relate to the affirmation in 23.10 that the 'Christ' is the one teacher? Verseput has demonstrated that, for Matthew, the divine Sonship of Jesus is inextricably linked with his Davidic Messiahship, such that Matthew can encompass the two Christological categories under the single term χριστός.[50] For Matthew, Jesus the Messiah is conceived of as Jesus the Son of God (Matt 16.16; 26.63).[51] Therefore, the reference to the Christ in 23.10 may point toward Jesus the Christ, the *Son of God* as the one who teaches with authority.[52]

Matthew's development of Jesus as the Son of God is the high point of his Christology. Kingsbury argues that Matthew's Son of God Christology has its roots in the Messiah, son of David, OT background but that it is 'far more elevated than anything found' in this background.[53] Verseput suggests that the title 'Son' in Matthew does not of itself signify divinity, but reaches in that direction, since it is Matthew's means of expressing the intimacy of Jesus with God.[54] In Matthew, Jesus' identity as the unique Son of the Father is the basis of his ability to convey perfectly the teaching of God.[55] This suggests that the close unity of Jesus and God in 23.8-10 is better explained by Matthew's Son of God Christology than by messianic categories. The link between Jesus as Son of God and Jesus as the 'one teacher' is strengthened

---

[48] Cf. Garland, *Intention*, 59, n. 97. Cf. Byrskog, *Teacher*, 301-2 on Matt 19.17. In *The Gospel of Matthew, Homily 72.3*, John Chrysostom argues that the 'one' master and guide refers both to the Father and to Christ. Cited in Simonetti, *Matthew*, 2.168.

[49] Cf. Byrskog, *Teacher*, 300.

[50] Verseput, 'Son,' 542-44.

[51] Cf. Kingsbury, *Matthew*, 79-80.

[52] Cf. Kingsbury, *Matthew*, 60-61.

[53] Kingsbury, *Matthew*, 80. On the high Christology of Matthew, cf. Kingsbury, *Matthew*, 78-83; Verseput, 'Son,' 532-56; Weren, 'Christology,' 447-65, esp. 465; Gerhardsson, 'Christology,' 14-32. Cf. Matt 1.23; 14.27; 18.20; 28.19-20. However, cf. Nolland, 'Christology,' 3-12, who argues against a Son of God Christology in Matt 1.23.

[54] Verseput, 'Son,' 541. Cf. Luz, 'Thetische,' 231, 234-35.

[55] Verseput, 'Son,' 538-41.

by 11.25-27, which suggests that it is as God's Son that Jesus is able to know and reveal God's eschatological plan. The intimate Father-Son relationship described in 11.27 grounds Jesus' call in 11.29 to μάθετε ἀπ᾽ ἐμοῦ. Other passages in Matthew make the same point, that as God's Son Jesus teaches with authority.[56]

This Matthean connection between Jesus as the Son of God and his identity as teacher is strikingly similar to the Fourth Gospel. In chapter 5, I suggested that the fourth evangelist develops a didactic storyline in which Jesus is the Son taught by his Father, and that this motif explains why Jesus' teaching is understood as the direct divine instruction of Isa 54.13. The high Christology of the Fourth Gospel (paradoxical though it is) thus accounts for Jesus' ability to give direct divine instruction. Something similar may be evident in Matt 23.8-10. Here, the διδάσκαλος is Jesus, who enjoys a unique intimacy with the Father as the Son of God, and therefore fulfills Jer 31.34. This accords with the remarkable claims regarding Jesus' teaching throughout Matthew's gospel, claims which equate his teaching with God's teaching.[57] The high authority accorded to Jesus as teacher in Matt 23.8-10, authority which is described in relation to the one God and in language reminiscent of the Shema, may be close to the Fourth Gospel's view that Jesus' teaching is divine instruction because of Jesus' unity with the Father.[58]

9.2 The content and function of divine instruction

If my argument in section 1 is correct (i.e. that Jesus' teaching is considered divine instruction), the content of divine instruction is, for Matthew, probably all of the teaching of Jesus recorded in his gospel, and particularly the five great discourses around which the gospel is structured (5.1-7.29; 10.5-42; 13.1-52; 18.1-35; 23.1-25.46).[59] This is, of course, different from the content of divine instruction in the Johannine writings and Pauline letters.

What is the function of the declarations that Jesus is the one teacher (23.8, 10)? Clearly, these declarations ground the commands that no one else in the community should be called teacher. The relevant question here is whether 23.8-10 is intended only for the Matthean community, or whether it can also be read as polemic against the Jewish community. Garland and van Tilborg have argued that Matthew's anti-Pharisaism serves a pedagogical function for

---

[56] Cf. Kingsbury, *Matthew*, 60-61; Yieh, *One Teacher*, 243-46. Cf. 17.5; 28.19-20.

[57] Cf. Byrskog, *Teacher*, 290-306.

[58] Cf. Athenagoras, *Leg.* 11.1: Jesus' words in Matt 5.44-45 are 'God-taught' wisdom.

[59] These five discourses are probably what Jesus' disciples are to 'teach' the nations (Matt 28.20). Cf. Stanton, *Gospels and Jesus*, 59, 74.

the Christian community by showing what it should not be like.[60] However, Stanton argues persuasively that the anti-Jewish polemic is real, not simply pedagogical, even though it is not directly addressed to the scribes and Pharisees in Matt 23.[61] Stanton's position does not rule out the possibility that Matthew's community is also addressed. In line with this interpretation, I suggest that Jesus' claim to be the one teacher may well have both a polemical and community-defining function. In this respect, it is similar to the Fourth Gospel – we saw in chapter 6 that the idea of divine instruction functions polemically and as a self-legitimation in the Fourth Gospel. In section 3, I will further elucidate the function of Jesus' claim to be the one teacher.

9.3 How does divine instruction affect human teaching?

Reading 23.8-10 as a triad (see above), there are three prohibitions: Jesus' followers are not to be called ῥαββί or καθηγηταί, and they are not to call anyone πατέρα. Opinion has differed as to what is prohibited in these verses. As in chapter 7, it is helpful to set out a continuum of positions, recognizing that some views may be partially compatible with others.

Interpretations of Matthew 23.8-10

Table 2. *What is prohibited in Matt 23.8-10?*

Church offices not prohibited		Church offices prohibited	
#1 At least titles are prohibited	#2 Ultimate authority of teachers prohibited	#3 Tension within Matthew: offices prohibited, but they existed anyway	#4 Special offices prohibited
Davies and Allison; Byrskog; Barbour? Newport; Luz?	Calvin; Reilly; Luz?	Viviano; Sim; Stanton; Duling; Saldarini; Bornkamm	Beare; Krentz; Derrett

(1) Those who hold view 1 agree that at least titles are prohibited. Davies and Allison argue that 23.8-10 constitutes a 'general prohibition against all ecclesiastical titles.'[62] This is explained by developments in emerging

---

[60] Garland, *Intention*, 117-23; van Tilborg, *Leaders*, 26, 97-98. Garland also emphasizes that Matt 23 functions to explain the fate of Israel.

[61] Stanton, *New People*, 154-57. Cf. Saldarini, 'Delegitimation,' 678-80; Luz, *Matthew*, 108; Newport, *Sources*, 68-75.

[62] Davies and Allison, *Matthew*, 3.275, 278.

rabbinic Judaism, as well as a growing *ecclesiastical* authority.[63] Similarly, Byrskog thinks titles are prohibited in order to establish the identity of Matthew's community over against the growing tendency of post-70 Judaism to legitimate teachers by bestowing didactic titles.[64] Barbour suggests the prohibition of titles, but is open to the view that Matthew favored an egalitarian community.[65] According to Newport, Matthew supports the continuing authority of the scribes and Pharisees (23.2-3) and the community's leaders, but does not allow either to be honored with titles.[66] Luz argues that 23.8-10 does not prohibit the existence of Christian scribes, but rather their 'preference for titles and the accompanying claims to honor and power.'[67] It is intended polemically against the Jewish leaders, and parenetically addressed to the community. Although there are variations in view 1, all these views suggest that it is possible to hold a teaching office in Matthew's community but not to be called by a didactic title.[68]

(2) View 2 suggests that what is prohibited is the assuming of ultimate didactic authority. Calvin argued that 23.8-10 was not about titles, but about the proper limits of teachers. Ultimate authority for human teachers is prohibited.[69] Similarly, Reilly suggests that the issue is not about titles, but rather about pride or humility in the use of titles, and whether or not a teacher is understood to be a teacher 'in Christ.'[70] Unlike Calvin and Reilly, Luz thinks the issue is *at least* about titles, but suggests that 23.8-12 also combats the claims to 'honor and power' of Christian scribes.[71]

(3) Views 3 and 4 are close to one another: they both argue that 23.8-10 prohibits church offices. However, view 3 more explicitly emphasizes a tension within Matthew due to the presence of teachers within the Matthean community. Viviano suggests that Matthew has a 'conflicted attitude' toward church office. He advocates a utopian vision of direct divine instruction (23.8-10), while at the same allowing for leadership structures in his community (23.34).[72] Sim argues similarly that 23.8-10 is 'clearly idealistic' given the strong evidence within the gospel that 'certain leadership roles and authoritative structures were beginning to emerge.'[73] Stanton suggests a

---

[63] Davies and Allison, *Matthew*, 3.280.

[64] Byrskog, 'Teacher,' 99.

[65] Barbour, 'Titles,' 141.

[66] Newport, *Sources*, 132.

[67] Luz, *Matthew*, 106.

[68] Cf. Becker, *Kathedra*, 202-3; Pesch, 'Theologische Aussagen,' 288-89.

[69] Calvin, *Matthew*, 79-80.

[70] Reilly, 'Titles,' 249-50.

[71] Luz, *Matthew*, 106.

[72] Vivianio, 'Social World,' 3-21.

[73] Sim, *Matthew*, 139-40. Cf. Sim, *Eschatology*, 188-89.

possible 'ambivalence concerning institutional structures.'[74] Duling concludes that, while 23.8-10 suggests a limited egalitarianism, this is contradicted by the actual situation of the Matthean community, in which there were probably some with authority. Duling speaks of a 'tension,' and a 'discontinuity between ideology and social reality.'[75] Finally, Bornkamm suggests that in Matthew 'all signs of special offices' are lacking, but notes that there is evidence in Matthew for 'order and particular functionaries' within the Matthean community. He suggests that the prohibitions of 23.8-10 indicate the presence of these functionaries.[76]

(4) View 4 also suggests that 23.8-10 prohibits teaching offices, but does not emphasize the tension highlighted by view 3. Beare argues that the prohibitions are meant to warn against the distinction between clergy and laity that was growing because of the move toward a church hierarchy.[77] Krentz suggests that Matthew opposes charismatic prophets and corrects the tendency of his community to adopt Jewish structures of authoritative teachers and leaders. Building part of his case on 23.8-10, Krentz argues that Matthew envisions an 'egalitarian church in which all members bear equal responsibility for leadership, edification, and service.'[78] On this reading, 'rank and office are unknown in the ideal community.'[79] Derrett also sees charismatic excess as one of the problems in view: Isa 54.13 and Jer 31.33-34 were being exploited by some in favor of charismatic gifts. Matthew responds by applying these passages to Jesus, showing that his mediation is, and remains, essential. Therefore, the Christian community is not to have 'professional exponents or patrons' like the synagogue.[80]

Critical assessment, and a way forward

What are we to make of these views? One of the most noticeable features of this survey is the variety of proposed backgrounds and settings for Matt 23.8-10. This is indicative of the kind of guess-work that has generated many of the views. It is important to heed the caution of Graham Stanton, who has highlighted the difficulties of reconstructing the social setting of Matthew's community from his gospel. Stanton notes that Matthew chose to write a gospel (not a letter), and that he likely wrote to 'loosely linked communities.'

---

[74] Stanton, *New People*, 104.

[75] Duling, 'Leadership,' 124-37, esp. 131, 134. Cf. also Saldarini, 'Delegitimation,' 671, 678.

[76] Bornkamm, 'Tradition,' 39. On this last point, cf. Stendahl, *School*, 30; Schweizer, 'Church,' 160.

[77] Beare, *Matthew*, 450-51.

[78] Krentz, 'Community,' 565-73, esp. 572.

[79] Krentz, 'Community,' 570.

[80] Derrett, 'Midrash,' 383, 385.

These factors of genre and geography warn against an uncritical reading of the narrative as a kind of 'allegory' within which to read the life of the community.[81] In chapter 6 above, I suggested that any attempt to read the story of the Johannine community from the narrative of the Fourth Gospel must be made with great methodological caution. This is also the case for Matthew's gospel.

In my judgment, even a methodologically cautious approach suggests that Matthew was probably not opposed to teachers within his community. This does not prove that teachers existed in the Matthean community, but it does suggest that they could have. Matthew reports Jesus' commission of his disciples to make disciples and teach (28.19-20). Matt 23.34 may suggest the presence of prophets, wise men, and scribes within the community (cf. 13.52), and the 'binding and loosing' of Matt 16.16 perhaps implies the presence of some didactic authority.[82] Furthermore, as noted above, the prohibitions of 23.8-10 may suggest that some members of the community had didactic functions.[83] These considerations indicate that view 4 is inadequate: Matthew is more positive toward the presence of teachers than this view suggests.

At the opposite end of the spectrum, view 1 seems correct as far as it goes. *Contra* Calvin and Reilly, 23.8-10 appears at least to prohibit titles. This is indicated by the immediate context (23.7) and the three-fold repetition of καλέω. The relevant question is whether it prohibits *more* than titles. The repeated use of καλέω does not require that only titles are in view, since Matthew can use the verb to denote not only what something is called but also what it is (or will become).[84] The prohibition of being 'called' rabbi, father, and master could therefore prohibit being a teacher. This latter prohibition is in fact assumed by view 3. However, it is never explicitly stated in 23.8-10, and to suggest that this passage confirms a 'utopian vision' of a radically egalitarian community is to go beyond the evidence. It seems unlikely that Matthew would have permitted contradictory visions of his community to come so close together in his narrative (23.8-10, 34).

These considerations suggest that an answer may lie in view 2. As noted above, Luz argues that 23.8-10 does not prohibit the existence of Christian scribes, but rather their 'preference for titles and the accompanying claims to honor and power.' Greater specificity can be brought to this suggestion if we consider the possibility that 23.8-10 not only promotes a vision of the Christian community, but polemicizes against Jewish didactic structures. One

---

[81] Stanton, 'Communities,' 9-23, esp. 9-13.

[82] Cf. Schweizer, 'Church,' 154-55. Orton, *Scribe*, 137-63 argues that Matthew characterizes the disciples as scribes.

[83] Cf. Schweizer, 'Church,' 160.

[84] Cf. Matt 5.9; 22.43, 45.

fundamental feature of the Jewish master-disciple relationship is so obvious that it is more often assumed than mentioned in the primary and secondary literature. That is the natural progression by which the disciple of a master eventually becomes a master with his own disciples.[85] Ordination came to be an important moment in this process, although it is not certain when ordination was first practiced.[86] The progression of an individual from disciple to master was necessitated by the fact that each generation of rabbis died and needed to be replaced by another generation, who made their own disciples.[87] Relatively little is known about how the rabbinic schools operated in the Tannaitic period, but it is seems that most early 'schools' were groups of disciples who gathered to a respected master, disbanding after his death.[88]

The vision of 23.8-10, in distinction to this practice, is of the gathering of a *multi-generational* community of disciples around one teacher who remains present with them (Matt 18.20; 28.18-20), namely Jesus the Messiah, the Son of God. The theme of Jesus' continuing presence with his disciples is a major one in Matthew's gospel.[89] The fundamental change of 23.8-10 is that Jesus' disciples, unlike those of the Pharisees, are to make disciples not for themselves but for their one teacher, Jesus (28.19).[90] 23.8-10 is therefore an exclusive claim that Jesus is the one teacher within the entire, multi-generational Christian community. Disciples of Jesus always remain disciples.[91] Within the Jewish master-disciple relationship it was possible to consider oneself the disciple of a great individual of the past (e.g. John 9.28; *m. 'Abot* 1.12) while remaining the disciple of one's own immediate master. Jesus' claim does not permit this. In 23.8-10 he claims to be the one rabbi/teacher such that no other masters even in future generations are permissible. There is no clear indication in Matt 23.8-10 that this prohibits teaching within the Matthean community, but it does seem at least to circumscribe that teaching. Ultimate authority does not reside in the Christian scribe. His teaching is simply a repeating of all that Jesus has commanded (28.18-20).

Importantly, the prohibitions of 23.8-10 are not grounded by allegations of corruption within the Jewish leadership (those are indeed stated in 23.1-7, and expanded in the woes of 23.13-36). Rather, the prohibitions are grounded by claims about the didactic authority of Jesus and God. Matthew's Jesus argues from the fact that he is the 'one teacher' and God is the 'one father' to

---

[85] Cf. Rengstorf, 'μαθητής,' *TDNT* 4.454. See *t. 'Ed.* 3.4.

[86] Cf. Stemberger, *Talmud and Midrash*, 13-14; Westerholm, *Jesus*, 31-39.

[87] On the trauma caused by a teacher's death, see Aberbach, 'Master,' 21.

[88] Cf. Stemberger, *Talmud and Midrash*, 10.

[89] Cf. Müller, 'Christology,' 166; especially Kupp, *Emmanuel, passim.*

[90] Cf. Keener, *Matthew*, 719.

[91] Cf. Bornkamm, 'Tradition,' 40.

the prohibition of his disciples possessing ultimate didactic authority and bearing didactic titles. In other words, the master-disciple relationship must change not simply because it is corrupt, but because the presence of God in the person of Jesus the Messiah calls for a restructuring of didactic relationships. This indicates the eschatological nature of Jesus' claims. His identity as the one (divine) teacher relativizes all other instruction.

9.4 Conclusion

In this chapter, I have argued that Matthew understands Jesus' identity as teacher in light of his identity as the Messiah and, ultimately, the Son of God. Jesus' intimacy with the Father is the basis of his teaching, and thus Jesus as teacher can be described in close conjunction with God, using the language of the Shema. Jesus' identity as the one teacher of the Matthean community serves both a polemical and a community-defining function. The Matthean community has one authoritative teacher, not the generational progression of masters and disciples. This does not appear to rule out all teaching in the Matthean community. But it does limit the authority of all teachers, whose job it is to disciple new believers to Jesus rather than themselves. If Jer 31.34 is in view in Matt 23.8-10, Matthew seems to have understood it not as an absolute prohibition of teaching, but as an affirmation of the unique status of Jesus, the one teacher.

Chapter 10

Conclusion

'Yonder in the better world, the inhabitants are independent of all creature comforts…They
need no teachers there; they doubtless commune with one another concerning the things of
God, but they do not require this by way of instruction; they shall all be taught of the Lord.'

Charles H. Spurgeon, *Morning and Evening*, the reading for August 9

This study represents the first comprehensive examination of the idea of divine instruction in the OT, early Jewish literature, and NT writings. In the introduction, I defined the parameters of the study as focusing on passages that combine a reference to God with didactic terminology. Within this group of passages, I was most interested in citations of, or allusions to, Isa 54.13 and Jer 31.34. As noted in the introduction, it is reasonably certain that Isa 54.13 is cited in John 6.45 and alluded to in 1 Thess 4.9. In chapters 7-9, I suggested that Jer 31.34 may have influenced 1 John 2.20, 27 and Matt 23.8-10, and that Isa 54.13 may stand behind 1 Cor 2.13. These cases are less certain. However, even if Isa 54.13 and Jer 31.34 have not influenced these passages, the idea of divine instruction is clearly present in them, so they remain relevant to this study.

The broader-than-normal sweep of the study has allowed the diversity of ideas about divine instruction to become apparent, and indeed, this is one of the striking features of the concept. However, some interesting commonalities have also emerged. In chapter 1, I claimed that early Christians' awareness that they had been, and were being, taught by God was an important aspect of their self-understanding, and that it had relevance for an understanding of the eschatology, Christology, pneumatology, ecclesiology and hermeneutics of the earliest Christian communities. In this concluding chapter, I highlight the significant findings of the study in these areas.

Eschatology

In chapter 2, I demonstrated that while most of the OT writings conceive of divine instruction as a past or present event, there is a prophetic development that promises eschatological divine instruction. My discussion in chapter 3 showed that early Jewish writers differed regarding when they understood divine instruction to occur. Some of the DSS understand it as a past or present event, while others may envision a future divine instruction. Even when divine instruction is understood as past or present, it is often seen as an eschatological event fulfilled within the community. This reflects the strong eschatological bent of the Scrolls. It is possible that CD 20.4 alludes to the eschatological promise of Isa 54.13 when it identifies members of the community as 'taught by God.' Similarly, *Pss. Sol.* 17.32 may allude to Isa 54.13 in its development of the idea of an end-time messianic figure who will offer instruction. Philo's development of the idea of divine instruction contrasts sharply with the eschatological emphases of these writings. Philo never cites or alludes to Isa 54.13 or Jer 31.34, and never appears to conceive of divine instruction as eschatological. Rather, Philo's development of the idea is heavily indebted to Greek educational ideas and his own observation.

The NT writings are more similar to the DSS and *Pss. Sol.* than to Philo in their development(s) of divine instruction. The NT writings draw upon Isa 54.13 and Jer 31.34, and highlight the idea of *eschatological* divine instruction. We saw this particularly in the fourth evangelist's redaction of Isa 54.13 and the eschatological emphases of 1 Cor 2.13 and Matt 23.8-10. Strikingly, our study uncovered no indication in the Johannine writings, Pauline letters, or Matthew of a future divine instruction. This contrasts with C. H. Spurgeon's futurist reading of Isa 54.13, cited above in the epigraph at the beginning of this chapter. In the Johannine writings, Pauline letters, and Matthew, the promise of eschatological divine instruction is considered as fulfilled. If there is a yet-future fulfillment, it is not spoken of in the NT writings studied here. This claim of the present fulfillment of Isa 54.13 and Jer 31.34 is explained by the belief of the earliest followers of Jesus that they were living in the last days, in the time of eschatological fulfillment.[1] In my view, the emphasis on present fulfillment is also explained by the *Christological* interpretation of divine instruction in the Fourth Gospel, Paul, and Matthew.

Christology

One of the most important contributions of this study is in Christology. I argued in chapter 5 that the fourth evangelist understands Isa 54.13 to promise direct, unmediated divine instruction. Further, I argued that the evangelist claims this promise is fulfilled through the teaching of Jesus. In chapters 7-9, I suggested that 1 John, 1 Thessalonians, and Matthew also interpret the promise of eschatological divine instruction as fulfilled through Jesus. In Matthew, this is likely connected with a Son of God Christology

---

[1] Cf. Johnson, *Writings*, 102-4.

that is similar to the Fourth Gospel. The idea of a teaching Messiah, examined in chapter 3, presents some continuity between Jewish expectation and Christian understanding. However, I argued that in Matthew 23, and especially in the Fourth Gospel, messianic categories are surpassed in favor of a higher Christology.

Indeed, the findings of this study suggest the presence of a high Christology in the earliest Christian communities. Multiple NT writers re-evaluated the prophetic promises of direct divine instruction, and concluded that Jesus, the teacher *par excellence*, had fulfilled those promises. In 1 Thessalonians, Paul prays to the resurrected Jesus to produce the very love he claims God teaches. In John 6, Jesus' teaching is the direct divine instruction promised by Isaiah. In Matthew 23, Jesus as the one teacher is understood in terms of God, the one father/teacher, using the language of the Shema. This study establishes an early trajectory to Clement of Alexandria's claim (sometime in the second century) that the 'holy God Jesus' is the instructor of Christians, and that the Lord instructs believers 'face to face' (see the epigraph at the beginning of chapter 4).

Pneumatology

In chapters 2-3, I noted a number of instances in the OT writings and early Jewish sources in which divine instruction was understood to occur through the Spirit of God. It is therefore perhaps unsurprising that the same idea occurs frequently in the NT writings. We saw that in the Fourth Gospel, the Holy Spirit/Paraclete teaches the disciples (John 14.26), and in 1 John 2.20, 27 the 'anointing' (i.e. the Spirit) teaches the whole community. Paul understands the Spirit as a teacher in 1 Thess 4.9 and 1 Cor 2.13. Only in Matt 23.8-10 is there no indication that the promise of divine instruction is fulfilled through the Spirit. Although there is agreement between the Johannine writings and the Pauline letters that the Spirit teaches, this is of course understood in different ways. In the Fourth Gospel and Johannine letters, divine instruction seems to be more cognitive. While this is similar to 1 Corinthians 2, our examination of 1 Thess 4.9 suggests that divine instruction may be understood there more as ethical empowerment than as revelatory.

Ecclesiology

One of the important questions raised by this study is whether divine instruction was considered in the earliest Christian communities to render otiose human teaching. When this question was addressed in the Johannine writings and Matthew, I urged a cautious methodological approach rather than the too-frequent readings of the gospels in which the lives of the gospel communities are read off the surface of the gospel narratives. In 1 John, divine instruction seems in some sense to render human teaching otiose. However, I suggested that, in light of the findings of chapter 4, 'teaching' in 1 John is ultimately understood as the direct revelation brought uniquely by Jesus. Moreover, Johannine ecclesiology is difficult to discern. These factors suggest that 1 John 2.27 should not be interpreted as the charter for a radically egalitarian community (e.g. Schweizer).

Paul's employment of divine instruction in 1 Thess 4.9 is noticeably different than the Johannine writings. Here, divine instruction is understood to come through the apostle rather than to obviate the need for his teaching. However, more of an antithesis between divine and human instruction is apparent in Paul's descriptions of his own divine 'education' (Gal 1.12; 1 Cor 2.13).

In Matthew, Jesus' identity as the one teacher does not require that no individuals in the Matthean community teach, but it does circumscribe the authority of teachers. No longer do teachers make disciples for themselves – rather, they disciple believers to Jesus, the one teacher. Thus, it seems that in the Johannine and Matthean communities there is more clearly a relativizing of human teaching in light of eschatological divine instruction. This same tendency is not as apparent in Paul.

Hermeneutics

Another significant finding of this study is that in the Fourth Gospel, the claim to be 'taught by God' functions polemically and as a self-legitimation, and is sometimes a claim to revealed interpretation of the Scriptures (chapter 6). This has been suggested previously by Borgen and Juel, but only in passing. I have strengthened their suggestion by showing that divine instruction may have been understood as a claim to revealed interpretation in the DSS (chapter 3), by reading John 6.45 in its context (chapter 6), and by demonstrating parallels between John 6.31-58 and the Qumran *pesharim*.[2] If my argument is valid, this has significant implications for the Fourth Gospel's approach to the Scriptures. The evangelist understood himself to be an inspired exegete of the Scriptures, able to understand their Christological content through the Spirit (14.26).

Although the idea of divine instruction is not used in order to claim revealed interpretation of the Scriptures in the other writings I have examined, it does function polemically and as a self-legitimation in 1 John, 1 Corinthians, Galatians, and Matthew. This is perhaps to be expected: the claim to be 'taught by God' has obvious potential for offering self-legitimation.

---

[2] Cf. Witmer, 'Approaches,' 313-28.

Conclusion

In *According to the Scriptures*, C. H. Dodd isolated several key OT passages that exercised a significant influence on the earliest followers of Jesus. Dodd's criterion for discerning early Christian *testimonia* was that a passage from the OT is, 'cited by two or more writers of the New Testament in *prima facie* independence of one another.'[3] Leaving aside discussion of Dodd's thesis of *testimonia*, I suggest that on his criterion, Isa 54.13 should be included: it appears to be present in the Pauline (1 Thess 4.9) and Johannine (John 6.45) writings.[4] Together with Jer 31.34, it seems to have influenced the thinking of various early Christians. This study confirms the suggestion of Traugott Holtz that there was an 'early Christian tradition' that Isa 54.13 was coming to fulfillment in the Christian community.[5] However, perhaps it would be better to say 'early Christian *traditions*.' While Isa 54.13 and/or Jer 31.34 influenced the Johannine writings, the Pauline letters, and Matthew, they are employed in noticeably different ways. I have found no evidence that any of these three bodies of writing drew upon the others in their development of divine instruction, so it seems likely that they are 'independent parallels.'[6] It is not surprising, then, that they differ in their development of divine instruction. What is striking is that they each re-interpret the prophetic promise of divine instruction in light of the teaching of Jesus and/or the Spirit.

As indicated by the epigraphs included throughout this thesis, Isa 54.13 and the other biblical texts relating to divine instruction have continued to influence later Christian (and Jewish) tradition since the writing of the NT. This history of interpretation demonstrates the importance of the subject for Christians (and Jews) of later periods, and surely warrants further study.

---

[3] Dodd, *Scriptures*, 28-29.

[4] Isa 54.13 is alluded to rather than cited in 1 Thess 4.9, but in my judgment the allusion is reasonably clear.

[5] Holtz, *Thessalonicher*, 174.

[6] Cf. Schuchard, *Scripture*, 47.

Bibliography

1. Primary sources

Ante-Nicene Fathers: The Writings of the Fathers down to A. D. 325. Edited by Alexander Roberts, James Donaldson, A. Cleveland Coxe, and Allan Menzies. 10 vols. Repr., Grand Rapids: Eerdmans, 1989-1990.

Apocrypha. Revised Standard Version. Oxford: Oxford University Press, 1977.

Baumgarten, Joseph M., and Michael T. Davis. 'Cave IV, V, VI Fragments Related to the Damascus Documents.' Pages 59-79 in *Damascus Document, War Scroll, and Related Documents*. Vol. 2 of *The Dead Sea Scrolls: Hebrew, Aramaic, and Greek Texts with English Translations*. Edited by James H. Charlesworth. Tübingen: J. C. B. Mohr (Paul Siebeck), 1995.

Baumgarten, Joseph M., and Daniel R. Schwartz. 'Damascus Document (CD).' Pages 4-57 in *Damascus Document, War Scroll, and Related Documents*. Vol. 2 of *The Dead Sea Scrolls: Hebrew, Aramaic, and Greek Texts with English Translations*. Edited by James H. Charlesworth. Tübingen: J. C. B. Mohr (Paul Siebeck), 1995.

Braude, William G. *The Midrash on Psalms*. YJS 13. 2 vols. New Haven: Yale University Press, 1959.

Chilton, Bruce D., ed. *The Isaiah Targum: Introduction, Translation, Apparatus and Notes*. Vol. 11 of *The Aramaic Bible*. Edited by Martin McNamara. Edinburgh: T & T Clark, 1987.

Darnell, D. R. and D. A. Fiensy. 'Hellenistic Synagogal Prayers.' Pages 671-97 in *The Old Testament Pseudepigrapha: Expansions of the "Old Testament" and Legends, Wisdom and Philosophical Literature, Prayers, Psalms, and Odes, Fragments of Lost Judeo-Hellenistic Works*. Edited by James H. Charlesworth. London: Darton, Longman & Todd, 1985.

de Selincourt, E., and J. C. Smith, eds. *Poetical Works of Spenser*. London: Oxford University Press, 1970.

Dio Chrysostom. *Discourses*. Translated by J. W. Cohoon and H. Lamar Crosby. LCL. 5 vols. Cambridge: Harvard University Press, 1932-1951.

Duhaime, Jean. 'Cave IV Fragments.' Pages 143-97 in *Damascus Document, War Scroll, and Related Documents*. Vol. 2 of *The Dead Sea Scrolls: Hebrew, Aramaic, and Greek Texts with English Translations*. Edited by James H. Charlesworth. Tübingen: J. C. B. Mohr (Paul Siebeck), 1995.

—. 'War Scroll.' Pages 80-141 in *Damascus Document, War Scroll, and Related Documents*. Vol. 2 of *The Dead Sea Scrolls: Hebrew, Aramaic, and Greek Texts with English Translations*. Edited by James H. Charlesworth. Tübingen: J. C. B. Mohr (Paul Siebeck), 1995.

Freedman, H., and Maurice Simon, eds. *Midrash Rabbah Song of Songs*. London: Soncino Press, 1961.

García Martínez, Florentino, and Eibert J. C. Tigchelaar, eds. *The Dead Sea Scrolls Study Edition*. 2 vols. Leiden: Brill, 1997.

García Martínez, Florentino, Eibert J. C. Tigchelaar, and Adam S. Van der Woude, eds. *Qumran Cave 11: 11Q2-18, 11Q20-31*. DJD 23. Oxford: Clarendon Press, 1998.

Holmes, Michael W., ed. *The Apostolic Fathers: Greek Texts and English Translations*. Rev. ed. Grand Rapids: Baker, 1999.

Josephus. Translated by H. St. J. Thackeray et al. 10 vols. LCL. Cambridge: Harvard University Press, 1926-1965.

Josephus. *The Works of Josephus*. Translated by William Whiston. Repr., United States of America: Hendrickson, 1987.

Lauterbach, Jacob Z., ed. *Mekilta de-Rabbi Ishmael*. 3 vols. Philadelphia: The Jewish Publication Society of America, 1961.

Luther's Works: American Edition. Edited by Jaroslav Pelikan and Helmut T. Lehmann. 55 vols. United States of America: Concordia Publishing House/Fortress, 1958-1986.

Mason, Steve, ed. *Flavius Josephus: Translation and Commentary*. Leiden: Brill, 2000–.

Michel, Otto, and Otto Bauernfeind, eds. *De Bello Judaico. Band III: Ergänzungen und Register*. München: Kösel-Verlag, 1969.

Neusner, Jacob, ed. *Pesiqta deRab Kahana*. CRD 11. 3 vols. Atlanta: Scholars Press, 1997.

Parry, Donald W., and Elisha Qimron, eds. *The Great Isaiah Scroll (1QIsa^a): A New Edition*. STDJ 32. Leiden: Brill, 1999.

Philo. Translated by F. H. Colson, G. H. Whitaker, and Ralph Marcus. 10 (+ 2 suppl.) vols. LCL. Cambridge: Harvard University Press, 1929-1962.

Robinson, James M., Paul Hoffmann, and John S. Kloppenborg, eds. *The Critical Edition of Q*. Leuven: Peeters, 2000.

Schuller, Eileen. '4QNon-Canonical Psalms B.' Pages 87-172 in *Qumran Cave 4: Poetical and Liturgical Texts, Part 1*. Edited by Esther Eshel, Hanan Eshel, Carol Newsom, Bilhah Nitzan, Eileen Schuller, and Ada Yardeni. DJD 11. Oxford: Clarendon Press, 1998.

Skehan, Patrick W., and Eugene Ulrich. 'Isaiah.' Pages 7-143 in *Qumran Cave 4: The Prophets*. Edited by Eugene Ulrich, Frank Moore Cross, Russell E. Fuller, Judith E. Sanderson, Patrick W. Skehan, and Emmanuel Tov. DJD 15. Oxford: Clarendon Press, 1997.

Sperber, Alexander, ed. *The Latter Prophets According to Targum Jonathan*. Vol. 3 of *The Bible in Aramaic*. Leiden: E. J. Brill, 1962.

Stenning, J. F., ed. *The Targum of Isaiah*. Oxford: Clarendon Press, 1953.

Townsend, John T., ed. *Midrash Tanhuma: Translated into English with Introduction, Indices, and Brief Notes (S. Buber Recension)*. Vol. II: Exodus and Leviticus. Hoboken, NJ: KTAV Publishing, 1989.

Vermes, Geza. *The Complete Dead Sea Scrolls in English*. London: Penguin Books, 1997.

Wise, M., Martin G. Abegg, Jr., E. Cook, and N. Gordon. 'Hodayot.' Pages 2-76 in *Poetic and Liturgical Texts*. Vol. 5 of *The Dead Sea Scrolls Reader*. Edited by Donald W. Parry and Emmanuel Tov. Leiden: Brill, 2005.

Wright, R. B. 'Psalms of Solomon: A New Translation and Introduction.' Pages 639-70 in *The Old Testament Pseudepigrapha: Expansions of the "Old Testament" and Legends, Wisdom and Philosophical Literature, Prayers, Psalms, and Odes, Fragments of Lost Judeo-Hellenistic Works*. Edited by James H. Charlesworth. London: Darton, Longman & Todd, 1985.

Yadin, Yigael, ed. *The Scroll of the War of the Sons of Light against the Sons of Darkness*. Oxford: Oxford University Press, 1962.

Ziegler, Joseph, ed. *Isaias*. Vol. 14 of *Septuaginta: Vetus Testamentum Graecum*. Göttingen: Vandenhoeck & Ruprecht, 1939.

2. Reference works

Abegg, Jr., Martin G., James E. Bowley, and Edward M. Cook, eds. *The Non-Biblical Texts from Qumran*. Vol. 1 of *The Dead Sea Scrolls Concordance*. Leiden: Brill, 2003.

Alexander, Patrick H. et al., eds. *The SBL Handbook of Style: for Ancient Near Eastern, Biblical, and Early Christian Studies*. Peabody: Hendrickson, 1999.

Balz, Horst, and Gerhard Schneider, eds. *Exegetical Dictionary of the New Testament*. 3 vols. Grand Rapids: Eerdmans, 1990-1993.

Bauer, W., F. W. Danker, W. F. Arndt, and F. W. Gingrich, eds. *Greek-English Lexicon of the New Testament and Other Early Christian Literature*. 3d ed. Chicago: University of Chicago, 1999.

Biblia Patristica: Supplément, Philon D'Alexandrie. Paris: Éditions du Centre National de la Recherche Scientifique, 1982.

Blass, F., A. Debrunner, and Robert W. Funk, eds. *A Greek Grammar of the New Testament and Other Early Christian Literature*. Chicago: University of Chicago, 1961.

Botterweck, G. J., Helmer Ringgren, and Heinz-Josef Fabry, eds. *Theological Dictionary of the Old Testament*. Translated by J. T. Willis, G. W. Bromiley, and D. E. Green. 13 vols. Grand Rapids: Eerdmans, 1974–.

Clines, D. J. A., ed. *Dictionary of Classical Hebrew*. Sheffield: Sheffield Academic Press, 1993–.

Delamarter, Steve. *A Scripture Index to Charlesworth's The Old Testament Pseudepigrapha*. Sheffield: Sheffield Academic Press, 2002.

Denis, Albert-Marie, ed. *Concordance Grecque des Pseudépigraphes D'Ancien Testament*. Louvain-la-Neuve: Université Catholique de Louvain, 1987.

Forestell, J. T. *Targumic Traditions and the New Testament: An Annotated Bibliography with a New Testament Index*. SBLAS 4. Chico: Scholars Press, 1979.

Freedman, David N., ed. *Anchor Bible Dictionary*. 6 vols. New York: Doubleday, 1992.

Hatch, Edwin, and Henry A. Redpath. *A Concordance to the Septuagint and the Other Greek Versions of the Old Testament (Including the Apocryphal Books)*. 2d ed., 2005 Repr. Grand Rapids: Baker Academic, 1998.

Jenni, Ernst, and Claus Westermann, eds. *Theological Lexicon of the Old Testament*. 3 vols. Peabody: Hendrickson, 1997.

Kittel, G., and G. Friedrich, eds. *Theological Dictionary of the New Testament*. Translated by G. W. Bromiley. 10 vols. Grand Rapids: Eerdmans, 1964-1976.

Koehler, Ludwig, Walter Baumgartner, and J. J. Stamm, eds. *The Hebrew and Aramaic Lexicon of the Old Testament*. Translated and edited under the supervision of M. E. J. Richardson. 5 vols. Leiden: E. J. Brill, 1994-2000.

Lausberg, Heinrich. *Handbook of Literary Rhetoric: A Foundation for Literary Study*. Edited by David E. Orton and R. Dean Anderson. Translated by Matthew T. Bliss, Annemiek Jansen, and David E. Orton. Leiden: Brill, 1998.

Liddell, Henry George, Robert Scott, and Henry Stuart Jones, eds. *A Greek-English Lexicon*. 9th ed. with revised supplement. Oxford: Clarendon, 1996.

Louw, Johannes P., and Eugene A. Nida, eds. *Greek-English Lexicon of the New Testament Based on Semantic Domains*. 2 vols. New York: United Bible Societies, 1988.

McLean, Bradley H. *Citations and Allusions to Jewish Scripture in Early Christian and Jewish Writings Through 180 C.E.* Lampeter: Edwin Mellen Press, 1992.

Rengstorf, Karl Heinrich, ed. *A Complete Concordance to Flavius Josephus*. 4 vols. Leiden: E. J. Brill, 1973-1983.

Bibliography

Robertson, A. T. *A Grammar of the Greek New Testament in the Light of Historical Research*. 3d ed. New York: Hodder & Stoughton, 1919.

Schiffman, Lawrence H., and James VanderKam, eds. *Encyclopedia of the Dead Sea Scrolls*. 2 vols. Oxford: Oxford University Press, 2000.

Schwertner, Siegfried, ed. *Internationales Abkürzungsverzeichnis für Theologie und Grenzgebiete*. 2d ed. Berlin: Walter de Gruyter, 1992.

VanGemeren, Willem A., ed. *New International Dictionary of Old Testament Theology & Exegesis*. 5 vols. Carlisle: Paternoster Press, 1996.

Wallace, Daniel B. *Greek Grammar Beyond the Basics*. Grand Rapids: Zondervan, 1996.

Waltke, Bruce K., and M. O'Connor. *An Introduction to Biblical Hebrew Syntax*. Winona Lake: Eisenbrauns, 1990.

3. Secondary literature

Aberbach, M. 'The Relations Between Master and Disciple in the Talmudic Age.' Pages 1-24 in *Essays presented to Chief Rabbi Israel Brodie on the occasion of his seventieth birthday*. Edited by H. J. Zimmels, J. Rabbinowitz, and I. Finestein. PJC n.s. 3. London: Soncino Press, 1967.

Agnon, S. Y. *Present at Sinai: The Giving of the Law*. Translated by Michael Swirksy. Philadelphia: Jewish Publication Society, 1994.

Alford, Henry. *The Epistles to the Galatians, Ephesians, Philippians, Colossians, Thessalonians, – to Timotheus, Titus, and Philemon*. Vol. 3 of *The Greek Testament*. Cambridge: Deighton, Bell, and Co., 1880.

—. *The Four Gospels*. Vol. 1 of *The Greek Testament*. Cambridge: Deighton, Bell, and Co., 1880.

Allison, Dale C., Jr. 'Two Notes on a Key Text: Matthew 11:25-30.' *JTS* ns. 39 (1988): 477-85.

Andersen, Francis I., and David Noel Freedman. *Micah*. AB 24E. London: Doubleday, 2000.

Anderson, A. A. *The Book of Psalms*. NCB. London: Marshall, Morgan & Scott, 1972.

Anderson, Paul N. *The Christology of the Fourth Gospel: Its Unity and Disunity in the Light of John 6*. WUNT 2.78. Tübingen: J. C. B. Mohr (Paul Siebeck), 1996.

—. 'The *Sitz im Leben* of the Johannine Bread of Life Discourse and Its Evolving Context.' Pages 1-59 in *Critical Readings of John 6*. Edited by R. Alan Culpepper. BIS 22. Leiden: Brill, 1997.

Ashton, John. *Understanding the Fourth Gospel*. Oxford: Clarendon Press, 1991.

Atkinson, Kenneth. *I Cried to the Lord: A Study of the Psalms of Solomon's Historical Background and Social Setting*. SJSJ 84. Leiden: Brill, 2004.

Aune, David E. 'Charismatic Exegesis in Early Judaism and Early Christianity.' Pages 126-50 in *The Pseudepigrapha and Early Biblical Interpretation*. Edited by James H. Charlesworth and Craig A. Evans. JSPSup 14. Sheffield: Sheffield Academic Press, 1993.

Austermann, Frank. *Von der Tora zum Nomos: Untersuchungen zur Übersetzungsweise und Interpretation im Septuaginta-Psalter*. MSU 27. Göttingen: Vandenhoeck & Ruprecht, 2003.

Bachmann, Michael. *Jerusalem und der Tempel: Die geographisch-theologischen Elemente in der lukanischen Sicht des jüdischen Kultzentrums*. BWA(N)T 109. Stuttgart: W. Kohlhammer, 1980.

Baker, David L. 'The Finger of God and the Forming of a Nation: The Origin and Purpose of the Decalogue.' *TynBul* 56 (2005): 1-24.

Ball, David Mark. *'I Am' in John's Gospel: Literary Function, Background and Theological Implications*. JSNTSup 124. Sheffield: Sheffield Academic Press, 1996.

Baltzer, Klaus. *Deutero-Isaiah*. Hermeneia. Translated by Margaret Kohl. Minneapolis: Fortress, 2001.

Barbour, R. S. 'Uncomfortable Words: Status and Titles.' *ExpTim* 82 (1970): 137-42.

Barclay, John M. G. 'The Family as the Bearer of Religion in Judaism and Early Christianity.' Pages 66-80 in *Constructing Early Christian Families: Family as Social Reality and Metaphor*. Edited by Halvor Moxnes. London: Routledge, 1997.

—. 'Πνευματικός in the Social Dialect of Pauline Christianity.' Pages 157-67 in *The Holy Spirit and Christian Origins: Essays in Honor of James D. G. Dunn*. Edited by Graham N. Stanton, Bruce W. Longenecker, and Stephen C. Barton. Grand Rapids: Eerdmans, 2004.

Barr, James. *The Semantics of Biblical Language*. Oxford: Oxford University Press, 1962.

Barrett, C. K. *The Gospel According to St. John: An Introduction with Commentary and Notes on the Gospel Text*. 2d ed. London: SPCK, 1978.

Bauckham, Richard. *God Crucified: Monotheism and Christology in the New Testament*. Carlisle: Paternoster, 1998.

—, ed. *The Gospels for All Christians: Rethinking the Gospel Audiences*. Grand Rapids: Eerdmans, 1998.

Beale, G. K. *1-2 Thessalonians*. IVPNTCS. Downers Grove: Intervarsity Press, 2003.

Beare, Francis Wright. *The Gospel according to Matthew*. Oxford: Basil Blackwell, 1981.

Beasley-Murray, George R. *John*. WBC 36. Waco: Word, 1987.

Becker, Hans-Jürgen. *Auf der Kathedra des Mose: Rabbinisch-theologisches Denken und antirabbinische Polemik in Matthäus 23, 1-12*. ANTZ 4. Berlin: Institut Kirche und Judentum, 1990.

Belleville, Linda L. '"Imitate Me, Just as I Imitate Christ": Discipleship in the Corinthian Correspondence.' Pages 120-42 in *Patterns of Discipleship in the New Testament*. Edited by Richard Longenecker. Grand Rapids: Eerdmans, 1996.

Bernard, J. H. *A Critical and Exegetical Commentary on the Gospel According to John*. ICC. 2 vols. Edinburgh: T & T Clark, 1928.

Best, Ernest. *A Commentary on the First and Second Epistles to the Thessalonians*. BNTC. London: A & C Black, 1986.

Betz, Hans Dieter. *Galatians*. Hermeneia. Philadelphia: Fortress, 1979.

Betz, Otto. *Offenbarung und Schriftforschung in der Qumransekte*. WUNT 6. Tübingen: J. C. B. Mohr (Paul Siebeck), 1960.

Beutler, Johannes. *Die Johannesbriefe*. RNT. Regensburg: Friedrich Pustet, 2000.

—. 'The Structure of John 6.' Pages 115-27 in *Critical Readings of John 6*. Edited by R. Alan Culpepper. BIS 22. Leiden: Brill, 1997.

Bicknell, E. J. *The First and Second Epistles to the Thessalonians*. WC. London: Methuen & Co., 1932.

Birnbaum, Ellen. 'What Does Philo Mean by "Seeing God"?: Some Methodological Considerations.' Pages 535-52 in *SBL Seminar Papers, 1995. SBLSP* 34. Atlanta: Scholars Press, 1995.

Black, David Alan. 'An overlooked stylistic argument in favor of πάντα in 1 John 2:20.' *FN* 5 (1992): 205-8.

Blenkinsopp, Joseph. *Isaiah*. AB 19, 19a. 2 vols. London: Doubleday, 2000-2002.

Bockmuehl, Markus N. A. *Revelation and Mystery in Ancient Judaism and Pauline Christianity*. WUNT 2.36. Tübingen: J. C. B. Mohr (Paul Siebeck), 1990.

Boismard, M.-E. 'La connaissance de Dieu dans l'Alliance Nouvelle d'après la première épître de S. Jean.' *RB* 56 (1949): 365-91.

Booth, Wayne C. *The Rhetoric of Fiction*. 2d ed. London: Penguin Books, 1983.

Borgen, Peder. *Bread From Heaven: An Exegetical Study of the Concept of Manna in the Gospel of John and the Writings of Philo*. NovTSup 10. Leiden: E. J. Brill, 1965.

—. 'Bread from Heaven: Aspects of Debates on Expository Method and Form.' Pages 32-46 in *Logos Was the True Light: And Other Essays on the Gospel of John*. Trondheim: Tapir, 1983.

—. 'God's Agent in the Fourth Gospel.' Pages 83-95 in *The Interpretation of John*. Edited by John Ashton. Edinburgh: T & T Clark, 1997. Repr. from *Religions in Antiquity*, ed. J. Neusner, 1968.

—. 'John 6: Tradition, Interpretation and Composition.' Pages 95-114 in *Critical Readings of John 6*. Edited by R. Alan Culpepper. BIS 22. Leiden: Brill, 1997.

—. 'Observations on the Midrashic Character of John 6.' *ZNW* 54 (1963): 232-40.

—. 'Philo of Alexandria.' Pages 333-42 in vol. 5 of *ABD*. Edited by David Noel Freedman. New York: Doubleday, 1992.

—. *Philo of Alexandria: An Exegete for His Time*. NovTSup 86. Leiden: Brill, 1997.

Bornkamm, Günther. 'End-Expectation and Church in Matthew.' Pages 15-51 in *Tradition and Interpretation in Matthew*. Edited by Günther Bornkamm, Gerhard Barth, and Heinz Joachim Held. NTL. London: SCM, 1963.

Bousset, Wilhelm. *Kyrios Christos*. Translated by John E. Steely. New York: Abingdon, 1970.

Bowman, John, ed. *Samaritan Documents Relating to their History, Religion and Life*. POTTS 2. Pittsburgh: Pickwick Press, 1977.

Braulik, Georg. 'Das Deuteronomium und die Gedächtniskultur Israels: Redaktionsgeschichtliche Beobachtungen zur Verwendung von למד.' Pages 119-46 in *Studien zum Buch Deuteronomium*. SBAB 24. Stuttgart: Katholisches Bibelwerk, 1997.

Breck, John. 'The Function of ΠΑΣ in 1 John 2:20.' *SVTQ* 35 (1991): 187-206.

Bréhier, Émile. *Les Idées Philosophiques et Religieuses de Philon D'Alexandrie*. EPhM 8. Paris: Librairie Philosophique, 1925.

Brooke, A. E. *A Critical and Exegetical Commentary on the Johannine Epistles*. ICC. Edinburgh: T & T Clark, 1912.

Brooke, George J. *Exegesis at Qumran: 4QFlorilegium in its Jewish Context*. JSOTSup 29. Sheffield: JSOT Press, 1985.

Brown, Raymond E. *The Community of the Beloved Disciple*. London: Geoffrey Chapman, 1979.

—. *The Epistles of John*. AB 30. Garden City: Doubleday, 1982.

—. *The Gospel According to John*. AB 29, 29a. 2 vols. New York: Doubleday, 1966-1970.

—. *An Introduction to the Gospel of John*. ABRL. London: Doubleday, 2003.

—. 'Johannine Ecclesiology – The Community's Origins.' *Int* 31 (1977): 379-93.

—. 'The relationship to the Fourth Gospel shared by the author of 1 John and by his opponents.' Pages 57-68 in *Text and Interpretation: Studies in the New Testament presented to Matthew Black*. Edited by Ernest Best and R. McL. Wilson. Cambridge: Cambridge University Press, 1979.

—. Review of Pierre Le Fort, *Les structures de l'Eglise militante selon saint Jean*. *Bib* 52 (1971): 454-56.

Brown, Tricia Gates. *Spirit in the Writings of John: Johannine Pneumatology in Social-scientific Perspective*. JSNTSup 253. London: T & T Clark, 2003.

Brownlee, William H. *The Midrash Pesher of Habakkuk*. SBLMS 24. Missoula: Scholars Press, 1979.

Bruce, F. F. *1 & 2 Thessalonians*. WBC 45. Waco: Word Books, 1982.

Büchsel, Friedrich. *Die Johannesbriefe*. ThHK 17. Leipzig: A. Deichertsche, 1933.

Bultmann, Rudolf. 'Die Eschatologie des Johannes-Evangeliums.' Pages 134-52 in *Glauben und Verstehen: Erster Band.* Tübingen: J. C. B. Mohr (Paul Siebeck), 1954.

—. *The Gospel of John: A Commentary.* Translated by G. R. Beasley-Murray. Oxford: Basil Blackwell, 1971.

—. *The History of the Synoptic Tradition.* Translated by John Marsh. Oxford: Basil Blackwell, 1972.

—. *The Johannine Epistles.* Translated by R. Philip O'Hara. Hermeneia. Philadelphia: Fortress, 1973.

—. *Theology of the New Testament.* Translated by Kendrick Grobel. 2 vols. London: SCM, 1955.

Burge, Gary M. *The Anointed Community: The Holy Spirit in the Johannine Tradition.* Grand Rapids: Eerdmans, 1987.

—. *The Letters of John.* NIVAC. Grand Rapids: Zondervan, 1996.

Burke, Trevor J. *Family Matters: A Socio-Historical Study of Kinship Metaphors in 1 Thessalonians.* JSNTSup 247. London: T & T Clark, 2003.

Burney, C. F. *The Aramaic Origin of the Fourth Gospel.* Oxford: Clarendon Press, 1922.

Byrskog, Samuel. 'Das Lernen der Jesusgeschichte nach den synoptischen Evangelien.' Pages 191-209 in *Religiöses Lernen in der biblischen, frühjüdischen und frühchristlichen Überlieferung.* Edited by Beate Ego and Helmut Merkel. WUNT 180. Tübingen: Mohr Siebeck, 2005.

—. 'Jesus as Messianic Teacher in the Gospel According to Matthew: Tradition History and/or Narrative Christology.' Pages 83-100 in *The New Testament as Reception.* Edited by M. Müller and H. Tronier. JSNTSup 230. Sheffield: Sheffield Academic Press, 2002.

—. *Jesus the Only Teacher: Didactic Authority and Transmission in Ancient Israel, Ancient Judaism and the Matthean Community.* ConBNT 24. Stockholm: Almqvist & Wiksell International, 1994.

Calvin, John. *1 & 2 Thessalonians.* CCC. Wheaton: Crossway Books, 1999.

—. *1, 2, & 3 John.* CCC. Wheaton: Crossway Books, 1998.

—. *Commentary on a Harmony of the Evangelists, Matthew, Mark, and Luke.* Translated by William Pringle. Grand Rapids: Baker, 1993.

Carleton Paget, James. 'Some Observations on Josephus and Christianity.' *JTS* 52 (2001): 539-624.

Carras, George P. 'Jewish Ethics and Gentile Converts: Remarks on 1 Thess 4,3-8.' Pages 306-15 in *The Thessalonian Correspondence.* BETL 87. Edited by Raymond F. Collins. Leuven: Leuven University Press, 1990.

Carson, D. A. *The Gospel According to John.* Leicester: InterVarsity Press, 1991.

—. 'John and the Johannine Epistles.' Pages 245-64 in *It is Written: Scripture Citing Scripture.* Edited by D. A. Carson and H. G. M. Williamson. Cambridge: Cambridge University Press, 1988.

—. 'Matthew.' in EBC. Edited by Frank E. Gaebelein. Grand Rapids: Zondervan, 1984.

—. 'Predestination and Responsibility: Elements of Tension-Theology in the Fourth Gospel against Jewish Background.' Ph.D. diss., University of Cambridge, 1975.

—. '"You Have No Need That Anyone Should Teach You" (1 John 2:27): An Old Testament Allusion That Determines the Interpretation.' Pages 269-80 in *The New Testament in Its First Century Setting: Essays on Context and Background.* Edited by P. J. Williams, Andrew D. Clarke, Peter M. Head, and David Instone-Brewer. Grand Rapids: Eerdmans, 2004.

Cerfaux, L. 'Le'Évangile de Jean et "Le Logion Johannique" des Synoptiques.' Pages 147-59 in *Le'Évangile de Jean: Études et Problèmes.* Edited by M. É. Boismard et al. RechBib 3. Louvain: Desclée de Brouwer, 1958.

Charlesworth, James H. 'Community Organization in the Rule of the Community.' Pages 133-36 in vol. 1 of *EDSS*. Edited by Lawrence H. Schiffman and James C. VanderKam. 2 vols. Oxford: Oxford University Press, 2000.

—. 'Old Testament Apocrypha.' Pages 292-94 in vol. 1 of *ABD*. Edited by David Noel Freedman. New York: Doubleday, 1992.

Chatman, Seymour. *Story and Discourse: Narrative Structure in Fiction and Film.* Ithaca: Cornell University Press, 1978.

Chazon, Esther. 'Words of the Luminaries.' Pages 989-90 in vol. 2 of *EDSS*. Edited by Lawrence H. Schiffman and James VanderKam. 2 vols. Oxford: Oxford University Press, 2000.

Chester, Andrew. *Messiah and Exaltation: Jewish Messianic and Visionary Traditions and New Testament Christology.* WUNT 207. Tübingen: Mohr Siebeck, 2007.

Childs, Brevard S. *Isaiah.* OTL. Louisville: Westminster John Knox, 2001.

Clark-Soles, Jaime. *Scripture Cannot Be Broken: The Social Function of the Use of Scripture in the Fourth Gospel.* Leiden: Brill, 2003.

Clines, David J. A. 'The Ten Commandments, Reading from Left to Right.' Pages 26-45 in *Interested Parties: The Ideology of Writers and Readers of the Hebrew Bible.* JSOTSup 205. Sheffield: Sheffield Academic Press, 1995.

Colless, Brian E. 'Divine Education.' *Numen* 17 (1970): 118-42.

—. 'The Divine Teacher Figure in Biblical Theology.' *JCE* 10 (1967): 24-38, 112-23, 151-62.

Collins, John J. 'Eschatology.' Pages 256-61 in vol. 1 of *EDSS*. Edited by Lawrence H. Schiffman and James VanderKam. 2 vols. Oxford: Oxford University Press, 2000.

—. Review of A.-M. Denis, *Concordance Grecque des Pseudépigraphes d'Ancien Testament. JBL* 109 (1990): 132-33.

—. *The Scepter and the Star: The Messiahs of the Dead Sea Scrolls and Other Ancient Literature.* ABRL. New York: Doubleday, 1995.

—. 'Teacher and Messiah? The One Who Will Teach Righteousness at the End of Days.' Pages 193-210 in *The Community of the Renewed Covenant: The Notre Dame Symposium on the Dead Sea Scrolls.* Edited by Eugene Ulrich and James VanderKam. Notre Dame: University of Notre Dame Press, 1994.

Collins, Raymond F. 'The Church of the Thessalonians.' Pages 285-98 in *Studies on the First Letter to the Thessalonians.* BETL 66. Leuven: Leuven University Press, 1984.

—. 'Paul's First Reflections on Love.' Pages 346-55 in *Studies on the First Letter to the Thessalonians.* BETL 66. Leuven: Leuven University Press, 1984.

Colson, F. H. 'Philo on Education.' *JTS* 18 (1917): 151-62.

Cothenet, Édouard. 'Témoignage de l'Esprit et interprétation de l'Ecriture dans le corpus johannique.' Pages 367-80 in *La vie de la Parole: de l'Ancien au Nouveau Testament.* Paris: Desclée, 1987.

Cotterell, Peter, and Max Turner. *Linguistics and Biblical Interpretation.* London: SPCK, 1989.

Couture, Paul. 'The Teaching Function in the Church of 1 John (1 John 2, 20. 27): A Contribution to Johannine Ecclesiology and Ecumenics.' Ph.D. diss., Pontifica Universitas Gregoriana, 1968.

Cowan, Christopher. 'The Father and the Son in the Fourth Gospel: Johannine Subordination.' *JETS* 49 (2006): 115-35.

Crawford, Sidnie White. 'Reworked Pentateuch.' Pages 775-77 in vol. 2 of *EDSS*. Edited by Lawrence H. Schiffman and James VanderKam. 2 vols. Oxford: Oxford University Press, 2000.

Crossan, John Dominic. 'It is Written: A Structuralist Analysis of John 6.' *Semeia* 26 (1983): 3-21.

Culpepper, R. Alan. *Anatomy of the Fourth Gospel: A Study in Literary Design.* NTFF. Philadelphia: Fortress, 1983.

—. *The Johannine School: An Evaluation of the Johannine-School Hypothesis Based on an Investigation of the Nature of Ancient Schools.* SBLDS 26. Missoula: Scholars Press, 1975.

—, ed. *Critical Readings of John 6.* BIS 22. Leiden: Brill, 1997.

Curtis, William A. *Jesus Christ the Teacher: A Study of His Method and Message Based Mainly on the Earlier Gospels.* London: Oxford University Press, 1943.

Dahl, Nils Alstrup. 'The Johannine Church and History.' Pages 124-42 in *Current Issues in New Testament Interpretation: Essays in Honor of Otto A. Piper.* Edited by William Klassen and Graydon F. Snyder. London: SCM, 1962.

—. 'The Neglected Factor in New Testament Theology.' Pages 153-63 in *Jesus the Christ: The Historical Origins of Christological Doctrine.* Edited by Donald H. Juel. Minneapolis: Fortress, 1991.

Dahood, Mitchell. *Psalms.* AB 16, 17, 17A. 3 vols. Garden City: Doubleday, 1965-1970.

Dalman, Gustaf. *The Words of Jesus.* Translated by D. M. Kay. Edinburgh: T & T Clark, 1902.

Davies, Philip R. *The Damascus Covenant: An Interpretation of the 'Damascus Document.'* JSOTSup 25. Sheffield: JSOT Press, 1982.

—. 'War of the Sons of Light against the Sons of Darkness.' Pages 965-68 in vol. 2 of *EDSS.* Edited by Lawrence H. Schiffman and James VanderKam. 2 vols. Oxford: Oxford University Press, 2000.

Davies, Stevan L. 'Who is Called Bar Abbas?' *NTS* 27 (1980): 260-62.

Davies, W. D. '"Knowledge" in the Dead Sea Scrolls and Matthew 11:25-30.' Pages 119-44 in *Christian Origins and Judaism.* London: Darton, Longman & Todd, 1962.

—. *The Setting of the Sermon on the Mount.* Cambridge: Cambridge University Press, 1964.

—. *Torah in the Messianic Age and/or the Age to Come.* Journal of Biblical Literature Monograph Series 7. Philadelphia: Society of Biblical Literature, 1952.

Davies, W. D., and Dale C. Allison, Jr. *A Critical and Exegetical Commentary on the Gospel According to Saint Matthew.* ICC. 3 vols. Edinburgh: T & T Clark, 1988-1997.

De Jonge, Marinus. 'Messiah.' Pages 777-88 in vol. 4 of *ABD.* Edited by David Noel Freedman. New York: Doubleday, 1992.

—. 'The Radical Eschatology of the Fourth Gospel and the Eschatology of the Synoptics.' Pages 481-87 in *John and the Synoptics.* Edited by Adelbert Denaux. BETL 101. Leuven: Leuven University Press, 1992.

de la Potterie, Ignace. 'The Truth in Saint John.' Pages 67-82 in *The Interpretation of John.* Edited by John Ashton. Edinburgh: T & T Clark, 1997. Repr. from *RivB* 11 (1963): 3-24.

de la Potterie, Ignace, and Stanislaus Lyonnet. *The Christian Lives by the Spirit.* Translated by John Morriss. Staten Island: Alba House, 1970.

De Moor, Johannes C., ed. *Synchronic or Diachronic? A Debate on Method in Old Testament Exegesis.* OtSt 34. Leiden: E. J. Brill, 1995.

Deasley, Alex R. G. 'The Holy Spirit in the Dead Sea Scrolls.' *WT* 21 (1986): 45-73.

Deidun, T. J. *New Covenant Morality in Paul.* AnBib 89. Rome: Biblical Institute Press, 1981.

Denaux, Adelbert. 'The Q-Logion Mt 11,27/Lk 10,22 and the Gospel of John.' Pages 163-99 in *John and the Synoptics.* Edited by Adelbert Denaux. BETL 101. Leuven: Leuven University Press, 1992.

Denney, James. *The Epistles to the Thessalonians*. ExpB. London: Hodder and Stoughton, 1892.

Derrett, J. Duncan M. 'Mt 23,8-10 a Midrash on Is 54,13 and Jer 31,33-34.' *Bib* 62 (1981): 372-86.

Dexinger, Ferdinand. 'Samaritan Eschatology.' Pages 266-92 in *The Samaritans*. Edited by Alan D. Crown. Tübingen: J. C. B. Mohr (Paul Siebeck), 1989.

Dibelius, Martin, and Hans Conzelmann. *The Pastoral Epistles*. Hermeneia. Philadelphia: Fortress, 1972.

Diedrich, Friedrich. 'Lehre mich, Jahwe! Überlegungen zu einer Gebetsbitte in den Psalmen.' Pages 59-73 in *Die alttestamentliche Botschaft als Wegweisung*. Edited by Josef Zmijewski. Stuttgart: Katholisches Bibelwerk, 1990.

Dillon, J. T. *Jesus as a Teacher: A Multidisciplinary Case Study*. Bethesda: International Scholars Publications, 1995.

Dimant, Devorah. 'Qumran Pesharim.' Pages 244-51 in vol. 5 of *ABD*. Edited by David Noel Freedman. New York: Doubleday, 1992.

Dodd, C. H. *According to the Scriptures: The Sub-Structure of New Testament Theology*. London: Nisbet & Co, 1952.

—. 'A Hidden Parable in the Fourth Gospel.' Pages 30-40 in *More New Testament Studies*. Manchester: Manchester University Press, 1968.

—. 'Jesus as Teacher and Prophet.' Pages 53-66 in *Mysterium Christi*. Edited by G. K. A. Bell and D. Adolf Deissmann. London: Longmans, Green and Col, 1930.

—. *The Johannine Epistles*. MNTC. London: Hodder and Stoughton, 1946.

—. 'Some Johannine "Herrnworte" with parallels in the Synoptic Gospels.' *NTS* 2 (1955/56): 75-86.

Donfried, Karl P. 'Ecclesiastical Authority in 2-3 John.' Pages 325-33 in *L'Évangile de Jean: Sources, rédaction, théologie*. Edited by M. De Jonge. BETL 44. Leuven: Leuven University Press, 1977.

Duhm, Bernhard. *Das Buch Jeremia*. KHC. Tübingen: J. C. B. Mohr (Paul Siebeck), 1901.

—. *Das Buch Jesaia*. HK. Göttingen: Vandenhoeck & Ruprecht, 1922.

Duling, Dennis C. '"Egalitarian" Ideology, Leadership, and Factional Conflict within the Matthean Group.' *BTB* 27 (1997): 124-37.

Dunn, James D. G. *Christology in the Making: A New Testament Inquiry into the Origins of the Doctrine of the Incarnation*. 2d ed. London: SCM Press, 1989.

Edwards, Mark. *John*. BBC. United Kingdom: Blackwell Publishing, 2004.

Edwards, Ruth B. 'XAPIN ANTI XAPIN (John 1.16): Grace and Law in the Johannine Prologue.' *JSNT* 32 (1988): 3-15.

Ego, Beate. 'Zwischen Aufgabe und Gabe: Theologische Implikationen des Lernens in der alttestamentlichen und antik-jüdischen Überlieferung.' Pages 1-26 in *Religiöses Lernen in der biblischen, frühjüdischen und frühchristlichen Überlieferung*. Edited by Beate Ego and Helmut Merkel. WUNT 180. Tübingen: Mohr Siebeck, 2005.

Ellicott, Charles J. *St Paul's Epistles to the Thessalonians: with a Critical and Grammatical Commentary, and a Revised Translation*. 4th ed. London: Longman, Green, Longman, Roberts & Green, 1880.

Elliger, Karl. *Deuterojesaja*. BKAT. Germany: Neukirchener, 1978.

Ellingworth, Paul, and Eugene A. Nida. *A Translator's Handbook on Paul's Letter to the Thessalonians*. London: United Bible Societies, 1976.

Esler, Philip F. *The First Christians in their Social Worlds: Social-scientific approaches to New Testament interpretation*. London: Routledge, 1994.

Estes, Daniel J. *Hear, My Son: Teaching and Learning in Proverbs 1-9*. NSBT 4. Leicester: Apollos, 1997.

Evans, Craig A. *Jesus and His Contemporaries: Comparative Studies.* Arbeiten zur Geschichte des Antiken Judentums und des Urchristentums 25. Leiden: E.J. Brill, 1995.

——. 'Messianic Hopes and Messianic Figures in Late Antiquity.' *JGRChJ* 3 (2006): 9-40.

——. 'Obduracy and the Lord's Servant: Some Observations on the Use of the Old Testament in the Fourth Gospel.' Pages 221-36 in *Early Jewish and Christian Exegesis: Studies in Memory of William Hugh Brownlee.* Edited by Craig A. Evans and William F. Stinespring. Atlanta: Scholars Press, 1987.

Fascher, Erich. 'Jesus der Lehrer: Ein Beitrag zur Frage nach dem "Quellort der Kirchenidee."' *TLZ* (1954): 326-42.

Fee, Gordon D. *The First Epistle to the Corinthians.* NICNT. Grand Rapids: Eerdmans, 1987.

——. *God's Empowering Presence: The Holy Spirit in the Letters of Paul.* Peabody: Hendrickson, 1994.

Finkel, Asher. *The Pharisees and the Teacher of Nazareth: A Study of Their Background, Their Halachic and Midrashic Teachings, the Similarities and Differences.* AGSU 4. Leiden: E. J. Brill, 1964.

Finsterbusch, Karin. '"Du sollst sie lehren, auf dass sie tun..." Mose als Lehrer der Tora im Buch Deuteronomium.' Pages 27-45 in *Religiöses Lernen in der biblischen, frühjüdischen und frühchristlichen Überlieferung.* Edited by Beate Ego and Helmut Merkel. WUNT 180. Tübingen: Mohr Siebeck, 2005.

——. *Weisung für Israel: Studien zu religiösem Lehren und Lernen im Deuteronomium und in seinem Umfeld.* FAT 44. Tübingen: Mohr Siebeck, 2005.

Fischer, Irmtraud. *Tora für Israel – Tora für die Völker.* SBS 164. Stuttgart: Katholisches Bibelwerk, 1995.

Fishbane, Michael. *Biblical Interpretation in Ancient Israel.* Oxford: Clarendon, 1985.

——. 'Revelation and Tradition: Aspects of Inner-Biblical Exegesis.' *JBL* 99 (1980): 343-61.

Fitzmyer, Joseph A. *Romans.* AB 33. London: Doubleday, 1993.

Flint, Peter. 'Book of Psalms: Apocryphal Psalms.' Pages 708-10 in vol. 2 of *EDSS.* Edited by Lawrence H. Schiffman and James VanderKam. 2 vols. Oxford: Oxford University Press, 2000.

Foster, Paul. 'Why Did Matthew Get the *Shema* Wrong? A Study of Matthew 22:37.' *JBL* 122 (2003): 309-33.

Frame, James E. *A Critical and Exegetical Commentary on the Epistles of St. Paul to the Thessalonians.* ICC. Edinburgh: T & T Clark, 1912.

France, R. T. 'Mark and the Teaching of Jesus.' Pages 101-36 in *Studies of History and Tradition in the Four Gospels.* Edited by R. T. France and David Wenham. Vol. 1 of *Gospel Perspectives.* Sheffield: JSOT Press, 1980-1986.

Freed, Edwin D. *Old Testament Quotations in the Gospel of John.* NovTSup 11. Leiden: E. J. Brill, 1965.

Frey, Jörg. *Die johanneische Eschatologie. Band I: Ihre Probleme im Spiegel der Forschung seit Reimarus.* WUNT 96. Tübingen: J.C.B. Mohr (Paul Siebeck), 1997.

——. *Die johanneische Eschatologie. Band II: Die johanneische Zeitverständnis.* WUNT 110. Tübingen: J.C.B. Mohr (Paul Siebeck), 1998.

——. *Die johanneische Eschatologie. Band III: Die eschatologische Verkündigung in den johanneischen Texten.* WUNT 117. Tübingen: J.C.B. Mohr (Paul Siebeck), 2000.

——. 'Eschatology in the Johaninne Circle.' Pages 47-82 in *Theology and Christology in the Fourth Gospel.* Edited by G. Van Belle, J.G. Van Der Watt and P. Maritz. BETL 184. Leuven: Leuven University Press, 2005.

Gaechter, Paul. 'Zur Form von Joh 5,19-30.' Pages 65-68 in *Neutestamentliche Aufsätze.* Edited by J. Blinzler, O. Kuss and F. Mußner. Regensburg: Friedrich Pustet, 1963.

Gaffin, Richard B., Jr. 'Some Epistemological Reflections on 1 Cor 2:6-16.' *WTJ* 57 (1995): 103-24.

Garland, David E. *The Intention of Matthew 23*. NovTSup 52. Leiden: E. J. Brill, 1979.

Gaston, Lloyd. 'The Messiah of Israel As Teacher of the Gentiles: The Setting of Matthew's Christology.' *Int* 29 (1975): 24-40.

Gaventa, Beverly Roberts. *First and Second Thessalonians*. IBC. Louisville: John Knox, 1998.

Geiger, Georg. 'Aufruf an Rückkehrende: Zum Sinn des Zitats von Ps 78,24b in Joh 6,31.' *Bib* 65 (1984): 449-64.

Gerhardsson, Birger. 'The Christology of Matthew.' Pages 14-32 in *Who Do You Say That I Am? Essays on Christology*. Edited by Mark Allan Powell and David R. Bauer. Louisville: Westminster John Knox, 1999.

—. *Memory and Manuscript: Oral Tradition and Written Transmission in Rabbinic Judaism and Early Christianity*. ASNU 22. Lund: C. W. K. Gleerup, 1961. Repr., BRS. Grand Rapids: Eerdmans, 1998.

—. 'The Shema' in Early Christianity.' Pages 275-93 in *The Four Gospels*. Edited by F. Van Segbroeck, C. M. Tuckett, G. Van Belle, and J. Verheyden. BETL 100. Leuven: Leuven University Press, 1992.

Glombitza, Otto. 'Die Titel διδάσκαλος und ἐπιστάτης für Jesus bei Lukas.' *ZNW* 49 (1958): 275-78.

Goff, Matthew J. *The Worldly and Heavenly Wisdom of 4QInstruction*. STDJ 50. Leiden: Brill, 2003.

Goldingay, John. *The Message of Isaiah 40-55: A Literary-Theological Commentary*. London: T & T Clark, 2005.

Green, Gene L. *The Letters to the Thessalonians*. PNTC. Grand Rapids: Eerdmans, 2002.

Green, Joel B. *The Gospel of Luke*. NICNT. Grand Rapids: Eerdmans, 1997.

Grimm, Werner, and Kurt Dittert. *Deuterojesaja*. CB. Stuttgart: Calwer, 1990.

Groß, Walter. 'Erneuerter oder Neuer Bund? Wortlaut und Aussageintention in Jer 31,31-34.' Pages 41-66 in *Bund und Tora: Zur theologischen Begriffsgeschichte in alttestamentlicher, frühjüdischer und urchristlicher Tradition*. Edited by Friedrich Avemarie and Hermann Lichtenberger. WUNT 92. Tübingen: J. C. B. Mohr (Paul Siebeck), 1996.

Hägerland, Tobias. 'John's Gospel: A Two-Level Drama?' *JSNT* 25 (2003): 309-22.

Hagner, Donald A. *Matthew*. WBC 33A, 33B. 2 vols. Dallas: Word Books, 1993-1995.

Hahn, Ferdinand. *The Titles of Jesus in Christology: Their History in Early Christianity*. Translated by Harold Knight and George Ogg. London: Lutterworth Press, 1969.

Hakola, Raimo. *Identity Matters: John, the Jews and Jewishness*. NovTSup 118. Leiden: Brill, 2005.

Hay, David M. 'Philo's View of Himself as an Exegete: Inspired, But Not Authoritative.' Pages 40-52 in *Heirs of the Septuagint: Philo, Hellenistic Judaism and Early Christianity*. Edited by David T. Runia, David M. Hay, and David Winston. SHJ 3. Atlanta: Scholars Press, 1991.

Hempel, Charlotte. 'Community Structures in the Dead Sea Scrolls: Admission, Organization, Disciplinary Procedures.' Pages 67-92 in *The Dead Sea Scrolls After Fifty Years: A Comprehensive Assessment*. Edited by Peter W. Flint and James C. VanderKam. 2 vols. Leiden: Brill, 1999.

—. *The Laws of the Damascus Document: Sources, Tradition and Redaction*. STDJ 29. Leiden: Brill, 1998.

Hengel, Martin. *The Charismatic Leader and His Followers*. Translated by James C. G. Greig. SNTW. Edinburgh: T & T Clark, 1981.

—. 'Eye-witness memory and the writing of the Gospels: Form criticism, community tradition and the authority of the authors.' Pages 70-96 in *The Written Gospel*. Edited by Markus Bockmuehl and Donald A. Hagner. Cambridge: Cambridge University Press, 2005.

—. 'Jesus as Messianic Teacher of Wisdom and the Beginnings of Christology.' Pages 73-117 in *Studies in Early Christology*. Edinburgh: T & T Clark, 1995.

—. *Judaism and Hellenism: Studies in their Encounter in Palestine during the Early Hellenistic Period*. 2 vols. London: SCM, 1974.

—. *The Zealots: Investigations into the Jewish Freedom Movement in the Period from Herod I Until 70 A.D.* Edinburgh: T & T Clark, 1989.

Herzog, William R., II. *Prophet and Teacher: An Introduction to the Historical Jesus*. Louisville: Westminster John Knox, 2005.

Hiebert, D. Edmond. 'An expositional study of 1 John. Pt 1, An exposition of 1 John 2:18-28.' *BSac* 146 (1989): 76-93.

Hodgson, Robert, Jr. '1 Thess 4:1-12 and the Holiness Tradition (HT).' Pages 199-215 in *SBL Seminar Papers, 1982*. SBLSP 21. Chico: Scholars Press, 1982.

Hoegen-Rohls, Christina. *Der nachösterliche Johannes: Die Abschiedsreden als hermeneutischer Schlüssel zum vierten Evangelium*. WUNT 2.84. Tübingen: J. C. B. Mohr (Paul Siebeck), 1996.

Hoet, Rik. *'Omnes autem vos fratres estis.' Etude du concept ecclésiologique des 'frères' selon Mt 23, 8-12*. AnGr 232. Rome: Universita Gregoriana Editrice, 1982.

Höffken, Peter. *Jesaja: Der Stand der theologischen Diskussion*. Germany: Wissenschaftliche Buchgesellschaft, 2004.

Hogg, C. F., and W. E. Vine. *The Epistles of Paul the Apostle to the Thessalonians: With Notes Exegetical and Expository*. Glasgow: Pickering & Inglis, 1914.

Holladay, William L. *Jeremiah*. Hermeneia. 2 vols. Minneapolis: Fortress, 1986-1989.

Holm-Nielsen, Svend. *Hodayot: Psalms from Qumran*. ATDan 2. Denmark: Universitetsforlaget I Aarhus, 1960.

Holtz, Traugott. *Der erste Brief an die Thessalonicher*. EKKNT 13. Zürich: Benziger, 1986.

Horgan, Maurya P. *Pesharim: Qumran Interpretations of Biblical Books*. CBQMS 8. Washington, D. C.: The Catholic Biblical Association of America, 1979.

Houlden, J. L. *A Commentary on the Johannine Epistles*. 2d ed. BNTC. London: A & C Black, 1994.

Hunter, A. M. 'Crux Criticorum – Matt. XI. 25-30 – A Re-Appraisal.' *NTS* 8 (1961-62): 241-49.

Instone-Brewer, David. *Techniques and Assumptions in Jewish Exegesis before 70 CE*. TSAJ 30. Tübingen: J. C. B. Mohr (Paul Siebeck), 1992.

—. *Prayer and Agriculture*. Vol. 1 of TRENT. Grand Rapids: Eerdmans, 2004.

Jenni, Ernst. *Das hebräische Piel: Syntaktisch-semasiologische Untersuchung einer Verbalform im Alten Testament*. Zürich: EVZ, 1968.

Jeremias, Joachim. *New Testament Theology. Part One: The Proclamation of Jesus*. NTL. Translated by John Bowden. London: SCM, 1971.

Johnson, Luke Timothy. *The Writings of the New Testament: An Interpretation*. London: SCM, 1999.

Juel, Donald H. *Messianic Exegesis: Christological Interpretation of the Old Testament in Early Christianity*. Philadelphia: Fortress, 1988.

—. 'Social Dimensions of Exegesis: The Use of Psalm 16 in Acts 2.' *CBQ* 43 (1981): 543-56.

Kammler, H.-C. *Christologie und Eschatologie. Eine exegetische Untersuchung zu Joh 5,17-30*. WUNT 126. Tübingen: Mohr Siebeck, 2000.

Karrer, Martin. 'Der lehrende Jesus – Neutestamentliche Erwägungen.' *ZNW* 83 (1992): 1-20.

Käsemann, Ernst. *The Testament of Jesus: A Study of the Gospel of John in the Light of Chapter 17*. NTL. London: SCM, 1968.

Keck, Leander E. 'Toward the Renewal of New Testament Christology.' *NTS* 32 (1986): 362-77.

Keener, Craig S. *A Commentary on the Gospel of Matthew*. Grand Rapids: Eerdmans, 1999.

—. *The Gospel According to John: A Commentary*. 2 vols. Peabody: Hendrickson, 2003.

Kennedy, H. A. A. 'The Covenant Conception in the First Epistle of St. John.' *ExpTim* 28 (1916): 23-26.

Keown, Gerald L., Pamela J. Scalise, and Thomas G. Smothers. *Jeremiah 26-52*. WBC 27. Dallas: Word Books, 1995.

Kingsbury, Jack Dean. *Matthew: Structure, Christology, Kingdom*. Philadelphia: Fortress, 1975.

Kirschner, Robert. 'Imitatio Rabbini.' *JSJ* 17 (1986): 70-79.

Klauck, Hans-Josef. 'Community, History, and Text(s): A Response to Robert Kysar.' Pages 82-90 in *Life in Abundance: Studies in John's Gospel in Tribute to Raymond E. Brown*. Edited by John R. Donahue. Collegeville: Liturgical Press, 2005.

—. *Der erste Johannesbrief*. EKKNT 23. Zürich: Benziger, 1991.

—. 'Gemeinde ohne Amt? Erfahrungen mit der Kirche in den johanneischen Schriften.' *BZ* 29 (1985): 193-220.

Kloppenborg, John S. 'ΦΙΛΑΔΕΛΦΙΑ, ΘΕΟΔΙΔΑΚΤΟΣ and the Dioscure: Rhetorical Engagement in 1 Thessalonians 4.9-12.' *NTS* 39 (1993): 265-89.

Knibb, Michael A. 'Community Organization in the Damascus Document.' Pages 136-38 in vol. 1 of *EDSS*. Edited by Lawrence H. Schiffman and James C. VanderKam. 2 vols. Oxford: Oxford University Press, 2000.

—. 'Interpreter of the Law.' Pages 383-84 in vol. 1 of *EDSS*. Edited by Lawrence H. Schiffman and James C. VanderKam. 2 vols. Oxford: Oxford University Press, 2000.

—. 'Teacher of Righteousness.' Pages 918-21 in vol. 2 of *EDSS*. Edited by Lawrence H. Schiffman and James C. VanderKam. 2 vols. Oxford: Oxford University Press, 2000.

Knowles, Michael. *Jeremiah in Matthew's Gospel: The Rejected-Prophet Motif in Matthaean Redaction*. JSNTSup 68. Sheffield: JSOT Press, 1993.

Koester, Helmut. '1 Thessalonians – Experiment in Christian Writing.' Pages 33-44 in *Continuity and Discontinuity in Church History: Essays Presented to George Huntston Williams on the Occasion of his 65th Birthday*. Edited by F. Forrester Church and Timothy George. SHCT 19. Leiden: E. J. Brill, 1979. Repr. pages 15-23 in *Paul & His World: Interpreting the New Testament in Its Context*. Minneapolis: Fortress Press, 2007.

Köstenberger, Andreas J. 'Jesus as Rabbi in the Fourth Gospel.' *BBR* 8 (1998): 97-128.

—. *John*. BECNT. Grand Rapids: Baker Academic, 2004.

Kothgasser, Alois M. 'Die Lehr-, Erinnerungs-, Bezeugungs- und Einführungsfunktion des Johanneischen Geist-Parakleten gegenüber der Christus-Offenbarung.' *Sal.* 33 (1971): 557-98.

Kraus, Hans-Joachim. 'Paedagogia Dei als theologischer Geschichtsbegriff.' *EvT* 8 (1948): 515-27.

Kraus, Thomas J. '"Uneducated," "Ignorant," or Even "Illiterate"?: Aspects and Background for an Understanding of ΑΓΡΑΜΜΑΤΟΙ (and ΙΔΙΩΤΑΙ) in Acts 4.13.' *NTS* 45 (1999): 434-49.

Kreitzer, L. Joseph. *Jesus and God in Paul's Eschatology*. JSNTSup 19. Sheffield: Sheffield Academic Press, 1987.

Krentz, Edgar. 'Community and Character: Matthew's Vision of the Church.' Pages 565-73 in *SBL Seminar Papers, 1987*. *SBLSP* 26. Atlanta: Scholars Press, 1987.

Kupp, David D. *Matthew's Emmanuel: Divine presence and God's people in the First Gospel*. SNTSMS 90. Cambridge: Cambridge University Press, 1996.

Kysar, Robert. *1, 2, 3 John*. ACNT. Minneapolis: Augsburg, 1986.

—. 'The Whence and Whither of the Johannine Community.' Pages 65-81 in *Life in Abundance: Studies in John's Gospel in Tribute to Raymond E. Brown*. Edited by John R. Donahue. Collegeville: Liturgical Press, 2005.

Lagrange, P. M.-J. *Évangile selon Saint Jean*. Paris: Librairie Victor Lecoffre, 1925.

Le Fort, Pierre. *Les structures de l'église militante selon saint Jean: Etude d'ecclésiologie concrète appliquée au IVe évangile et aux épîtres johanniques*. Genève: Labor et Fides, 1970.

Leaney, A. R. C. *The Rule of Qumran and its Meaning: Introduction, Translation and Commentary*. NTL. London: SCM, 1966.

Lemaire, André. 'Education (Israel).' Pages 305-12 in vol. 2 of *ABD*. Edited by David Noel Freedman. New York: Doubleday, 1992.

Levenson, Jon D. 'The Sources of Torah: Psalm 119 and the Modes of Revelation in Second Temple Judaism.' Pages 559-74 in *Ancient Israelite Religion*. Edited by Patrick D. Miller, Jr., Paul D. Hanson, and S. Dean McBride. Philadelphia: Fortress, 1987.

Levin, Christoph. *Die Verheißung des neuen Bundes in ihrem theologiegeschichtlichen Zusammenhang ausgelegt*. FRLANT 137. Göttingen: Vandenhoeck & Ruprecht, 1985.

Levison, John R. *The Spirit in First Century Judaism*. AGJU 29. Leiden: Brill, 1997.

Lieu, Judith M. *Image and Reality: The Jews in the World of the Christians in the Second Century*. Edinburgh: T & T Clark, 1996.

—. *The Theology of the Johannine Epistles*. NTT. Cambridge: Cambridge University Press, 1991.

—. 'What Was from the Beginning: Scripture and Tradition in the Johannine Epistles.' *NTS* 39 (1993): 458-77.

Lightfoot, J. B. *Notes on the Epistles of St Paul from Unpublished Commentaries*. London: MacMillan and Co., 1895.

Lightfoot, R. H. *St. John's Gospel: A Commentary*. Edited by C. F. Evans. Oxford: Clarendon Press, 1956.

Lim, Timothy H. 'Midrash Pesher in the Pauline Letters.' Pages 280-92 in *The Scrolls and the Scriptures: Qumran Fifty Years After*. Edited by Stanley E. Porter and Craig A. Evans. JSPSup 26. Sheffield: Sheffield Academic Press, 1997.

Lincoln, Andrew T. 'Matthew – A Story for Teachers?' Pages 103-25 in *The Bible in Three Dimensions*. Edited by David J. A. Clines, Stephen E. Fowl, and Stanley E. Porter. JSOTSup 87. Sheffield: Sheffield Academic Press, 1990.

Lindars, Barnabas. *New Testament Apologetic: The Doctrinal Significance of the Old Testament Quotations*. London: SCM, 1961.

—. Review of Peder Borgen, *Bread from Heaven*. *JTS* 18 (1967): 192-94.

Longenecker, Richard N. *Galatians*. WBC 41. Dallas: Word Books, 1990.

Louw, Johannes P. 'Narrator of the Father – ΕΧΗΓΕΙΣΘΑΙ and Related Terms in Johannine Christology.' *Neot* 2 (1968): 32-40.

Lundbom, Jack R. *Jeremiah*. AB 21A, 21B, 21C. 3 vols. London: Doubleday, 1999-2004.

Lünemann, Gottlieb. *Critical and Exegetical Handbook to the Epistles of St. Paul to the Thessalonians*. MCNT. Translated by Paton J. Gloag. Edinburgh: T & T Clark, 1880.

Luz, Ulrich. *Das Evangelium nach Matthäus*. EKKNT 1. 5 vols. Düsseldorf: Benziger Verlag, 1985-2002.

—. 'Eine thetische Skizze der Matthäischen Christologie.' Pages 221-35 in *Anfänge der Christologie*. Edited by Cilliers Breytenbach and Henning Paulsen. Göttingen: Vandenhoeck & Ruprecht, 1991.

—. *Matthew 21-28*. Hermeneia. Minneapolis: Fortress, 2005.

Macdonald, John. *The Theology of the Samaritans*. NTL. London: SCM, 1964.

Mach, Michael F. 'Lerntraditionen im hellenistischen Judentum unter besonderer Berücksichtigung Philons von Alexandrien.' Pages 117-39 in *Religiöses Lernen in der biblischen, frühjüdischen und frühchristlichen Überlieferung*. Edited by Beate Ego and Helmut Merkel. WUNT 180. Tübingen: Mohr Siebeck, 2005.

—. 'The Social Implications of Scripture-Interpretation in Second Temple Judaism.' Pages 166-79 in *The Sociology of Sacred Texts*. Edited by Jon Davies and Isabel Wollaston. Sheffield: Sheffield Academic Press, 1993.

Magness, Jodi. *The Archaeology of the Qumran and the Dead Sea Scrolls*. SDSSRL. Grand Rapids: Eerdmans, 2002

Malatesta, Edward. *Interiority and Covenant: A Study of εἶναι ἐν and μένειν ἐν in the First Letter of Saint John*. AnBib 69. Rome: Biblical Institute Press, 1978.

Malbon, Elizabeth Struthers. '"No Need To Have Anyone Write"?: A Structural Exegesis of 1 Thessalonians.' *Semeia* 26 (1983): 57-83.

Malherbe, Abraham J. 'Exhortation in First Thessalonians.' *NovT* 25 (1983): 238-56.

—. *The Letters to the Thessalonians*. AB 32B. London: Doubleday, 2000.

—. *Moral Exhortation, A Greco-Roman Sourcebook*. LEC. Philadelphia: Westminster, 1986.

Malina, Bruce J., and Jerome H. Neyrey. *Portraits of Paul: An Archaeology of Ancient Personality*. Louisville: Westminster John Knox, 1996.

Mansoor, Menahem. *The Thanksgiving Hymns*. STDJ 3. Leiden: E. J. Brill, 1961.

Marcus, Joel. 'Authority to Forgive Sins upon the Earth: The *Shema* in the Gospel of Mark.' Pages 196-211 in *The Gospels and the Scriptures of Israel*. Edited by Craig A. Evans and W. Richard Stegner. JSNTSup 104. Sheffield: Sheffield Academic Press, 1994.

Marshall, I. Howard. *1 and 2 Thessalonians*. NCB. Grand Rapids: Eerdmans, 1983.

—. *The Epistles of John*. NICNT. Grand Rapids: Eerdmans, 1978.

Martyn, J. Louis. *Galatians*. AB 33A. London: Doubleday, 1997.

—. *History & Theology in the Fourth Gospel*. Nashville: Abingdon, 1979.

—. Review of Peder Borgen, *Bread from Heaven*. JBL 86 (1967): 244-45.

McKane, William. *A Critical and Exegetical Commentary on Jeremiah*. ICC. 2 vols. Edinburgh: T & T Clark, 1986-1996.

Meeks, Wayne A. *The First Urban Christians: The Social World of the Apostle Paul*. 2d ed. New Haven: Yale University Press, 2003.

—. 'The Man from Heaven in Johannine Sectarianism.' *JBL* 91 (1972): 44-72.

—. *The Prophet-King: Moses Traditions and the Johannine Christology*. NovTSup 14. Leiden: E. J. Brill, 1967.

—. 'Social Functions of Apocalyptic Language in Pauline Christianity.' Pages 687-705 in *Apocalypticism in the Mediterranean World and the Near East*. Edited by David Hellholm. Tübingen: J. C. B. Mohr (Paul Siebeck), 1983.

Mendelson, Alan. *Secular Education in Philo of Alexandria*. HUCM 7. Cincinnati: Hebrew Union College Press, 1982.

Menken, M. J. J. 'The Old Testament Quotation in John 6,45. Source and Redaction.' *ETL* 64 (1988): 164-72.

—. *Old Testament Quotations in the Fourth Gospel: Studies in Textual Form*. CBET 15. Kampen: Kok Pharos Publishing, 1996.

Metso, Sarianna. *The Textual Development of the Qumran Community Rule*. STDJ 21. Leiden: Brill, 1997.

Meye, Robert P. *Jesus and the Twelve: Discipleship and Revelation in Mark's Gospel.* Grand Rapids: Eerdmans, 1968.

—. 'Messianic Secret and Messianic Didache in Mark's Gospel.' Pages 57-68 in *Oikonomia: Heilsgeschichte als Thema der Theologie.* Edited by Felix Christ. Hamburg: Herbert Reich, 1967.

Michaels, J. Ramsey. 'Christian Prophecy and Matthew 23:8-12: A Test Exegesis.' Pages 305-10 in *SBL Seminar Papers, 1976. SBLSP* 10. Missoula: Scholars Press, 1976.

Michl, Johann. 'Der Geist als Garant des rechten Glaubens.' Pages 142-51 in *Vom Wort des Lebens.* Edited by Nikolaus Adler. Münster: Aschendorffsche, 1951.

Millard, Alan. *Reading and Writing in the Time of Jesus.* Sheffield: Sheffield Academic Press, 2000.

Milligan, George. *St. Paul's Epistles to the Thessalonians.* London: Macmillan and Co., 1908.

Mitchell, Margaret M. 'Patristic Counter-Evidence to the Claim that "The Gospels Were Written for All Christians."' *NTS* 51 (2005): 36-79.

Moloney, Francis J. *The Gospel of John.* SP 4. Collegeville: Liturgical Press, 1998.

Montefiore, C. G. 'Florilegium Philonis.' *JQR* 7 (1895): 481-545.

Moo, Douglas J. *The Old Testament in the Gospel Passion Narratives.* Sheffield: Almond Press, 1983.

Moore, A. L. *1 and 2 Thessalonians.* NCeB. London: Nelson, 1969.

Morgenstern, Julian. 'Jesus the "Teacher."' Pages 1-7 in *Some Significant Antecedents of Christianity.* StPB 10. Leiden: E. J. Brill, 1966.

Morris, Leon. *The Gospel According to John.* NICNT. Grand Rapids: Eerdmans, 1995.

—. *The First and Second Epistles to the Thessalonians.* NICNT. Grand Rapids: Eerdmans, 1991.

Motyer, Stephen. 'The Fourth Gospel and the Salvation of Israel: An Appeal for a New Start.' Pages 83-100 in *Anti-Judaism in the Fourth Gospel.* Edited by R. Bieringer, Didier Pollefeyt, and Frederique Vandecasteele-Vanneuville. London: Westminster John Knox, 2001.

Moule, C. F. D. 'The Individualism of the Fourth Gospel.' *NovT* 5 (1962): 171-90.

Müller, Mogens. 'The Theological Interpretation of the Figure of Jesus in the Gospel of Matthew: Some Principal Features in the Matthean Christology.' *NTS* 45 (1999): 157-73.

Neil, William. *The Epistle of Paul to the Thessalonians.* MNTC. London: Hodder and Stoughton, 1950.

Neirynck, F. 'John and the Synoptics.' Pages 73-106 in *L'Évangile de Jean: Sources, rédaction, théologie.* Edited by M. De Jonge. BETL 44. Leuven: Leuven University Press, 1977.

—. 'John and the Synoptics: 1975-1990.' Pages 3-62 in *John and the Synoptics.* Edited by Adelbert Denaux. BETL 101. Leuven: Leuven University Press, 1992.

Neugebauer, Fritz. 'Miszelle zu John 5.35.' *ZNW* 52 (1961): 130.

Neusner, Jacob. *A History of the Jews in Babylonia: III. From Shapur I to Shapur II.* StPB. Leiden: E. J. Brill, 1968.

—. *A History of the Jews in Babylonia: IV. The Age of Shapur II.* StPB. Leiden: E. J. Brill, 1969.

—. *A History of the Jews in Babylonia: V. Later Sasanian Times.* StPB. Leiden: E. J. Brill, 1970.

—. 'The Phenomenon of the Rabbi: (2) The Ritual of "Being a Rabbi."' Pages 61-77 in *Talmudic Judaism in Sasanian Babylonia: Essays and Studies.* Leiden: E. J. Brill, 1976.

Newport, Kenneth G. C. *The Sources and Sitz im Leben of Matthew 23.* JSNTSup 117. Sheffield: Sheffield Academic Press, 1995.

Neyrey, Jerome H. 'John III – A Debate Over Johannine Epistemology and Christology.' *NovT* 23 (1981): 115-27.

—. 'The Trials (Forensic) and Tribulations (Honor Challenges) of Jesus: John 7 in Social Science Perspective.' *BTB* 26 (1996): 107-24.

Nicholl, Colin R. *From Hope to Despair in Thessalonica.* SNTSMS 126. Cambridge: Cambridge University Press, 2004.

Nicholson, E. W. 'The Decalogue as the Direct Address of God.' *VT* 27 (1977): 422-33.

Nickelsburg, George W. E. 'Revelation.' Pages 770-72 in vol. 2 of *EDSS*. Edited by Lawrence H. Schiffman and James C. VanderKam. 2 vols. Oxford: Oxford University Press, 2000.

Noack, Bent. *Zur Johanneischen Tradition: Beiträge zur Kritik an der literarkritischen Analyse des vierten Evangeliums.* København: Rosenkilde Og Bagger, 1954.

Nolland, John. *Luke.* WBC 35A, 35B, 35C. 3 vols. Dallas: Word Books, 1989-1993.

—. 'No Son-of-God Christology in Matthew 1.18-25.' *JSNT* 62 (1996): 3-12.

Normann, Friedrich. *Christos Didaskalos: Die Vorstellung von Christus als Lehrer in der christlichen Literatur des ersten und zweiten Jahrhunderts.* MBTh 32. Münster: Aschendorff, 1967.

O'Grady, J. 'Individualism and Johannine Ecclesiology.' *BTB* 5 (1975): 227-61.

—. 'Johannine Ecclesiology: A Critical Evaluation.' *BTB* 7 (1977): 36-44.

Obermann, Andreas. *Die christologische Erfüllung der Schrift im Johannesevangelium.* WUNT 2.83. Tübingen: J. C. B. Mohr (Paul Siebeck), 1996.

Odeberg, Hugo. *The Fourth Gospel.* Uppsala, 1929. Repr., Amsterdam: B. R. Grüner, 1968.

Olson, K. A. 'Eusebius and the Testimonium Flavianum.' *CBQ* 61 (1999): 305-22.

Olson, Stanley N. 'Pauline Expressions of Confidence in His Addressees.' *CBQ* 47 (1985): 282-95.

Orton, David E. *The Understanding Scribe: Matthew and the Apocalyptic Ideal.* JSNTSup 25. Sheffield: JSOT Press, 1989.

Painter, John. *1, 2, and 3 John.* SP 18. Collegeville: Liturgical Press, 2002.

—. 'Jesus and the Quest for Eternal Life.' Pages 61-94 in *Critical Readings of John 6.* Edited by R. Alan Culpepper. BIS 22. Leiden: Brill, 1997.

Pancaro, Severino. *The Law in the Fourth Gospel.* NovTSup 42. Leiden: E. J. Brill, 1975.

Patte, Daniel. *Early Jewish Hermeneutic in Palestine.* SBLDS 22. Missoula: Scholars Press, 1975.

—. *The Gospel According to Matthew: A Structural Commentary on Matthew's Faith.* Philadelphia: Fortress, 1987.

Pearson, Birger A. 'Gnosticism.' Pages 313-17 in vol. 1 of *EDSS*. Edited by Lawrence H. Schiffman and James C. VanderKam. 2 vols. Oxford: Oxford University Press, 2000.

Perkins, Pheme. *Jesus as Teacher.* UJT. Cambridge: Cambridge University Press, 1990.

Pesch, Wilhelm. 'Theologische Aussagen der Redaktion von Matthäus 23.' Pages 286-99 in *Orientierung an Jesus.* Edited by Paul Hoffmann. Wien: Herder, 1973.

Phillips, Gary A. '"This is a Hard Saying. Who Can Be Listener to It?": Creating a Reader in John 6.' *Semeia* 26 (1983): 23-56.

Phipps, William E. *The Wisdom and Wit of Rabbi Jesus.* Louisville: Westminster John Knox, 1993.

Plevnik, Joseph. 'Pauline Presuppositions.' Pages 50-61 in *The Thessalonian Correspondence.* Edited by Raymond F. Collins. BETL 87. Leuven: Leuven University Press, 1990.

Plummer, Alfred. *A Commentary on St. Paul's First Epistle to the Thessalonians.* London: Robert Scott, 1918.

Polak, F. 'Theophany and Mediator: The Unfolding of a Theme in the Book of Exodus.' Pages 113-47 in *Studies in the Book of Exodus: Redaction - Reception - Interpretation.* Edited by Marc Vervenne. BETL 126. Leuven: Leuven University Press, 1996.

Potter, H. D. 'The New Covenant in Jeremiah XXXI.31-34.' *VT* 33 (1983): 347-57.

Poythress, Vern S. 'Testing for Johannine Authorship by Examining the Use of Conjunctions.' *WTJ* 46 (1984): 350-69.

Prete, Benedetto. 'L'unzione (XPIΣMA) ricevuta dai credenti (1 Giov 2,20-27).' Pages 199-234 in *Fede e sacramenti negli scritti giovannei.* Rome: Edizioni Abbazia S. Paulo, 1985.

Puech, Émile. 'Hodayot.' Pages 365-69 in vol. 1 of *EDSS.* Edited by Lawrence H. Schiffman and James VanderKam. 2 vols. Oxford: Oxford University Press, 2000.

Rabin, Chaim. *The Zadokite Documents.* Oxford: Clarendon Press, 1954.

Reicke, Bo. 'Traces of Gnosticism in the Dead Sea Scrolls?' *NTS* 1 (1954-55): 137-41.

Reif, Stefan C. *Judaism and Hebrew Prayer: New perspectives on Jewish liturgical history.* Cambridge: Cambridge University Press, 1995.

Reilly, Wendel S. 'Titles in Mt. 23:8-12.' *CBQ* 1 (1939): 249-50.

Reim, Günter. *Studien zum Alttestamentlichen Hintergrund des Johannesevangeliums.* SNTSMS 22. Cambridge: Cambridge University Press, 1974.

Reitzenstein, Richard. *Hellenistic Mystery-Religions: Their Basic Ideas and Significance.* Translated by John E. Steely. PTMS. Pittsburgh: Pickwick Press, 1978.

Rensberger, David. *1 John, 2 John, 3 John.* ANTC. Nashville: Abingdon, 1997.

Richard, Earl. *First and Second Thessalonians.* SP. Collegeville: Liturgical Press, 1995.

Richter, Georg. *Studien zum Johannesevangelium.* Edited by Josef Hainz. BU 13. Regensburg: Friedrich Pustet, 1977.

Ridderbos, Herman. *The Gospel according to John: A Theological Commentary.* Translated by John Vriend. Grand Rapids: Eerdmans, 1997.

Riesner, Rainer. *Jesus als Lehrer: Eine Untersuchung zum Ursprung der Evangelien-Überlieferung.* WUNT 2.7. Tübingen: J. C. B. Mohr (Paul Siebeck), 1981.

——. 'Jesus as Preacher and Teacher.' Pages 185-210 in *Jesus and the Oral Gospel Tradition.* Edited by Henry Wansbrough. JSNTSup 64. Sheffield: Sheffield Academic Press, 1991.

Rigaux, B. *Saint Paul les Épitres aux Thessaloniciens.* Paris: Librairie Lecoffre, 1956.

Ringgren, Helmer. *The Faith of Qumran: Theology of the Dead Sea Scrolls.* Translated by Emilie T. Sander. 2d ed. New York: Crossroad, 1995.

Robbins, Vernon K. *Jesus the Teacher: A Socio-Rhetorical Interpretation of Mark.* Philadelphia: Fortress, 1984.

Roetzel, Calvin J. 'Theodidaktoi and Handwork in Philo and 1 Thessalonians.' Pages 324-31 in *L'Apotre Paul. Personnalite, Style et Conception du Ministere.* Edited by A. Vanhoye. BETL 73. Leuven: Leuven University Press, 1986.

Rofé, Alexander. 'Revealed Wisdom: From the Bible to Qumran.' Pages 1-11 in *Sapiential Perspectives: Wisdom Literature in Light of the Dead Sea Scrolls.* Edited by John J. Collins, Gregory E. Sterling, and Ruth A. Clements. *STDJ* 51. Leiden: Brill, 2004.

Runia, David T. 'How to read Philo.' *NedTT* 40 (1986): 185-98.

Sabbe, Maurits. 'Can Mt 11,27 and Lk 10,22 Be Called a Johannine Logion?' Pages 363-71 in *Logia: Les Paroles de Jésus – the Sayings of Jesus.* Edited by Joël Delobel. BETL 59. Leuven: Leuven University Press, 1982.

Safrai, S. 'Education and the Study of the Torah.' Pages 945-70 in *The Jewish People in the First Century: Historical Geography, Political History, Social, Cultural and Religious Life and Institutions.* Edited by S. Safrai and M. Stern. CRI 1. 2 vols. Amsterdam: Van Gorcum, 1974.

Saggin, L. 'Magister vester unus est, Christus. (Mt 23,10).' *VD* (1952): 205-13.

Saldarini, Anthony J. 'Delegitimation of Leaders in Matthew 23.' *CBQ* 54 (1992): 659-80.

Sanders, Boykin. 'Imitating Paul: 1 Cor 4:16.' *HTR* 74 (1981): 353-63.

Sanders, E. P. *Jewish Law from Jesus to the Mishnah: Five Studies*. London: SCM, 1990.

Sawyer, John F. A. Review of *Theological Dictionary of the New Testament*, Volume V, Ξ-Πα. *SJT* 23 (1970): 240-42.

Schawe, Erwin. *Gott als Lehrer im Alten Testament: Eine semantisch-theologische Studie*. Fribourg: F. Stettler, 1979.

Schlatter, Adolf. *Der Evangelist Johannes: Wie er spricht, denkt und glaubt*. Stuttgart: Calwer, 1975.

Schnackenburg, Rudolf. *The Church in the New Testament*. London: Burns & Oates, 1965.

—. *The Gospel According to St. John*. Translated by Kevin Smyth, Cecily Hastings, Francis McDonagh, David Smith, Richard Foley, and G. A. Kon. HTC. 3 vols., Wellwood: Burns & Oates, 1968-1982.

—. *The Johannine Epistles*. Translated by Reginald Fuller and Ilse Fuller. Wellwood: Burns & Oates, 1992.

—. Review of Peder Borgen, *Bread from Heaven*. *BZ* 12 (1968): 143-45.

Schnelle, Udo. *The History and Theology of the New Testament Writings*. London: SCM, 1998.

—. 'Johannes als Geisttheologe.' *NovT* 40 (1998): 17-31.

Schniewind, Julius. *Das Evangelium nach Matthäus*. NTD. Göttingen: Vandenhoeck and Ruprecht, 1956.

Scholtissek, Klaus. *Die Vollmacht Jesu: Traditions- und redaktionsgeschichtliche Analysen zu einem Leitmotiv markinischer Christologie*. NTAbh 25. Münster: Aschendorff, 1992

Schrage, Wolfgang. *Der erste Brief an die Korinther*. EKKNT 7. 4 vols. Zürich: Benziger, 1991-2001.

Schuchard, Bruce G. *Scripture within Scripture: The Interrelationship of Form and Function in the Explicit Old Testament Citations in the Gospel of John*. SBLDS 133. Atlanta: Scholars Press, 1992.

Schürer, Emil. *The History of the Jewish People in the Age of Jesus Christ (175 B. C. – A. D. 135)*. Rev. and ed. by Geza Vermes, Fergus Millar, Martin Goodman, and Matthew Black. A New English Version. 3 vols. Edinburgh: T & T Clark, 1979-1987.

Schweizer, Eduard. *Church Order in the New Testament*. SBT. London: SCM, 1961.

—. 'The Concept of the Church in the Gospel and Epistles of St. John.' Pages 230-45 in *New Testament Essays: Studies in Memory of Thomas Walter Manson*. Edited by A. J. B. Higgins. Manchester: Manchester University Press, 1959.

—. *Das Evangelium nach Matthäus*. NTD. Göttingen: Vandenhoeck & Ruprecht, 1973.

—. 'Matthew's Church.' Pages 149-77 in *The Interpretation of Matthew*. Edited by Graham Stanton. 2d ed. Edinburgh: T & T Clark, 1995. Repr. from *Matthäus und seine Gemeinde*. Stuttgart: Katholisches Bibelwerk, 1974.

Silva, Moisés. *Biblical Words and Their Meaning: An Introduction to Lexical Semantics*. Grand Rapids: Zondervan, 1994.

Sim, David C. *Apocalyptic Eschatology in the Gospel of Matthew*. SNTSMS 88. Cambridge: Cambridge University Press, 1996.

—. *The Gospel of Matthew and Christian Judaism: The History and Social Setting of the Matthean Community*. SNTW. Edinburgh: T & T Clark, 1998.

Simonetti, Manlio, ed. *Matthew 14-28*. ACCS 1b. Downers Grove: InterVarsity Press, 2002.

Smalley, Stephen S. *1, 2, 3 John*. WBC 51. Waco: Word Books, 1984.

—. 'The Johannine Community and the Letters of John.' Pages 95-104 in *A Vision for the Church: Studies in Early Christian Ecclesiology in Honour of J. P. M. Sweet*. Edited by Markus Bockmuehl and Michael B. Thompson. Edinburgh: T & T Clark, 1997.

Smith, D. Moody. *First, Second, and Third John*. IBC. Louisville: John Knox, 1991.

—. *Johannine Christianity: Essays on Its Setting, Sources, and Theology.* Columbia: University of South Carolina Press, 1984.

—. *John.* ANTC. Nashville: Abingdon, 1999.

Spicq, C. 'Une Allusion au Docteur de Justice dans Matthieu, XXIII, 10?' *RB* 66 (1959): 387-96.

—. *Agape in the Epistles of St. Paul, the Acts of the Apostles and the Epistles of St. James, St. Peter, and St. Jude.* Vol. 2 of *Agape in the New Testament.* Translated by Marie Aquinas McNamara and Mary Honoria Richter. London: B. Herder, 1965.

Stanley, Christopher D. 'The Social Environment of "Free" Biblical Quotations in the New Testament.' Pages 18-27 in *Early Christian Interpretation of the Scriptures of Israel: Investigations and Proposals.* Edited by Craig A. Evans and James A. Sanders. JSNTSup 148. Sheffield: Sheffield Academic Press, 1997.

Stanton, Graham N. *A Gospel for a New People: Studies in Matthew.* Edinburgh: T & T Clark, 1993.

—. *The Gospels and Jesus.* 2d ed. OBS. Oxford: Oxford University Press, 2002.

—. 'Revisiting Matthew's Communities.' Pages 9-23 in *SBL Seminar Papers, 1994. SBLSP* 33. Atlanta: Scholars Press, 1994.

Stein, Robert H. 'The "Redaktionsgeschichtlich" Investigation of a Markan Seam (Mc 1 21f.).' *ZNW* 61 (1970): 70-94.

Stemberger, Günter. *Introduction to the Talmud and Midrash.* Translated by Markus Bockmuehl. 2d ed. Edinburgh: T & T Clark, 1996.

Stendahl, Krister. *The School of St. Matthew and Its Use of the Old Testament.* ASNU 20. Lund: CWK Gleerup, 1968.

Steudel, Annette. '"Bereitet den Weg des Herrn": Religiöses Lernen in Qumran.' Pages 99-116 in *Religiöses Lernen in der biblischen, frühjüdischen und frühchristlichen Überlieferung.* Edited by Beate Ego and Helmut Merkel. WUNT 180. Tübingen: Mohr Siebeck, 2005.

—. '"End of Days" in the Texts from Qumran.' *RevQ* 16 (1993): 225-46.

Stott, John R. W. *The Letters of John.* 2d ed. TNTC. Leicester: InterVarsity Press, 1988.

—. *The Message of Thessalonians: Preparing for the Coming King.* BST. Leicester: InterVarsity Press, 1991.

Stowers, Stanley K. *Letter Writing in Greco-Roman Antiquity.* LEC. Philadelphia: Westminster, 1986.

Strecker, Georg. *The Johannine Letters.* Translated by Linda M. Maloney. Hermeneia. Minneapolis: Fortress, 1996.

Stuhlmacher, Peter. 'Spiritual Remembering: John 14.26.' Pages 55-68 in *The Holy Spirit and Christian Origins.* Edited by Graham N. Stanton, Bruce W. Longenecker, and Stephen C. Barton. Grand Rapids: Eerdmans, 2004.

Swancutt, Diana M. 'Hungers Assuaged by the Bread from Heaven: "Eating Jesus" as Isaian Call to Belief: The Confluence of Isaiah 55 and Psalm 78 (77) in John 6.22-71.' Pages 218-51 in *Early Christian Interpretation of the Scriptures of Israel: Investigations and Proposals.* Edited by Craig A. Evans and James A. Sanders. JSNTSup 148. Sheffield: Sheffield Academic Press, 1997.

Swetnam, James. 'Why was Jeremiah's New Covenant New?' Pages 111-15 in *Studies on Prophecy.* Edited by G. W. Anderson. VTSup 26. Leiden: Brill, 1974.

Tambyah, T. Isaac. 'θεοδίδακτοι. A Suggestion of an Implication of the Deity of Christ." *ExpTim* 44 (1933): 527-28.

Thatcher, Tom. 'Literacy, Textual Communities, and Josephus' *Jewish War.*' *JSJ* 29 (1998): 123-42.

Theobald, Michael. 'Gezogen von Gottes Liebe (Joh 6,44f): Beobachtungen zur Überlieferung eines johanneischen "Herrenworts."' Pages 315-41 in *Schrift und Tradition: Festschrift für Josef Ernst zum 70. Geburtstag.* Edited by Knut Backhaus and Franz Georg Untergassmair. München: Ferdinand Schöningh, 1996.

——. *Herrenworte im Johannes-Evangelium.* HBS 34. Freiburg: Herder, 2002.

——. 'Schriftzitate im "Lebensbrot"-Dialog Jesu (Joh 6): Ein Paradigma für den Schriftgebrauch des Vierten Evangelisten.' Pages 327-66 in *The Scriptures in the Gospels.* Edited by C. M. Tuckett. BETL 131. Leuven: Leuven University Press, 1997.

Thiselton, Anthony. *The First Epistle to the Corinthians.* NIGTC. Grand Rapids: Eerdmans, 2000.

Thompson, J. A. *The Book of Jeremiah.* NICOT. Grand Rapids: Eerdmans, 1980.

Thompson, Marianne Meye. *The God of the Gospel of John.* Grand Rapids: Eerdmans, 2001.

Thompson, Michael. *Clothed with Christ: The Example and Teaching of Jesus in Romans 12.1-15.13.* JSNTSup 59. Sheffield: JSOT Press, 1991.

Townsend, John T. 'Ancient Education in the Time of the Early Roman Empire.' Pages 139-63 in *Early Church History: The Roman Empire as the Setting of Primitive Christianity.* Edited by Stephen Benko and John J. O'Rourke. London: Oliphants, 1971.

——. 'Education (Greco-Roman Period).' Pages 312-17 in vol. 2 of *ABD.* Edited by David Noel Freedman. New York: Doubleday, 1992.

——. 'Matthew XXIII.9.' *JTS* 12 (1961): 56-59.

Tuckett, C. M. Review of Rik Hoet, *"Omnes autem vos fratres estis." Etude du concept ecclésiologique des 'frères' selon Mt 23, 8-12. JTS* 35 (1984): 508-9.

——. 'Synoptic Tradition in 1 Thessalonians?' Pages 160-82 in *The Thessalonian Correspondence.* Edited by Raymond F. Collins. BETL 87. Leuven: Leuven University Press, 1990.

Untergassmair, Franz Georg. '"Du bist der Lehrer Israels und verstehst das nicht?" (Joh 2,10b) [*sic*] – Lernen bei Johannes.' Pages 211-33 in *Religiöses Lernen in der biblischen, frühjüdischen und frühchristlichen Überlieferung.* Edited by Beate Ego and Helmut Merkel. WUNT 180. Tübingen: Mohr Siebeck, 2005.

Van Der Watt, Jan G. *Family of the King: Dynamics of Metaphor in the Gospel According to John.* BIS 47. Leiden: Brill, 2000.

van Tilborg, Sjef. *Imaginative Love in John.* BIS 2. Leiden: E. J. Brill, 1993.

——. *The Jewish Leaders in Matthew.* Leiden: E. J. Brill, 1972.

VanderKam, James. 'Book of Jubilees.' Pages 434-38 in vol. 1 of *EDSS.* Edited by Lawrence H. Schiffman and James VanderKam. 2 vols. Oxford: Oxford University Press, 2000.

——. 'Messianism in the Scrolls.' Pages 211-34 in *The Community of the Renewed Covenant: The Notre Dame Symposium on the Dead Sea Scrolls.* Edited by Eugene Ulrich and James VanderKam. Notre Dame: University of Notre Dame Press, 1994.

Vermes, Geza. 'The Jesus Notice of Josephus Re-Examined.' *JJS* 38 (1987): 2-10.

Verseput, Donald J. 'James 1:17 and the Jewish Morning Prayers.' *NovT* 39 (1997): 177-91.

——. 'The Role and Meaning of the "Son of God" Title in Matthew's Gospel.' *NTS* 33 (1987): 532-56.

Viviano, Benedict T. 'Rabbouni and Mark 9:5.' *RB* 97 (1990): 207-18.

——. 'Social World and Community Leadership: The Case of Matthew 23.1-12, 34.' *JSNT* 39 (1990): 3-21.

——. 'Study and Education.' Pages 896-98 in vol. 2 of *EDSS.* Edited by Lawrence H. Schiffman and James C. VanderKam. 2 vols. Oxford: Oxford University Press, 2000.

Völker, Walther. *Fortschritt und Vollendung bei Philo von Alexandrien: Eine Studie zur Geschichte der Frömmigkeit.* TUGAL. Leipzig: J. C. Hinrich, 1938.

von Dobschütz, Ernst. *Die Thessalonicher-Briefe*, 1909. Repr., Göttingen: Vandenhoeck & Ruprecht, 1974.

Wach, Joachim. 'Master and Disciple: Two Religio-Sociological Studies.' *JR* 42 (1962): 1-21.

Waltke, Bruce K. *The Book of Proverbs*. NICOT. 2 vols. Grand Rapids: Eerdmans, 2004-2005.

Wan, Sze-Kar. 'Charismatic Exegesis: Philo and Paul Compared.' Pages 54-82 in *The Studia Philonica Annual*. SHJ 6. Edited by David T. Runia. Atlanta: Scholars Press, 1994.

Wanamaker, Charles. *The Epistles to the Thessalonians: A Commentary on the Greek Text*. NIGTC. Grand Rapids: Eerdmans, 1990.

Watts, John D. W. *Isaiah*. WBC 24, 25. 2 vols. Waco: Word Books, 1985-1987.

Weatherly, Jon A. *1 & 2 Thessalonians*. CPNIVC. Joplin: College Press, 1996.

Wegner, Paul D. 'Discipline in the Book of Proverbs: "To Spank or Not to Spank?"' *JETS* 48 (2005): 715-32.

Weima, Jeffrey A. D. '"How You Must Walk to Please God": Holiness and Discipleship in 1 Thessalonians.' Pages 98-119 in *Patterns of Discipleship in the New Testament*. Edited by Richard N. Longenecker. Grand Rapids: Eerdmans, 1996.

Weinfeld, Moshe. 'Jeremiah and the Spiritual Metamorphosis of Israel.' *ZAW* 88 (1976): 17-56.

Wengst, Klaus. *Das Johannesevangelium*. THKNT 4. 2 vols. Berlin: W. Kohlhammer, 2000.

Wenthe, Dean O. 'The Social Configuration of the Rabbi-Disciple Relationship: Evidence and Implications for First Century Palestine.' Pages 143-74 in *Studies in the Hebrew Bible, Qumran, and the Septuagint Presented to Eugene Ulrich*. Edited by Peter W. Flint, Emmanuel Tov, and James C. VanderKam. VTSup 101. Leiden: Brill, 2006.

Weren, Wim. 'Quotations from Isaiah and Matthew's Christology (Mt 1,23 and 4,15-16).' Pages 447-65 in *Studies in the Book of Isaiah*. Edited by J. van Ruiten and M. Vervenne. BETL 132. Leuven: Leuven University Press, 1997.

Westcott, Brooke Foss. *The Epistles of St John*. 1883. Repr., Appleford: Marcham Manor Press, 1966.

Westerholm, Stephen. *Jesus and Scribal Authority*. ConBNT 10. Lund: CWK Gleerup, 1978.

Westermann, Claus. *Isaiah 40-66: A Commentary*. OTL. London: SCM, 1969.

Whealey, Alice. *Josephus on Jesus: The Testimonium Flavianum Controversy from Late Antiquity to Modern Times*. SBLit 36. New York: Peter Lang, 2003.

Whiteley, D. E. H. *Thessalonians*. NCB. Oxford: Oxford University Press, 1969.

Wildberger, Hans. *Isaiah: A Commentary*. CC. 2 vols. Translated by Thomas H. Trapp. Minneapolis: Fortress, 1991-1997.

—. *Jesaja*. BKAT 10. 3 vols. Germany: Neukirchener Verlag, 1972-1982.

Wilkins, Michael J. *The Concept of Disciple in Matthew's Gospel As Reflected in the Use of the Term Μαθητής*. NovTSup 59. Leiden: E. J. Brill, 1988.

Williams, Catrin H. 'Isaiah in John's Gospel.' Pages 101-16 in *Isaiah in the New Testament*. Edited by Steve Moyise and Maarten J. J. Menken. Edinburgh: T & T Clark, 2005.

Williams, David J. *1 and 2 Thessalonians*. NIBCNT. Peabody: Hendrickson, 1992.

Williams, H. H. Drake, III. *The Wisdom of the Wise: The Presence and Function of Scripture within 1 Cor. 1:18-3:23*. AGJU 49. Leiden: Brill, 2001.

Williamson, H. G. M. 'Synchronic and Diachronic in Isaian Perspective.' Pages 211-26 in *Synchronic or Diachronic? A Debate on Method in Old Testament Exegesis*. Edited by Johannes C. De Moor. OtSt 34. Leiden: E. J. Brill, 1995.

—. *The Book Called Isaiah: Deutero-Isaiah's Role in Composition and Redaction*. Oxford: Clarendon Press, 1994.

Wilson, Stephen G. *Related Strangers: Jews and Christians 70-170 C. E.* Minneapolis: Fortress, 1995.

Winter, Bruce W. *After Paul Left Corinth: The Influence of Secular Ethics and Social Change.* Grand Rapids: Eerdmans, 2001.

—. 'The Entries and Ethics of Orators and Paul (1 Thessalonians 2:1-12).' *TynBul* 44 (1993): 55-74.

—. 'The Messiah as the Tutor: The Meaning of καθηγητής in Matthew 23:10.' *TynBul* 42 (1991): 152-57.

—. *Philo and Paul Among the Sophists.* 2d ed. Grand Rapids: Eerdmans, 2002.

Witherington, Ben, III. *John's Wisdom: A Commentary on the Fourth Gospel.* Louisville: Westminster John Knox, 1995.

Witmer, Stephen E. 'Approaches to Scripture in the Fourth Gospel and the Qumran *Pesharim.*' *NovT* 48 (2006): 313-28.

—. 'Overlooked Evidence for Citation and Redaction in John 6,45a.' *ZNW* 97 (2006): 134-38.

—. 'θεοδίδακτοι in 1 Thessalonians 4.9: A Pauline Neologism.' *NTS* 52 (2006): 239-50.

Yieh, John Yueh-Han. *One Teacher: Jesus' Teaching Role in Matthew's Gospel Report.* BZNW 124. Berlin: Walter de Gruyter, 2004.

Young, Franklin W. 'A Study of the Relation of Isaiah to the Fourth Gospel.' *ZNW* 46 (1955): 215-33.

Zenger, Erich. 'JHWH als Lehrer des Volkes und der Einzelnen im Psalter.' Pages 47-67 in *Religiöses Lernen in der biblischen, frühjüdischen und frühchristlichen Überlieferung.* Edited by Beate Ego and Helmut Merkel. WUNT 180. Tübingen: Mohr Siebeck, 2005.

Zimmerman, Alfred F. *Die urchistlichen Lehrer.* WUNT 2.12. Tübingen: J. C. B. Mohr (Paul Siebeck), 1984.

Zimmermann, Johannes. *Messianische Texte aus Qumran: Königliche, priesterliche und prophetische Messiasvorstellungen in den Schriftfunden von Qumran.* WUNT 2.104. Tübingen: Mohr Siebeck, 1998.

Zuck, Roy B. 'Greek Words for Teach.' *BSac* 122 (1965): 158-68.

—. 'Hebrew Words for "Teach."' *BSac* 121 (1964): 228-35.

Zumstein, Jean. 'Die Schriftrezeption in der Brotrede (Joh 6).' Pages 123-39 in *Israel und seine Heilstraditionen im Johannesevangelium.* Edited by Michael Labahn, Klaus Scholtissek, and Angelika Strotmann. Paderborn: Ferdinand Schöningh, 2004.

Index of sources

Old Testament

Old Testament Apocrypha

Old Testament Pseudepigrapha

Dead Sea Scrolls

New Testament

Philo

Rabbinic literature

Greco-Roman literature

Early Christian literature

Index of modern authors

Index of key-words and subjects

Wissenschaftliche Untersuchungen zum Neuen Testament

Alphabetical Index of the First and Second Series

Bieringer, Reimund: see *Koester, Craig.*

Bittner, Wolfgang J.: Jesu Zeichen im Johannesevangelium. 1987. *Vol. II/26.*

Bjerkelund, Carl J.: Tauta Egeneto. 1987. *Vol. 40.*

Blackburn, Barry Lee: Theios Aner and the Markan Miracle Traditions. 1991. *Vol. II/40.*

Blanton IV, Thomas R.: Constructing a New Covenant. 2007. *Vol. II/233.*

Bock, Darrell L.: Blasphemy and Exaltation in Judaism and the Final Examination of Jesus. 1998. *Vol. II/106.*

Bockmuehl, Markus N.A.: Revelation and Mystery in Ancient Judaism and Pauline Christianity. 1990. *Vol. II/36.*

Bøe, Sverre: Gog and Magog. 2001. *Vol. II/135.*

Böhlig, Alexander: Gnosis und Synkretismus. Vol. 1 1989. *Vol. 47* – Vol. 2 1989. *Vol. 48.*

Böhm, Martina: Samarien und die Samaritai bei Lukas. 1999. *Vol. II/111.*

Böttrich, Christfried: Weltweisheit – Menschheitsethik – Urkult. 1992. *Vol. II/50.*

– */ Herzer, Jens* (Ed.): Josephus und das Neue Testament. 2007. *Vol. 209.*

Bolyki, János: Jesu Tischgemeinschaften. 1997. *Vol. II/96.*

Bosman, Philip: Conscience in Philo and Paul. 2003. *Vol. II/166.*

Bovon, François: Studies in Early Christianity. 2003. *Vol. 161.*

Brändl, Martin: Der Agon bei Paulus. 2006. *Vol. II/222.*

Breytenbach, Cilliers: see *Frey, Jörg.*

Brocke, Christoph vom: Thessaloniki – Stadt des Kassander und Gemeinde des Paulus. 2001. *Vol. II/125.*

Brunson, Andrew: Psalm 118 in the Gospel of John. 2003. *Vol. II/158.*

Büchli, Jörg: Der Poimandres – ein paganisiertes Evangelium. 1987. *Vol. II/27.*

Bühner, Jan A.: Der Gesandte und sein Weg im 4. Evangelium. 1977. *Vol. II/2.*

Burchard, Christoph: Untersuchungen zu Joseph und Aseneth. 1965. *Vol. 8.*

– Studien zur Theologie, Sprache und Umwelt des Neuen Testaments. Ed. by D. Sänger. 1998. *Vol. 107.*

Burnett, Richard: Karl Barth's Theological Exegesis. 2001. *Vol. II/145.*

Byron, John: Slavery Metaphors in Early Judaism and Pauline Christianity. 2003. *Vol. II/162.*

Byrskog, Samuel: Story as History – History as Story. 2000. *Vol. 123.*

Cancik, Hubert (Ed.): Markus-Philologie. 1984. *Vol. 33.*

Capes, David B.: Old Testament Yaweh Texts in Paul's Christology. 1992. *Vol. II/47.*

Caragounis, Chrys C.: The Development of Greek and the New Testament. 2004. *Vol. 167.*

– The Son of Man. 1986. *Vol. 38.*

– see *Fridrichsen, Anton.*

Carleton Paget, James: The Epistle of Barnabas. 1994. *Vol. II/64.*

Carson, D.A., O'Brien, Peter T. and *Mark Seifrid* (Ed.): Justification and Variegated Nomism.
Vol. 1: The Complexities of Second Temple Judaism. 2001. *Vol. II/140.*
Vol. 2: The Paradoxes of Paul. 2004. *Vol. II/181.*

Chae, Young Sam: Jesus as the Eschatological Davidic Shepherd. 2006. *Vol. II/216.*

Chapman, David W.: Ancient Jewish and Christian Perceptions of Crucifixion. 2008. *Vol. II/244.*

Chester, Andrew: Messiah and Exaltation. 2007. *Vol. 207.*

Chibici-Revneanu, Nicole: Die Herrlichkeit des Verherrlichten. 2007. *Vol. II/231.*

Ciampa, Roy E.: The Presence and Function of Scripture in Galatians 1 and 2. 1998. *Vol. II/102.*

Classen, Carl Joachim: Rhetorical Criticsm of the New Testament. 2000. *Vol. 128.*

Colpe, Carsten: Iranier – Aramäer – Hebräer – Hellenen. 2003. *Vol. 154.*

Crump, David: Jesus the Intercessor. 1992. *Vol. II/49.*

Dahl, Nils Alstrup: Studies in Ephesians. 2000. *Vol. 131.*

Daise, Michael A.: Feasts in John. 2007. *Vol. II/229.*

Deines, Roland: Die Gerechtigkeit der Tora im Reich des Messias. 2004. *Vol. 177.*

– Jüdische Steingefäße und pharisäische Frömmigkeit. 1993. *Vol. II/52.*

– Die Pharisäer. 1997. *Vol. 101.*

Deines, Roland and *Karl-Wilhelm Niebuhr* (Ed.): Philo und das Neue Testament. 2004. *Vol. 172.*

Dennis, John A.: Jesus' Death and the Gathering of True Israel. 2006. *Vol. 217.*

Dettwiler, Andreas and *Jean Zumstein* (Ed.): Kreuzestheologie im Neuen Testament. 2002. *Vol. 151.*

Dickson, John P.: Mission-Commitment in Ancient Judaism and in the Pauline Communities. 2003. *Vol. II/159.*

Dietzfelbinger, Christian: Der Abschied des Kommenden. 1997. *Vol. 95.*

Dimitrov, Ivan Z., James D.G. Dunn, Ulrich Luz and *Karl-Wilhelm Niebuhr* (Ed.): Das Alte Testament als christliche Bibel in orthodoxer und westlicher Sicht. 2004. *Vol. 174.*

Dobbeler, Axel von: Glaube als Teilhabe. 1987. *Vol. II/22.*

Dryden, J. de Waal: Theology and Ethics in 1 Peter. 2006. *Vol. II/209.*

Dübbers, Michael: Christologie und Existenz im Kolosserbrief. 2005. *Vol. II/191.*

Dunn, James D.G.: The New Perspective on Paul. 2005. *Vol. 185.*

Dunn, James D.G. (Ed.): Jews and Christians. 1992. *Vol. 66.*

– Paul and the Mosaic Law. 1996. *Vol. 89.*

– see *Dimitrov, Ivan Z.*

–, *Hans Klein, Ulrich Luz* and *Vasile Mihoc* (Ed.): Auslegung der Bibel in orthodoxer und westlicher Perspektive. 2000. *Vol. 130.*

Ebel, Eva: Die Attraktivität früher christlicher Gemeinden. 2004. *Vol. II/178.*

Ebertz, Michael N.: Das Charisma des Gekreuzigten. 1987. *Vol. 45.*

Eckstein, Hans-Joachim: Der Begriff Syneidesis bei Paulus. 1983. *Vol. II/10.*

– Verheißung und Gesetz. 1996. *Vol. 86.*

Ego, Beate: Im Himmel wie auf Erden. 1989. *Vol. II/34.*

Ego, Beate, Armin Lange and *Peter Pilhofer* (Ed.): Gemeinde ohne Tempel – Community without Temple. 1999. *Vol. 118.*

– and *Helmut Merkel* (Ed.): Religiöses Lernen in der biblischen, frühjüdischen und frühchristlichen Überlieferung. 2005. *Vol. 180.*

Eisen, Ute E.: see *Paulsen, Henning.*

Elledge, C.D.: Life after Death in Early Judaism. 2006. *Vol. II/208.*

Ellis, E. Earle: Prophecy and Hermeneutic in Early Christianity. 1978. *Vol. 18.*

– The Old Testament in Early Christianity. 1991. *Vol. 54.*

Endo, Masanobu: Creation and Christology. 2002. *Vol. 149.*

Ennulat, Andreas: Die 'Minor Agreements'. 1994. *Vol. II/62.*

Ensor, Peter W.: Jesus and His 'Works'. 1996. *Vol. II/85.*

Eskola, Timo: Messiah and the Throne. 2001. *Vol. II/142.*

– Theodicy and Predestination in Pauline Soteriology. 1998. *Vol. II/100.*

Fatehi, Mehrdad: The Spirit's Relation to the Risen Lord in Paul. 2000. *Vol. II/128.*

Feldmeier, Reinhard: Die Krisis des Gottessohnes. 1987. *Vol. II/21.*

– Die Christen als Fremde. 1992. *Vol. 64.*

Feldmeier, Reinhard and *Ulrich Heckel* (Ed.): Die Heiden. 1994. *Vol. 70.*

Fletcher-Louis, Crispin H.T.: Luke-Acts: Angels, Christology and Soteriology. 1997. *Vol. II/94.*

Förster, Niclas: Marcus Magus. 1999. *Vol. 114.*

Forbes, Christopher Brian: Prophecy and Inspired Speech in Early Christianity and its Hellenistic Environment. 1995. *Vol. II/75.*

Fornberg, Tord: see *Fridrichsen, Anton.*

Fossum, Jarl E.: The Name of God and the Angel of the Lord. 1985. *Vol. 36.*

Foster, Paul: Community, Law and Mission in Matthew's Gospel. *Vol. II/177.*

Fotopoulos, John: Food Offered to Idols in Roman Corinth. 2003. *Vol. II/151.*

Frenschkowski, Marco: Offenbarung und Epiphanie. Vol. 1 1995. *Vol. II/79* – Vol. 2 1997. *Vol. II/80.*

Frey, Jörg: Eugen Drewermann und die biblische Exegese. 1995. *Vol. II/71.*

– Die johanneische Eschatologie. Vol. I. 1997. *Vol. 96.* – Vol. II. 1998. *Vol. 110.* – Vol. III. 2000. *Vol. 117.*

Frey, Jörg and *Cilliers Breytenbach* (Ed.): Aufgabe und Durchführung einer Theologie des Neuen Testaments. 2007. *Vol. 205.*

– and *Udo Schnelle (Ed.):* Kontexte des Johannesevangeliums. 2004. *Vol. 175.*

– and *Jens Schröter* (Ed.): Deutungen des Todes Jesu im Neuen Testament. 2005. *Vol. 181.*

–, *Jan G. van der Watt,* and *Ruben Zimmermann* (Ed.): Imagery in the Gospel of John. 2006. *Vol. 200.*

Freyne, Sean: Galilee and Gospel. 2000. *Vol. 125.*

Fridrichsen, Anton: Exegetical Writings. Edited by C.C. Caragounis and T. Fornberg. 1994. *Vol. 76.*

Gäbel, Georg: Die Kulttheologie des Hebräerbriefes. 2006. *Vol. II/212.*

Gäckle, Volker: Die Starken und die Schwachen in Korinth und in Rom. 2005. *Vol. 200.*

Garlington, Don B.: 'The Obedience of Faith'. 1991. *Vol. II/38.*

– Faith, Obedience, and Perseverance. 1994. *Vol. 79.*

Garnet, Paul: Salvation and Atonement in the Qumran Scrolls. 1977. *Vol. II/3.*

Gemünden, Petra von (Ed.): see *Weissenrieder, Annette.*

Gese, Michael: Das Vermächtnis des Apostels. 1997. *Vol. II/99.*

Gheorghita, Radu: The Role of the Septuagint in Hebrews. 2003. *Vol. II/160.*

Gordley, Matthew E.: The Colossian Hymn in Context. 2007. *Vol. II/228.*

Gräbe, Petrus J.: The Power of God in Paul's Letters. 2000. *Vol. II/123.*

Gräßer, Erich: Der Alte Bund im Neuen. 1985. *Vol. 35.*

– Forschungen zur Apostelgeschichte. 2001. *Vol. 137.*

Grappe, Christian (Ed.): Le Repas de Dieu / Das Mahl Gottes.2004. *Vol. 169.*

Green, Joel B.: The Death of Jesus. 1988.
Vol. II/33.

Gregg, Brian Han: The Historical Jesus and
the Final Judgment Sayings in Q. 2005.
Vol. II/207.

Gregory, Andrew: The Reception of Luke and
Acts in the Period before Irenaeus. 2003.
Vol. II/169.

Grindheim, Sigurd: The Crux of Election. 2005.
Vol. II/202.

Gundry, Robert H.: The Old is Better. 2005.
Vol. 178.

Gundry Volf, Judith M.: Paul and Perseverance.
1990. *Vol. II/37.*

Häußer, Detlef: Christusbekenntnis und Jesus-
überlieferung bei Paulus. 2006. *Vol. 210.*

Hafemann, Scott J.: Suffering and the Spirit.
1986. *Vol. II/19.*

– Paul, Moses, and the History of Israel. 1995.
Vol. 81.

Hahn, Ferdinand: Studien zum Neuen Testa-
ment.
Vol. I: Grundsatzfragen, Jesusforschung,
Evangelien. 2006. *Vol. 191.*
Vol. II: Bekenntnisbildung und Theologie in
urchristlicher Zeit. 2006. *Vol. 192.*

Hahn, Johannes (Ed.): Zerstörungen des Jeru-
salemer Tempels. 2002. *Vol. 147.*

Hamid-Khani, Saeed: Relevation and Conceal-
ment of Christ. 2000. *Vol. II/120.*

Hannah, Darrel D.: Michael and Christ. 1999.
Vol. II/109.

Hardin, Justin K.: Galatians and the Imperial
Cult? 2007. *Vol. II /237.*

Harrison; James R.: Paul's Language of Grace
in Its Graeco-Roman Context. 2003.
Vol. II/172.

Hartman, Lars: Text-Centered New Testament
Studies. Ed. von D. Hellholm. 1997.
Vol. 102.

Hartog, Paul: Polycarp and the New Testament.
2001. *Vol. II/134.*

Heckel, Theo K.: Der Innere Mensch. 1993.
Vol. II/53.

– Vom Evangelium des Markus zum vierge-
staltigen Evangelium. 1999. *Vol. 120.*

Heckel, Ulrich: Kraft in Schwachheit. 1993.
Vol. II/56.

– Der Segen im Neuen Testament. 2002.
Vol. 150.

– see *Feldmeier, Reinhard.*

– see *Hengel, Martin.*

Heiligenthal, Roman: Werke als Zeichen. 1983.
Vol. II/9.

Heliso, Desta: Pistis and the Righteous One.
2007. *Vol. II/235.*

Hellholm, D.: see *Hartman, Lars.*

Hemer, Colin J.: The Book of Acts in the Setting
of Hellenistic History. 1989. *Vol. 49.*

Hengel, Martin: Judentum und Hellenismus.
1969, ³1988. *Vol. 10.*

– Die johanneische Frage. 1993. *Vol. 67.*

– Judaica et Hellenistica. Kleine Schriften I.
1996. *Vol. 90.*

– Judaica, Hellenistica et Christiana. Kleine
Schriften II. 1999. *Vol. 109.*

– Paulus und Jakobus. Kleine Schriften III.
2002. *Vol. 141.*

– Studien zur Christologie. Kleine Schriften IV.
2006. *Vol. 201.*

– and *Anna Maria Schwemer:* Paulus zwischen Damaskus und Antiochien. 1998.
Vol. 108.

– Der messianische Anspruch Jesu und die
Anfänge der Christologie. 2001. *Vol. 138.*

– Die vier Evangelien und das eine Evangelium von Jesus Christus. 2008. *Vol. 224.*

Hengel, Martin and *Ulrich Heckel* (Ed.): Paulus
und das antike Judentum. 1991. *Vol. 58.*

– and *Hermut Löhr* (Ed.): Schriftauslegung
im antiken Judentum und im Urchristentum.
1994. *Vol. 73.*

– and *Anna Maria Schwemer* (Ed.): Königs-
herrschaft Gottes und himmlischer Kult.
1991. *Vol. 55.*

– Die Septuaginta. 1994. *Vol. 72.*

–, *Siegfried Mittmann* and *Anna Maria Schwemer* (Ed.): La Cité de Dieu / Die Stadt Gottes. 2000. *Vol. 129.*

Hentschel, Anni: Diakonia im Neuen Testament.
2007. *Vol. 226.*

Hernández Jr., Juan: Scribal Habits and Theological Influence in the Apocalypse. 2006.
Vol. II/218.

Herrenbrück, Fritz: Jesus und die Zöllner. 1990.
Vol. II/41.

Herzer, Jens: Paulus oder Petrus? 1998.
Vol. 103.

– see *Böttrich, Christfried.*

Hill, Charles E.: From the Lost Teaching of Polycarp. 2005. *Vol. 186.*

Hoegen-Rohls, Christina: Der nachösterliche
Johannes. 1996. *Vol. II/84.*

Hoffmann, Matthias Reinhard: The Destroyer
and the Lamb. 2005. *Vol. II/203.*

Hofius, Otfried: Katapausis. 1970. *Vol. 11.*

– Der Vorhang vor dem Thron Gottes. 1972.
Vol. 14.

– Der Christushymnus Philipper 2,6–11.
1976, ²1991. *Vol. 17.*

– Paulusstudien. 1989, ²1994. *Vol. 51.*

– Neutestamentliche Studien. 2000.
Vol. 132.

– Paulusstudien II. 2002. *Vol. 143.*

– Exegetische Studien. 2008. *Vol. 223.*

– and *Hans-Christian Kammler:* Johannesstu-
dien. 1996. *Vol. 88.*

Holmberg, Bengt (Ed.): Exploring Early
Christian Identity. 2008. *Vol. 226.*

– and *Mikael Winninge* (Ed.): Identity Formation in the New Testament. 2008. *Vol. 227.*

Holtz, Traugott: Geschichte und Theologie des Urchristentums. 1991. *Vol. 57.*

Hommel, Hildebrecht: Sebasmata. Vol. 1 1983. *Vol. 31.* Vol. 2 1984. *Vol. 32.*

Horbury, William: Herodian Judaism and New Testament Study. 2006. *Vol. 193.*

Horst, Pieter W. van der: Jews and Christians in Their Graeco-Roman Context. 2006. *Vol. 196.*

Hvalvik, Reidar: The Struggle for Scripture and Covenant. 1996. *Vol. II/82.*

Jauhiainen, Marko: The Use of Zechariah in Revelation. 2005. *Vol. II/199.*

Jensen, Morten H.: Herod Antipas in Galilee. 2006. *Vol. II/215.*

Johns, Loren L.: The Lamb Christology of the Apocalypse of John. 2003. *Vol. II/167.*

Jossa, Giorgio: Jews or Christians? 2006. *Vol. 202.*

Joubert, Stephan: Paul as Benefactor. 2000. *Vol. II/124.*

Judge, E. A.: The First Christians in the Roman World. 2008. *Vol. 229.*

Jungbauer, Harry: „Ehre Vater und Mutter". 2002. *Vol. II/146.*

Kähler, Christoph: Jesu Gleichnisse als Poesie und Therapie. 1995. *Vol. 78.*

Kamlah, Ehrhard: Die Form der katalogischen Paränese im Neuen Testament. 1964. *Vol. 7.*

Kammler, Hans-Christian: Christologie und Eschatologie. 2000. *Vol. 126.*

– Kreuz und Weisheit. 2003. *Vol. 159.*

– see *Hofius, Otfried.*

Karakolis, Christos: see *Alexeev, Anatoly A.*

Karrer, Martin und *Wolfgang Kraus* (Ed.): Die Septuaginta – Texte, Kontexte, Lebenswelten. 2008. *Vol. 219.*

Kelhoffer, James A.: The Diet of John the Baptist. 2005. *Vol. 176.*

– Miracle and Mission. 1999. *Vol. II/112.*

Kelley, Nicole: Knowledge and Religious Authority in the Pseudo-Clementines. 2006. *Vol. II/213.*

Kieffer, René and *Jan Bergman (Ed.)*: La Main de Dieu / Die Hand Gottes. 1997. *Vol. 94.*

Kierspel, Lars: The Jews and the World in the Fourth Gospel. 2006. *Vol. 220.*

Kim, Seyoon: The Origin of Paul's Gospel. 1981, ²1984. *Vol. II/4.*

– Paul and the New Perspective. 2002. *Vol. 140.*

– "The 'Son of Man'" as the Son of God. 1983. *Vol. 30.*

Klauck, Hans-Josef: Religion und Gesellschaft im frühen Christentum. 2003. *Vol. 152.*

Klein, Hans: see *Dunn, James D. G.*

Kleinknecht, Karl Th.: Der leidende Gerechtfertigte. 1984, ²1988. *Vol. II/13.*

Klinghardt, Matthias: Gesetz und Volk Gottes. 1988. *Vol. II/32.*

Kloppenborg, John S.: The Tenants in the Vineyard. 2006. *Vol. 195.*

Koch, Michael: Drachenkampf und Sonnenfrau. 2004. *Vol. II/184.*

Koch, Stefan: Rechtliche Regelung von Konflikten im frühen Christentum. 2004. *Vol. II/174.*

Köhler, Wolf-Dietrich: Rezeption des Matthäusevangeliums in der Zeit vor Irenäus. 1987. *Vol. II/24.*

Köhn, Andreas: Der Neutestamentler Ernst Lohmeyer. 2004. *Vol. II/180.*

Koester, Craig and *Reimund Bieringer* (Ed.): The Resurrection of Jesus in the Gospel of John. 2008. *Vol. 222.*

Konradt, Matthias: Israel, Kirche und die Völker im Matthäusevangelium. 2007. *Vol. 215.*

Kooten, George H. van: Cosmic Christology in Paul and the Pauline School. 2003. *Vol. II/171.*

Korn, Manfred: Die Geschichte Jesu in veränderter Zeit. 1993. *Vol. II/51.*

Koskenniemi, Erkki: Apollonios von Tyana in der neutestamentlichen Exegese. 1994. *Vol. II/61.*

– The Old Testament Miracle-Workers in Early Judaism. 2005. *Vol. II/206.*

Kraus, Thomas J.: Sprache, Stil und historischer Ort des zweiten Petrusbriefes. 2001. *Vol. II/136.*

Kraus, Wolfgang: Das Volk Gottes. 1996. *Vol. 85.*

– see *Karrer, Martin.*

– see *Walter, Nikolaus.*

– and *Karl-Wilhelm Niebuhr* (Ed.): Frühjudentum und Neues Testament im Horizont Biblischer Theologie. 2003. *Vol. 162.*

Kreplin, Matthias: Das Selbstverständnis Jesu. 2001. *Vol. II/141.*

Kuhn, Karl G.: Achtzehngebet und Vaterunser und der Reim. 1950. *Vol. 1.*

Kvalbein, Hans: see *Ådna, Jostein.*

Kwon, Yon-Gyong: Eschatology in Galatians. 2004. *Vol. II/183.*

Laansma, Jon: I Will Give You Rest. 1997. *Vol. II/98.*

Labahn, Michael: Offenbarung in Zeichen und Wort. 2000. *Vol. II/117.*

Lambers-Petry, Doris: see *Tomson, Peter J.*

Lange, Armin: see *Ego, Beate.*

Lampe, Peter: Die stadtrömischen Christen in den ersten beiden Jahrhunderten. 1987, ²1989. *Vol. II/18.*

Landmesser, Christof: Wahrheit als Grundbegriff neutestamentlicher Wissenschaft. 1999. *Vol. 113.*

– Jüngerberufung und Zuwendung zu Gott. 2000. *Vol. 133.*

Lau, Andrew: Manifest in Flesh. 1996. *Vol. II/86.*

Lawrence, Louise: An Ethnography of the Gospel of Matthew. 2003. *Vol. II/165.*

Lee, Aquila H.I.: From Messiah to Preexistent Son. 2005. *Vol. II/192.*

Lee, Pilchan: The New Jerusalem in the Book of Relevation. 2000. *Vol. II/129.*

Lichtenberger, Hermann: Das Ich Adams und das Ich der Menschheit. 2004. *Vol. 164.*

– see *Avemarie, Friedrich.*

Lierman, John: The New Testament Moses. 2004. *Vol. II/173.*

– (Ed.): Challenging Perspectives on the Gospel of John. 2006. *Vol. II/219.*

Lieu, Samuel N.C.: Manichaeism in the Later Roman Empire and Medieval China. ²1992. *Vol. 63.*

Lindgård, Fredrik: Paul's Line of Thought in 2 Corinthians 4:16–5:10. 2004. *Vol. II/189.*

Loader, William R.G.: Jesus' Attitude Towards the Law. 1997. *Vol. II/97.*

Löhr, Gebhard: Verherrlichung Gottes durch Philosophie. 1997. *Vol. 97.*

Löhr, Hermut: Studien zum frühchristlichen und frühjüdischen Gebet. 2003. *Vol. 160.*

– see *Hengel, Martin.*

Löhr, Winrich Alfried: Basilides und seine Schule. 1995. *Vol. 83.*

Luomanen, Petri: Entering the Kingdom of Heaven. 1998. *Vol. II/101.*

Luz, Ulrich: see *Alexeev, Anatoly A.*

–: see *Dunn, James D.G.*

Mackay, Ian D.: John's Raltionship with Mark. 2004. *Vol. II/182.*

Mackie, Scott D.: Eschatology and Exhortation in the Epistle to the Hebrews. 2006. *Vol. II/223.*

Maier, Gerhard: Mensch und freier Wille. 1971. *Vol. 12.*

– Die Johannesoffenbarung und die Kirche. 1981. *Vol. 25.*

Markschies, Christoph: Valentinus Gnosticus? 1992. *Vol. 65.*

Marshall, Peter: Enmity in Corinth: Social Conventions in Paul's Relations with the Corinthians. 1987. *Vol. II/23.*

Martin, Dale B.: see *Zangenberg, Jürgen.*

Mayer, Annemarie: Sprache der Einheit im Epheserbrief und in der Ökumene. 2002. *Vol. II/150.*

Mayordomo, Moisés: Argumentiert Paulus logisch? 2005. *Vol. 188.*

McDonough, Sean M.: YHWH at Patmos: Rev. 1:4 in its Hellenistic and Early Jewish Setting. 1999. *Vol. II/107.*

McDowell, Markus: Prayers of Jewish Women. 2006. *Vol. II/211.*

McGlynn, Moyna: Divine Judgement and Divine Benevolence in the Book of Wisdom. 2001. *Vol. II/139.*

Meade, David G.: Pseudonymity and Canon. 1986. *Vol. 39.*

Meadors, Edward P.: Jesus the Messianic Herald of Salvation. 1995. *Vol. II/72.*

Meißner, Stefan: Die Heimholung des Ketzers. 1996. *Vol. II/87.*

Mell, Ulrich: Die „anderen" Winzer. 1994. *Vol. 77.*

– see *Sänger, Dieter.*

Mengel, Berthold: Studien zum Philipperbrief. 1982. *Vol. II/8.*

Merkel, Helmut: Die Widersprüche zwischen den Evangelien. 1971. *Vol. 13.*

– see *Ego, Beate.*

Merklein, Helmut: Studien zu Jesus und Paulus. Vol. 1 1987. *Vol. 43.* – Vol. 2 1998. *Vol. 105.*

Metzdorf, Christina: Die Tempelaktion Jesu. 2003. *Vol. II/168.*

Metzler, Karin: Der griechische Begriff des Verzeihens. 1991. *Vol. II/44.*

Metzner, Rainer: Die Rezeption des Matthäusevangeliums im 1. Petrusbrief. 1995. *Vol. II/74.*

– Das Verständnis der Sünde im Johannesevangelium. 2000. *Vol. 122.*

Mihoc, Vasile: see *Dunn, James D.G..*

Mineshige, Kiyoshi: Besitzverzicht und Almosen bei Lukas. 2003. *Vol. II/163.*

Mittmann, Siegfried: see *Hengel, Martin.*

Mittmann-Richert, Ulrike: Magnifikat und Benediktus. *1996. Vol. II/90.*

Miura, Yuzuru: David in Luke-Acts. 2007. *Vol. II/232.*

Mournet, Terence C.: Oral Tradition and Literary Dependency. 2005. *Vol. II/195.*

Mußner, Franz: Jesus von Nazareth im Umfeld Israels und der Urkirche. Ed. von M. Theobald. 1998. *Vol. 111.*

Mutschler, Bernhard: Das Corpus Johanneum bei Irenäus von Lyon. 2005. *Vol. 189.*

Nguyen, V. Henry T.: Christian Identity in Corinth. 2008. *Vol. II/243.*

Niebuhr, Karl-Wilhelm: Gesetz und Paränese. 1987. *Vol. II/28.*

– Heidenapostel aus Israel. 1992. *Vol. 62.*

– see *Deines, Roland*

– see *Dimitrov, Ivan Z.*

– see *Kraus, Wolfgang*

Nielsen, Anders E.: "Until it is Fullfilled". 2000. *Vol. II/126.*

Nissen, Andreas: Gott und der Nächste im antiken Judentum. 1974. *Vol. 15.*

Noack, Christian: Gottesbewußtsein. 2000. *Vol. II/116.*

Noormann, Rolf: Irenäus als Paulusinterpret. 1994. *Vol. II/66.*

Novakovic, Lidija: Messiah, the Healer of the Sick. 2003. *Vol. II/170.*

Obermann, Andreas: Die christologische Erfüllung der Schrift im Johannesevangelium. 1996. *Vol. II/83.*

Öhler, Markus: Barnabas. 2003. *Vol. 156.*
– see *Becker, Michael.*

Okure, Teresa: The Johannine Approach to Mission. 1988. *Vol. II/31.*

Onuki, Takashi: Heil und Erlösung. 2004. *Vol. 165.*

Oropeza, B. J.: Paul and Apostasy. 2000. *Vol. II/115.*

Ostmeyer, Karl-Heinrich: Kommunikation mit Gott und Christus. 2006. *Vol. 197.*
– Taufe und Typos. 2000. *Vol. II/118.*

Paulsen, Henning: Studien zur Literatur und Geschichte des frühen Christentums. Ed. von Ute E. Eisen. 1997. *Vol. 99.*

Pao, David W.: Acts and the Isaianic New Exodus. 2000. *Vol. II/130.*

Park, Eung Chun: The Mission Discourse in Matthew's Interpretation. 1995. *Vol. II/81.*

Park, Joseph S.: Conceptions of Afterlife in Jewish Insriptions. 2000. *Vol. II/121.*

Pate, C. Marvin: The Reverse of the Curse. 2000. *Vol. II/114.*

Pearce, Sarah J.K.: The Land of the Body. 2007. *Vol. 208.*

Peres, Imre: Griechische Grabinschriften und neutestamentliche Eschatologie. 2003. *Vol. 157.*

Philip, Finny: The Origins of Pauline Pneumatology. 2005. *Vol. II/194.*

Philonenko, Marc (Ed.): Le Trône de Dieu. 1993. *Vol. 69.*

Pilhofer, Peter: Presbyteron Kreitton. 1990. *Vol. II/39.*
– Philippi. Vol. 1 1995. *Vol. 87.* – Vol. 2 2000. *Vol. 119.*
– Die frühen Christen und ihre Welt. 2002. *Vol. 145.*
– see *Becker, Eve-Marie.*
– see *Ego, Beate.*

Pitre, Brant: Jesus, the Tribulation, and the End of the Exile. 2005. *Vol. II/204.*

Plümacher, Eckhard: Geschichte und Geschichten. 2004. *Vol. 170.*

Pöhlmann, Wolfgang: Der Verlorene Sohn und das Haus. 1993. *Vol. 68.*

Pokorný, Petr and *Josef B. Souček:* Bibelauslegung als Theologie. 1997. *Vol. 100.*
– and *Jan Roskovec* (Ed.): Philosophical Hermeneutics and Biblical Exegesis. 2002. *Vol. 153.*

Popkes, Enno Edzard: Das Menschenbild des Thomasevangeliums. 2007. *Vol. 206.*
– Die Theologie der Liebe Gottes in den johanneischen Schriften. 2005. *Vol. II/197.*

Porter, Stanley E.: The Paul of Acts. 1999. *Vol. 115.*

Prieur, Alexander: Die Verkündigung der Gottesherrschaft. 1996. *Vol. II/89.*

Probst, Hermann: Paulus und der Brief. 1991. *Vol. II/45.*

Räisänen, Heikki: Paul and the Law. 1983, ²1987. *Vol. 29.*

Rehkopf, Friedrich: Die lukanische Sonderquelle. 1959. *Vol. 5.*

Rein, Matthias: Die Heilung des Blindgeborenen (Joh 9). 1995. *Vol. II/73.*

Reinmuth, Eckart: Pseudo-Philo und Lukas. 1994. *Vol. 74.*

Reiser, Marius: Bibelkritik und Auslegung der Heiligen Schrift. 2007. *Vol. 217.*
– Syntax und Stil des Markusevangeliums. 1984. *Vol. II/11.*

Rhodes, James N.: The Epistle of Barnabas and the Deuteronomic Tradition. 2004. *Vol. II/188.*

Richards, E. Randolph: The Secretary in the Letters of Paul. 1991. *Vol. II/42.*

Riesner, Rainer: Jesus als Lehrer. 1981, ³1988. *Vol. II/7.*
– Die Frühzeit des Apostels Paulus. 1994. *Vol. 71.*

Rissi, Mathias: Die Theologie des Hebräerbriefs. 1987. *Vol. 41.*

Roskovec, Jan: see *Pokorný, Petr.*

Röhser, Günter: Metaphorik und Personifikation der Sünde. 1987. *Vol. II/25.*

Rose, Christian: Theologie als Erzählung im Markusevangelium. 2007. *Vol. II/236.*
– Die Wolke der Zeugen. 1994. *Vol. II/60.*

Rothschild, Clare K.: Baptist Traditions and Q. 2005. *Vol. 190.*
– Luke Acts and the Rhetoric of History. 2004. *Vol. II/175.*

Rüegger, Hans-Ulrich: Verstehen, was Markus erzählt. 2002. *Vol. II/155.*

Rüger, Hans Peter: Die Weisheitsschrift aus der Kairoer Geniza. 1991. *Vol. 53.*

Sänger, Dieter: Antikes Judentum und die Mysterien. 1980. *Vol. II/5.*
– Die Verkündigung des Gekreuzigten und Israel. 1994. *Vol. 75.*
– see *Burchard, Christoph*
– and *Ulrich Mell* (Hrsg.): Paulus und Johannes. 2006. *Vol. 198.*

Salier, Willis Hedley: The Rhetorical Impact of the Semeia in the Gospel of John. 2004. *Vol. II/186.*

Salzmann, Jorg Christian: Lehren und Ermahnen. 1994. *Vol. II/59.*

Sandnes, Karl Olav: Paul – One of the Prophets? 1991. *Vol. II/43.*

Sato, Migaku: Q und Prophetie. 1988. *Vol. II/29.*

Schäfer, Ruth: Paulus bis zum Apostelkonzil. 2004. *Vol. II/179.*

Schaper, Joachim: Eschatology in the Greek Psalter. 1995. *Vol. II/76.*

Schimanowski, Gottfried: Die himmlische Liturgie in der Apokalypse des Johannes. 2002. *Vol. II/154.*

– Weisheit und Messias. 1985. *Vol. II/17.*

Schlichting, Günter: Ein jüdisches Leben Jesu. 1982. *Vol. 24.*

Schließer, Benjamin: Abraham's Faith in Romans 4. 2007. *Vol. II/224.*

Schnabel, Eckhard J.: Law and Wisdom from Ben Sira to Paul. 1985. *Vol. II/16.*

Schnelle, Udo: see *Frey, Jörg.*

Schröter, Jens: Von Jesus zum Neuen Testament. 2007. *Vol. 204.*

– see *Frey, Jörg.*

Schutter, William L.: Hermeneutic and Composition in I Peter. 1989. *Vol. II/30.*

Schwartz, Daniel R.: Studies in the Jewish Background of Christianity. 1992. *Vol. 60.*

Schwemer, Anna Maria: see *Hengel, Martin*

Scott, Ian W.: Implicit Epistemology in the Letters of Paul. 2005. *Vol. II/205.*

Scott, James M.: Adoption as Sons of God. 1992. *Vol. II/48.*

– Paul and the Nations. 1995. *Vol. 84.*

Shum, Shiu-Lun: Paul's Use of Isaiah in Romans. 2002. *Vol. II/156.*

Siegert, Folker: Drei hellenistisch-jüdische Predigten. Teil I 1980. *Vol. 20* – Teil II 1992. *Vol. 61.*

– Nag-Hammadi-Register. 1982. *Vol. 26.*

– Argumentation bei Paulus. 1985. *Vol. 34.*

– Philon von Alexandrien. 1988. *Vol. 46.*

Simon, Marcel: Le christianisme antique et son contexte religieux I/II. 1981. *Vol. 23.*

Smit, Peter-Ben: Fellowship and Food in the Kingdom. 2008. *Vol. II/234.*

Snodgrass, Klyne: The Parable of the Wicked Tenants. 1983. *Vol. 27.*

Söding, Thomas: Das Wort vom Kreuz. 1997. *Vol. 93.*

– see *Thüsing, Wilhelm.*

Sommer, Urs: Die Passionsgeschichte des Markusevangeliums. 1993. *Vol. II/58.*

Sorensen, Eric: Possession and Exorcism in the New Testament and Early Christianity. 2002. *Vol. II/157.*

Souček, Josef B.: see *Pokorný, Petr.*

Southall, David J.: Rediscovering Righteousness in Romans. 2008. *Vol. 240.*

Spangenberg, Volker: Herrlichkeit des Neuen Bundes. 1993. *Vol. II/55.*

Spanje, T.E. van: Inconsistency in Paul? 1999. *Vol. II/110.*

Speyer, Wolfgang: Frühes Christentum im antiken Strahlungsfeld. Vol. I: 1989. *Vol. 50.*

– Vol. II: 1999. *Vol. 116.*

– Vol. III: 2007. *Vol. 213.*

Sprinkle, Preston: Law and Life. 2008. *Vol. II/241.*

Stadelmann, Helge: Ben Sira als Schriftgelehrter. 1980. *Vol. II/6.*

Stenschke, Christoph W.: Luke's Portrait of Gentiles Prior to Their Coming to Faith. *Vol. II/108.*

Sterck-Degueldre, Jean-Pierre: Eine Frau namens Lydia. 2004. *Vol. II/176.*

Stettler, Christian: Der Kolosserhymnus. 2000. *Vol. II/131.*

Stettler, Hanna: Die Christologie der Pastoralbriefe. 1998. *Vol. II/105.*

Stökl Ben Ezra, Daniel: The Impact of Yom Kippur on Early Christianity. 2003. *Vol. 163.*

Strobel, August: Die Stunde der Wahrheit. 1980. *Vol. 21.*

Stroumsa, Guy G.: Barbarian Philosophy. 1999. *Vol. 112.*

Stuckenbruck, Loren T.: Angel Veneration and Christology. 1995. *Vol. II/70.*

– *, Stephen C. Barton* and *Benjamin G. Wold* (Ed.): Memory in the Bible and Antiquity. 2007. *Vol. 212.*

Stuhlmacher, Peter (Ed.): Das Evangelium und die Evangelien. 1983. *Vol. 28.*

– Biblische Theologie und Evangelium. 2002. *Vol. 146.*

Sung, Chong-Hyon: Vergebung der Sünden. 1993. *Vol. II/57.*

Tajra, Harry W.: The Trial of St. Paul. 1989. *Vol. II/35.*

– The Martyrdom of St.Paul. 1994. *Vol. II/67.*

Theißen, Gerd: Studien zur Soziologie des Urchristentums. 1979, [3]1989. *Vol. 19.*

Theobald, Michael: Studien zum Römerbrief. 2001. *Vol. 136.*

Theobald, Michael: see *Mußner, Franz.*

Thornton, Claus-Jürgen: Der Zeuge des Zeugen. 1991. *Vol. 56.*

Thüsing, Wilhelm: Studien zur neutestamentlichen Theologie. Ed. von Thomas Söding. 1995. *Vol. 82.*

Thurén, Lauri: Derhethorizing Paul. 2000. *Vol. 124.*

Thyen, Hartwig: Studien zum Corpus Iohanneum. 2007. *Vol. 214.*

Tibbs, Clint: Religious Experience of the Pneuma. 2007. *Vol. II/230.*

Toit, David S. du: Theios Anthropos. 1997. *Vol. II/91.*

Tolmie, D. Francois: Persuading the Galatians. 2005. *Vol. II/190.*

Tomson, Peter J. and *Doris Lambers-Petry* (Ed.): The Image of the Judaeo-Christians in Ancient Jewish and Christian Literature. 2003. *Vol. 158.*

Trebilco, Paul: The Early Christians in Ephesus from Paul to Ignatius. 2004. *Vol. 166.*

Treloar, Geoffrey R.: Lightfoot the Historian. 1998. *Vol. II/103.*

Tsuji, Manabu: Glaube zwischen Vollkommenheit und Verweltlichung. 1997. *Vol. II/93.*

Twelftree, Graham H.: Jesus the Exorcist. 1993. *Vol. II/54.*

Ulrichs, Karl Friedrich: Christusglaube. 2007. *Vol. II/227.*

Urban, Christina: Das Menschenbild nach dem Johannesevangelium. 2001. *Vol. II/137.*

Vahrenhorst, Martin: Kultische Sprache in den Paulusbriefen. 2008. *Vol. 230.*

Vegge, Ivar: 2 Corinthians – a Letter about Reconciliation. 2008. *Vol. II/239.*

Visotzky, Burton L.: Fathers of the World. 1995. *Vol. 80.*

Vollenweider, Samuel: Horizonte neutestamentlicher Christologie. 2002. *Vol. 144.*

Vos, Johan S.: Die Kunst der Argumentation bei Paulus. 2002. *Vol. 149.*

Wagener, Ulrike: Die Ordnung des „Hauses Gottes". 1994. *Vol. II/65.*

Wahlen, Clinton: Jesus and the Impurity of Spirits in the Synoptic Gospels. 2004. *Vol. II/185.*

Walker, Donald D.: Paul's Offer of Leniency (2 Cor 10:1). 2002. *Vol. II/152.*

Walter, Nikolaus: Praeparatio Evangelica. Ed. von Wolfgang Kraus und Florian Wilk. 1997. *Vol. 98.*

Wander, Bernd: Gottesfürchtige und Sympathisanten. 1998. *Vol. 104.*

Waters, Guy: The End of Deuteronomy in the Epistles of Paul. 2006. *Vol. 221.*

Watt, Jan G. van der: see *Frey, Jörg*

Watts, Rikki: Isaiah's New Exodus and Mark. 1997. *Vol. II/88.*

Wedderburn, A.J.M.: Baptism and Resurrection. 1987. *Vol. 44.*

Wegner, Uwe: Der Hauptmann von Kafarnaum. 1985. *Vol. II/14.*

Weissenrieder, Annette: Images of Illness in the Gospel of Luke. 2003. Vol. II/164.

–, *Friederike Wendt* and *Petra von Gemünden* (Ed.): Picturing the New Testament. 2005. *Vol. II/193.*

Welck, Christian: Erzählte ‚Zeichen'. 1994. *Vol. II/69.*

Wendt, Friederike (Ed.): see *Weissenrieder, Annette.*

Wiarda, Timothy: Peter in the Gospels. 2000. *Vol. II/127.*

Wifstrand, Albert: Epochs and Styles. 2005. *Vol. 179.*

Wilk, Florian: see *Walter, Nikolaus.*

Williams, Catrin H.: I am He. 2000. *Vol. II/113.*

Wilson, Todd A.: The Curse of the Law and the Crisis in Galatia. 2007. *Vol. II/225.*

Wilson, Walter T.: Love without Pretense. 1991. *Vol. II/46.*

Winninge, Mikael: see *Holmberg, Bengt.*

Wischmeyer, Oda: Von Ben Sira zu Paulus. 2004. *Vol. 173.*

Wisdom, Jeffrey: Blessing for the Nations and the Curse of the Law. 2001. *Vol. II/133.*

Witmer, Stephen E.: Divine Instruction in Early Christianity. 2008. *Vol. II/246.*

Wold, Benjamin G.: Women, Men, and Angels. 2005. *Vol. II/2001.*

– see *Stuckenbruck, Loren T.*

Wright, Archie T.: The Origin of Evil Spirits. 2005. *Vol. II/198.*

Wucherpfennig, Ansgar: Heracleon Philologus. 2002. *Vol. 142.*

Yeung, Maureen: Faith in Jesus and Paul. 2002. *Vol. II/147.*

Zangenberg, Jürgen, Harold W. Attridge and *Dale B. Martin* (Ed.): Religion, Ethnicity and Identity in Ancient Galilee. 2007. *Vol. 210.*

Zimmermann, Alfred E.: Die urchristlichen Lehrer. 1984, ²1988. *Vol. II/12.*

Zimmermann, Johannes: Messianische Texte aus Qumran. 1998. *Vol. II/104.*

Zimmermann, Ruben: Christologie der Bilder im Johannesevangelium. 2004. *Vol. 171.*

– Geschlechtermetaphorik und Gottesverhältnis. 2001. *Vol. II/122.*

– see *Frey, Jörg*

Zumstein, Jean: see *Dettwiler, Andreas*

Zwiep, Arie W.: Judas and the Choice of Matthias. 2004. *Vol. II/187.*

For a complete catalogue please write to the publisher
Mohr Siebeck • P.O. Box 2030 • D–72010 Tübingen/Germany
Up-to-date information on the internet at www.mohr.de